THE LONG CAMPAIGN

The History of the 15th Fighter Group in World War II

Cover artwork by Steve Ferguson, Burlington, VT.

ONE MORE TAPP-ED OUT

After three and half years holding on in reserve to defend of the very ground where their war had begun, the 15th Fighter Group finally was afforded the chance to exact their own special vengeance. Their measured air assault to date had been the tactical mopping up the residual battle sites of the Pacific war, but now their mission was against the enemy's home islands. From Iwo Jima, literally the enemy's front step, the Yanks would prove their worth on those tedious long-range sorties, and none more ably than 78 Sqdn. CO Major Jim "Tapper" Tapp. The Major would be confirmed as the Group's first ace on April 12 over Yokohama and on May 25, Tapper was back over Tokyo aboard his P-51D MARGARET IV causing more trouble. After proving out the newest airborne artillery in a grass cutting rocket attack on Matsuda airfield, he rose upward into a swarm of interceptors to "Tapp down" his seventh aerial victim. Tapper and MARGARET are seen breaking off from point blank range against the torched TOJO. Another TOJO would likewise be heavily damaged upon Tapper's withdrawal.

Maps courtesy of USAF.
Cover design by Robert Biondi.
Book design by Robin Higham and Lori Daniel.

Library of Congress Catalog Number: 2005934708.

Printed in China.
ISBN: 0-7643-2428-4

We are always looking for people to write books on new and related subjects. If you have an idea for a book, please contact us at the address below.

Published by Schiffer Publishing Ltd.
4880 Lower Valley Road
Atglen, PA 19310
Phone: (610) 593-1777
FAX: (610) 593-2002
E-mail: Info@schifferbooks.com.
Visit our web site at: www.schifferbooks.com
Please write for a free catalog.
This book may be purchased from the publisher.
Please include $3.95 postage.
Try your bookstore first.

In Europe, Schiffer books are distributed by:
Bushwood Books
6 Marksbury Ave.
Kew Gardens
Surrey TW9 4JF
England
Phone: 44 (0)20 8392-8585
FAX: 44 (0)20 8392-9876
E-mail: Bushwd@aol.com.
Free postage in the UK. Europe: air mail at cost.
Try your bookstore first.

THE LONG CAMPAIGN

The History of the 15th Fighter Group in World War II

John W. Lambert

Schiffer Military History
Atglen, PA

TABLE OF CONTENTS

LIST OF MAPS

GLOSSARY

AA, ack-ack, flak — Anti-aircraft fire
Ace — An unofficial status achieved by the destruction of five enemy planes in aerial combat.
ASR — Air/Sea Rescue
Bandit — Enemy aircraft
Biscuit Gun — Landing signal light
Bogey — Any unidentified aircraft
BOQ — Bachelor Officer's Quarters
CAP — Combat air patrol
CINCPAC — Commander-in-Chief Pacific
CO — Commanding Officer
CV — Aircraft Carrier
CVE — Escort Aircraft Carrier
DD — Destroyer
DE — Destroyer-Escort
Departure Point — The point of approach to the attack run
DU — Directional Unit
Dumbo — Catalina flying-boat
E/A — Enemy aircraft
Element — Two supporting aircraft in a flight
ETA — Estimated time of arrival
Exec — Executive officer (Non-pilot, top administrator)
Flak — Anti-aircraft fire
Flat Hatting — Low-level flying i.e., buzzing
Flight — A basic four-plane formation
HVAR — High-velocity aircraft rockets
IAS — Indicated Air Speed
IFF — Identification-friend-or-foe transponder
IP — Initial Point, where attack run commences
KPC — Killed in plane crash, non-combat
Lifeguard league — Unofficial term used to describe U.S. Navy subs assigned to rescuing downed airmen in 1945
NAS — Naval Air Station
OD — Officer of the day
Rally Point — A gathering or rendezvous point after completion of the attack
R-and-R — Rest and recuperation leave
Rendezvous Point — Assembly area after mission takeoff
SOI — Standard operating instructions
Sortie — One individual aircraft mission
SS — Submarine in U.S. Navy terms; steamship in merchant marine terms
Super Dumbo — B-17 fitted with drop lifeboat
VHF — Very high frequency
VP — Navy patrol squadron designator

Note

Military (0000-2400 hour) times and local zones are used throughout this history; this conforms to U.S. and Allied usage, but differs from Japanese.

INTRODUCTION

While writing the narrative history of the Seventh Fighter Command, I came to the conclusion that the project was impossible unless I first defined the historic role of the 15th Fighter Group. Hence this volume. It is an introduction, as it were, to the full history of the Seventh Fighter Command now in preparation.

Both the 15th and 18th Fighter Groups formed the nucleus of the Seventh Fighter Command. However, the 18th was permanently assigned to the Thirteenth Air Force in March 1943 and served the balance of the war in the Southwest Pacific. The rest of the Command was largely spawned by the 15th.

The assembly of the information contained in this volume involved conclusions based on deduction as much as on research. The difficulties encountered were immense. Material available in Air force archives for the years 1941 through 1943 was fragmentary at best. Group records for the period from June through August 1945, the wind-up of World War II, were incomplete and, in some instances, inaccurate. Squadron records, if they were maintained at all during that period, were lost to posterity, except for those of the 47th Squadron.

Secondly, in attempting to fill in the documentary gaps with military personnel records, I was effectively thwarted by an official obstruction, the Privacy Act. Vital personnel records, sometimes the only remaining source of accurate data, are guarded in the National Personnel Records Center, St. Louis, when they are not on fire, as happened in 1973. More zealous fervor is employed in protecting these historic documents than is expended on Pentagon secrets. While this effectively shields the veteran from junk mail, it also insulates him from participating in historical projects, whether he wants the protection or not.

Even when official records were available, I encountered certain inevitable human errors which made the interpretation of data akin to detective work. To cite just one example: the Group history noted that 1st Lt. Robert L. White was among those lost on 8 July 1945. His name is listed at the beginning of the July monthly summary of operations and in a list of all officers killed or missing in an August 1945 summary. The Command consolidated combat mission report for 8 July 1945 notes that the 15th lost two planes and pilots that day. One was clearly Al Sherran.

A year of searching finally convinced me that there was no such person as Robert L. White. He simply didn't exist. The Veterans' Administration cooperated in verifying this. Some Group clerk had erred in listing White and then repeated the error a second time. But since two P-51s had gone down and there was no reported ASR rescue, who was lost? Looking through the Squadron battle honors roster, Sandy Sanders searched scores of names for a similarity in first names and middle initials. Robert L. Carr, 1st Lt., 78th Squadron, drew his attention. Then I recalled a note in Jim Vande Hey's scrapbook that Carr had been lost over Tokyo.

However, Carr was not mentioned in combat mission reports as missing, nor was he on the August 1945 Group record of those lost during the Iwo campaign. The U.S. Battle Monuments Commission has three volumes the size of the New York City phone book ostensibly listing the dead and missing of World War II. Carr was not listed there. However, this source has proven fallible in the past; it had not carried Lt. Colonel Jack Thomas' name.

In the search to verify Thomas' certain death, I had discovered that there was yet one more set of archives. The U.S. Army's Casualty and Memorial Affairs Branch has a musty dog-eared stack of computerized names of the honored dead of World War II, assuming they had been buried by a graves registration unit. There, in a twelve-inch stack of papers among tens of thousands of names were the coded numbers that said Robert L. Carr was killed and buried in Japan, then reburied in Fort Bliss, Texas. Thus was one small mystery resolved.

Finally, though I received the greatest courtesy and co-operation from dozens of officers and enlisted men whom I interviewed or with whom I corresponded, that they were drawing on their memories. Thirty-five or forty years had dimmed many recollections. Men who had participated in the same action or event often remembered the facts in different and conflicting ways. In those cases, it took a third party or some independent verification to substantiate the actual circumstances.

In conclusion, this history is a blend of sometimes incomplete records and personal reflections into a narrative history that combines the best available information.

Despite the culling of some details to enhance the story line, it is a sincere effort to give the members of the 15th and their families, as well as history, a sense of the sacrifice and accomplishment of these men. I have felt a compulsion to see that this chapter of our national heritage not be left in fragments stacked in government storerooms nor in the attics of the mind. This extraordinary story needed to be told.

John W. Lambert
Mendota Heights, Minnesota

ACKNOWLEDGEMENTS

It would be difficult to list the many former members of the 15th Fighter Group who assisted me in this undertaking. I corresponded with and interviewed dozens of them and am afraid a listing might inadvertently omit someone. They are all mentioned at some point in *The Long Campaign*, and my sincerest hope is that after closing the book they will say, "That's the way it was."

The help rendered by the Office of Air Force history was crucial to the research. Major General John W. Huston and his Bolling Field staff, as well as the team at Maxwell Field, were all courteous and cooperative. However, Mr. Bill Heimdahl, in the Chief's office at Bolling, gave much more than responses to my requests. He offered guidance in the pursuit of information and suggested avenues of approach with other government agencies when I ran into blind alleys. His help was absolutely invaluable.

Mr. James Taylor at the National Archives in Washington and his associates at the Modern Military Branch were always supportive and responsive as was Mr. Jim Trimble at the photo library in the 19th floor attic.

The people at the USAF's 1361st Audio-Visual Squadron in Arlington assisted with some of my photos. That office's Mr. Dana Bell, a fellow historian, was most generous in sharing his vast knowledge with me during his off hours.

Staff members of the Naval Historical Center in Washington, D.C. helped me solve some interface problems between the Navy and Army in World War II.

Colonel Shinji Kondo of the National Defense College in Tokyo resolved many of my questions regarding the other side, and Lieutenant Commander Haruki Iki, IJN (Retired) supplied me with many valuable contacts among veteran Japanese air officers.

Copies of *Brief* and *The Fighter*, wartime newsmagazines of the Central Pacific published by the Army were useful sources of information.

I am indebted to my friend, Bob Lemm, an aviation artist supreme, for his two beautiful action works which add another dimension to the book.

When I was first fumbling to get myself organized Bill Hess, the dean of World War II air historians, was unusually kind and supportive. Don Woerpel and Jack Ilfrey also gave me advice learned through the publication of their two excellent war histories.

Early in the project I talked to Dr. Robin Higham, the driving force behind *Aerospace Historian*. His scholarly guidance has given me direction and purpose.

Several friends, John Loosbrock, Larry Zoeller, Steve Ellis, and Ramsay Potts offered encouragement at various steps. I am grateful to all of them and any others among the legion who have played any part in the production of this history.

The research for this volume took about 35 years and the writing only two, but the latter was the more formidable task. While I have written more than a few magazine articles, speeches, economic studies and congressional testimony, I have never engaged in any literary effort as demanding as this. Through seven drafts I have been assisted by my wife, Dolly, who was both typist and collaborator. Without her patient criticism this would have been a collection of historical facts, rather than a narrative history.

J.W.L.

86
4B
15P
B1219
BOB LEMM ©

Chapter I

FROM ACTIVATION TO BAPTISM OF FIRE 1 December 1940 to 7 December 1941

This is the wartime chronicle of a military unit that engaged the enemy on the first and last days of World War II and intermittently between those dates.

While airmen in other theaters of combat displayed no less bravery or dedication than the subjects of this history, their tours of duty were generally defined in months and numbers of missions. For the men of the 15th Fighter Group — those who survived — the shift was generally accounted by the years.

Although the 15th was not continuously engaged with the Japanese, it was constantly confronted by those enemies for whom there was no book of tactics; the weather and the sea. Even during periods of relative inaction, when the Group was both a replacement training unit for the entire Pacific, and Hawaii's primary air defense force, the toll of lives was inordinately high. With the collateral effects of combat, weather, and over water operations, the attrition rate was staggering.

The 15th's environment, the Central Pacific, is of such awesome proportions that no one can look at it and grasp its vastness. Each horizon merely relinquishes to another more distant horizon. Navigation over these trackless, featureless expanses of water became an all-consuming science for the pilots. The only land mass they ever approached in four years was the hostile Home Islands of Japan. Reflecting on operations, their late chief, Major General E. M. "Mickey" Moore, said, "Every time they pulled their wheels up, they were over water."

The thought of a bail-out was objectionable to all air-crews, but particularly to fighter pilots. Pushing out of the cramped cockpit of a disabled fighter plane reeling inevitably toward earth was a singular achievement. Once free, there was the danger of being struck a fatal blow by the tail of the beast that had lately borne them.

A successful parachute jump was, however, only the prelude to survival. A landing on the ground, even enemy soil, increased the odds of ultimately living. Those odds were dramatically reduced by a landing at sea. For, despite the herculean efforts of air sea rescue units, a man down in the Pacific had two strikes against him. He not only had to be located, like a lost soul in limbo, but also he had to fight for his life in the angry ocean.

These were the perils that shadowed the Group's wartime venture. They combined to take the lives of 134 officers and enlisted men between the attack on 7 December 1941 and victory on 14 August 1945.

Paradise before "The Blitz," early 1941: Waikiki Beach. (Source: Joe Powell)

The 15th was a Hawaiian product, born at Wheeler Field, Oahu Island on 1 December 1940. It was originally designated a "Pursuit Group", a hold-over term from World War I.

Its first Commanding Officer was Captain Lorry N. Tindal. The balance of the original cadre came from other units of the Hawaiian Air Force, primarily the 18th Pursuit Group also stationed at Wheeler Field.

Original command of the Group's three Squadrons, the 45th, 46th, and 47th, was vested in Captains Aaron W. Tyer, Thomas C. Musgrave, Jr., and Gordon H. Austin, respectively. Only Musgrave, transferred from the 19th Pursuit Squadron of the 18th Group, was a fighter pilot. Aside from this handful of veteran officers, most of the 15th's pilots were youngsters fresh from the 1940 flight classes of Kelly Field, San Antonio.

Prior to their Air Cadet experience, most of these Depression era boys had never strayed beyond the borders of their native states. In those days, a trip from a Midwest farm to Des Moines or Omaha, or a move from a West Texas ranch to college in Fort Worth was an historic journey. When these same boys were awarded their silver wings and gold bars at Kelly Field, it was indeed heady stuff. The assignment to Hawaii and the trip from San Francisco to Honolulu on a Matson steamship was like a voyage to another planet.

In the "old Army", Hawaii was considered among the choicest of military posts. It was a world unto itself and Paradise to boot, even for a private at thirty dollars per month. War was raging in Europe and Africa. There was war and rumors of war in the Orient, but that was

Paradise before "The Blitz," early 1941: Officer's Club Patio at Wheeler Field. (Source: Joe Powell)

thousands of miles from Hawaii and seemed even more remote.

As 1941 dawned there was still a festive air about the business of soldiering in the Hawaiian Department. Parades by the 25th Division at Schofield Barracks were grand spectacles. The fleet returned to Pearl Harbor every weekend to stand down, and the arrival or departure of any dignitary was ample justification for a magnificent display of formation flying by the Hawaiian Air Force. Equally popular among aviators was the buzzing of arriving liners from the States. Although such maneuvers were strictly against orders, it was done frequently and with some flourish. Certain Air Corps lotharios were prone to dipping low over the great steamships and dropping their names and phone numbers to admiring lady passengers. Variations of these aerial hi-jinks were extended to competition between the services. The buzzing of Navy airfields by Army planes and reciprocal flat-hatting by the Navy was routine. The use of flour sacks for mock bombings was an unsanctioned but accepted bit of military barnstorming.

Early aircraft employed by the 15th Pursuit Group were the Boeing P-26 and the Curtiss P-36 "Hawk". The former was a 234 m.p.h. maximum speed, open cockpit, antique. The P-36, a 314 m.p.h. aircraft, was a dramatic improvement over the P-26 and was considered a top performer in 1941. The French Air Force had used export models of the Curtiss fighter against the Luftwaffe in Europe with reasonable success. It was, therefore, popularly held that the P-36 could outperform the aircraft of any Asiatic power. The events of 7 December 1941 exploded that myth, along with many others and relegated the P-36 to the trash heap of outmoded weapons.

The 15th Group was strengthened by the arrival of 31 additional pilots and aircraft in February 1941. This P-36 contingent was drawn from volunteers in existing mainland pursuit squadrons. First Lieutenant Lewis M. Sanders (later to command the 46th Squadron) led one 12 plane formation from the 27th Squadron, 1st Pursuit Group, Selfridge Field, Michigan. Another flight came from Hamilton Field, California. The planes, pilots, and crew chiefs gathered at North Island Naval Air Station, San Diego, where they boarded the aircraft carrier, *Enterprise*. After being ferried across the Pacific the P-36s were flown from the deck of the *Enterprise* off Oahu on February 21.

Although the launching of Army fighters from the deck of an aircraft carrier was an historic "first", it generated no official recognition. In fact, the deck log of the *Enterprise* devoted considerably more space to the loading of produce from the farmer's market in San Diego than to the transport of Army fighters.

By April 1941 limited numbers of Curtiss P-40B aircraft began to be shipped to Hawaii and were assigned first to those units still operating the P-26. The 47th Squadron drew the first of these new fighters for the 15th Group. The P-40 was greeted by the men who had to fly it with something between breathless anticipation and elation. With a maximum speed of 352 m.p.h. the P-40 was not merely superior to the P-26, it represented major design and technological advances that made the little Boeing fighter look like a flying dinosaur. The mechanics, all radial engine men, were less enthusiastic about the P-40 with its in-line liquid cooled Allison engine, but bent to the task of learning how to service these new planes.

War clouds may have been gathering in the Far East, but a peacetime, business-as-usual attitude continued to dominate the Hawaiian military establishment. Late in July the Group participated in an aerial review marking the dedication of the first United States Post Office at Wheeler Field, an extraordinary exercise for a command only five months from catastrophe.

By October, as the amount of war talk increased, the Group's new commander, Major Paul Blanchard, decided to conduct an interception test with the P-36. A performance test was devised based on the confidence in this plane, still dominant in numbers, and a concern over its ability to challenge high level attackers. Six aircraft of the 46th Squadron, 1st Lt. Malcolm A. "Mike" Moore leading, took off from Wheeler Field in an attempt to determine the time necessary to reach 30,000 feet. The rate of climb was 2,000 feet per minute up to 12,000 feet, then fell off as follows:

1,200 feet per minute at 18,000 feet
800 feet per minute at 24,000 feet
300 feet per minute at 30,000 feet

Moore and the second element leader dropped out with fuel pressure problems, but the remainder of the flight reached the designated 30,000 foot level in 29 minutes. It was easy to see that without considerable warning the Hawk was ill-equipped to place a defensive umbrella over Oahu. As events unfolded, the Group would never be given the opportunity for its P-36s to engage in such a langorous interception.

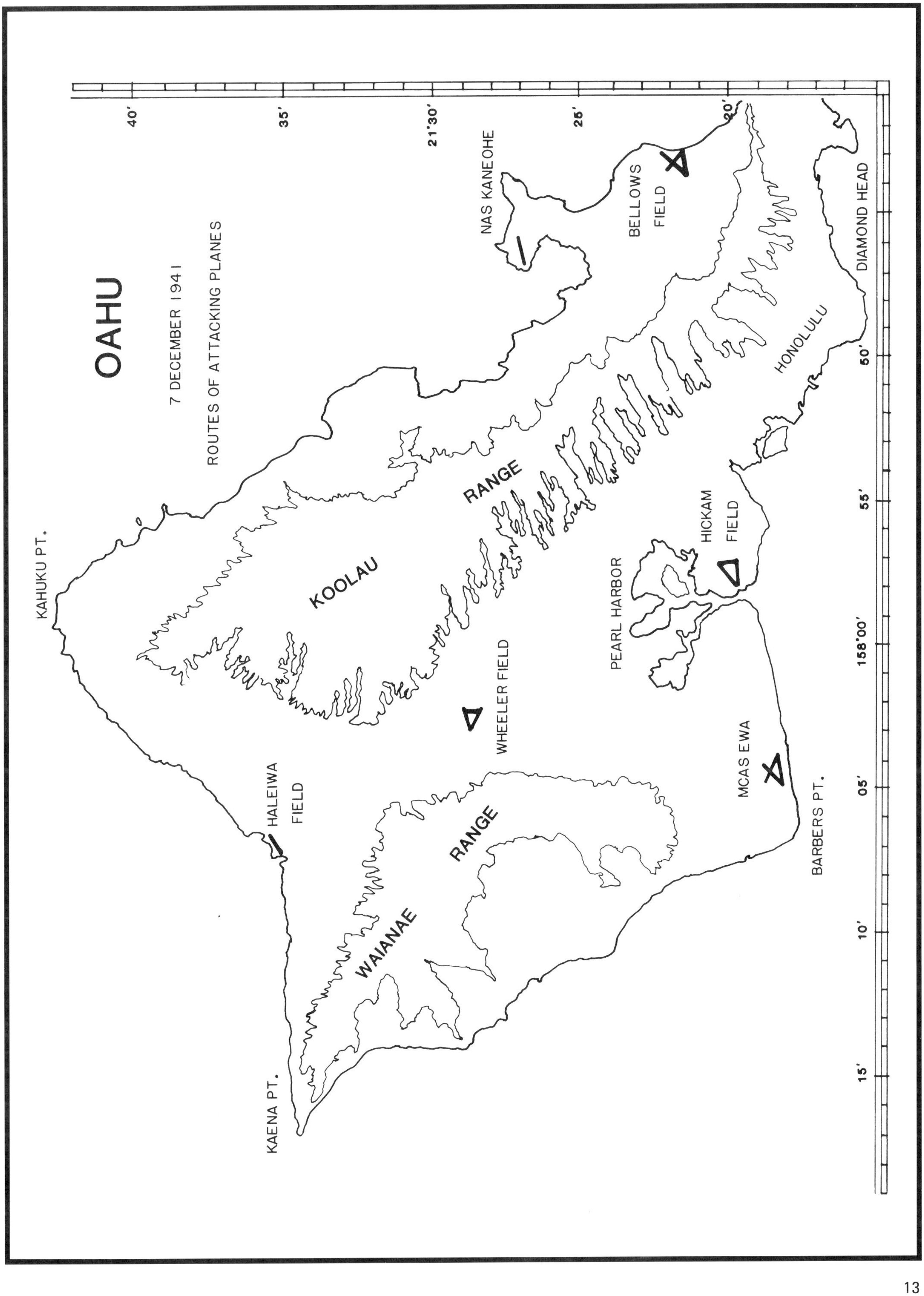
OAHU
7 DECEMBER 1941
ROUTES OF ATTACKING PLANES
KAHUKU PT.
NAS KANEOHE
BELLOWS FIELD
KOOLAU RANGE
WHEELER FIELD
HALEIWA FIELD
WAIANAE RANGE
PEARL HARBOR
HICKAM FIELD
HONOLULU
DIAMOND HEAD
MCAS EWA
BARBERS PT.
KAENA PT.
40'
35'
21°30'
25'
20'
50'
55'
158°00'
05'
10'
15'

The 15th Group's strength was augmented by the creation of a fourth squadron on 5 October 1941. The 72nd Squadron, equipped with the latest P-40D aircraft, was placed under the command of 1st Lt. James O. Beckwith. Jim had been one of the Selfridge Field reinforcements. Within a month of its organization the 72nd was alerted for posible assignment to the islands of Wake or Guam. The Squadron moved into a tent area at Wheeler behind Hangar I while senior officers debated the move.

The later months of 1941 involved a series of training alerts based on a general belief that war somewhere in the Pacific was imminent. Throughout this period the men and planes of the 15th alternated duty on alert status.

Lew Sanders recalls the ordeal: "We sat out on the field in revetments night after night with crew chiefs on the wings ready to start the engines and pilots resting under the wings to stay out of the dew. There was a guy in the tower with a 'Biscuit Gun' ready to give the green light in case there was a raid."

Lieutenant General Short, commanding Army forces, had a fixation with sabotage for which he had been conditioned by his predecessor, the intelligence servies, and all of official Washington.

So far as the 15th Group was concerned, this subversive hysteria reflected adversely on flight operations. Aircraft continued to be dispersed about the perimeter of Wheeler Field guarded by Air Corps ground personnel. Eventually pilots and ground crews became worn out from this ritual. Both flying proficiency and aircraft maintenance suffered.

General Short's prediliction toward the native Japanese uprising theory was reinforced by Washington's vaguely worded "war warning" of November 27th. It seemed to Short a certain signal that his primary threat came from within. Accordingly, he ordered an anti-sabotage alert.

Complying with these orders Major General Frederick L. Martin, Chief of the Hawaiian Air Force, ordered all aircraft to be brought in from designated dispersal areas. Bombers and fighters not participating in flight operations or undergoing major maintenance were concentrated on the Hangar lines. Planes of the 14th Pursuit Wing were lined up by squadron, wing tip to wing tip, and dove tailed in precise rows on the ramp

Haleiwa, a training airstrip on the North coast of Oahu, October 1941. Japanese intelligence overlooked this airfield. (Source: National Archives)

Lew Sanders' 46th Sq was assigned to Haleiwa for gunnery training in November: Lew (paddling) and Phil Rasmussen try some dry land canoeing. (Source: Joe Powell)

at Wheeler Field. Exceptions to the Wheeler concentration were a squadron of the 18th Group stationed at Bellows Field and the 47th Squadron which replaced the 46th at Haleiwa Field on December 3rd for gunnery training.

Saturday, December 6, found the planes of the 45th, 46th, and 72nd Squadrons clustered on the ramp at Wheeler. A routine weekend stand-down was ordered. Except for a handful of sentries, the 15th Pursuit Group was on peacetime weekend pass.

Captain Austin, commander of the 47th Squadron, went wild boar hunting for the weekend. Everyone else not assigned to the skeletal duty roster relaxed with the single men mostly embarked on girl hunting.

Late on Saturday night, while driving back from Honolulu to Wheeler Field, 2nd Lt. Philip M. Rasmussen of the 46th Squadron slowed his Chevy convertible to admire the display of lights below him at Pearl Harbor. It was Battleforce Pacific in all its majesty including seven battleships at the quays off Ford Island. He nudged his drowsing double date, 2nd Lt. Joe Powell, "Joe, look at that. Isn't it a beautiful sight?"

Powell stirred from his slumber to gaze at the great fleet and uttered a prophetic, "Boy! What a target that would make."

Those up past midnight were surprised to find that KGMB, Radio Honolulu, was broadcasting past its customary sign-off time. The "Night Owls" show had stayed on the air at the request of the Army. Its radio music would serve as a navigation aid to assist Major Truman H. Landon's flight of twelve B-17E heavy bombers winging in from Hamilton Field, California. These Philippines bound "Flying Fortresses" had an ETA of 0800 December 7 at Hickam Field.

At 0600, at latitude 26 degrees North, longitude 158 degrees West, 230 miles due north of Oahu, Admiral Chuichi Nagumo turned his great carrier task force into the wind. With battle flags flying and repeated shouts of "Banzai" sounding over the roar of many engines, the Japanese strike force was launched from *Kaga, Akagi, Shokaku, Hiryu, Soryu,* and *Zuikaku*.

As the first rays of sunlight began to streak the eastern horizon, Commander Mitsuo Fuchida assembled his first attack wave and climbed to altitude. Fuchida commanded a force of 181 aircraft consisting of 88 Nakajima B5N "Kates" (40 loaded with torpedoes and 48 with armor piercing bombs), 51 Aichi D3A "Val" dive bombers, and 42 escorting Zero-sen or "Zeke" fighters.

In the unfolding dawn of December 7 Fuchida's alert attack force and Landon's weary bomber crews were both homing in on Radio Honolulu. Only a few miles separated the two formations.

At 0749, off Oahu's North coast, the Japanese units began their attack runs on pre-assigned targets. Unchallenged, Commander Fuchida sent a pre-arranged signal to the *Akagi* indicating achievement of surprise: "Tora! Tora! Tora!"

Within a few minutes of 0800 Fuchida's superbly trained China veterans plunged to the attack. Almost simultaneously they hit the fleet at Pearl Harbor, the Ford Island Naval Station (NAS), Kaneohe NAS, the Marine Corps Air Station at Point Ewa, and Hickam and Wheeler Army air fields.

Led by Lt. Akira Sakamoto, the 16th Attack Unit swept through Kole-Kole Pass in the Waianae Mountains toward Wheeler Field. As the 27 Vals and nine Zekes nosed over for the attack, personnel of the 15th Pursuit Group were engaged in a variety of inconsequential activities. The recollections of those seemingly mundane moments are indelibly etched in their memories.

Second Lieutenants Harry Brown and John Dains, of the 47th Squadron, were having a nightcap in the Bachelor Officers Quarters (BOQ) concluding an all-night celebration that had started in Honolulu. The festivities were occasioned by their completion of aerial gunnery qualifications at Haleiwa on Friday.

Phil Rasmussen, a senior 2nd Lt., (date of rank was a precious commodity in the old peacetime Army) had just ambled out of bed and was heading for the bathroom in the 46th Squadron BOQ.

At Wheeler's married officer's quarters Lew Sanders had just strolled out to pick up the Sunday morning newspaper. The headline and the subhead of the *Honolulu Advertiser* read: "FDR WILL SEND MESSAGE TO EMPEROR ON WAR CRISIS — Japanese Deny Massing Troops for Thai War — Hirohito Holds Power to Stop Japanese Army."

Gordon Sterling enjoys the beach at Haleiwa between training exercises. (Source: Joe Powell)

Ken Taylor and George Welch were first in the air to engage the Japanese on 7 December 41. (Source: Ken Taylor)

Lew Sanders' 46th Sq was assigned to Haleiwa for gunnery training in November: Above — The tent existence was a bit primitive but the luxury of Wheeler Field was just 10 miles down the road. (Source: Joe Powell) Left — Mike Moore (Source: Alec Streete)

Everyone who heard the roar of the approaching attackers immediately concluded that Navy carrier planes were buzzing Wheeler, part of the horseplay that characterized pre-war Hawaiian life.

John Dains and Harry Brown heard the first explosion and stepped outside on the assumption that one of those mischievous Navy boys had crashed.

From the bathroom, in the midst of his morning ablutions, Phil Rasmussen heard the sound of an engine lugging a plane out of a dive. He looked out the window and, in an instant, saw both the orange blossom of the first bomb explosion and the red "meatball" insignia on a Val clawing for altitude.

"We're being attacked by the Japs!" he yelled down the hall. The immediate response from an unknown but irritated pilot was, "Go to bed, you son-of-a-bitch, it's too early."

Standing in front of his house, Lew Sanders heard the multiple engines of the attackers with their unfamiliar stacatto sounding exhaust as the Japanese pilots rapidly changed throttle settings. He ran through the house, knowing intuitively that his long held fears were about to become a reality. From his west window he saw a wave of Japanese planes passing over Schofield Barracks. Then he heard the first bomb detonations.

Sergeant James M. Davenport, a 72nd Squadron aircraft mechanic, was walking toward the enlisted mess when he heard an airplane in a steep dive. Looking toward the sound, he saw a strange looking plane pulling out of a dive as its bomb was released. In a split second he saw the Japanese insignia and "knew we were at war."

Staff Sergeant Clayton M. Westhaver, also of the 72nd, was catapulted from his bunk by the first bomb explosion. He ran from his tent to see Japanese planes skimming over Wheeler Field as low as 50 feet.

Private First Class Robert R. Shattuck was caught in the open on his way to morning duty at the 15th Group

Communications Section. One of his legs was severed by a bomb fragment and the young Wisconsin soldier became Wheeler's first fatality.

Within a few minutes Sakamoto's dive bombers had unloaded their 550-pound general-purpose bombs with devastating accuracy on the hangar line, base engineering, and ordnance building, the older stucco barracks, and the temporary tent city. The same force then began a reckless strafing attack, racing back and forth over Wheeler, raking aircraft, barracks, houses, vehicles, and anyone daring enough to expose himself.

Lew Sanders gave his wife and a visiting Air Corps wife instructions to head for the hills. He headed for the air field. As he left home he observed the attackers making low level runs over the quarters. "Machine gun fire was deafening. Empty shell casings clattered off roofs and against trash cans. Looking south I could see heavy columns of black smoke rising from Pearl Harbor."

Second Lieutenant John Thacker drove up, and Sanders bounded into the car. Through enemy fire they raced to the flight line.

First Lieutenant Jim Beckwith placed some heavy metal furniture on top of a bed, had his wife and baby daughter get underneath, then reported to the hangar line. His 72nd Squadron, housed in tents, suffered heavy casualties from both shrapnel and strafing.

Despite the continuous fire from Sakamoto's force, officers and enlisted men spewed forth from the barracks to the flight line, to assist the wounded, or to man duty stations. A flurry of frantic personal decisions produced a number of impromptu but generally inspired actions.

First Lieutenant John J. Webster, 47th Squadron, shouldered a .30 caliber Garand rifle and, from an exposed position, commenced a modest but satisfying counter fire.

Sergeants Westhaver and Charles A. Fay raced to the blazing flight line together. Westhaver was clipped by a bomb fragment and headed for the dispensary while Fay began to taxi aircraft away from the inferno. His reckless action drew the attention of Japanese attackers and he was hit twice by machine gun bullets but he still continued his efforts.

Sergeant Jim Davenport was helping in the dispersal of planes when his left leg was hit by shrapnel. A few

The carnage at Wheeler Field as photographed from the cockpit of a Japanese attacker. (Source: National Archives)

minutes later, still exposed, his right leg was torn by a machine-gun bullet.

Private Donald Plant was carrying a wounded man from another unit when he was cut down and killed by a strafing plane.

First Lieutenant "Mike" Moore drove to the hangar line during the attack and began to fight the raging fires until he could get a fighter airborne.

Phil Rasmussen buckled his Colt .45 pistol over his pajamas and made his way to the flight line. He began taxiing airplanes to dispersal areas with Japanese strafers in hot pursuit. As enemy aircraft roared overhead Phil banged away with his pistol in a defiant but largely futile response.

Burning P-40s and P-36s on the ramp were now igniting adjacent planes. Whole rows were going off like strings of giant firecrackers.

Hangar I, housing some two million rounds of ammunition, was afire and began to cook off the stored rounds, adding to the hazard of Japanese machine-gun fire.

Dead and wounded men were being pulled free of bombed and burning buildings. Exploding .50 caliber ammunition in Hangar I made the job of removing casualties particularly dangerous in the 72nd Squadron area. Jim Beckwith concenrated the efforts of his men on the wounded. All 12 of his P-40s had been destroyed beyond salvage.

While fire fighting crews poured water into burning hangars, aircraft tugs were used to batter in the warped doors. Once inside, personnel worked to salvage essential tools and equipment while wading through tepid water and working around fires.

Ground crews at Haleiwa had witnessed the approach of Fuchida's first wave and assumed it was a flight of U.S. Navy carrier planes. It seems likely that the distance which did not permit correct aircraft recognition also prevented the Japanese from observing the grass airstrip.

A few minutes after the "Navy" planes had disappeared to the South, the sergeant who had Charge of Quarters at Haleiwa came running out of the orderly room tent. In a state of frenzy, he approached a group of enlisted men. His arms were windmilling and his mouth was moving, but he wasn't saying anything. Finally he blurted out the word, "Japs!"

There were only two officers present at Haleiwa. One was Lt. Charles Kneen. A newly arrived "yardbird", Charlie had joined the Air Force to "fly a P-40" but had yet to be given the opportunity. However, he took charge like a veteran and began directing the ground crews. With feverish activity they fueled, armed, and warmed up the engines of the Squadron's P-40 and P-36 aircraft.

Second Lieutenants Ken Taylor and George Welch had gotten on the phone to alert Haleiwa as soon as the attack on Wheeler Field began. They were astonished to learn that Haleiwa was, so far, untouched. With a minimum of conversation they jumped in a car and sped for the field some ten miles to the north.

Crew chiefs, S/Sgts George Wilson and Cecil Goodroe, had gotten Taylor and Welch's P-40Bs prepared in record time. The two young 2nd Lieutenants scrambled into their cockpits and were airborne about 0820. However, the planes had been engaged in gunnery practice the previous week using only the four wing-mounted .30 caliber guns. The two fuselage mounted .50 caliber guns on each plane were inoperative.

Heading due south for their home base at Wheeler, the two P-40 pilots soon overtook a B-17, one of the twelve which had just arrived from California in the midst of the attack.

Passing over Wheeler, Taylor and Welch found no air action, only a panoramic view of the awesome destruction and the still raging fires. Proceeding toward the towering columns of smoke at Pearl Harbor which were the funeral pyres of the great battleships, they caught sight of fifteen to twenty Aichi dive-bombers battering the Marine Base at Ewa.

The P-40s ripped into the unsuspecting Japanese, each flaming a Val and passing through the formation before the startled enemy could bring their rear cockpit guns into firing position.

Their first pass broke the discipline of the Japanese formation and a general melée ensued. Taylor pursued and destroyed a Val that was heading seaward, but a rear gunner from another Val scored hits on Welch and his P-40 began smoking.

Welch pulled up through a cloud layer to assess his damage, but, when the smoke abated and he found the plane handled properly, he renewed the pursuit.

Taylor was pounding another dive-bomber as the Japanese formation scattered for the open sea. Taylor's target dropped out of the fight. Without taking time to observe results, both Tomahawks swung their sights onto other retreating Japanese. Welch's next victim dove into the ocean and Taylor's headed out to sea losing altitude and trailing a streamer of smoke.

Low on ammunition and fuel, the two pilots gave up the chase and headed back to a landing at Wheeler, periodically drawing the fire of U.S. forces.

Harry Brown and John Dains, who had stepped from their barracks celebration to find the Japanese mauling Wheeler Field, had the same idea as Taylor and Welch — get to Haleiwa. They jumped into Harry's pride and joy, a robin's egg blue Ford Coupe, and started for the married officer's quarters to pick up 1st Lt. Robert J. Rogers, their 47th Squadron instructor. En route, a Japanese plane tried to strafe the car but couldn't get its nose down enough and shot out the windows of a house. A brief detour to the chaotic flight line convinced them that Haleiwa was their best bet. They scooped up Rogers and headed north.

Driving the narrow winding road at breakneck speed, Brown attracted another Val intent on perforating his Ford. The Japanese pilot made repeated passes firing his two forward firing machine guns and then chandelled to give his rear gunner a shot. Luckily he and his gunner kept missing as Brown veered from one side of the road to the other praying he would encounter no southbound traffic.

"He was taking full deflection shots but wasn't doing very well," said Brown, disparagingly. It seems unlikely that the Japanese had ever engaged in low-level combat with an automobile.

Bob Rogers, becoming dubious about the outcome of this uneven duel, was yelling at Brown to pull off into a cane field for cover. Johnny Dains was laughing uncontrollably at the Mack Sennett-like chase scene.

Brown bore on, determined to exchange his coupe for a fighter plane. Shortly after they arrived at the field a Japanese dive bomber appeared from the south angling toward Haleiwa. Rogers had just ordered two P-36s to be rolled out.

Private Ralph Wright, a mechanic, was on an aircraft tug in the middle of the field when he spotted the Val.

> For just a moment I thought he was one of ours, but as it banked and dove on the field, it became clear what was about to happen.
>
> From that point on, everything seemed to move in slow motion. I was off the tug and running for cover, the airplane was getting bigger all the time and I thought I would never reach the protection of those palm trees. When I got there the trees didn't seem nearly large enough.

The Haleiwa ground crews, now fully alerted, unleashed a volley of machine-gun and small-arms fire at the Val. Charlie Kneen, knowing he wouldn't get in the air, engaged the enemy with his .45. The Japanese made one half-hearted pass, damaging a single P-36 and Kneen's car, and vanished over the ocean to the north. This enemy aircraft was the only one to locate and attack Haleiwa. Once rid of him, all personnel turned to the work of getting Rogers, Brown, and Dains into the air.

Back at Wheeler Field the reality of the stunning attack began to filter through the initial shock. It had taken Sakamoto's unit just 15 minutes to turn Oahu's main air defense base into a shambles. Casualties were heavy. Lew Sanders observed men "who had been blown out of second story windows to the ground below. They had suffered broken legs, arms, and other wounds. Many were lying dead where they had caught a burst of bullets or shrapnel. Death and injury in the tent area was horrendous. Men had attempted to escape the strafing by digging through wooden tent floors with their bare hands. Hands and fingers were severely lacerated, and in many instances fingernails were torn out."

Nearly 100 neatly parked aircraft, mostly P-40s, were destroyed or disabled. A huge black cloud of smoke from the burning fighters and hangars served as a screen to protect Lt. Sanders' P-36s, now dispersed in their revetments downwind. Only one of the 46th's planes had been damaged.

Officers, mechanics, armorers and clerks worked with grim determination to salvage machine-guns, ammo belts, and parachutes, and to prepare several 46th Squadron planes for action. The two fuselage guns, one .30 caliber and one .50 caliber, were installed hastily in each plane. There was no time to test or boresight.

Lew Sanders held an impromptu briefing of officers and enlisted men regarding their precarious position, ground defense, and the enormous task necessary to get the Squadron fully operational since maintenance

Burned out P-40Bs in front of Hangars 3 and 4. (Source: USAF)

and supply had been disrupted. "Bravery and courage had already been amply demonstrated, so there was no need to mention unflinching response and resistance."

Sanders selected three of the most qualified and disciplined pilots in his command to accompany him in the first four P-36s that had been prepared — Lieutenants John Thacker, Phil Rasmussen, and Othneil Norris.

The pilots mounted their planes, fired up their engines, and prepared for the first sortie from Wheeler. At the last minute, leaving his engine running, Norris climbed out of his cockpit and ran to get a better fitting parachute. Seeing the rest of the formation beginning to taxi out, 2nd Lt. Gordon H. Sterling, who had been standing by hoping to get into the fight, bounded into the empty cockpit of the fourth P-36. He handed his wrist watch to an astonished mechanic, and said, "See that my mother gets this. I won't be coming back," slammed the canopy and gunned the plane down the field.

It was about 0850 when Sanders' flight cleared Wheeler, entered a cloud base at 2,000 feet and headed southeast. As they broke out of the clouds at 8,500 feet Sanders advised the fighter control center of his position and availability. The fighter director reported many bogeys over Kaneohe and Bellows Fields. Sanders acknowledged, increased his climb at full throttle to 11,000 feet, and turned north.

By this time the first wave of the Japanese attack force was streaming back to their carriers. Fuchida, cruising at 15,000 feet over Pearl Harbor, was surveying his handiwork and directing the next wave. This force, led by Lt. Commander Shigekazu Shimazaki of the *Zuikaku*, had been launched at 0715. It consisted of 167 Kates, Vals, and escorting Zekes. About 0850 they began to deploy for the attack run on their targets off the East Coast of Oahu.

Shimazaki's units struck Kaneohe and Bellows airfields and renewed the attacks on Hickam and the badly wounded fleet at Pearl Harbor. These Vals with Zekes flying top cover were the bogeys identified by fighter control who had directed the 46th Squadron's P-36s to rendezvous. Lew Sanders relates the action:

> In a slight dive at near maximum throttle, we sighted a formation of 11 enemy planes at about 6,000 feet. I rocked my wings and the formation tightened up around me. As I began to give hand signals to my flight I saw that Sterling had somehow taken over Norris' plane. It was quite a shock to discover this youngster in formation under such dire circumstances. However, there was no alternative but to signal him to take my right wing position. Then I directed the left element pilots to take agressive action.
>
> We dived, coming in on the enemy formation at an overtaking speed, from about level flight. I fired at the leader, watched tracers enter the fuselage, saw him pull up slightly, and then fall off the the right, smoking. I made a fast 360 degree turn to clear my tail and, at a very short distance ahead, saw a P-36 I thought to be my wingman. Sterling was shooting at a burning enemy plane in a near vertical dive. An instant later another enemy fighter split S-ed on Sterling's tail. I pushed over on the three planes below me and began firing at the one on Sterling. Soon the P-36 ahead of me was on fire and spiraling slowly out of control. The Japanese fighter in my sights was in a dive, trailing white smoke.
>
> I began my pull-out at around 1500 feet, came close to the water, and did a steep climbing turn while looking over the area. All three planes had vanished into the sea. There was no fire and no smoke. Nor did I see any airborne aircraft, friendly or enemy.
>
> I crusied north for a few minutes before turning back south, and, as I leveled off I saw an unidentified plane headed in my direction. When closer I saw the Japanese insignia, applied full throttle, and as we closed, I did a steep climbing turn and rollout in an effort to get on his tail. In a matter of seconds, this fighter was at my level and still climbing. Soon he had a hundred or more feet advantage, and the only way I could stay opposite the enemy aircraft, which was higher and gaining altitude, was to 'walk rudder' and pull my nose up and around.
>
> The disparate performance characteristics of the Japanese plane were bewildering and frightening. I realized that if the pilot had any ability, sooner or later he would be able to use his superior performance and altitude advantage to maneuver behind me for a shot. It also occurred to me that he had to be low on gas and probably would turn back north if I succeeded in breaking off.
>
> After considering that discretion was the better part of valor, and the possibility of my becoming a casualty was the most likely alternative, I decided to end the engagement. I dropped the nose of my P-36 and rolled out beneath the enemy and headed

Enlisted personnel of the 72nd Sq suffered heavy casualties in their tent quarters behind Wheeler's hangar line.(Source: Signal Corps, USA)

Harry Brown, in his P-36, sortied from Haleiwa scoring a victory and one probable. (Source: Harry Brown)

Phil Rasmussen was jumped by Japanese Zeros after shooting down a Val. He brought his P-36A back to Wheeler where it was junked. (Source: Phil Rasmussen)

for shore at full throttle. I observed no pursuit, so I made a tight 180, cleared my tail, and climbed for altitude in a turn.

Lew Sanders had just taken on the new Mitsubishi Zero in a head-to-head dogfight, a violation of future U.S. fighter doctrine. Recalling the historic duel, he said:

> I had logged several hundred hours in the P-36 and was getting the most out of it. But my plane was simply outclassed by the Japanese fighter. Our intelligence later advised that the enemy had no such aircraft, but I knew better.

Returning to Wheeler, Sanders located one of his own flock.

> As I leveled off, I saw another plane headed toward me with puffs of smoke coming from one gun. It was a 46th Squadron plane flying somewhat erratically. I slipped up behind it unnoticed. The plane was badly shot up. The tail wheel was drooping, and there were countless bullet and 20 mm elongated holes in the fuselage and wings. I moved in closer and the pilot, Phil Rasmussen, acknowledged my presence by hand signals. It was astonishing that he was alive and still in the air. A 20 mm cannon shell had shattered his canopy, the radio, and other equipment located directly behind his head.
>
> We returned to Wheeler together, made a direct approach, wheels and flaps down, and received small-arms fire during the landing.

Enroute to the battle over the ocean off Keneohe Bay, Phil Rasmussen had routinely attempted to charge his .50 caliber gun manually and it began to run away on him. (This antiquated procedure was a throw-back to World War I aircraft.) He had to keep that gun cocked until he needed it.

> I uncocked my .50 as we dove on the enemy formation because I wanted the fire power even though that gun was running wild. A Val flew right into that damn stream of .50s, and watching my tracers enter him, I shot him down.
>
> Then, in a flash, I saw a Zeke diving down in flames, with Sterling following in flames, and another Zeke on fire following Sterling, and Lew behind the last Japanese. I watched, like a spectator, as the first three planes all plunged into the waters off the coast.
>
> At that instant I was hit broadside, apparently by two Zeros. They laced my catwalk on both wings with 7.7 mm machine gun fire, and with 20 mm cannon fire, shot off my tail wheel, severed my rudder cables, and shattered my canopy. The canopy hit blew up the radio right behind my head with a deafening explosion.
>
> Immediately, I ducked into a convenient cloud. I thought I had been killed. I was sure that the top of my head had been shot off. I could feel a mass up there and felt sure it was my brains, but I was having such a fight to control the plane that it took a minute or two before I could gingerly put a hand to the top of my helmet. All that was there was a pile of Plexiglass; no blood, not a scratch.

John Thacker's guns jammed on the first pass at the Japanese formation. He continued in the wild dogfight, making dry runs, until his P-36 was hit by cannon fire. Thacker succeeded in breaking off and returned to Wheeler, but a flurry of ground fire convinced him that it was safer in the sky with the Japanese for the moment, so he climbed back up out of range of anti-aircraft fire and waited for things to cool off.

The swirling air battle over Keneohe Bay had ended with both sides retiring, but Rasmussen still had a memorable struggle ahead of him to return in one piece. Seeing Sanders join him was comforting, but he had all he could handle with both feet and both hands just to keep his battered P-36, belching .50 caliber bullets, in the air.

Phil continued to struggle desperately with his disabled plane. It contained over 500 bullet and cannon holes, the latter appeared to be caused by repeated blows with an ax. With the wind howling through the shattered canopy, rudder inoperative, and the engine sputtering, the wounded beast was trying to demonstrate the law of gravity.

With Wheeler Field in sight, Rasmussen was perplexed by the reception: "As we came in over Schofield Barracks I saw a lot of winking lights. They were shooting at us! Fortunately, they weren't well enough organized yet and missed both planes."

Rasmussen stretched his glide and made the Field, skidding on the wet grass. His plane kept trying to ground loop because of the smashed tail wheel and the lack of rudder control. Like the old state fair stunt pilot doing the flying drunk act, he lurched the reluctant P-36 from side to side across the field, eventually stopping at his revetment. The plane was a washout, good only for spare parts, but Phil, still in his pajamas and Colt .45, was full of fight and asking for another plane.

John Thacker, made a second wary approach and landed just after Sanders and Rasmussen. The 46th's four-plane flight had shot down one Val and two Zekes and probably destroyed another Zeke. They lost one plane and its pilot, Gordon Sterling. Lew Sanders seriously questioned "if the cost was attributable to the enemy or our own lack of preparedness."

The diligent ground crews of the 47th Squadron had gotten Brown, Rogers, and Dains all off Haleiwa individually by about 0850. But each P-36 aircraft had only one gun; the solenoid switch for the .50 caliber had been disconnected for gunnery practice. Rogers and Brown, in P-36s, found each other near Kahuku Point and went into a wary Lufbery Circle trying to get on each others' tails before they made mutual identification.

As Brown joined up on his wing, Rogers pointed down toward the water. There were three or four Japanese airplanes headed north out to sea. Harry Brown recalled:

> We did a momentary Alphonse and Gaston act looking at the Japanese and looking back at each other. Then my leader peeled off and dove on the formation, firing a sharp burst and ending up in a screaming chandelle.
>
> I closed with my target, a bomber I first thought, but went all over the sky with him for quite a long time. I had gotten some shots and may have hit him but I couldn't be sure. Finally he started straight down, chopped his throttle dumped his flaps, and I went by him like an express train and almost hit the water. I must have bent the stick, because I pulled so many G's that I blacked out as I rolled into some clouds.

Harry later reasoned that he, too, had tangled with a highly maneuverable Mitsubishi Zeke.

Finding no further action along the north coast, Rogers and Brown headed for Kaena Point on Oahu's northwest tip.

John Webster had abandoned his Garand rifle and gotten to Haleiwa where he took off in a P-36, and Mike Moore had turned in his fire hose for a P-36 and taken off from Wheeler. Both Webster and Moore in independent sorties were directed to the Kaena point area where the enemy force seemed to be concentrating in a withdrawal corridor. In fact, the Japanese plan had designated a rally point 20 nautical miles and 340 degrees from the western extremity of Kaena Point.

While Sanders' flight was engaging part of the Japanese second wave near Bellows Field, another portion of the same strike force attacked Wheeler Field. It was about 0900 when nine Vals were observed approaching the smoldering base in column from the south. The attack force eventually grew to fifteen.

Taylor and Welch were in the process of refueling and reloading their guns when the alarm was raised.

"Welch had already rearmed and was able to get into the air very quickly," recalls Ken Taylor. "However, the ground crews had just barely finished servicing my plane and scattered for cover."

Despite an ammunition dolly parked in front of him, Taylor gunned his engine and began a desperate take off run without regard to impediments or wind direction. Pushing the ammo cart aside, he began rolling across Wheeler's grass directly at the oncoming enemy force. Spotting the P-40 in its vulnerable take off roll the Vals began maneuvering for position to take a crack at him before he could gain the air.

"The Japanese were beginning to strafe the field and my plane in particular. However, we were closing so rapidly that it was impossible for them to lead me enough to get any hits without flying into the ground. I, on the other hand, lifted the nose of my P-40 and was getting in good bursts before my wheels were up."

Taylor made a steep chandelle right in the middle of the Japanese traffic and "came around on what I thought was the last airplane in the string."

Rolling out on the tail of a Val, Ken was pumping bullets into the target at close range. In the midst of this dangerous low level encounter his P-40 came under fire from behind. The last of the Japanese attackers was right on Taylor's tail.

"One bullet came through the canopy, through my left arm, and shattered on the stabilizer control putting several fragments in my leg." Climbing for altitude and jinxing the plane to shake the Aichi dive bomber, Taylor got a welcome glimpse of his pursuer being shot off his tail by George Welch. With his airplane still flyable and his adrenal glands temporarily overriding his wounds, Ken renewed the defense of Wheeler. Pursuing the enemy force to the north, he expended the rest of his ammunition on the Vals before returning to base.

George Welch, with ammo still in his guns, chased the retreating raiders and knocked down one more for his fourth confirmed kill of the day. This second attack on Wheeler Field caused little damage, thanks to the

Charlie Kneen was one of only two officers of the 47th Sq at Haleiwa when the Japanese hit Wheeler. (Source: Charles Kneen)

tenacious counterthrust by Taylor and Welch.

As the final Japanese wave withdrew, Moore, Webster, Rogers, and Brown met the heavy enemy traffic near Kaena Point. Moore and Webster each damaged an enemy aircraft, were themselves jumped and damaged, and Webster was wounded.

Two Japanese went after Bob Rogers as he attacked the enemy formations. Harry Brown said:

> I saw one plane high and banking toward Rogers, who was heading down at 45 degrees with a Val hard on his tail shooting the hell out of him. I feinted for the high one and he cut inside to avoid me, taking him off Rogers. Then I put my prop up the tail of the second one and he made a fatal error, turning away from me right into my line of fire.

Brown was only fifteen yards from the Val when he fired a fatal burst into the plane. He retained a "vivid image" of the terrified rear gunner on the receiving end of his volley. The action was witnessed by men of the 15th Infantry who confirmed the victory.

Bob Rogers dove out of this engagement and headed his crippled P-36 toward Haleiwa. But Harry Brown peeled upward and found himself

> face to face with a covey of 13 or 14 planes. We met head-on in an unscheduled game of 'chicken', and all of us were so surprised and closed so fast that neither side fired a shot. The Japanese soon remedied that and fell all over themselves trying to get at me, all shooting, but I was running pretty hard and they didn't get any hits.

Brown spotted one lonely airplane between himself and Haleiwa and, overtaking it, found it was Mike Moore. Before leaving the Kaena area, Moore spotted a single Japanese plane and attacked it aggressively until he ran out of ammunition. Brown then took up the pursuit and scored several hits as the harried Japanese angled northwest toward Kauai. Harry broke off the engagement well out to sea and claimed the Japanese as a probable since it was emitting a cloud of smoke and losing altitude. It was also off course for its carrier. Brown, Moore, Rogers and Webster all made it safely back to Haleiwa.

Johnny Dains, of the 47th, had flown two lone sorties in a P-40B by about 0930. Dains mixed it up with the Japanese with unknown results. He sustained damage to his own plane but brought it back to Haleiwa.

By about 0945 the Japanese attack had spent its fury. The stragglers of the second wave rendezvoused off Kaena Point and set course for the task force.

About this same time, the irrespressible George Welch in his P-40 and John Dains in a fresh P-36 scrambled off Haleiwa, each for their third mission of the day. It was an ill-fated final flight. The Japanese raiders were gone, scurrying off to the north, but every gun on the Island of Oahu was now aimed skyward and fired at anything with wings. Dains was hit by a volley of ground fire over Schofield Barracks. His plane crashed on the golf course and he was killed. Welch landed unscathed.

The surprise Japanese aerial attack on Hawaii had been a masterpiece of planning and execution. The results were devastating. In the great fleet anchorage at Pearl Harbor the Navy had lost the use of eight battleships, which were either sunk or severely damaged. In addition, the Navy suffered severe damage to three light cruisers and three destroyers. The old battleship *Utah*, used as a target ship, was sunk at the regular berth of the carrier *Saratoga*. A repair ship and a seaplane tender were damaged and a minelayer was sunk.

The combined loss of Army, Navy, and Marine aircraft was 188, and an additional 160 were damaged.

Some of the heroes of 7 December 41, (left to right) Harry Brown, Phil Rasmussen, Lew Sanders, Ken Taylor and John Webster (KIA). (Source: Lew Sanders)

Fewer than 90 Army planes of all types survived on four airfields.

American military and civilian casualties totaled 2,403 dead and 1,178 wounded.

Japanese losses were modest by comparison. One fleet submarine and five midget subs operating in the approaches to Pearl Harbor were sunk. Twenty nine aircraft — five Kates, 15 Vals, and nine Zekes — with 55 aircrew members, failed to regain their carriers. Nineteen additional planes were jettisoned on return to the IJN task force due to battle damage or landing accidents.

The 15th Pursuit Group had provided the only real aerial opposition offered by U.S. forces. Eleven of the Group's pilots got into the air during the attack and flew a total of 14 sorties. Those pilots were credited with ten confirmed kills. They definitely scored hits on nine other Japanese planes. Some of these "probables" were undoubtedly part of the 29 that failed to return to the enemy carriers. Lieutenants Sterling and Dains were killed in the battle, but only Sterling was lost as a result of enemy action. (See Appendix 2)

The 15th sustained heavy losses on the ground at Wheeler Field. Two hangars were heavily damaged and many other facilities received light to moderate damage. All of the aircraft of the 45th and 72nd Squadrons were destroyed or damaged. Many of the Group's remaining aircraft sustained varying degrees of damage from air action or friendly ground fire, and some of these were later cannibalized for spare parts. But the most stunning loss to the 15th was the 57 enlisted men who were casualties of the bombing and strafing attacks. The Group suffered 23 dead and 34 wounded. (See Appendix 3)

The agony of 7 December 1941 did not end with the departure of Fuchida's last wave. Another air attack was imagined or expected with each passing hour.

Fighter control ordered the 46th Squadron to put a combat air patrol (CAP) over Pearl Harbor. About noon Lew Sanders dutifully took off, leading a three-plane flight. Army and Navy officers either could not or would not control their heavy anti-aircraft batteries, and the 46th's planes were subjected to an infuriating barrage of ack-ack as high as 12,000 feet. The mission was called off, and the P-36s drew machine-gun fire at lower altitudes on the return to Wheeler. Both Sanders' and Moore's aircraft sustained damage.

Other units made equally fruitless and similarly dangerous flights during the day. A final mission was flown at dusk by ten 15th Group fighters escorting single B-17s on a search north-northwest of Oahu in a 200-mile sweep. They were airborne for about one and one half hours.

While landing from this third sortie of the day, Lew Sanders was momentarily terrified as tracers arched over his plane from behind. He assumed he had touched down in the midst of another deadly strafing attack. Again, it proved to be friendly fire, this time from another P-36 landing in Sanders' wake. Fred Shiflett had forgotten to put his guns back on 'safe' and had given the trigger a squeeze as he pulled the stick back to land. Fortunately for everyone involved, it was a short burst and it missed the Squadron CO.

A detail of non-coms from the 47th Squadron were dispatched from Haleiwa to Wheeler for ammo and supplies. Stopping briefly at their regular barracks at Wheeler Field they found reason to be thankful that they had been in tents at Haleiwa on that fateful day. Ralph Wright found "the barracks a shambles. My bunk was covered with rubble and my wall locker was riddled with shrapnel."

That evening, back at Haleiwa, Captain Gordon Austin gave his Squadron a grim assessment. The Japanese were expected to land in force. Since the 47th possessed nothing but rifles and sidearms, they were not expected to stem an invasion. Austin gave his young soldiers and pilots sobering orders: "If we are invaded, take to the mountains with whatever provisions you can carry and hold out as long as possible."

As darkness settled on Oahu, terror of the unknown became almost as intense as the reality of the daring daylight raids. Tension fed by rumors of invasion, paratroop landings, and subversive outbreaks gripped the island.

The clean white barracks, which made inviting targets, were evacuated and personnel were dispersed to outlying temporary shelters or to spend a night camped out. Ground crews labored in the revetments to repair, refuel and arm the few remaining fighters in anticipation of the next onslaught. Food was scarce and nerves were frayed. It was especially tough for married men who agonized over the fate of their families. All women and children on the base had been evacuated to an uncomfortable but secure area in the Koolau Mountains.

George Welch and Harry Brown drove in from Haleiwa seeking the fate of their downed comrade, John Dains, but in the chaos at Wheeler they could determine nothing and returned glumly to their airstrip.

When darkness fell, a total blackout was imposed and stark horror was constantly intermingled with grim humor.

Phil Rasmussen loaded his car with a commandeered Garand rifle, bandoleers of ammunition and C-Rations. "We were prepared to fight it out in the hills as gueril-las, so convinced were we that we would be invaded. For weeks we ran around with all that stuff in our trunks."

Guard posts were set up all over Wheeler, but lacking sufficient time to prepare foxholes or set up barricades, sentries had to improvise. Some put ladders down street manholes, and stood guard on the ladder with only their heads and rifles at street level.

A sign and counter-sign arrangement had been established at Wheeler. The challenge was "Thomas," to be answered by the countersign, "Jefferson," but few people got a chance to use the response. Lew Sanders said, "All night you could hear the sentries challenging loudly, 'Thomas,' and then 'Bang'. So when you heard that sign you'd better be dropping to the ground because there was a bullet following."

Sergeant Westhaver, bandaged but "still able to get about", settled into a guard post for the night like many other soldiers. Nestled into some bushes on Wheeler's perimeter, he had a Springfield "03" rifle and one five-round clip to repel a rumored ground assault by Japanese paratroops. He was "scared as Hell, and thought the night would never end."

The trigger happy guards shot a lot of people that night, including each other. Cows and dogs suffered heavy casualties as they magically took the form of invaders or saboteurs. Indeed sentry fire crackled at imiginary enemies all over Oahu through the night.

On the afternoon of 7 December, fate, in the form of Admiral Nagumo's cautious apprehension and limited expectations, preordained the future course of the war. While the Americans on Oahu were bracing for the next blow, haunted by the possibility that it might be fatal, Nagumo was withdrawing his forces to preserve a bloody, but incomplete, victory.

At 1330, after recovering the last stragglers on his carriers, Nagumo turned the great Japanese task force to a northwesterly direction and, still maintaining radio silence, withdrew at high speed.

For the 15th Pursuit Group the long campaign had just begun. The war would last another three years and eight months, and the dark journey between that first brutal action and the last battle would be marked by the rosters of the dead.

Chapter II

DEFENSE, TRAINING, BOREDOM 8 December 1941 to March 1943

The stunning surprise attack of Sunday, December 7th, sowed destruction, but it also planted the seeds of certain retribution. Never again would Hawaii be left naked to aggression. The Japanese attack had left a legacy of perpetual vigilance. "The Blitz", as it was known to the survivors, fused the determination of Hawaii's military and civilian populations.

The 15th Group's maintenance personnel performed round-the-clock miracles, repairing and refitting damaged aircraft. Working at temporary locations, dispersed from the heart of Wheeler's facilities, they adapted and adjusted, but they got ready. Even the old P-36 fighters were refitted with two .50 caliber guns and armor plating salvaged from wrecked P-40s.

Combat air patrols were flown day and night, though none of the pilots had any experience in night tactics. Night air fighting was an art yet to be fashioned. "The night patrols were scary as Hell at first," said Phil Rasmussen. "With the adrenaline charging through us, we imagined seeing enemy aircraft constantly."

As soon as communications and transportation were sorted out, the Group scattered its Squadrons to outlying airfields. The 45th went to Mokuleia and the 46th to Ewa. The 47th remained at Haleiwa and the 72nd at Wheeler. They were determined not to forget the lesson of dispersal.

The men realized losing battles were being fought elsewhere in the Pacific Theatre and this heightened the tension on Oahu. The Philippine Air Force had suffered a nearly identical fate. Most of their planes had been destroyed on the ground in the first attack. Luzon and the Malay Penninsula had been invaded. Guam had fallen on 10 December, and Wake Island, battered by superior forces for 16 days, was finally overwhelmed on 23 December.

A nearly continuous CAP was maintained over and around Oahu in full expectation of another assault and invasion. This air of expectancy was heightened by the knowledge that the Japanese forces had retired to their corner before the end of the bout. U.S. forces in Hawaii were on the ropes, but still in the fight.

Since many junior pilots had joined the Group only a few days before the Blitz, a crash training program was started with the limited resources at hand. However, gunnery training was not part of the curriculum because ammunition was in short supply. Two CAP missions per day were common assignments for the veterans. This intensive combination of air defense missions and

Bob Kaempfer, in a PR shot for stateside consumption, poses before his 72nd Sq P-36 in late December 41. Ground crewmen (left to right) are: Cpl. Scheer, radioman, Sgt. McLaughlin, parachute rigger, S/Sgt. Knox, crew chief, and Sgt. Mettlin, armorer. (Source: Robert Kaempfer)

A newly delivered P-40D of the 46th Sq parked in a revetment at Wheeler. Camouflage netting came into use only after the Japanese attack. (Source: Alec Streete)

advanced combat training took an unavoidable toll in men and machines. Second Lieutenant Karl F. Harris was the first operational fatality. His 47th Squadron P-40B spun into the ocean off Oahu on 20 December.

Christmas Day 1941 was an all time low for morale. Military dependents sailed from Honolulu for the mainland aboard the *S. S. Mariposa*. While married men could feel a measure of relief that their families were being evacuated from a war zone, it was still a bitter Noel.

On Oahu 1942 was ushered in with news of continued Allied reverses in the Western Pacific. However, replacement aircraft were beginning to arrive from the Mainland, and the 15th was getting back to full strength. New P-40D and E models and Bell P-39D, "Aircobras", had been received. For the less experienced pilots each aircraft was like a new girl, every one an original design with exceptional traits. For the veteran flyers, the adjustment was more subtle.

The venerable Curtiss P-36 was an honest plane with good handling characteristics. It took to aerobatics and recovered well from a spin. At 5,470 lbs. gross weight, it was one of the smallest Army fighters of World War II and it landed at a modest 70 m.p.h.

One of the Hawk's hidden hazards showed itself only when the plane was grounded. The P-36 had one of the last radial-engine shotgun starters. The breach mechanism was located just under the center of the instrument panel between the pilot's legs. If the first shell didn't kick the engine over, it was necessary to snap the breech open, clear the spent cartridge and insert a live one. Being too casual about this exercise could cause an unpleasant experience. The breech mechanism was aimed at the pilot's crotch, and unless one bled off the pressure with great care, the empty shell casing would fly back, doing injury to a critical part of the anatomy. Positioning the control stick in front of the breech as a deflctor was a necessary precaution if a P-36 pilot did not wish to sing soprano.

The P-40, while a direct descendant of the Curtiss P-36, was a very different aircraft. It had a long, liquid-cooled, in-line engine. Though not much bigger in outward appearance that its sire, it weighed in at 7,645 lbs. loaded, a ton more than the P-36. The B model, with an Allison engine, had a maximum speed of 352 m.p.h. and landed at 80 m.p.h.

The long nosed P-40 developed considerable torque as it gained power on take off, and pilots were obliged to apply increasing amounts of right rudder to compensate. There were airmen who maintained you could spot a P-40 pilot in shorts by his overdeveloped right leg. Like all the Curtiss Hawk line, the P-40B and later models were good in combat aerobatics and generally had no bad spin characteristics.

In a dive, the P-40 was like a stone rolling downhill; it could quickly exceed its maximum straight and level speed roaring to over 450 m.p.h. This was to become one of its tactical advantages. It was usually not able to dogfight the nimble Zeke but it could always outdive and outdistance the enemy.

The armament on the P-40B was much improved over that of the two gun P-36. The B had two .50 caliber and four .30 caliber guns. All later models of the P-40 carried six .50 caliber guns.

The Bell P-39 was an airplane of radical design. Its needle-nose housed a 37 mm cannon. The Allison power plant sat behind the cockpit. Though its dimensions were slightly smaller than the P-40, it weighed more, at 7,830 lbs. gross.

The Aircobra, as it was grandly named by the manufacturer, had a maximum speed of 368 m.p.h. It was faster than most fighters in 1942, Allied or enemy, but top performance was only attained while flying at low altitude. The lack of a supercharger doomed the P-39 to tactial roles at or near deck level. It had a critical altitude of about 12,000 feet and rapidly lost power and performance at higher altitudes.

The firepower of the P-39D was made awesome by its 30-round 37 mm cannon, used as an anti-tank weapon in surface combat. Secondary armament consisted of two .50 caliber guns set into the fuselage over the cannon and four .30 caliber guns in the wings.

Another unique feature of the P-39 was its tricycle landing gear. Learning to work with this required some adjustment for both rookie and veteran pilots. It was the first tricycle-type plane in the Army Air Force.

Generally called the "Cobra" by its pilots, the Bell P-39 was the engineering marvel of its day in many respects. But the plane was bedeviled by stability problems. Center of gravity problems were created by locating the engine behind the cockpit and aft of the middle of the wing. This gave the ship a tendency to enter into unscheduled aerobatics, including high-speed stalls and rumored end-over-end tumbles. Even the P-39 flight manual prohibited "outside loops and spins" and recommended against "snap rolls and spinning". In other words, you weren't likely to pull out of a spin in this plane.

The same flight manual advised, "Warning: Pullouts

Cockpit of a P-36A showing the starter breech aimed at the pilot. (Source: USAF)

from dives are to be started at 10,000 feet minimum altitude;'' an extraordinary restriction for an aircraft employed in low-level attacks and often called on to engage enemy fighters at whatever altitude survival dictated.

Still, many pilots were partial to the P-39. One of these was Lt. Charles Bryant who would later fly it in combat. ''If you respected its limitations, it was a good plane,'' recalled Charlie. ''Some people were apprehensive about flying it because of rumors more than reality. I figured I had to fly it — they didn't offer me a selection — so why worry about it?''

Charlie Bryant and a few others were the exception. Generally speaking, the P-39 was never a popular plane. On the contrary, it was unloved. An old AAF rhyme about the Cobra seemed more like an elegy:

''Don't give me a P-39
With an engine that's mounted behind.
It will tumble and roll
And dig a big hole.
Don't give me a P-39.

The aged Boeing P-26, an open cockpit relic, was still used for training and target towing. Mercifully, none of them were sent against the Japanese at Pearl Harbor. They were in the Philippines where results were predictably disastrous.

The appearance of new planes involved the 15th Group not only in major training exercises, but in monumental technical problems. The variety of aircraft still operational in early 1942 presented a parts and maintenance nightmare to engineering officers, line chiefs, and mechanics. All of the ground crews performed their duties with exceptional devotion and total disregard for hours worked. Periodic sightings of Japanese submarines and a random night shelling by enemy subs at scattered points in the Islands seemed to suggest the possible return of the IJN carrier divisions. Thusly, were nerves kept tightly wound until mid 1942.

Though new equipment and training procedures occupied most of their time, the pilots of the 15th spent many unlogged hours discussing the Blitz. Enemy planes and tactics were reviewed in formal briefings as well as countless informal bull sessions. The Japanese had displayed good air discipline and aggressiveness. The outstanding performance and superior firepower of the new Mitsubishi Zero, or Zeke, was totally unexpected.

The combination of Japanese equipment and tactics encountered over Oahu and in other Pacific battlegrounds necessitated the formulation of new tactical doctrines. It quickly became Air Force dogma that you never tried to dogfight a Zeke. The P-40 could neither outclimb nor outmaneuver the Mitsubishi product, but it could outdive and outrun it. Though the P-40 could take more punishment than the Zeke, it was apparent, early on, that the Japanese naval aviators flying this plane were superb airmen. Therefore the 15th's fighter pilot training program aimed at excellence. In the early years of the war the margin between aircraft was not sufficient to provide any assurance of victory. Discipline and training usually decided survival and victory.

In a March 1942 report to Headquarters, Seventh Fighter Command, leaders of the 15th Group reviewed "lessons learned" and rendered their opinions as to future training and tactics.

Jim Beckwith, CO of the 72nd Squadron declared: "We need extensive landing training to insure the utmost conservation of equipment. Formation flying instills flight discipline, confidence in one's ability, and enables a flight or element leader to direct a concentrated fire from two or more aircraft at an objective."

Sandy Kofahl, CO of the 45th Squadron added: "We need much practice on formation flying and simulated aerial attacks by all types of aircraft. Hit and run tactics are the only technique that can be used with our present type of equipment."

January 42. The 72nd Sq reequipped with new P-40Ds. (Left to Right) Front row: Bill Waldman, Joe Powell, Jim Beckwith, CO, Bob McCabe, Pappy Sawyer, Bill Feiler; back row: Bill Haney, Roy Wigley (KIA), Bill Martin, John Cox (KPC), John Simonton. The plane was named "Squirt" for Beckwith's daughter. (Source: Jim Beckwith)

Lew Sanders, the battle tested CO of the 46th said: "Gunnery training requires the most emphasis." Regarding tactics, Sanders had many suggestions and observations. He viewed hit-and-run as essential, "because Japanese aircraft are vastly more maneuverable than our own." Commenting on the importance of dispersal and revetments, Sanders noted, "All reports from the Far East indicate that more aircraft are lost as a result of ground strafing than aerial combat." Sanders considered height a paramount matter if interception was the mission, but found that "Altitude is one of the most vital factors to be considered in the employment of the P-39D. They are medium altitude interceptors only and cannot be expected to give a good account against Japanese fighters of the Zero type."

Group CO, Bill Steele, philosophized on the beginnings of a new era in aerial warfare: "The days of individual combat are gone. All pilots must be taught the technique of the hit-and-run attack which is best suited for our heavy fast equipment. They can outdive and outrun anything they might be up against, but we cannot dogfight with the highly maneuverable fighters used by the Japanese. Above all else, dogfighting must be avoided."

The year 1942 brought a realignment of commands and commanders. The old Hawaiian Air Force was redesignated the Seventh Air Force. The new Navy command had been vested in Admiral Chester W. Nimitz. As Commander-in-Chief Pacific Fleet (CINC-PAC) and Commander Pacific Ocean Area, he would retain a close relationship with the Seventh Air Force for the duration of the war. The Seventh would literally be the Navy's Army Air Force.

Major Blanchard left the 15th for reassignment to the States on 12 February 1942 and Major William S. Steele became Group commander, a position he was to hold for over a year. The 15th Pursuit Group was redesignated the 15th Fighter Group, dropping the archaic term.

A 45th Sq P-40B on Stanley Field, an airstrip carved out of the Schofield Barracks golf course. Pilot (far left) is Fred Stoffel. (Source: National Archives)

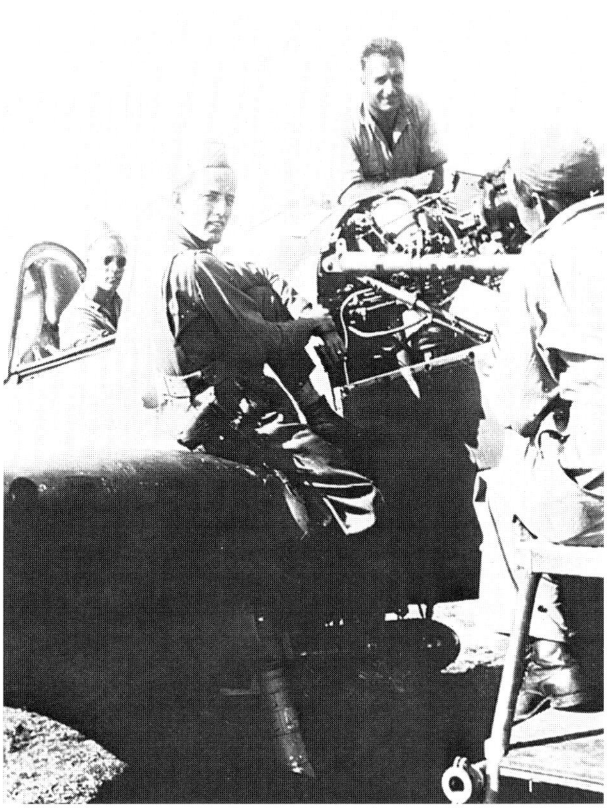

Above — "Pandora's Box Maru" a P-39D of the 46th Sq., is unbuttoned to reveal unique behind cockpit engine. (Source: Lew Sanders)

The conversion to liquid cooled engines and new planes taxed the ability of ground crews: Left — Jim Cox (KPC), sits the wing of his 72nd Sq P-40D during maintenance. (Source: Alec Streete)

Armed and Alert: Left to right — Ken Workman, Bob Rogers, John Babel and Charlie Kneen of the 47th Sq at Haleiwa. (Source: Charles Kneen)

Armed and Alert: Left to right — Front row: Homer Forsythe, Eldon "Scrap Iron" Stratton(KIA); middle row sitting: John Thacker, Frank Tomkins, Paul Fojtik, John Thorgerson; middle row standing: Fred Shifflet(KIA), George Welch(KPC), Joel Zabel, Dick Toole; back row: Mike Moore, H. H. Cords, George Abel at the 46th Squadron's alert tent on Mokuleia.(Source: Paul Fojtik)

The months following the Blitz were heavy with honors and sad tributes to the men of the 15th. (See Appendix 4) Award ceremonies were highly formal affairs with a review by officers and enlisted men of the Group. Uniforms were "Steel helmets, gas masks, side arms (pistols with belts complete)."

Many extraordinary deeds were never recognized by any official awards or citations. Some only much later. Master Sergeant Clayton Westhaver received a Bronze Star 39 years after his heroic actions. Others were also honored many years after 7 December 1941.

The presentation ceremonies for fallen members of the Group were somber occasions and evoked bitter memories. Gordon Sterling was awarded the Distinguished Flying Cross and the Purple Heart posthumously. John Dains won posthumous awards of the Silver Star and Purple Heart. The 72nd Squadron's deceased First Sergeant, Edward Burns, was honored with a posthumous Purple Heart as were other enlisted men killed in the 7 December attack. All wounded personnel received the Purple Heart. In an additional tribute, three roads at Wheeler Field were renamed for First Sgt. Burns and Lts. Sterling and Dains. On the evening of 3 May 1942, in Post Chapel No. 3, a newly organized chapter of the Veterans of Foreign Wars was named and dedicated to the memory of Gordon Sterling. As a final sweeping recognition of their courageous service, the War Department awarded Battle Honors to the 15th Group for 7 December 1941.

The great carrier task force engagement of 5-7 June 1942, the Battle of Midway, was fought and won by U.S. forces with the sinking of the Japanese carriers,*Kaga*, *Akagi*, *Hiryu*, and *Soryu*. The United States Navy lost the aircraft carrier *Yorktown*. The destruction of the four IJN carriers and one heavy cruiser suddenly and dramatically tipped the balance of naval power. It was the key naval battle of the Pacific war and it signaled the 'turning of the tide.'

The 15th Fighter Group was in a high state of readiness on Oahu as the struggle off Midway unfolded. But Nagumo and his great ships never came closer than 1200 miles. From this date on, Hawaii was in the backwash of the war.

It was not until July 1942 that the last of the Old P-36 Hawks were retired to the Hickam Depot. Yet the last P-26 had only been phased out of operational use in April. Their passing was not lamented. The Squadrons were then fully equipped with late model P-40s (including F and K models) and P-39D Cobras.

However, the November 1942 loss of the Group hack, a venerable and rare Sikorsky OA-8 twin-engined flying-boat, caused general gloom even though there were no fatalities. It had been used to shuttle personnel to and from Hilo and other out-island locations. The plane had caught a wave while landing in Kaneohe Bay and flipped over on its back. The pilot, nameless in

P-39Ds of the 46th Sq taxi out at Hilo, Hawaii, in January 43. Note bombs slung under fuselages. (Source: Ken Powell)

records, dove out safely, but Radio Operator Melvin Hendricks had to abandon ship through the floor which had suddenly become the ceiling. Technical Sergeant Hendricks made a satisfactory adjustment from this unnerving experience and stayed on to become Section Chief of Group Communications.

While continuing in its role as a defensive force, the 15th Fighter Group assumed a dual role. It began a long and unspectacular mission as a "Farm Club" to the entire Pacific Theatre for trained fighter pilots. The Group served as a replacement training unit and reserve pool to be drawn on by the Fifth, Seventh, and Thirteenth Air Forces. Some pilots also returned to the United States to flesh out new groups destined for Europe and Africa. (See Appendix 5)

Promotions and wholesale reassignments characterized 1942 for the 15th. Its veteran officers advanced in the organization or became the glue that bonded together new units.

Organizational changes also afflicted the Group as the Command utilized it as a stragetic reserve. In October it was stripped of the 72nd Squadron which was assigned to the 318th Fighter Group, a new outfit in the Seventh Fighter Command. A few weeks later, the 12th Fighter Squadron was transferred from the 15th to the 18th Fighter Group and shipped out from an uneventful garrison job at Christmas Island to the heart of the fighting in the Solomon Islands. The 18th Group, long a fixture in the Hawaiian air establishment, thus left the Seventh Air Force for good and fought the rest of the war with the Thirteenth Air Force in the Southwest Pacific islands campaign.

With the end of 1942 came the bitter anniversary of the Blitz and the end of the first year of the war in the Pacific. Intensive training had caused a terrible toll of men and planes. These operational fatalities would ultimately exceed the 15th's future combat losses. (See Appendix 6) The Group had experienced the loss of 13 pilots and 31 of its fighter aircraft in operational accidents in 1942. (See Appendix 7)

All in all, 1942 had been a year of major events in the Pacific War. The Japanese advance across New Guinea had been halted by Australian troops along the Kokoda Trail just short of Port Moresby. Guadalcanal in the Solomons had been invaded by U.S. Marines. The Japanese Navy had been mauled at the Battle of Midway, and the entire Allied strategic picture was vastly improved. But those who remained with the 15th Fighter Group had no part in these great conflicts. They served their assigned roles in obscurity and without glory, many of them dying in seemingly routine training and defense missions. The price of vigilance remined high.

The year 1943 dawned with the Group's Squadrons

Right: Mechanics John Rega (on wing) and Russ Bishop (in cockpit) boresight a 47th Sq P-40 at Haleiwa. (Source: Fred Arnold)

Below: 47th Sq P-40s during a demonstration flight over Honolulu in mid-1943 spell out Morse Code V for Victory. (Source: W. H. Sparks)

still scattered about the Hawaiian Islands; the 45th at Bellows Field, the 46th at Hilo on the big island, and the 47th still at Haleiwa. In January 1943 Major Jim Beckwith was sent Down Under on 30 days temporary duty as an observer of fighter operations. He flew five escort and strafing missions from Port Moresby with units of the Fifth Fighter Command.

In addition to viewing the war from a cockpit, Jim held extensive discussions with fighter leaders of both Fifth and Thirteenth Air Forces regarding tactics and air combat techniques. The firsthand knowledge he acquired was incorporated into the Group's training program and foreshadowed his future leadership role in the unit.

The combat training of pilots by well defined and repeated procedures, followed by critiques, reflected the deadly nature of the busines. Formation flying, formation aerobatics, the "rat race" (simulated dogfighting), and gunnery practice were hammered into new pilots. Day after day the skies over the Hawaiian islands were filled with dozens of diving tumbling planes as young flyers honed their skills for future action.

"In the 45th Squadron, I was the teacher," said Sandy Kofahl. "Anyone who wanted to challenge me was welcome. Just come into the Ops Tent and say so. Gabreski was the toughest to defeat." First Lieutenant Francis S. Gabreski became one of the Group's most renowned alumni by downing 28 German aircraft while serving in Europe with the 56th Fighter Group.

Two-plane elements practiced attacks on other two and four ship formations. Both Army and Navy bombers were fair game for a simulated pass. The tight four-ship string formation was found to be the ultimate in training wingmen. A pilot who had learned to stay in formation through loops, rolls, and prolonged high speed dives was hard to lose in the most violent mutual support maneuvers.

Navigation was also high on the list of essential courses. "Time, heading, and airspeed" were hammered into newcomers. Navigational errors might be tolerated in other war zones with large land masses and distinguishing landmarks, but in the Pacific's vastness, men flew into oblivion based on a few degrees of deviation from their heading.

Training continued at an intensive pace while the 15th fulfilled its assignment as a fighter pilot reservoir for units engaged in the Southwest Pacific area. Pilots passing through the Group's training program would live and fly together for a time, establishing enigmatic bonds. Then, singly or in small clusters, they would be separated and shipped off to some secret base in the war zone. It was often years before their paths crossed again or they learned each other's fate.

Many of the veteran pilots of the 15th left to form the backbone of new fighter groups. They served not only in the Southwest Pacific but in many other theaters of combat.

In March of 1943 there was a stirring of activity as the 78th Fighter Squadron, long a part of the 18th Group, transferred to the 15th while on station at Midway Island. Later in the month Lt. Colonel Steele left for reassignment to Mitchel Field, Long Island, and Lt. Colonel Sherwood E. Buckland became boss of the 15th Group.

Training accidents and fatalities mounted alarmingly with ten deaths in the first five months of 1943. The Group Flight Surgeon observed that pilots were becoming "overtrained." Many were accumulating 60 to 100 hours monthly flying time in fighter type aircraft, and it was thought that this instensity of operations was contributing to pilot error.

The atmosphere of frenzied training generally masked the boredom and vexation of men seeking to use their skills against the enemy. Unlike ground troops waiting quietly for battle, these soldiers persisted in flinging themselves about the sky at 400 m.p.h. in mechanical monsters which periodically dragged them to their deaths.

However, the United States was marshalling its strength for major offensive operations. There were signs that lifted the spirits of young men yearning for action. Aircraft modifications were undertaken including the introduction of VHF radio sets, the appearance of the new IFF (Identification Friend or Foe) transponder, and installation of ignition pressurization systems. Catapult launching equipment was being fashioned for the P-40s and P-39s.

At long last, units of the 15th Fighter Group would begin to catch up with the war. Those who were poised for action and those who would continue to wait exhibited a special sort of devotion to duty displayed by men who serve in seemingly empty roles.

Aviators were never forced into the profession of fighter pilot. It was relatively easy to be transferred out. Those who followed the profession had a consuming desire to engage the enemy. So, it was an almost intolerable frustration for those who stayed on to guard Hawaii. They dubbed themselved the Pineapple Air Force.

Chapter III

PINPOINTS IN THE PACIFIC March 1943 to March 1944

Hawaii and Australia anchored the Allies' invisible front in a theatre that involved an ocean of incomprehensible proportions interspersed by widely scattered and incredibly small pinpoints of land — the Pacific atolls. It was 4800 miles between Hawaii and Australia. These two bases served both as flank defense posts and staging areas for the offensive operations that would be needed to sever Japan's vital raw material supply lines, pave the way for the liberation of the Philippines, and ultimately allow a thrust at the heart of the enemy's homeland.

However, between the two anchors, on the perimeter of the Japanese line, were the Gilbert and Marshall Islands. Administration of this vast archipelago, geographically referred to as Micronesia, had been awarded to Japan in 1920 by a League of Nations mandate. For twenty years the Japanese had been cautiously but deliberately militarizing these islands. By 1943 they posed a formidable perimeter defense and a bulge in our shipping lanes with which the Allies were compelled to deal.

CINCPAC, Admiral Nimitz, determined on a plan to attack and secure certain bases in the Gilbert Island group as a prelude to the Central Pacific offensive. The operation was labeled GALVANIC, and began with carrier strikes and a detailed reconnaissance of the intended targets by Seventh Air Force long-range bombers.

In an atmosphere of restless exhilaration, the 15th Group prepared to play a role in this great undertaking. By mid-March the 46th Squadron, Major Ken Powell commanding, received orders to relieve the 333rd Fighter Squadron on Canton Island. The two units left their equipment in place and prepared to exchange aircraft as well as base assignments.

The 46th had been at Hilo, Hawaii, for three months. They prepared to leave this paradise of beauty and civilized amenities for a place the 333rd had dubbed "The Isle of Atonement".

The pilots, the air echelon, were to be ferried to Canton courtesy of the Seventh's Southern Cross Airways. The ground echelon, consisting of four officers and 234 enlisted men, embarked on the *S. S. Comet* from Hilo on 19 March 1943.

46th Sq portrait, January 43, Hilo: (Left to right) Front row: Paul Montrose, Tom Kephart (KPC), Bob Boal, Norman Lipman, Bob Fetch, Ken Newell; middle row: Keith Rasmussen, Jack Davis, Don Peck, Keith Brown, Smith, Friederick, Travis Wells (KIA), Jim Beckwith, Deputy Group CO; back row: Dr. George Hart, Flight Surgeon, Clifford Erdman (KIA), F. R. Daugherty, Lt. Col. Bill Steele, Group CO, Bill Southerland (KPC), Paul Fojtik, Unknown, Ken Powell, Sq CO. (Source: Ken Powell)

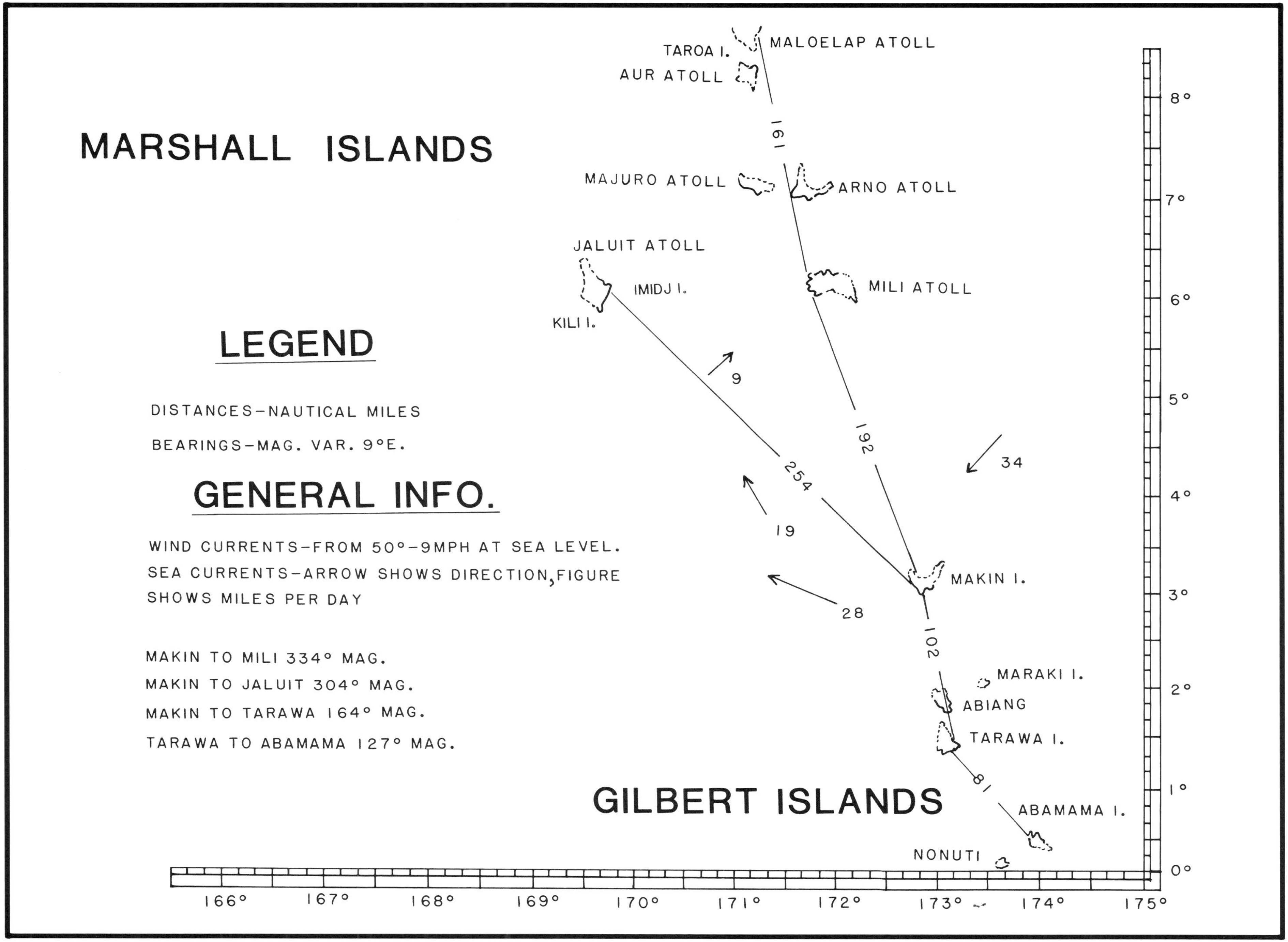
MARSHALL ISLANDS
LEGEND
DISTANCES–NAUTICAL MILES
BEARINGS–MAG. VAR. 9°E.
GENERAL INFO.
WIND CURRENTS–FROM 50°–9MPH AT SEA LEVEL.
SEA CURRENTS–ARROW SHOWS DIRECTION, FIGURE SHOWS MILES PER DAY
MAKIN TO MILI 334° MAG.
MAKIN TO JALUIT 304° MAG.
MAKIN TO TARAWA 164° MAG.
TARAWA TO ABAMAMA 127° MAG.
TAROA I.
MALOELAP ATOLL
AUR ATOLL
161
MAJURO ATOLL
ARNO ATOLL
JALUIT ATOLL
IMIDJ I.
KILI I.
MILI ATOLL
9
192
254
34
19
MAKIN I.
28
102
MARAKI I.
ABIANG
TARAWA I.
81
GILBERT ISLANDS
ABAMAMA I.
NONUTI
8°
7°
6°
5°
4°
3°
2°
1°
0°
166°
167°
168°
169°
170°
171°
172°
173°
174°
175°

The *Comet*, hardly an ocean liner, had been formerly a night boat in the Boston — Providence — New York run. She was a small vessel, 2500 tons, and had only a 15 foot draft. Old salts among the soldiers made a dash for the top bunks. They had experienced seasickness and, understanding the iron laws of gravity, expected the worst from a ride on this oversized ferry boat.

The *Comet* stopped in Honolulu the following morning for fuel and supplies, and all members of the 46th were given a pass with orders to return by 1600. When the ship sailed next day with the convoy, everyone had sampled the joys of Honolulu and, incredibly, every man had mustered for the trip to Canton Island. Packed like sardines, under oppressive heat, with only two meals per day, the ground crews made the seven-day trip without interference from either Japanese submarines or the weather.

Major Powell and the pilots left Hilo Airport on the morning of 25 March in an LB-30 and landed on Canton about 1700 that evening. At 0100 the next morning the Japanese greeted their arrival with an air raid. This unwelcome visit by a long range Kawanishi H8K, "Emily", flying boat of the 802nd Japanese Naval Air Group was to become all too routine on Canton.

On 27 March the *Comet* dropped anchor off Canton and the ground crews and staff of the Squadron joined the air echelon.

The briefings had not been sufficient to prepare the men of the 46th for this shocking change in their environment. Canton was a desolate coral atoll protruding from the Pacific in a narrow circular ring. Prior to the arrival of U.S. forces its native population consisted primarily of rats and hermit crabs. Lying barely 200 miles south of the Equator, its blistering heat and lack of rain had permitted the growth of just one single palm tree. Coral revetments bulldozed along the east side of the airstrip were the only prominent nobs on the otherwise featureless landscape.

Canton, like a thousand other atolls, is a geological mutation found chiefly in the Pacific Ocean. These island rings are the coral encrusted by-product of ancient volcanos scattered among the ocean ranges. As the mountains sank into the sea or erupted, losing their caps, the limestone slopes spawned millions of years of coral stratum that formed delicate island reefs. While the outer depths are often fathomless, the inner lagoons are mere lakes protruding from the high seas.

Conditions on the atoll were primitive. A few wooden shacks were in evidence as were many tents. Foxholes were scattered throughout the living and working areas.

According to the official Squadron records, Canton was hardly a tropical resort:

> The food during that time was fair. There seemed to be a fairly good supply of meat, potatoes, and canned vegetables, and sometimes there were eggs for breakfast, but bread was rationed most of the time. The evening meal consisted of leftovers from the noon mess with the addition of C rations, hash or beans. Fish, which had been caught by the men, was used frequently to vary the diet and was served at the evening meal. Officers and enlisted men ate in the same mess hall. An ice plant had been set up on the Island shortly before the arrival of the Squadron, and cooled drinks for the noon mess could be had when the plant was working. Each officer and enlisted man received a ration of six bottles of beer and four bottles of coke per week.

Canton was a paradox. Rainfall was nil, so despite the surrounding ocean, the island was a dust bowl. Lieutenant Frederick H. Deamant, Squadron Intelligence Officer, noted, "High excitement was being first away from the outdoor movies. Everyone else was left in a cloud of dust in the dark."

The fresh-water situation was a continuing problem that caused exasperating personal problems. "We were all dehydrated," said Fred Deamant, "since there was no fresh water and we had to depend on juices. This led to personal embarrassment. We had been issued three pairs of shorts. Whenever anyone wore long khakis, it was apparent he had to take a dose of mineral oil."

"Washing hair with salt water also was an experience. Your hair turned into wire unless Halo Shampoo was used. I wrote this information to the manufacturer who sent me a case."

An air alert sounded shortly after midnight on 4 April, but no bombs were dropped nor was the enemy flying-boat sighted. However, the Japanese inadvertently scored a casualty as one officer cut himself on barbed wire while sprinting to his foxhole. This was to be the only air-raid wound during the Squadron's nine months on Canton.

Although the Japanese never laid a single bomb on Canton's runways, a P-39 pilot landing from a dusk submarine patrol managed the job quite nicely. As he touched down, his left landing gear collapsed. In a shower of sparks, he skidded along the runway on his 250 lb. depth charge.

Major Powell watched the five-point landing, braced himself for the explosion, and agonized over the fate of his pilot. The P-39 came to a grinding halt with little damage. The depth charge had proved to be an excellent landing skid. Unfortunately, history does not record the name of the pilot who rode that depth charge back to base in such dramatic fashion.

On 21 April 1943 the 78th Squadron was relieved of its air defense assignment at Midway and bid that post an enthusiastic farewell. The Squadron's 22 P-40K aircraft took off for Barking Sands, Kauai, a trek of 1033 nautical miles, with Major Gordon R. Hyde leading. Three LB-30s served as navigators and a Navy flying-boat went along to provide air/sea rescue if needed.

The flight had been well planned and went off without a hitch. Rigid cruise control procedures were followed,

Top — A partial view of Canton Atoll. Note 46th Sq P-39s on flight line and in revetments to left of runway. (Source: National Archives) Some of Canton's spartan facilities: Left — First "O" Club. (Source: Tony Deangelo) Above — Operations shack. (Source: Tony Deangelo)

with the pilots maintaining a speed of 170 m.p.h. at 10,000 feet. Average flying time was just over 7 hours, a long day in a cramped cockpit, and a preview of future long-range fighter missions.

The 78th's ground personnel returned to Kauai both by ship and air transport, and there the Squadron took up temporary residence.

Another series of command changes took place that shuffled the Commanding Officers of the Group's Squadrons. Major Julian E. "Jack" Thomas assumed command of the 45th Squadron. Ken Powell moved up to Group headquarters as Deputy Commander. Major Norval K. Heath took over as CO of the 47th. Major Gordon Hyde also moved upstairs to Group and Captain Bill Southerland took command of the 78th Squadron on Kauai island.

During its lonely tour on Midway Island, the 78th had become a crack unit, and was intensely proud of its ability. When the new CO, Bill Southerland, prepared to shape up his new charges with practice join-ups, the Midway smoothies were a little insulted. First Lieutenant Rich W. "Hogan" Birk recollects, "We formed up so fast that Southerland barely had his gear up when we were tucked into formation. We made a 78th man out of him."

Before the month was out Hogan Birk had participated in an adventure worthy of mention in the *National Geographic*. When the engine on his P-40 caught fire he was forced to bail out over the ocean near Barking Sands. He also demonstrated the prevailing belief that parachuting from an uncontrolled fighter was a high-risk enterprise.

> I hit the horizontal stabilizer with one leg as I left the plane. I landed all right and inflated my Mae West and life raft without any problem, but the water was so rough that I damn near drowned before I could board the raft. My leg was cut to the bone, as if I'd been hit with an axe, and I was bleeding badly. After I was in the raft and had a chance to examine the leg, I was suddenly aware that several sharks were circling closer and closer. Then a huge whale appeared and nuzzled right up to my raft. I couldn't believe it. He was 40 feet long. I touched him with my hand to make sure I wasn't hallucinating. The whale stayed with me, like a mother cow, until a rescue boat arrived. As long as the whale was with me, the sharks stayed away.

Meanwhile, the big excitement on Canton was a 27 June move to new homes on the west side of the island — eight-man shacks. New mess halls, showers, and latrines turned the 46th Squadron's accommodations from wretched to merely dismal.

Always anxious to participate in these joyous events, the Japanese sent an H8K "Emily" over the island the next night. This greatly facilitated the rapid location of new foxholes.

The 46th Sq erected a more palatial Officer's Club. (Left to right) Ben and Charlie Bryant, otherwise known as No. 1 and No. 2. (Source: Charlie Bryant)

While the shacks were a step up from tents, it still burned the Army that the Navy detachment on the other side of the island lived in Quonset huts. The P-39s buzzed the Navy early every morning just to wake them up.

The 46th even had the luxury of a Post Exchange, but its stock of goods, dutifully managed by Sgt. William S. Johnson, made Mother Hubbard's cupboard look like a supermarket. The official history confirms this:

> Supplies for the Island's post exchanges were sent to the atoll about every five to seven weeks, and were never adequate (a situation that was bad under these conditions for there were no drugstores just around the corner). Candy and cigars had to be rationed but still usually lasted for only two or three days. For almost two months the island was out of matches and for five weeks there were no cigarettes. During the latter part of this cigarette crisis the Air Transport Command began flying a small quantity to the atoll daily, with a ration allowance of one package per day per man. Eventually a large shipment was received and once again, everyone could smoke to their heart's content.

Bob Clark gives a demonstration of going "rock Happy."(Source: Charlie Bryant)

The Fourth of July 1943 was a red letter day for the 46th. An aircraft-carrier dropped anchor in the harbor and delivered 25 brand new P-39Q-1 aircraft. They replaced the old P-39Ds which had been on Canton for so long that their olive drab paint jobs had turned to something approximating a dirty Nile Green.

The Q models had arrived with the same standard olive drab paint job. They were soon given a buff or sand colored coating to blend in with the coral atoll. Half a world away this same paint scheme was applied to planes operating in North Africa. There it was called "desert pink".

Just as the sun and salt wore away paint on airplanes and trucks, it took its toll on men. Minor cuts and bruises that would have been insignificant in another environment became infected and troublesome on Canton. A slight outbreak of dysentery added to the general misery of July and outranked the annoyance of nocturnal visits by Japanese patrol bombers.

On 18 and 22 July Emilys approached the island. John Thacker and others gave chase in the new P-39Q but never made contact over the dark ocean in the black of night.

Japanese flying-boats stalked Canton in the dark three times in August and twice more in September but neither side could locate the other. It was a tiresome little campaign in which boredom seemed the only victor.

Back at Bellows Field on Oahu, the 45th Fighter Squadron had received orders that would send them into the war. Major Jack Thomas called a meeting to advise his jubilant squadron that they had been placed on alert, pending movement to the Central Pacific. None of the pilots knew where they were going, but no one seemed to care.

Equipped with P-40Ns, the pilots left Bellows and flew to Ford Island. Their planes were loaded aboard the escort carrier, *Prince William* (CVE 31). They sailed for Canton Island on 18 August. The ground echelon boarded the transport *USS President Tyler*, and followed several days behind the air echelon.

During the seven-day voyage to Canton,45th officers were forced to suffer the indignities of the Shellback Ceremony. This bit of Navy sadism was inflicted on those making their first crossing of the Equator. Neither war nor peace can deter the Navy from this bizarre ritual. It is best conducted, in the most satanic manner, when the subjects are Army personnel and makes a fraternity initiation look like a garden party.

Lieutenants Art Bridge and Bob Jackson were detailed to attack a Navy torpedo bomber — crawling on their hands and knees armed with spit balls. Lieutenants Bruce Campbell, George Hunter, Dwight Butler and Dennis Rooney, arms outstretched and engines running, were to patrol the ship searching for bogeys during the entire hour preceding sunset. Captain Jim Vande Hay and Lt. Herb Boone were nominated for non-stop hula dancing and sporadic singing in the wardroom.

No one, regardless of rank, escaped these or similar humiliations unless he could produce the Shellback Certificate to prove a previous Equator crossing. And, while it was all done in a spirit of good humor, the Navy seemed to go to extravagant lengths when the helpless victims wore Army khaki.

On 24 August 1943 the *Prince William* arrived at Canton where the P-40s were slung over the side to barges and ferried ashore.

The pilots of the 45th Squadron barely had time to develop a loathing for Canton when they were ordered to move. On 11 September they departed for a forward base. Accompanied by three escorting B-24s of the 26th Bomb Squadron they lifted off for a 352-mile over water trip to their new base, Baker Island.

There was an air of gloom at Canton as the 46th watched their brethern depart for what they assumed was a superior station. Anything had to be better than Canton. The gloom deepened a few days later when the 46th suffered a fatality. Second Lieutenant Murray L.

P-39D crash-landed with depth charge still attached in April 43. (Source: Ken Powell)

After months of furtive night raids the Japanese flying boats finally blew up a shack on Canton. (Source: Joe Miner)

Hurlbert, flying a P-39Q went into a spin shortly after takeoff and crashed into the ocean.

The ground echelon of the 45th Squadron had arrived at Baker on 1 September along with the occupying force and aviation engineers. For several days the unit worked as stevedores unloading vital gear to prepare for the arrival of their P-40s. This proved to be no simple task since the island rose like a pinnacle from the surrounding deep. Ships could neither beach nor anchor with ease, and the cargo transfer proved to be dangerous and gruelling work. Once ashore the ground echelon subsisted on "K" rations and a water quota for several days.

Baker Island was part of the Ellice Island Group, a possession of the United States since mid-1800s. Sitting precisely astride the Equator, Baker Island was another tiny coral outcropping. It had little vegetation but had an abundance of bat guano. For reasons lost in the mists of history, a lighthouse had been built on Baker and was its sole distinguishing feature until Seventh Air Force engineers built a 5700 by 150 foot steel mat runway.

Just 40 miles northwest of Baker was an equally depressing atoll named Howland. Its dubious claim to fame was a 2400-foot runway built in 1937 as a refueling station for Amelia Earhart's round-the-world flight. She never made it to Howland, and though the runway had never been used, both the Americans and Japanese had bombed it to keep it out of service.

As soon as the entire 45th Squadron was functional, the unit began flying CAP missions and kept P-40s on alert both day and night for Japanese subs and snoopers. While eating their meals outside on the ground or on benches, the men had to fight off swarms of flies that seemed to increase by geometric progressions. Baker was proving as inhospitable as Canton.

Early in October there was an outbreak of bacillary dysentery on the island. Despite frantic preventive measures taken by the Flight Surgeon, Captain John J. Bunting, the epidemic hit the Squadron on 8 October. Thirty men were stricken on that one day, and before the scourge had run its course, 91 officers and enlisted men, including the CO, Jack Thomas, had become casualties of the common house fly. It took one month to control the problem with flying completely suspended for one four day period. Captain Bunting worked round the clock with the sick and supervised the development of new sanitary measures. He noted that his prior scoldings about sanitary conditions had now taken effect and "each man suddenly became fearfully health conscious."

The Baker Island occupation had brought units of the 15th Group to within 600 miles of Japanese bases in the Gilbert Islands. Somehow the enemy seemed to have missed the arrival of new folks in the neighborhood.

On 23 October, Baker's SC2 radar picked up a bogey passing south of the Island at 12,000 feet ambling toward Canton island. It was 1145 when Captain Gilmer L. "Buck" Snipes and 2nd Lieutenant Russell L. Hendrickson were scrambled to intercept. Captain Harry W. "Tommy" Thompson, acting as controller, vectored the two P-40Ns toward the radar plot. Twenty-two minutes later, some 70 miles south of Baker, Snipes' "Tally-Ho" was heard in the 45th operations shack. For the first time since 7 December 1941, the 15th Fighter Group was about to come to grips with the enemy.

Buck Snipes, leading Hendrickson, had found a four-engined Emily flying-boat lumbering along at about 205 m.p.h. indicated air speed. While climbing to gain an altitude advantage, the two P-40s were spotted by the Japanese crew. The Emily put its nose down and dove for a cloud layer at 2,000 feet building up its air speed to a respectable 375 m.p.h. Snipes' element gained rapidly on the enemy aircraft and the P-40 pilots began making passes from both sides and underneath.

"That plane had so many holes on the underside," said Buck, "that had it made a water landing it would have sunk immediately. On two passes underneath I fired until breaking off at about 100 feet."

Firing back from its beam and ventral rear window turets, the giant Kawanishi patrol bomber holed Snipes' P-40 in the exhaust stacks before reaching the low-lying cloud layer.

Buck plunged through the undercast and came out firing at the Emily. His final burst hit a fuel tank causing the big plane to blow up "like a giant firecracker." The P-40 flew through debris that caused some damage to its left wing root.

Snipes and Hendrickson circled the wreckage on the water, then returned to base and a jubilant reception.

Late November saw the loss of a P-40 when a battle damaged B-24 crash landed at Baker and destroyed one of the 45th's new planes. A second P-40 was thought to be lost a few days later after 2nd Lieutenant John W.

Canton's equatorial sun darkened men and bleached airplanes. (Left to right) Tony Deangelo, Ben Warren and Fred Gibson. (Source: Ken Powell)

Polk made an emergency wheels up landing on Howland's ghostly air strip. However, a contingent from the 45th decided to give the precious P-40N enough first aid to get it on its feet and try to return to base. Under the most primitive conditions they made an engine and prop change, locked and wired the landing gear into the down position, wired the cowl shutters and stripped the P-40 of excess equipment. Lieutenant Robert W. "Todd" Moore flew the cripple off Howland with a 600-foot takeoff run and nursed it back to Baker at 1500-feet altitude.

As Thanksgiving 1943 approached, things began to happen that signaled the 45th's departure from dreary Baker Island. Harry Thompson and twelve other pilots returned to Hickam via the 19th Troop Carrier Squadron to pick up 13 dditional P-40s.

First Lieutenant William K. Prichett, the Squadron's scholarly S-2, began a series of lectures to acquaint personnel with the geography, location, population, and conditions of the Ellice, Gilbert, and Marshall Island groups. Doc Bunting gave concurrent lectures about the native diseases at those locations. Pilots and enlisted men alike were suitably terrorized by his description of syphilis, yaws, and elephantiasis, but no one was sorry to be leaving Baker Island in their slipstream.

Back at Group headquarters on Oahu, a new boss had taken over the front office. Lieutenant Colonel Jim Bechwith had become CO as Lt. Colonel Sherwood Buckland took operational command of all Army fighter units destined for the campaign in the Mandated Islands.

The 78th Fighter Squadron stationed in Mokuleia suffered a tragic loss when its CO, Major Bill Southerland, crashed to his death after a mid-air collision with Lieutenant Howard M. Edmondson. The latter was able to parachute to safety. Captain Emmett L. "Pilot Ben" Kearney succeeded Major Southerland.

A big new fighter plane, the razor-back Republic P-47D, was arriving in Hawaii to replace the older aircraft of the 47th and 78th Squadrons. The "Thunderbolt" was a strange new bird with a variety of undiagnosed problems. They were destined to be unraveled via the costly learn-by-doing process.

Life for the 46th on Canton had proceeded at the same level of tedium under the pitiless equatorial sun. The men refused to eat Australian mutton after a time, so fresh meat became a memory. Coffee became scarce, and the refrigeration equipment failed more often than it functioned. Adapting to the situation, the men varied their meager rations by catching fish, lobster, and turtles "that tasted like veal" from the lagoon.

The inner lagoon at Canton also provided a major source of recreation. After swimming classes were held, everyone seemed to go native — diving, shell hunting, and gathering material for necklaces. Along with basketball and softball it all helped to break the otherwise crushing monotony. After nine months of confinement on Canton only two members of the 46th Squadron had to be returned because of mental problems. One man understandably went "atoll happy" in front of the messhall.

Movement orders to Makin finally came in early December and were greeted like an emancipation proclamation. Nobody knew what Makin was like, and there was a certainty of combat ahead, but there was unbridled joy within the Squadron. The solitary regret was that the 46th's softball team, led by star pitcher, Sgt. Lawrence Rust, was on top in the Canton Island League.

On 10 December 1943 the ground echelon of the 46th Squadron boarded the transport *S. S. Mormacport* bound for Butaritari Island in Makin Atoll. U.S. forces had invaded the Gilbert islands of Makin, Tarawa, and Abemama on 19 November. The air echelon remained to cover Canton, repaint the planes back to olive drab, and await the occupation and completion of Makin's airfield.

Meanwhile the 45th Fighter Squadron's contingent, led by Harry Thompson, were at sea on the escort carrier *Breton* (CVE 23), bound for the Gilberts via Canton. They brought thirteen worn P-40Ks from the 47th and 78th Squadrons. It was one of those mystifying logistical exercises that supplied used aircraft to the

When the 46th got new P-39Q models in mid-1943 they were painted coral on the upper surfaces and sky blue on the bottom. Examples are: Left — "Texas Ed" with pilot, Felix Scott. Right — Serial No. 4-218545 with pilot, Charlie Bryant. (Source: Charlie Bryant)

Canton's equatorial sun darkened men and bleached airplanes. (Left to right) Front row; Bill Higgins, Tony Deangelo, Bob Reiser, Tom Lewis; Back row: Arpod Artwohl, Paul Fojtik, John Thacker, 46th Sq CO, Lamar Ramos, Whitey Betner, (Source: Paul Fojtik)

The 78th Sq poses on Midway Island after being absorbed into the 15th Group: (Left to right) Front row: Rich Birk, Ray Obenshain, Harold Pace, John Vogt, Ed Markham, Summerside, Vic Mollan, Arthur "Red Dog" Nash, Armament Officer, Fred (red dog wearing earphones), Todd Moore; middle row: Gordon Hyde, Sq CO, Wild Ivan Viers, Art Bridge, Harold Collins, Dr. Charles Sokol, Flight Surgeon, Bill Mannon, Lew Nelson, Louie Strihafka, Engineering Officer, Unknown, Scallop O'Hare, Dale Laughlin, Skeeter Long, W/O Beaman; top row: Unknown, Jim Downey, Marshall Crispen, Ben Kearney, Windy Johnson, Jim Tapp. (Source: Robert W. Moore)

units headed for combat while rear area units got new equipment. Three top mechanics loaned from the 47th and 78th worked onboard the *Breton* to get them in shape. With the prospect of seeing action in the future, none of the pilots complained about the hand-me-down aircraft.

Getting the P-40Ks off the *Breton* was a prospect more disturbing to the pilots than pending combat. The planes weren't going to be slung over the side to barges. This time the Army fliers were going to be catapulted off the aircraft-carrier.

The 45th pilots were downright dubious. While the theory of catapulting seemed technically possible, it still struck them as unnatural that a slingshot and a steam contraption could fling four tons of aircraft into the sky. Although the operation was billed as a joint exercise, the Navy was a bit impatient about the whole thing, lending an additional air of apprehension to the launch.

First Lieutenant Lyman F. "Skinny" Ennis was in the cockpit of the last (and one of the weariest) P-40s spotted on the deck of the *Breton*. His view of the operation on 10 December 1943 off Canton Island was:

> Twelve planes took off. The last ones to be catapulted were about to overheat. The Navy was not at all familiar with in-line engines. By the time I, the 13th, was finally hooked up, my coolant was spewing out, and it was necessary to wait for the engine to cool off.
>
> In the meantime, the carrier was steaming at full speed into the wind and about 180 degrees off course. The Captain, looking down from the bridge, was furious. We were 'taking too much time,' forcing him 'off course,' and 'the planes didn't fit the ship,' etc. After maybe 15 minutes, I started the engine again, gave it full throttle, dropped my hand to signal release — and the launch officer canceled the shot. The engine had lost power and revved down so audibly that he stopped the sequence.
>
> I remember it so well. Another 15 or 20 minutes waiting, the *Breton* at full speed, last plane, Canton Island now lost over the horizon, we were 16 to 17 miles off course, and the Captain was fuming.
>
> We tried it once more. I restarted the engine, gave it full throttle, dropped my arm to signal 'ready' — and I was on my way. The bow of the ship was rising as I went forward, and I was thrown up into a climb, more than normal, and suddenly the engine revved down and leveled off at about 2,200 r.p.m.
>
> I stalled. Then I flipped, and completed a roll that came out at about wave-top level. My wheels were down and I had full flaps. I was furious that I was sent off, ready-or-not, and in an angry mood,

A tight formation of 78th P-40Ks led by Jim Tapp over Midway. (Source: Jim Vande Hey)

but never doubting that I would make it. I flew for at least 20 minutes, milking up the flaps, the wheels, and gaining enough altitude to find the island. I landed and had a stiff drink and that was that.

Ennis' P-40 was apparently a "hangar queen", a red-line special. It had the carburetor of another model and several parts that were never intended for a P-40K in a combat zone. It was used for spare parts from that time onward.

On 16 December 1943 Major Harry Thompson led his detachment from Canton to Baker and then to Nanomea Island. The air echelon from Baker with their P-40Ns, the ground echelon from Baker aboard ship, and a remaining group of 65 personnel left on Oahu had now all assembled as a full squadron on Nanomea.

The 45th's family reunion was marred by the death of 2nd Lt. Verne B. Snyder who crashed and was killed during a routine training flight on 28 December.

The 46th Squadron arrived in the combat zone in bits and pieces like the 45th. Seven pilots with replacement aircraft had left from Oahu with another P-39 unit (the 72nd Fighter Squadron) and a squadron of A-24s (the 531st Fighter Bomber) aboard the escort carrier, *Nassau* (CVE 16).

The 46th pilots with brand new P-39Q-1 aircraft aboard the Nassau were: Lieutenants Clifford S. Erdman, William A. Higgins, Thomas W. Lewis, Raymond B. Kessler, Cranston B. Rader, Edward H. Bryant, and J. G. Rattigan.

There were three Bryants, not related to each other in the 46th; Ben, Charlie, and Ed, generally referred to by the CO as Bryant 1, 2, or 3. The assignment of men with similar last names to the same unit resulted from an old service foible. Personnel officers habitually selected people for assignment in bunches, like grapes, from alphabetical lists. While commanders, operations officers, and administrative staff looked on such assignments as plots to complicate their lives and confuse paper work, it was usually the inadvertant act of a personnel officer following the path of least resistance.

The 46th pilots on the *Nassau* experienced the same combination of terror and exhilaration as the 45th when they were catapulted off Makin with the rest of the 72nd and the 531st. The launch took place without incident on 14 December. Ed Bryant had only logged 10 hours in a P-39 prior to this cat shot trip.

The ground echelon of the 46th had boarded their transport off Canton on 10 December but hadn't departed until the 12th. Sailing to an uncertain fate on another primitive island, some members of the Squadron had decided an ice-making machine would likely be useful and stashed one in the bottom of the hold on the *Mormacport*. It seems the machine had been the prior property of the island commander, a humorless man, who held up the Pacific war for one day in a fruitless search.

The rest of the Squadron, led by Major Thacker, left Canton on 27 December. Twenty-three P-39s, escorted by LB-30s of Southern Cross Airways, island-hopped to Baker and then to Makin. The 1148 mile flight was made without mishap, although the planes flew through a tropical deluge that took some paint off the prop-spinners. When Thacker's planes landed at Makin that afternoon the entire 46th Fighter Squadron had finally been reunited within 200 miles of the enemy.

In the thirteen days prior to John Thacker's arrival his seven orphaned pilots were attached to the 72nd Squadron. During that time they flew on three missions to attack the Japanese base at Mili, scrambled to search for Japanese night raiders on ten sorties, and had been on the receiving end of several air raids.

The detachment thus gained valuable combat experience to share with the rest of the Squadron, but the seasoning was not without its price. On 18 December, returning from the first Mili mission, Lt. Rattigan jettisoned his 75 gallon belly tank, then began losing fuel from his wing tanks due to a fuel transfer malfunction. Some 65 miles from Makin he ran out of gas and bailed out successfully.

Maj. Gordon Hyde (tail No. 10) leads the 78th on the long overwater flight from Midway to Kauai on 21 April 43. (Source: Rich Birk)

Todd Moore in his P-40K1 off Kauai Island in July 43. (Source: Robert W. Moore)

With several P-39s circling him, Rattigan climbed into his one man life raft and waved. A PBY-5A Catalina of the Navy's Patrol Squadron 53 was dispatched from Makin on what appeared to be a routine rescue mission.

The PBY, known as "Dumbo", both in service slang and code, was piloted by Lt. (j.g.) Charles B. Bremer. The big Navy flying boat spotted Rattigan, and despite mounting seas, Bremer made a determined effort to land. A fifteen-foot wave stove a hole in the hull. Before he could maneuver, another giant wave engulfed the port engine causing the propeller to break off and tearing the engine loose from its mounting. A third wave smashed in the bow compartment and the plane began to sink rapidly.

With two of his own crew members now injured, Bremer got his group into their large life raft and began to paddle toward Rattigan. As they came near, Rattigan, buffeted by towering seas, left his one man life raft and began swimming toward the navy crewmen. Before he could reach them he vanished in the trough of a wave. The PBY crew was rescued by a crash boat from Makin, but two days of searching for Lt. Rattigan proved ineffectual.

The 46th Fighter Squadron had regressed to tents and C rations but the climate was vastly improved and they were shooting at the enemy instead of fishing.

The only target within range of the P-39s was Mili, an important Japanese airbase in the Marshall Islands, 220 miles from Makin. The 46th escorted A-24s of the 531st Squadron and B-25s of the 41st Bomb Group to Mili and, though finding no aerial opposition, they sprayed the enemy island liberally with .50 caliber and 37 mm cannon fire. Despite the almost daily attacks on Mili the enemy used it as a staging area for the nightly marauders attacking the newly acquired U.S. bases in the Gilberts.

On Christmas Eve these heckler flights caused four air raid alerts on Makin between 0215 and 1200. To the chagrin of the 46th, it was a CAP from the 72nd Squadron which first made contact with the enemy and knocked down two.

By the end of December 1943 living conditions and the food had improved on Makin and morale was high. The 46th was flying missions to Mili almost every day. One or two were aborted by massive buildups of weather that towered to heights far above the operating altitudes of the P-39.

On 3 January 1944 the Squadron put up 24 of its 29 aircraft in a maximum effort to escort the 531st's A-24s to Mili. Major Thacker led.

Major DeWitt S. Spain took the first flight over the target at 100 feet catching and strafing a twin-engined Japanese bomber observed in front of bunkers on the southwest-northeast runway.

While other flights accompanied the A-24s, Captain Clifford Erdman led his high-cover flight down from 15,000 feet in a strafing run at an indicated air speed of 550 m.p.h. Anti-aircraft fire was heavy from the deck to 8,000 feet.

Suddenly Captain Erdman's plane was in trouble. Tom Quinn, his wingman, thought he saw the tail come off Erdman's P-39. Raymond J. Popson and Robert E. Clark in the next element thought Erdman was on the deck strafing when his plane dropped out of their line of sight. On join-up Erdman was missing, but no one in the Squadron had actually seen him crash.

The cold details of the obscure 3 January 1944 mission report masked a drama involving the missing Captain Erdman. It was not until 1968, almost 25 years after the mission that the final chapter was disclosed.

There was a legend among the natives of the Southern Marshalls, a story passed along from those who survived the war and the brutal Japanese occupation. The bizarre account described a reckless American flyer who would periodically land his fighter on the runway at Mili and taxi about pumping machine-gun bullets and cannon fire into targets that suited his fancy. Before the Japanese could raise their heads from their slit trenches he would roar down the runway and take to the sky. Frustrated with the American's defiant attacks, the Japanese defenders finally set up a cross fire of concealed automatic weapons which shot down the next lone fighter as it approached the runway threshold at Mili.

The native story tells that the P-39 crashed and the pilot was dragged from the wreckage and beaten to death by the enraged Japanese. He was then buried near the ruins of his plane. One of the witnesses was a 14-year-old boy who is, today, a doctor on the neighboring island of Majuro.

In 1967, Lt. Colonel Joseph C. Wright USAF, was told this astonishing tale while visiting on Majuro. His curiosity led him to an inspection of Mili where natives pointed the way to a rusting heap of indistinguishable wreckage that bore a faded white star on a blue field.

First, Wright established that the power plant was an Allison engine. Then, as he cut away the encroaching jungle and probed the mold and rust of the disintegrating wreck, he found a brass plate with a radio call sign, "22 0373."

After months of obsessive investigation it was verified that the P-39Q lost by the 46th Squadron in the 3 January 1944 attack on Mili was aircraft number 42-20373, piloted by Captain Clifford G. Erdman of San Diego.

This relentless search by Colonel Wright also uncovered the fact that in 1945 the Japanese commander of the Mili garrison committed suicide rather than face war atrocity charges.

Amelia Earhart and Fred Noonan are now believed to have made a water landing off Mili in 1937. They were captured there and first interrogated. The reluctance of the Mili commander to face interrogation could have been influenced by his knowledge of the Earhart incident or the Erdman matter.

Former members of the 46th and 72nd (both P-39 units) are dubious that any P-39, at that point in time, could have landed on the bomb-pocked runway of Mili and survived the inevitable hail of automatic weapons and small-arms fire. Yet the natives had led Colonel Wright to the wreckage, much of which survived the crash. Erdman's P-39 had not rolled into a fiery ball, as expected in such uncontrolled crashes. It is quite possible that he had survived the crash landing.

None of those who served with the 46th place any stock in the native story about the American fighter that periodically landed and savaged the garrison with its gun fire. But the natives had, with certainty, pinpointed the wreckage of Erdman's Cobra. The story of his death at the hands of the Japanese is both technically plausible and not totally impossible based on circumstantial evidence and the later suicide of the island commander.

The "Bushmasters" well stocked bar at Barking Sands manned by Sgt. Frank Fusco. (Source: Rich Birk)

CO of the 78th, Maj. Gordon Hyde at Barking Sands, Kauai in mid-43. (Source: Robert W. Moore)

Chaplain Tom Norton held a joint service for Rattigan and Erdman. There was a tinge of bitterness within the 46th that they had already lost two of their own without having dealt the enemy any substantial damage.

There was a comparative lull for the next week interspersed by uneventful reconnaissance flights over Mili. There was no letup in the Japanese night-intruder missions. The tactic seemed primarily designed to keep everyone on Makin from sleeping. Again P-39s scrambled and again they demonstrated their weakness as high-altitude interceptors. The bogeys all departed before contact could be made.

Living conditions on Makin improved steadily as individual quarters were improved and an "O" Club began to take shape. Though the climate was vastly improved from that of Canton, there was still the potential threat of dengue and dysentery. Dr. George Hart, the 46th Squadron Flight Surgeon, and a team of medical personnel decided on the necessity of medical examinations. Thus a Squadron formation was ordered where all personnel suffered the mass indignity of a rear-end inspection.

The bitching and complaining of men standing with their pants around their ankles was bordering on mutiny when some wag broke the tension. A record player began to blare, over and over, a song entitled, "Don't give me a goose for Christmas, Grandma. A goose makes me nervous as the deuce."

Another source of humor involved an official attempt at enforced modesty among the natives. The pleasant Gilbertese generally wore nothing above the waist. The island commander, doubtless a stuffy chap, issued G.I. undershirts to all the women. Those who wore them did so briefly as a novelty or curiosity. Both the natives and the Americans viewed the whole exercise as welcome comedy relief.

Relationships between the Makin natives and the 46th were extremely pleasant. Those who served there have fond memories of these happy people. "The natives, particularly the children, were a delight," said Fred Deamant. "They spoke English, having gone to the British King George V School. They were also very accommodating. They would climb to the top of a coconut tree, those that still had tops, and pick one for you. They loved to ride in Jeeps. The kids were as sharp as could be. They could play aircraft recognition games with the aircraft identification flash cards faster than the pilots. And at Christmas time we were thrilled with their British-taught hymn singing. They were good looking and intelligently curious.

On 10 January the 46th was off to attack Mili, this time carrying bombs on one aircraft as an experiment. Lieutenant Ben Warren's plane had been specially fitted with wing racks for two 500 lb. general purpose bombs. With this load and its 540 lb. belly tank, Ben's P-39Q was carrying an unprecedented load over 200 miles of water.

The four-plane flight of Lts. Warren, Carl Murray, Fred Gibson and James Burrows arrived over Mili an hour before midnight, returning the nightly calls made to Makin by the Japanese. Warren dove on the fuel storage area, releasing his bombs from 1500 feet, and was rewarded with a column of smoke that rose 100 feet into the air. After the bomb release Warren and Murray strafed the main island and received return fire from automatic weapons.

As tracers arched around his P-39 Carl Murray called to Warren that he had been hit. On the deck over Mili, the situation for Murray was serious.

With Ben Warren on his wing and talking to him, Murray fought with his stricken plane to gain altitude and distance. At a point only 5 miles southeast of Mili at 6,000 feet, the P-39, leaking coolant, began to heat up and started to smoke. Though he was dangerously close

Formal portrait of the 47th Squadron's "Dogpatchers" in June 43 at Haleiwa: (Left to right) Front row: Ed Glascock, John Piper, Verne Snyder (KPC), Walter Powell (KIA), Maj. Norval Heath, CO, John Hudson, Hayden Sparks, Ormal Kiesling, Milton Mitchell, Tom Holstien; middle row: Billy Gresham (KPC), Howard Hedrick, Frank Gromada (KPC), Joe Cohen, Bob Mallin, Tom Mackey (KPC), Clarence Strother, Executive Officer, Don Anderson, John Apple; back row: John Hartsfield (KIA), Herb Swigert, Percy Donack (KPC), Harold Place (KPC), Phil Oronsky, Dr. Lloyd Kaiser, Flight Surgeon, Tom Leaver, Ordnance Officer, Charles Blandford, Ernest Thomas, Charles Ross. (Source: Ken Powell)

A "Dogpatchers" party: (Left to right) Front row: Ed Markham, John Piper, Norval Heath, CO, Doc Kaiser; back row: Bob Mallin, Tom Blandford, Unknown, Clarence Strother. (Source: John Whitcomb)

to the Japanese base, Carl Murray was about to burn up with his plane so he released the door and bailed out.

Warren, Gibson, and Burrows raced back to Makin to alert a rescue mission, though uncertain of Murray's fate. Warren's planes landed at midnight and within 30 minutes another flight was airborne.

Captain Paul Fojtik, leading a four-plane flight, reached the approximate area of Murray's bailout at 0120. They orbited the area at low altitude in the dark for 30 minutes looking for the downed pilot and ready to ward off any approaching Japanese. However, Fojtik's team saw neither friend nor foe and returned home.

Because of the great distance involved, the P-39s could only orbit for a few minutes. Therefore relays of aircraft were established, the 72nd Squadron pitched in to help, and the Navy was called for assistance.

The next four-plane flight, led by 1st Lt. Jack Garnett, was aloft shortly after 0200. A Navy Gruman J2F "Duck" amphibian joined the 46th. Fred Gibson rode with the two man Navy crew hoping to pinpoint Murray's location.

The J2F, with its enormous hull pontoon had the speed of a wounded pelican. "He was so damn slow," recalls Charlie Bryant, "that we had to scissor behind him occasionally dropping wheels and flaps. We were frequently at stalling speed."

Garnett's escort flight was still orbiting the area southeast of Mili when the next relay of 46th planes appeared on the scene. This eight-plane formation, led by Major Thacker, reached the rescue area at 0300 and sighted Murray in his life raft. The gutsy Navy pilot in his small amphibian was trying to effect a landing in the waves and the P-39s of the 46th were keeping one eye on Murray and one eye on Mili. Occasionally they sprayed the island with machine-gun fire to inform any would-be prisoner missions that the task would be unhealthy.

Like the cavalry to the rescue, a PBY flying boat and an escort of P-39s from the 72nd Fighter Squadron arrived just as dawn began to break. The Catalina circled twice, landed under the orbiting J2F and scooped Carl Murray from the waters off Mili. One more flight of P-39s had been put in the air to escort the "Duck" back to Makin. The weary J2F pilot, with his crewman and Fred Gibson, had been up for over four hours.

Besides the Dumbo and the Duck, a total of 31 Coras from two squadrons had participated in the rescue operation.

Second Lieutenant George E. Dunstan, who flew in one of the last flights to orbit Murray and discourage expeditions from Mili, reminisced about the massive operation: "Needless to say, we had quite a party that night to celebrate Murray's return. I recall thinking that the U.S. will go to any degree to save the life of one man. It was very good for morale."

Thr pounding of Mili continued with missions on January 12 and 13. A-24s were escorted and the 46th added its own .50 caliber and 37 mm fire to the ordnance laid on every visible target. Still the Japanese seemed to get the airfield repaired for staging nightly raiders into Makin.

On January 15 and 16 the 46th Squadron finally got in a position to intercept the intruders. Radar had picked up several bogeys just after dark on the 15th. Several planes were scrambled and F/O Felix P. Scott was able to nurse his P-39, "Texas Ed", to an incredible 27,000 feet over Makin. When the twin-engined Japanese bomber stumbled into the searchlights at 22,000 feet it was illuminated and Scott spotted the heckler.

A collection of Dogpatch P-40s of the Pineapple Air Force in mid-43: Above — "Moonbeam McSwine" (Source: H. G. Smith) Below — "Adam Lazonga" (Source: H. G. Smith) Left — "Sadie Hawkins" (Source: Fred Arnold)

Diving on the enemy plane, he made a head-on pass at the Mitsubishi "Nell", firing two long bursts as the gap closed. Pieces of the bomber were seen to break off near the port engine which began to smoke and flame. As numerous ground observers watched the action, Scott began to prepare for another run on the target, but the Nell was already out of control and plunged into the ocean.

After additional forays by Japanese aircraft that night, Major John Thacker took off before dawn on January 16 in an effort to track the raiders to their home base. Lieutenants Ben Warren, Jack Garnett, and Tom Lewis accompanied Thacker. They were rewarded by spotting two Mitsubishi "Betty" bombers. "It was still so dark when I spotted the two bombers above their own field, I was afraid they might be some of ours." Thacker pulled in for positive identification alerting both the Japanese bomber crews and the Mili anti-aircraft defense.

The twin-engined Mitsubishis were approaching Mili Atoll from the south, apparently intending to land. The P-39s followed the Bettys north of the island, drawing AA fire from Japanese ground batteries. Thacker, who had flown through U.S. fire during the Blitz, was undaunted by the Japanese flak. He bore in on the nearest bomber and fired a 30 degree deflection shot without results, then made another pass from 500 feet dead astern. This time his fire hit home and the Betty burst into flames and plunged into the ocean.

The rest of the flight was busily jockeying for position behind the other Japanese bomber. Warren, Lewis, and Garnett all took an over eager pass at the Betty with no apparent results. Then Warren and Lewis lined up for another attack from astern and saw their fire tear into the wings. With its port engine aflame, the second Betty crashed on the northern reef of the Mili lagoon. Warren and Lewis shared the victory.

The tight air patrols at Makin and the success of John Thacker's intruders apparently discouraged the Japanese from any further offensive air action in the region. Not only were the air raids on Makin halted but Japanese aircraft were never again seen on the airfield at Mili.

As the Mili missions took their toll of P-39s and the 45th Squadron languished in inactivity at Abemama and Nanomea, it became apparent that the P-40s could lend a hand. It was also obvious that the P-40 with its greater range, could reach targets beyond the operational capability of the Bell Aircobra. The Seventh

Formal portrait of the 45th Sq at Bellows Field in June 43: (Left to right) Front row: Dr. John Bunting, Flight Surgeon, David Kyzer, Bob Clark, Ralph Cleague, Al Williams, Gordon Lewis (KPC), Harry Thompson, Art Bridge, Bob Tomberg, Travis Wells (KIA), Bob Jackson, Gene Horton; middle row: Dick Hintermeier, Bill Pritchett, Intelligence Officer, Dwight Butler, Skinny Ennis, Al Maltby, Jim Haglund, Charlie Hefelfinger, Wilbur Tews (KPC), Morton Knox (KIA), Phil Kriechbaum (KIA); back row: Peter Samuels, Bill Morrow, Clarence Sibbernsen, Maj. Jack Thomas (KIA), CO, Cliff Rohan, Fred Shirley, Gilmer Snipes, Bruce Campbell, Lloyd Harvey (KIA). (Source: Ken Powell)

Fighter Command ordered that a rear echelon be left at Abemama and sent a forward echelon of the 45th to Makin.

The Squadron, with Major Thomas leading, got their first chance to lay some fire on the Japanese at Mili on 17 January 1944 when eight P-40s flew out of Makin. They accompanied Seventh Air Force A-24s and P-39s. The pilots of the 45th bombed and strafed barracks and anti-aircraft emplacements, learning that the AA over Mili could be both intense and accurate.

The 72nd Squadron lost two P-39s and one pilot to enemy ground fire while the 46th Squadron sustained damage on one P-39. Paul Fojtik's plane took a single 7.7 mm round through the cockpit shattering his gas gauge and cutting his hand. Fojtik's eight plane formation strafed hangars and assorted gun positions with liberal doses of .50 caliber machine gun and 37 mm cannon fire.

The Cobra's cannon was a substantial weapon. On wheels it was an anti-tank gun with armor piercing capability. The Russians, who received many lend-lease P-39s, had a positive affinity for the plane and its heavy artillery. Most pilots of the 46th, however, thought it an "ineffective" gun with a low, short trajectory and a propensity to malfunction.

Charlie Bryant said, "It seemed to slow you down. You'd get off one or two rounds, then the damn think would jam. You had to let go of everything, grab the recharge T-bone ahead of the control column with both hands and pull to clear the jam. Sometimes you'd get 5 or 6 more rounds off but more likely another two."

October 43. Eurich Bright crashed on takeoff from Barking Sands, flipped over in a drainage ditch, completely demolishing his 47th Sq P-40, but he walked away. (Source: John Whitcomb)

In flight the cannon emitted a gentle "pat-pat-pat" sound which made it seem deceptively impotent, but on those rare occasions when a pilot could observe the results of a 37 mm shell hitting something more substantial than jungle, it was a real can opener.

The longer legged P-40s of the 45th Squadron reached out to hit Jaluit on January 18. This target, 298 statute miles from Makin, was beyond the range of the 46th's

Aircobras. Eight P-40s escorted A-24s of the 531st in this initial strike both bombing and strafing oil storage areas and the Jaluit radio station. Again Jack Thomas led the 45th Squadron.

Jaluit's defenses proved formidable. Two A-24s were downed by intense, accurate AA fire. One crashed over the target carrying both crewmen to their death. The pilot was CO of the 531st and a former member of the 15th Fighter Group, Major Roy Wigley.

The second A-24 crew bailed out 10 miles south of Jaluit. A PBY and an escort from the 46th Squadron were dispatched on the rescue mission. Rescue was successful with the P-39 cover using 175 gallon belly tanks for the first time on the three hour mission.

The bulbous 175 gallon ferry tanks could not be dropped. They were bonded to the fuselage of the P-39 making it look like a pregnant shark. While providing greater range, the new auxiliary fuel tanks did nothing to enhance the airplane's performance. Commenting on the big tanks, Charlie Bryant said, "When you were half out of fuel the remaining gas, amounting to some considerable weight, would slosh around despite baffles. You would throw the plane into a turn intending to go one way and the remaining gas would go the other way. The result was an unplanned skid."

Ben Warren, the 46th Squadron's Engineering Officer, was a bundle of energy and a wonder to his Squadron mates. When he wasn't flying missions he was supervising the expert maintenance which the unit had come to expect. These parallel duties would have been more than a platterful for a normal mortal, but Warren had to have side projects to fill his time.

On Canton he had built an extension onto the Ready Shack for Fred Deamant, the Intelligence Officer. His first project on Makin was the 500 pound bomb racks on the P-39Q. It was Warren's brainchild. His collaborator in the design and installation was S / Sgt. Jonas Orrell.

Warren outdid himself when he pulled a damaged P-39 from the junk heap and decided to resurrect it into a flying machine. The 72nd Squadron plane had crash landed with extensive damage to wing, horizontal stabilizer, main gear, and nose wheel strut. It had been set aside for delivery to a sub-depot, but was further damaged as mechanics scavenged the wreck for parts and souvenir hunters picked at its bones. Warren received permission to adopt the wrecked orphan and, with a crew of master mechanics, headed by T/ Sgt. Harry Stahlke, they spent every spare hour nursing the derelict back to life. Some new parts had to be hand made, no simple task under the primitive conditions at Makin. Other parts that Warren considered extraneous were stripped. With all due respect to the manufactuer, no one at Bell had ever flown a P-39 in combat. Ben had. After 10 days of hard work the P-39Q, renamed "Spare Parts", was nursed back to health and test hopped. Warren's baby was the hottest Cobra in the Pacific. At 2600 RPM and 30 inches of mercury, she could outclimb a standard Q Model by 600 feet per minute. "Spare Parts" became the 46th's ready night fighter.

On 20 January Major Thomas led his 45th Squadron back to Jaluit and caught two vessels: a 75 foot armed service vessel and a 65 foot wooden sailing schooner. The nine P-40s burned the larger vessel and turned the smaller into kindling. "It was a real pretty sailing vessel," said Todd Moore with a twinge of regret, "all painted up. Probably the property of the island commander."

Another flight of the 45th led by Art Bridge bombed and strafed Mili on what seemed to be a routine and uncontested mission. On the return flight Bridge's P-40N began siphoning off gasoline. He had apparently taken a random hit and his engine sputtered dead 75 miles from Makin.

Art bailed out successfully and was orbited by a flight

The 45th Squadron's unpretentious Hq on Baker Island on 10 September 43 shortly after the advance ground echelon landed and set up camp. (Source: USAF)

Everybody worked to assemble the camp on Baker. The ready room takes shape with this assortment of workers: (Left to right) Rooney, Fred Shirley, Todd Moore, Art Bridge, Jim Vande Hey. (Source: Robert W. Moore)

The 45th's P-40Ns flew CAP and sub patrol at the same time. A 500 pound depth charge is slung under this Warhawk on Baker. (Source: Robert W. Moore)

of P-39s from the 46th. They left when a PBY approached, but the Catalina found the seas too rough to land. With darkness developing, two more P-39s left Makin and Major Thacker succeeded in dropping a larger two-man life raft right on target to Bridge. He spent a wet but safe night and was rescued by a patrol craft from Makin the next morning.

Most of the 45th Squadron was now operating from Makin with only a single flight left to guard Abemama. Pilots of the 45th were rotated for the Abemama duty and, through life was a quiet R and R in this idyllic setting, the pilots thirsted for the action out of Makin.

The climax of Operations FLINTLOCK, and CATCHPOLE, the invasions of Kawjalein, and Eniwetok, and the storming of Majuro were approaching. D-Day for the assault on the Marshall Islands was scheduled for the 31st of January, 1944. The P-40s of the 45th Squadron and the P-39s of the 46th battered Jaluit and Mili with almost daily regularity making these bases useless for Japanese air units. Hale's B-24 heavy bombers and B-25 medium bombers were hitting targets deeper in the Marshalls beyond the range of fighter escorts. Here Japanese resistance was stiffening and B-25s of the 41st Bomb Group were encountering aggressive Japanese interceptors and began taking heavy losses. As many as 50 Japanese fighters were sighted on one occasion, and while the gunners in the Seventh Air Force bombers claimed many victories, eleven of the big Liberators and seven B-25 Mitchells were lost and over 100 bombers were damaged by enemy interceptors.

Battle damaged B-24s and B-25s occasionally limped into Makin and their plight caused anguish to the fighter pilots. The Japanese fighters routinely followed the bombers out of Taroa, Maloelap Atoll, to a point just beyond the assumed range of Seventh Air Force fighters. Several fighter pilots, watching the removal of a crewman from a damaged Mitchell recall a bleeding gunner who said, "If you guys want to come along, you'd sure be welcome." The 45th and 46th were furious and frustrated, but were powerless to intercede. Their sense of helplessness reached new heights on 25 January. A B-25 of the 41st Bomb Group was down in the water off Arno Atoll. This was almost halfway between Mili and Taroa, deep in enemy territory. The fighters were needed to cover rescue operations.

While it was theoretically possible to fly to Arno with cruise control, the P-40s and P-39s had to pass over Mili. Any enemy action would cause them to jettison drop-tanks. Even if undetected, their orbit time over the rescue scene would be only a few minutes. Despite these known risks, Majors Thomas and Thacker began a series of relay flights to cover the downed bomber crew and escort the Navy Catalina.

This whole operation took place on the evening of 25 - 26 January. It involved two PBYs, two Navy Venturas, 15 aircraft from the 45th Squadron and four from the 46th. The exercise covered a round trip of some 600 statute miles, with heavy frontal conditions, rain showers and limited visibility north of Mili. The P-40s, carrying 75-gallon drop-tanks, had forty minutes to orbit the downed flyers and returned with as little as 22 gallons of gas. The P-39s carried their 175 gallon "bathtub" tanks. They orbited 15 minutes over the rescue site and landed with an average of 100 gallons each.

Careful planning, no Japanese interference, and some luck were the ingredients in the dramatic rescue of this B-25 crew from the heart of enemy waters. The intolerable circumstances which had resulted in the loss of so many Seventh bombers caused the fighters to think about operational alternatives. Those involved with the previous rescue mission stated that the fighters had been placed at a severe tactical disadvantage while orbiting low over the downed bomber crew. An attack by Zeros under those circumstances could have had tragic consequences.

Lieutenant Colonel Sherwood Buckland, Director of the Fighter command at Makin, began to plot. Reason-

"Buck" Snipes climbs from the cockpit on 23 October 43 after downing an Emily flying boat south of Baker. Note bullet hole in exhaust stack. (Source: Gilmer Snipes)

*The crew of the **Breton** initiate the 45th's pilots in the Shellback ceremony crossing the equator. There were no fatalities. (Source: Gilmer Snipes)*

*Left: The CVE 23, **Breton,** ferrying thirteen P-40Ks from Oahu to Canton in December 43 to augment the 45th Squadron's inventory. (Source: National Archives)*

ing that the P-40s could reach as far as Arno Atoll, he decided to set a trap for the Japanese with the B-25s of the 41st Bomb Group as bait. If the Japanese fighters at Maloelap strayed a bit too far south, the P-40s might get a crack at them. It would have to be a short combat — neither side would have sufficient fuel for a lengthy engagement — Buckland's force would have the advantage of altitude and the element of surprise.

On 26 January 1944 nine B-25s of the 41st Bomb Group headed out from Makin to attack Taroa's airfield and radar on Maloelap Atoll. As usual, the bombers went in unescorted, but this time the 45th Fighter Squadron was close behind.

With Major Harry M. Thompson leading, twleve P-40Ns took off from Makin 30 minutes after the slower B-25s had departed. Carrying 75 gallon belly tanks, the 45th climbed to altitude and, at 2000 RPMs and an indicated air speed of 170 m.p.h., they trailed the Mitchells on a heading of 340 degrees. P-39s from the 72nd Squadron would arrive over Mili at a predetermined hour to ensure that the B-25s and P-40s had no interference on their return trip.

Thompson had arrayed his force at three levels. He led the lower flight, including Lts. Robert Jackson, Dwight Butler, and Morton Knox at 8,000 feet. Captain Jim Vande Hey's flight, consisting of Lts. John Apple, Richard Hintermeier, and Albert Maltby, flew at 10,000 feet. Deployed at 12,500 feet was the top cover flight led by 1st Lt. Robert W. Moore and including Lts. William Fisher, Herbert Boone and John Basham.

Flying toward their first major aerial action since Pearl Harbor, they skirted Mili to the west. Lieutenant Bob "Todd" Moore recalls the silent tension in twelve P-40 cockpits:

> Even though Major Thompson and Captain 'Van' had seen Japanese planes at Pearl Harbor, this was our first anticipated encounter with Japanese fighter opposition.

*10 December 43. The **Breton** catapult launches 45th P-40s off Canton Island: Left — Capt. Harry "Tommy" Thompson is first off in No. 215. (Source: George Hunter) Right — No. 220 is shot over the bow in a good attitude of flight. (Source: National Archives)*

The 45th Sq was scattered to Abemama and Nanumea Atolls for unneeded air defense. Shown here are P-40Ns at Nanumea, Ellice Islands. (Source: USAF)

> It is impossible to describe the full range of feelings. You could include apprehension, fear of capture, mouth turning to cotton. Probably our prime motivation then, as it was in combat generally, was the fear of individual failure before our contemporaries, letting down those with whom we lived from day to day.

While the P-40s were plodding along under rigid cruise control conditions, the B-25s reached Maloelap Atoll and found the anticipated welcoming committee of Japanese ack-ack and fighters. After running the anti-aircraft gauntlet and competing their attack, the bombers were jumped by about 15 Zekes of the 252nd Naval Air Group. Fighting their way out, the Mitchells departed from the target on the prescribed retirement course that led them south over Aur Atoll. The Zekes were making leisurely high side passes on the bombers, then doing 360 degree turns and repeating the maneuver.

With perfect co-ordination and nearly empty belly tanks, Tommy Thompson's P-40s arrived over Aur Atoll to witness the approach of the B-25s being savaged by many Zekes and a couple of Kates that had decided to join in the fun.

Jim Vande Hey was first to spot the harassed Mitchells and called out the bogies on his radio.

> The B-25s were strung out near the deck running like Hell with one cripple trailing behind the main formation, flying on one engine. Tommy didn't want to spoil the ambush so he was saying, 'Wait . . . Wait.' But I didn't think that straggler could take any more punishment, and as five Japanese stacked up on a parallel course to take one more pass at him, I called into my mike, 'Can't wait!'
>
> I put my flight into echelon left and we peeled off. As we dove on the battle the B-25 crews spotted us: 'Here they come! Those beautiful fighters! Those beautiful bastards! We'll never say another bad thing about you.'

Jim Vande Hey was first to reach the retreating formation of Mitchells and pursuing Mitsubishis. He bore in on the leader with a 10-degree deflection shot. "I had been told that Zeros blew up easily," said Jim. "I pumped so much lead into the first one I thought I'd go right through him if he didn't explode. All of a sudden he blew and it popped the pilot right out and he opened his chute."

Vande Hey rolled slightly to his left and flamed another Zeke with a short burst. He was closing on the third when his wingman, Al Maltby, squeezed off a burst over his wing and sent the Zeke diving toward the sea trailing smoke.

Dick Hintermeier and John Apple, the second element in Vande Hey's flight, had a slightly different view of the opening action:

> With my interest fixed on the action below, we started a large circle over the tops of the bombers.

Meeting the new neighbors: Left to right — George Morey and Joe Riley of the 45th at Abemama. (Source: Gilmer Snipes) Below — Joe Miner and Tom Quinn represent the 46th at Makin. (Source: Joe Miner)

> We dropped our tanks as we peeled off and I was suddenly aware of other belly tanks showering down around us from the high flight. We each picked a target, and I fired a long burst into mine, pulling up to avoid a collision.

Hintermeier's Zeke flamed and spun into the water; Apple's fell away in apparent trouble. Vande Hey's flight had shot down or probably destroyed the entire five-plane unit that was assaulting the crippled B-25. It had all happened in less than a minute of air-to-air combat.

The 45th Squadron had been silent until the action broke — the cotton mouthed syndrome — but as they dove on the Japanese fighters from a point in the Pacific sky where P-40s simply weren't supposed to be, their radios exploded: "I got one! I got one! He's on your tail!"

Meanwhile Thompson and his wingman, Bob Jackson, had waded into the startled Japanese at 1500 feet. Jackson hit a Zeke that never smoked, flamed, or took evasive action, but remained in a diving bank until it hit the water. Thompson got on the tail of another and saw his tracers hit the fuselage and chew off pieces of rudder. The Zeke pulled up into a gentle climbing turn and Thompson pulled up with him, firing another burst. Chunks of the enemy plane broke off as the P-40 passed over. The Mitsubishi rolled over and dove into the ocean.

Butler and Knox closed quickly on a Zeke and Knox got in a pointblank belly shot which caused the Japanese fighter's landing gear to drop. The crippled plane began to burn and crashed into the water. Lieutenant Butler pursued a Zeke that was breaking down and away. He fired one 90 degree deflection shot and observed his target burst into flames and dive into the water. Todd Moore recalls his part:

> On letting down from flying top cover, I spotted a Zeke climbing out of the fight. I turned into him and he turned into me attempting to return to Maloelap. I outbluffed him and fired head-on, observing hits in the engine and wing root area. I knew better than to dogfight a Zero with a P-40, but our Ns were pretty maneuverable. I managed to turn tightly on his tail as he continued toward Maloelap. As I closed in, the Zero turned over slowly on its back as though the pilot were already dead. From about 700 feet I gave him a slight lead and exploded the fighter with a very short burst.

Lieutenant Boone's element, the last to go in, spotted two enemy planes scurrying away from the fight. They dove after them, coming up astern and found that they were pursuing a pair of Kate torpedo bombers apparently out to bell the cat. Despite the fire from the rear seat gunners, Boone climbed right up the tail of his Kate and fired a long burst. The bomber exploded. Lieutenant Basham chased his target back toward Maloelap and saw his tracers enter the plane. The Kate began to smoke and lose altitude but fuel and distance precluded further pursuit.

The Japanese attack force now destroyed or com-

Felix Scott, 46th Sq, claimed the Group's first Makin Island victory on the night of 15 January 44. (Source: Charlie Bryant)

pletely scattered, the P-40s rejoined the B-25 flight and adjusted their throttles and mixture for the 380-mile return flight. A quick nose count showed that all twelve P-40s and all nine Mitchells were heading back to Makin. The fighters pancaked onto the Makin airstrip after an overall flight of 800 statute miles, many with as little as 25 gallons of gas.

In just three minutes of swirling combat the 45th Squadron had destroyed 9 Zekes, one Kate and probably destroyed another Zeke and Kate. The B-25 gunners nailed five more of the distracted Japanese fighters.

There was a big party at the 45th that night. They were celebrating a victory won by superior airmanship, discipline, and perfect coordination, but the most exhilirating aspect was having survived to toast one another. Todd Moore put it in perspective: "We all knew that in the event of a prolonged running fight, none of us would have enough fuel to return to Makin."

Commendations and accolades were received from General Landon, CG of the Bomber Command, General Hale, Chief of the Seventh Air Force, and even from CINCPAC, Admiral Nimitz. It was indeed a superb three minutes in the 15th Fighter Group's long campaign.

The 45th tried to conjure up a repeat performance the next day. They trailed behind nine B-25s of the 48th Bomb Squadron slated to attack Wotje. The rendezvous point was Majuro Atoll, 310 statute miles from Makin.

However, things seemed to go wrong from the beginning of this mission. Todd Moore's prop malfunctioned, forcing him and his wing man to abort.

The remaining ten P-40Ns arrived at the designated rendezvous point on schedule only to have the bombers radio that they were 45 minutes late. Major Thompson orbited his planes in the area for over an hour with no contact. The B-25s refused to communicate their position until they were past Majuro.

With no small amount of standard Army cussing, the 45th started the long slow homeward trek. They pancaked at Makin after 4 hours and 35 minutes of pointless flying under rigid fuel discipline. The mission report flatly states, "The mission can be considered a failure."

On the same day, 27 January, Major Spain led a flight of the 46th Squadron to Mili as escort for A-24s. Despite a month and a half of bombing and strafing the Mili garrison was still putting up flak that was "considerable and accurate". The Japanese shot down one A-24 over the target.

On 28 January the 45th Squadron set off an another exercise with the 47th Bomb Squadron to attempt a reenactment of the "Maloelap trap." There was much, 'Now this time let's get it right', discussion after the fiasco of the Majuro mission.

Fourteen P-40Ns were sent out. Four aborted because of mechanical problems, but the remainder hit the rendezvous point, Aur Atoll, on the nose, on schedule.

The B-25s were attacked over Taroa Island by Japanese fighters as expected and one of the Mitchells was shot down. Only seven Zekes were airborne and not one ventured near the waiting trap over Aur Atoll. They had learned their lesson from the battle of 26 January.

The 45th picked up the B-25s over Aur Atoll and escorted them back to Makin. While it was a moral victory of sorts, the pilots of the 45th tended to view the mission as 4 hours and 48 minutes of sweaty flying with nothing to show for it. From that date, however, Japanese fighter aircraft were withdrawn from Taroa. The B-25s were never again to see Zekes in that combat zone.

Beginning 29 January, the 45th and 46th Squadrons hammered Jaluit and Mili daily to deny the use of their airfields to any Japanese aircraft that might attempt to interfere with the invasion of the Marshall Islands. On 31 January, D-Day at Kwajalein, Eniwetok, and Majuro, the P-40s hit Jaluit while both Squadrons sent relays of planes to put a virtual CAP over Mili. None of these flights met any resistance and it began to appear that the enemy garrisons were being sandpapered down to impotence.

After hauling two 500 lb. bombs on each P-40 on target strikes for the better part of a month, the energetic Jack Thomas decided to experiment with heavier loads. On the 5th and 7th flights to Jaluit, the 45th Squadron lugged two 1,000 lb. bombs along with their 75-gallon belly tanks. It was the biggest load of ordnance ever carried by a P-40 in tactical operations.

The target of both raids was the pier and oil installation on Jaluit. Hauling the 1,000 pounders was one thing, placing them on the target with a degree of accuracy proved difficult except at very low altitudes. Those that did hit near the target created some fire, a

"Spare Parts" and its builders: (Left to right) Front row: Eldrige Norton and Leo Sanchez; back row: Ben Warren, 46th Engineering Officer, Harry Stahlke, Emil Zaph, and George Wolfe. (Source: National Archives)

P-40s of the 45th Sq pitching out over Makin's fighter strip. P-39s can be seen parked on the perimeter. (Source: Fred Erbele)

smoke column to 500 feet and some gratifying holes in the enemy landscape.

The old P-40, Warhawk, handled the load quite nicely with no loss of lateral or longitudinal stability. It was discovered that the successful dive-bombing run had to be on target from the peel off. Since the heavily loaded P-40 built up tremendous speed, major corrections were impossible. On release of the bomb load the plane "jumped 15 feet."

Award ceremonies on 5 February broke the usual routine. Major General Willis Hale showed up to honor the fighter pilots among his "handful."

Those old timers who received Air Medals, and some who didn't, were nonetheless frequently decorated with Fox Holer Medals. These prized awards were lovingly struck from the tin of a Prince Albert tobacco can. Wearing one entitled the bearer to jibe newcomers with, "Why son, I have more time in a fox hole than you have in the Army."

The Seventh Air Force was so confident of its mastery of the air, that P-39s made the long trip to Jaluit on 6 February 1944. Carrying their 175-gallon belly tanks, 1st Lt. Joe McHale led a flight of the 46th in a strafing attack on the radio station and other buildings around the Atoll.

The 46th continued armed reconnaissance over Mili but targets of opportunity on the battered base were scarce and AA was non-existent except at deck level.

On 8 February 1944 Lts. Joe McHale and Tom Quinn

flew the 46th Squadron's last recon mission to Mili. Orders came through withdrawing the 46th from combat.

The move from Makin proved to be a windfall for the Gilbertese natives. "We had a ball when we were getting ready to depart," said Fred Deamant. "They inherited all our extra personal gear. I remember explaining the use of such wonders as toothpaste and hair oil with animated demonstrations that broke up everyone."

In its tour at Makin the 46th had flown a total of 1,801 hours on various missions. They had rained 15,301 rounds of .50 caliber ammunition and 794 rounds of 37 mm shells on a weary enemy. (See Appendix 8 for individual pilot combat records.)

The 45th Sq plans a strike on Jaluit Atoll in January 44. (Left to right) Maj. Jack Thomas, CO, Maj. Gordon Hyde, Group Operations Officer, Harry Thompson, Dan Boone, and Bill Pritchett, Intelligence Officer. (Source: Gilmer Snipes)

With the departure of the P-39s, the 45th Fighter Squadron was left the task of interdicting Mili and Jaluit and escorting the A-24s of the 531st Fighter Bomber Squadron. Led by Jack Thomas, recently promoted to Lieutenant Colonel, they hit the enemy islands on an almost daily basis.

Bombing with 500-pounders on 9 February the 45th finally succeeded in firing the oil storage tanks on Jaluit. A heavy column of black smoke rose to a height of 2,000 feet.

On 16 February Jaluit yielded the most Japanese shipping in a month. Fifteen P-40Ns damaged a 150-foot transport and a 100-foot corvette, and sank three small 30-foot launches with a bombing and strafing attack. The same mission caused damage to the radio station, antiaircraft installations and buildings. Bombs again hit the target area of the island's aviation gas storage and started a fire larger than the one set off on the 9th. Smoke could still be observed when the formation was 50 miles away from the target. Antiaircraft fire was the heaviest yet encountered over Jaluit Atoll but only Lt. Bruce Campbell's aircraft was hit. Although his left wing was struck twice, he returned safely.

Not content with merely damaging the shipping at Jaluit Atoll, Jack Thomas returned, refueled, and rearmed his planes, and asked for volunteers to go back after the Japanese transport that same afternoon.

Eight P-40s went in to strafe flak positions, while four others carried two 500 lb. bombs each. At 400 m.p.h. Jim Vande Hey and John Apple led their elements in a deck level skip bombing attack on the enemy transport. Both Vande Hey and Apple scored hits with undetermined results.

Antiaircraft fire was exceptionally heavy. Some pilots reported the entire surface of Emidj Island flashing with gunfire. The Japanese gunners had found the

Officers of the 46th pose for one last unit photo in February 44 as they return to Hawaii. (Source: Charlie Bryant)

Awards for the Marshall Islands campaign: Maj. Gen. Willis Hale pins Air Medals on 46th Sq members Ben Warren (sunglasses) and Charlie Bryant. (Source: Charlie Bryant)

Lt. Col. Sherwood Buckland presenting medals to 45th officers: (Left to right) Skinny Ennis, Todd Moore, Bruiser Dunlap, and Bill Fisher. (Source: Robert W. Moore)

range. For the second time in a day Bruce Campbell was hit. His engine began to smoke, and he fought his plane southeast 15 miles from Jabor Island before baling out. He landed safely, climbed into his life raft and waved to circling P-40s.

Dick Hintermeier was the next casualty but he wasn't sure who victimized him. Roaring across Jaluit Lagoon on his skip bombing run, he released on the target and soon saw two bombs porpoising in front of him.

> They had gone through the wrecked ship and come out the other side. I pulled up sharply, the Japanese were shooting at me, and I don't know if I was hit by enemy fire or my own bomb blast. But I definitely had been hit in my engine, as I began to lose coolant. I determined to stay with the plane as long as I could, but my resolve faded as the plane started to burn up front. I got rid of the canopy and stood partially in the seat to gain visibility. I wanted to get as far away from that damned Island as fast as I could, but the fire soon got too hot and I had to bail out.
>
> As I jumped, at about 2,500 feet, I hit the horizontal stabilizer a glancing blow with my knee. I landed in the water with no problem, got into my life raft, and waved to the Squadron. They dipped their wings, waved back, and headed home.
>
> Darkness soon set in, then the sea got rough and I was periodically being thrown out of the raft by huge waves. Late that night a plane flew low right over me. I fumbled for a flare, and with everything soaked, it just came in half. It might have been a Japanese plane so maybe I was lucky, but right at that stage I was seasick, my knee hurt, and I was down near an enemy base on my 21st birthday. It was hard to be optimistic.

With two of his boys in the water not far from Jaluit Atoll, Lt. Colonel Thomas raced back to organize a search effort. The Navy dispatched the destroyer *McCalla* (DD 488), and readied a search by two PBY Catalinas of Patrol Squadron 72. The 45th began the now familiar routine of sending off four-man flights at staggered intervals to search for and orbit the downed airmen and protect Dumbo.

The first two flights had no success, and the initial sweep by the Catalinas was negative, but two single-engined float biplane fighters were spotted moored near Emidj Island. First Lieutenant Bob Williams led the next flight on a strafing attack which ensured that the Japanese Petes would not interfere with rescue operations. They also searched for Campbell and Hintermeier without success.

Dick Hintermeier had survived the ordeal of the first night, and with the coming of daylight, he knew his comrades were searching for him. He could hear the Allison engines in the distance and occasionally caught sight of them on the horizon, but they were searching vast areas of ocean for two bobbing souls, and the day long search of the 17th was negative.

The day was waning and Dick Hintermeier was beginning to despair. It was bad enough that he hadn't been sighted, but sharks had found him and started rubbing their backs on his raft. "About sunset I spotted a Dumbo in the distance going back and forth. I set off a smoke bomb, it ignited, to my surprise and delight, and they spotted my smoke."

Lieutenant (j.g.) Vernon H. Osburn, pilot of the Catalina from VP-72, had about given up for the day when his crew spotted Hintermeier's flare close to Jaluit Atoll. Osburn located the downed Army pilot and dropped him some water. Then he made a careful

45th Sq P-40Ns, March 44: Left — Tommy Thompson and "Miss Flo." (Source: Spencer Olsen) Right — Cpl. Vernon Wollin and Dan Boone's "Lackanooki." (Source: Spencer Olsen)

survey of the sea, landing conditions, and the proximity of the enemy. The situation was perilous.

The ocean was rough. Hintermeier, from his vantage point among the troughs of the waves, didn't think that a landing was possible. Osburn was also mindful of directives following the loss of a PBY in the disastrous Rattigan rescue. The Navy had ordered that patrol planes and crews not be endangered in valiant but hopeless sea rescues. He was singularly aware that there was no fighter cover over him and that he was uncomfortably close to Jaluit — some 18 miles. As if to underscore the point, the Japanese fired a few rounds of anti-aircraft at the PBY during one of its wide circuits of the rescue scene. The fire was distant and ineffective but the implication was clear.

With all conditions for failure present, the indomitable Navy pilot began to prepare an improbable rescue attempt. He dropped a smoke bomb to gauge wind direction, then began to crank down flaps, adjust power and mixture, and line up for a landing, quartering between the white crested waves.

Dick Hintermeier became detached enough from his own grim circumstances to scrutinize the landing with professional admiration. The big Catalina knifed through the first wave tops, then slammed hard into a maturing swell. Lieutenant Osburn quickly taxied his big plane over to the raft. The crew plucked the Army pilot from the Pacific and secured him in the topmost bunk of a rack of cots. Hintermeier was asleep almost instantly.

Osburn taxied into the wind and began the tricky task of getting the massive flying boat airborne. With the twin engines revved to the firewall the Dumbo surged forward breasting several swells, then the bottom dropped out of a huge wave and the plane came down with a resounding crash. Hintermeier plunged from his top bunk through two canvas cots to the floor, but Osburn kept pouring on the coal and ultimately gained the air. The exhausted fighter pilot slept through the whole thing.

By the time Makin was reached, Hintermeier was awake and relishing his salvation from what seemed to be death or imprisonment. "The minute we touched down on the lagoon all Hell broke loose. That last bump on takeoff had stove a hole in the hull and the plane began taking on water. The pilot applied full throttle again and told us to start throwing things overboard."

45th Sq P-40Ns, March 44: Bruce Campbell's "Geronimo." (Source: Fred Erbele)

Dick Hintermeier's adrenaline was flowing. Determined to survive again, he threw himself into the job of jettisoning loose gear through the side blisters. At near takeoff speed, Osburn taxied the Catalina right up to the seaplane tender, *Mackinac*, in a beautiful but harrowing approach and chopped the throttles.

Hintermeier reported to the *Mackinac* sick bay where he was treated and put to bed. The Dumbo was rolled onto a shore ramp at Makin for salvage work on its cracked hull. Both survived to serve again.

One of Jack Thomas' lost brood was back but Bruce Campbell was still missing after two days. While Thomas continued to badger the Navy about rescue efforts, he sent another mission to Jaluit to make certain that the Japanese kept their heads down.

After the 18 February bombing and strafing operation were complete, Buck Snipes and Fred Shirley led two four-plane flights of P-40s in another search for Campbell. Again they came up empty handed. A pervasive gloom began to descend on the 45th Squadron. Campbell had been lost for three days. The odds for his survival seemed remote.

Then the Navy command on Makin relayed a signal

Doc Drane decorated 45th pilots (left to right) Ennis, Hunter and Bridge with a homemade DFC. (Source: George Hunter)

Lt. Col. Julian "Jack" Thomas leader of the 45th Sq during the Marshall Island campaign. (Source: Gilmer Snipes)

from the destroyer *McCalla*. Bruce Campbell was aboard and alive. On the last leg of the last day of the destroyer's last search pattern, they had accomplished the rescue. In three days in his one-man life raft, Campbell had drifted 60 miles from the point where he had parachuted. Again and again, during the 15th Group's history the United States Navy would serve them well.

The near routine bombing and strafing of Japanese bases stimulated the inventiveness of the 45th Squadron. They decided to augment their arsenal with rockets. They concocted a launching scheme by attaching two M-1 "Bazookas" to the outboard sway braces of a P-40N. These infantry anti-tank weapons were rigged to be fired by pressing the gun-camera button. On 22 February the 45th attacked Mili with bombs, machine guns, and for the first time, rockets. Captain Fred Shirley flew the specially adapted N. While the Japanese likely viewed the experiment as unnecessary bedevilment, the Squadron wrote it off as a failure. One launcher failed to fire. The other exhibited such a low muzzle velocity that the 4½ lb. missile had no more trajectory than a hand thrown rock. Results were unobserved and unimpressive.

The supply situation for the Japanese garrisons on Mili and Jaluit deteriorated and became more desperate as the campaign ground on and their isolation became more complete. On almost every mission the 45th was shooting up boats, but the size of those boats was almost pathetic. They were mostly of the 30-foot variety and some were native-designed outriggers.

Japanese return fire was diminishing. It appeared that a shortage of ammunition was causing them to hold their fire for selective use. Though permanently bypassed, these Japanese garrison units still anticipated invasion.

The mission of 25 February 1944 to Jaluit seemed disarmingly routine. Eleven P-40Ns arrived over the atoll and commenced their dive bombing runs on Tiniet Island. Since there were no specific targets left, it was simply a saturation strike. Great gouts of dust and some smoke resulted, but no fires; nor did the enemy waste any of his precious antiaircraft ammunition.

After all bombing runs had been completed, the three flights broke up to search designated portions of the atoll from both the lagoon and ocean sides. At altitudes of 50 feet they literally looked under every tree for boats.

Al Williams' flight found and destroyed a camouflaged 30-footer off Imrol Island. Art Bridge had discovered a 35-foot cabin-cruiser at anchor and sank it with several hundred rounds of fire from his flight.

Dwight Butler, leading another flight, found fourteen outriggers around Tiniet and Imrol and set up a pattern to strafe these boats. Bridge's P-40s joined in the fun and began to follow Butler. Light Japanese automatic weapon fire seemed to emerge from somewhere.

Suddenly Lloyd Harvey's P-40 was smoking, but he circled back toward the target for another pass. Art Bridge thought Harvey might have drawn enemy fire from a church. "I sensed that he was irritated by the fire and was turning back for another pass to silence it."

Skinny Ennis, leading an element, recalls that the strafing was an "overkill. We were wasting our effort. I was following Butler and Harvey onto the target. I was firing as Harvey was pulling away. I can't help but wonder if my richochets might have hit his plane."

With his aircraft in trouble, Harvey began to pull up. Ennis was among the helpless spectators. "We cried out for him to bail out. He leveled off, then he stalled over the target. He made a slow turn to the left and plunged straight down into the ocean."

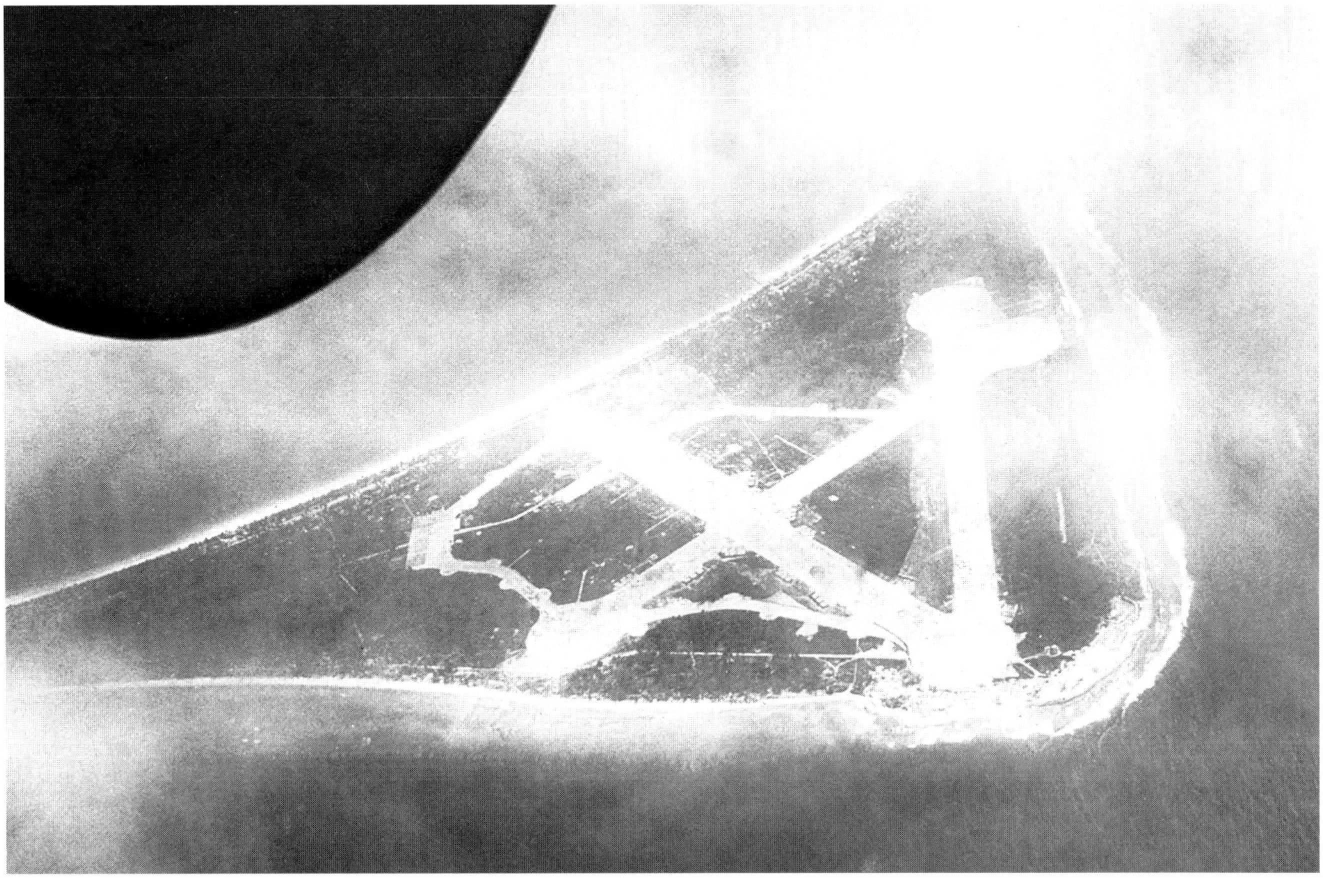

Mili Atoll as seen at the start and the end of the battle for control of the Marshalls: Above — November 43. Left — 10 March 44. (Source: USAF).

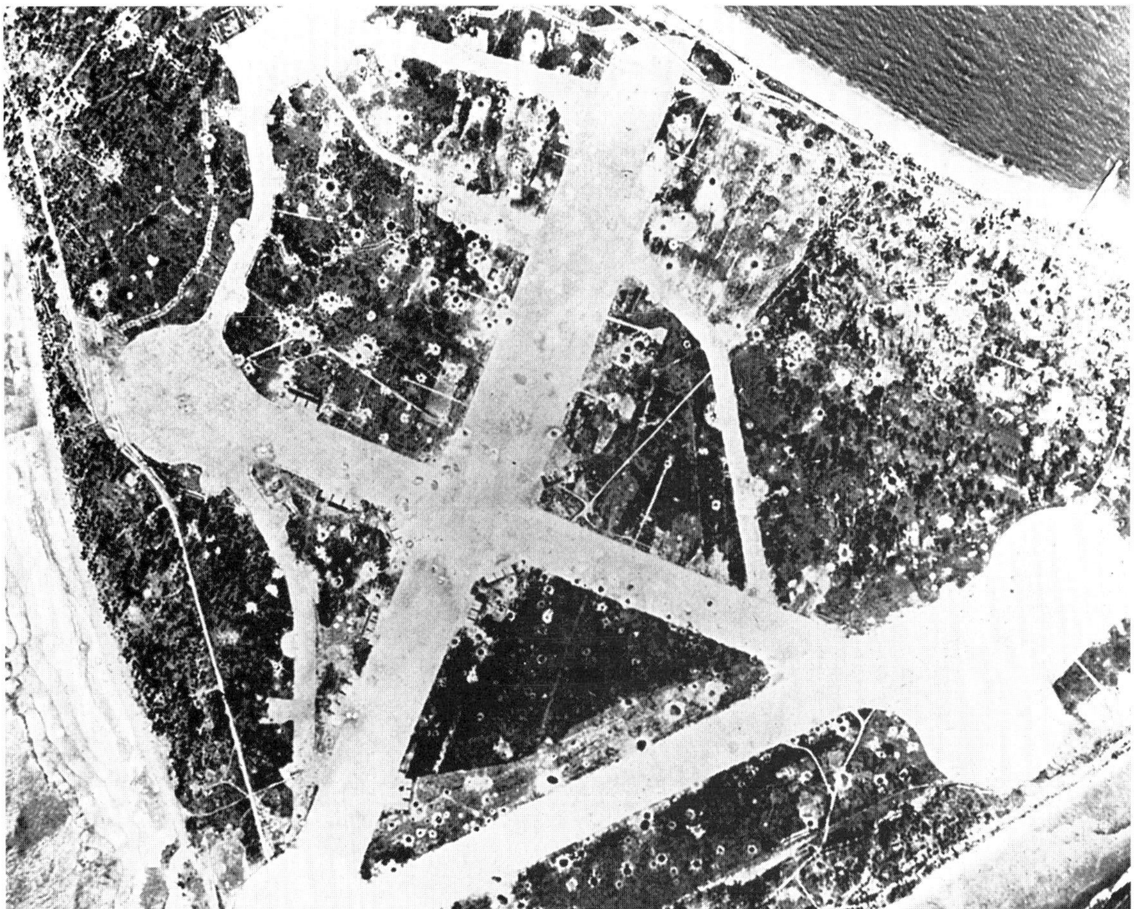

The 15th Fighter Group staff, December 43 at Wheeler Field: (Left to right) Front row: Capt. P. B. Deily, Asst. Adjutant, Maj. C. R. Sokol, Flight Surgeon, Maj. L. B. Knouse, S-4, Lt. Col. James O. Beckwith, CO, Frederic, the dog (VII Fighter Command mascot), Lt. Col. Kenneth R. Powell, Deputy CO, Maj. H. C. Ward, Adjutant, Maj. Tom Mackey (KPC), S-3; back rows: Lt. James Quinn, Asst. Stat. Officer, Lt. Herb Swigert, S-2, Capt. Emerson Johnson, Engineering Officer, Lt. B. L. Parker, Asst. S-3, Lt. Daniel J. Mahaney (KIA), Asst. Stat. Officer, Lt. Olson Fields, Asst. Engineering Officer, Capt. Art "Red Dog" Nash, Armament Officer, Lt. C. J. Duellman, CO, Hq Detachment, Lt. Nich Hubbuch, Asst. Communications Officer, Capt. Y. Y. Kam, Special Services Officer, Lt. H. M. Frye, Transportation Officer, Capt. Hyman Lipsitz, Dental Officer, Capt. Jim McNevins, Communications Officer, and Capt. Albert Jamison, Chaplain. (Source: Jim Beckwith)

The stunned pilots of the 45th circled the spot where Lloyd Harvey and his P-40 went down for half an hour, finally accepting that there would be no miracle rescue this time.

Unwilling to accept the loss of Harvey, Major Thompson immediately led an afternoon search flight back to Jaluit. Dwight Butler went along to pinpoint the crash site, but forty minutes over the Atoll produced no sign of pilot or plane. Thompson and his flight vented their frustration on the enemy with almost 2000 rounds of .50 caliber.

Reflecting bitterly on their first and last combat fatality of the Mandates Campaign, Art Bridge said. "There wasn't a target on the whole atoll worth a second pass."

Every day during the rest of February the 45th rained 500-pound bombs, 20-pound fragmentation bombs, and a dousing of .50 caliber slugs on enemy installations and boats at Mili or Jaluit.

Mili's anti-aircraft came to life on 1 March and proved it still had some sting. While cratering runways and strafing guns, Lyman Ennis' P-40K was hit.

> We continued in a slow dive firing at anything along the edge of the runway. I have a memory of bouncing a soldier out of his gunpit — the poor bastard.
>
> I was close to the runway when the plane rolled left. I brought it back to level and found that my left aileron was in full 'up' position while the right aileron was normal. I thought it was just broken, and I had a very slow trip home. One small bullet had severed a cable. Again, I was very lucky.

The last strike on Jaluit Atoll was conducted on 1 March 1944. Eleven P-40Ns of the 45th escorted nine A-24s of the 531st Squadron in an uneventful mission. The base had been so thoroughly battered that there were no more targets available.

Turning their full attention to Mili, the 45th Squadron visited it on an almost daily basis in March. Enemy gunners continued to respond, but two and a half months of bombing and strafing had left little for them to defend.

On 10 March the 45th escorted the 531st Squadron's A-24s and brutalized Mili for what was to be the last time. They bombed antiaircraft gun emplacements and radio installations, then turned their machine-guns loose on a 30-foot boat and three outriggers.

The next day, Captain Jim Vande Hey leading, the Squadron launched another strike on Mili with seventeen P-40Ns and Ks, but old "Devil Weather" spared the Japanese. Vande Hey encountered a long towering front with a wall of rain en route to Mili. Going down to the deck, they ducked under the weather, arriving at a position north of Mili, but unable to see the target. They jettisoned bombs and started to return to Makin but this atmospheric disturbance was a developing giant that soon enveloped their return route.

Since most of these P-40s had been stripped of everything but needle, ball, and climb indicator, they weren't equipped for instrument flight. Jim Vande Hey said:

> We put on our lights and called for a heading. I'd fly on the water until the rain was so heavy I couldn't see the surface. Then I'd pull up and try to fly simulated instruments at about 300 feet with all the formation stacked tightly about me. As we got nearer the base, still in the soup and uncertain of our location, the other planes began to call me, 'Captain Van, I'm down to 20 gallons. My fuel warning light has come on.'

Vande Hey was calling for a homer but there was no response from Makin. Either his low altitude or the weather were interfering with radio transmission.

> I was contemplating a mass bail-out, wondering how I could get the Squadron in a circle so we could jump and come down together. I was also praying like mad and sweating like Hell. All at once we broke out into a big hole. I looked up through the clouds and there was blue sky. The top of the overcast was about 10,000 feet. I put the boys in a string and we corkscrewed our way up through this vertical tunnel. On reaching the top I called again for a homer and Makin answered giving me the exact heading I was on. We were just 20 miles from the Island and it was clear over the field.
>
> We all landed and many of us got out and kissed the ground. Some of our tanks were just plain flat empty.

They had flown through intense weather with full combat loads over half the distance for three and one half hours. On its last mission, the Squadron had narrowly averted disaster. Leadership and discipline had provided the margin for survival.

Thus ended the air campaign in the Marshall Islands for the 15th Fighter Group. The reduction of bypassed Mili and Jaluit had evolved into nothing more than flogging a dead horse.

The unit had completed 501 combat sorties, dropping 216 tons of bombs and expending over 158,000 rounds of .50 caliber on the enemy. They had shot down or probably destroyed 13 Japanese planes (including Snipes' Baker Island victory) and probably destroyed two on the ground. In the category of shipping destroyed or damaged, they accounted for 6 medium-sized vessels and 33 small boats. (See Appendix 9 for individual pilot combat records.)

With an enthusiastic "Well done" from the U.S. Navy, the 45th Fighter Squadron was withdrawn from combat and returned to Oahu.

It was the "Jug" era and the Group's P-47Ds wore some of the most colorful trappings in the Central Pacific: A beautifully tight formation from the 78th Sq. (Source: Jim Vande Hey)

Chapter IV
THE PINEAPPLE AIR FORCE
April 1944 to January 1945

The return of the 45th and 46th Squadrons from combat reunited the 15th Fighter Group on Oahu. To the atoll soldiers it was like returning home, an R-and-R to familiar places with all the amenities. To the men of the 47th and 78th Squadrons, who had yet to fire a shot in anger, the Spring of 1944 was just another exercise in boredom. One of the stay-at-homes had struck a Pineapple Cluster Award for those involved in the seemingly endless ritual of training and defense. Yet events were under way which would reshape the 15th fighter Group and prepare it for its final campaign. Chief among the changes was the transfer of the 46th Squadron to the newly formed 21st Fighter Group in April 1944. Lieutenant Colonel Ken Powell, the 15th's Deputy Commander, became CO of the new 21st Group. He took several 15th Group staff officers with him to flesh out the organization of the new unit, spreading the roots of the 15th Group through the Seventh Fighter Command.

The three remaining squadrons had their strength beefed up from 27 pilots to 39 each, but Jim Beckwith, Group CO had a rebuilding problem as many of the unit's veteran flyers rotated back to the States for reassignment. Notable among those old soldiers who left the Group were John Thacker, Jack Thomas and Harry Thompson. In command changes within the unit, Buck Snipes took over the 45th Squadron and Jim Vande Hey the 78th, while Major Thomas W. Mackey

It was the "Jug" era and the Group's P-47Ds wore some of the most colorful trappings in the Central Pacific: Left—Personal aircraft of 47th Sq CO, Capt. John Piper. (Source: Gilmer Snipes). Right — Bob Scamara's Thunderbolt shows the 47th Sq insignia. (Source: Bob Scamara)

became CO of the 47th.

While replacements from the States built up the 15th's pilot strength, the Group lacked sufficient aircraft to outfit two full squadrons. Constantly playing a combination of Dutch Uncle and Godfather to the 21st and 318th fighter Groups caused a drawdown on aircraft, service equipment, supplies, and experienced personnel. Adding insult to injury, the 318th had been alerted for movement to a combat zone. Envy mixed with the "prevalent state of confusion" left the Group in a depressed state of mind. A move in June 1944 from Wheeler to Bellows Field did nothing to improve morale. The official history records that the 15th inherited the former home of the 318th less a lot of necessary equipment, but with the same old bed bugs.

Although still short of crew chiefs and aircraft, the Group was now equipped with 93 Republic P-47D Thunderbolt aircraft. Pilots had dubbed the big plane "The Jug."

For experienced pilots, transitioning to the razor-backed P-47 was a modest challenge. To the less qualified, it was a formidable task. Nearly twice the gross weight of the P-39 or P-40, the big Thunderbolt was considered akin to a dump truck by some, but it proved to be a reliable plane. The big elliptical wing provided great stability and, with its 2,000 h.p. Pratt & Whitney engine, the plane had enormous power. The widetread landing gear made it far less susceptible to ground looping than the old Warhawk. From a performance standpoint, the P-47 could do most everything better than the P-39 or P-40. It was faster in level flight, climbed quicker, had better range and altitude, and with eight .50 caliber guns, had greater firepower.

The D model did have some bugs and some character traits that had to be mastered. Tail wheels malfunctioned and the factory installed Curtiss 836 propellers caused vibration. Modification of the former and replacement of the latter were undertaken. More deadly was the tendency of the P-47 to achieve a flat spin if handled improperly. Once this condition developed, bailout was mandatory.

Hogan Birk was testing a new P-47D over the west coast of Oahu when he heard a young replacement pilot, 2nd Lt. Robert E. Green, call out a "May Day!" over the same area.

> He told me he was in trouble, in a spin at 28,000 feet just off Waianie. I told him I was there, too, and looking for him. It was a perfectly clear day. I tried to calm him down and told him, "Don't cut your throttle. Use spin procedure, but don't cut that damn throttle.' I was twisting my neck off looking for him but couldn't spot a thing. I told him to bail out at 10,000 feet if he couldn't correct the spin. Finally he said he was in a flat spin and getting set to bail out at 10,000. I told him I'd find him and stay with him, but he must have been disoriented because I never saw a chute, the plane, or an oil slick.

Over thirty years later the P-47 wreckage was found in a remote section of the Waianae Mountain Range.

For the mechanics and maintenance personnel of the Group, the P-47 offered a veritable galaxy of unwonted and disparate problems. A crew chief who had tended a P-40 for almost two and a half years could overhaul it about as deftly as he could field-strip a rifle. Old grease monkeys who had learned their trade on radial engines and then learned the mysteries of the P-40 in-line engine were now reacquainting themselves with the P-47's big radial powerplant. A spark plug change on a P-40 took one hour, while the same job on the Jug took four to six hours. Being a more advanced and complex plane in every respect, the P-47 required greater care.

With the advent of the P-47, the many personnel changes, and the move to Bellows, the general tempo of bitching reached new heights in the Group in June. Tension was relieved somewhat by a training exercise that was considered a classic in rear-echelon mentality.

Some higher authority decided that it would be beneficial for Army nurses to experience simulated com-

The 45th Sq was filled with Makin veterans: Left—Buck Snipes, Sq CO, (Source: Spencer Olsen) Above — (Left to right) Bruce Campbell, Bruiser Dunlap, George Hunter and Art Bridge at Bellows Field. (Source: George Hunter)

Left — Oldtimers, (left to right) "Pilot Ben" Kearney and "Hogan" Birk were on the Group staff by 1944. (Source: Don Broesamle) Right — Jim Vande Hey, who served on Makin with the 45th, became CO of the 78th at Bellows Field. Jim's P-47D was "Jeanne VII." (Source: Jim Vande Hey)

bat. A bevy of them, in fatigues and steel helmets, were deposited on Waimanalo Beach to be subjected to a mock strafing attack.

Such good fortune had not proffered itself to Hawaiian flyers since pre-Pearl Harbor days. Buzzing and flat-hatting had long since been outlawed. The assignment of fighter pilots to make authorized low-level runs on the entrenched nurses was a license to cavort. There were more volunteers than the mission required.

Captain Jim Tapp led the flight. They conducted what has been described as one of the most spectacular, death-defying, low-level displays of tomfoolery since barnstorming was invented.

Everyone on Waimanalo Beach was in a picnic mood and all were more or less observers until the first deafening pass. They dove for cover as Tapp's flight clipped their hair and left them in their prop wash. Dynamite charges set off near the beach contributed to the reality of simulated bombing. Passes were made from all directions in coordinated four-plane runs, and then in two-plane elements. One pair of fighters would come in from the sea, speeding low over the beach while the other element hedgehopped over land, "attacking" the beach from behind.

The mission was adjudged a great training success. The nurses were properly terrified, so much so that four became casualties of hysteria and had to be removed from the area by ambulance.

July 1944 found the Group still short of aircraft mechanics and specialists, but more pilots were arriving from the States and the 15th had 122 Jugs by month's end. The most popular reading material was the 318th Group's mission reports from Spain. Better still were the first-hand experiences of the twenty members of the 15th who went to Saipan on Detached Service with Sanders' outfit. They returned from the battle area with coveted gems of information.

Jim Beckwith, just promoted to full Colonel, led a 48-plane formation of 15th P-47s over Wheeler Field on 26 July 1944 to honor a visit from President Roosevelt. Major Warren Roeser, Operations Officer of the 47th Squadron, commanded a separate 16-plane unit that flew in a giant Lufbery Circle over Honolulu during the President's stay. Readiness had become a state of mind on Oahu.

Spirits and morale were lifted by rumors of impending deployment to a combat zone. The appearance of an officer of the Royal Australian Air Force to lecture on various island groups lent credibility to the gossip. However, the best news was the granting of a limited number of furloughs to a few ranking non-coms. Although these men had put in 3½ years in the Hawaiian-Air Force, their leaves at least displayed a "light at the end of the tunnel" for other enlisted men.

August was a hectic month. The tempo of deployment activity was increased though no shipping orders were received. Packing began for operations in an undisclosed forward area. Classes on escape and survival were conducted and all personnel completed qualifications in small arms. The unit records indicate that a "few Sgt. Yorks were unearthed."

Flight training was intensified and napalm was used in practice bombing for the first time. Although five aircraft were lost in accidents during August, the Group had no fatalities and could still muster 128 P-47s by month's end. The balance of those on Detached Service with the 318th returned with glimpses of adventure. Still playing the role of farm club, the Group sent several replacement pilots to join the 318th Fighter Group on Saipan.

Morale was at a new high as the 15th Group awaited the impending move. The signs of departure were everywhere with packing, orientation classes, and "final" three-day passes. Even the Chaplain's section reported that Captain Jamison had taken a three-day pass "with beneficial effects on his physical and spiritual welfare." On 30 August the Group was alerted for movement, and speculation centered on their assignment to the Philippines. The official unit history sounded an exhilarating note: "The Group and its Squadrons are now ready and primed for mortal combat."

Colonel Beckwith and staff members shipped out with a Navy task force under secret orders, and the rest of the Group began to pack and load their gear on a vessel at Honolulu. The Marines had invaded the Palau Islands as the 15th bade goodbye to Bellows Field. Officers and enlisted men had a feeling that they were about to play a role in history. However, on 18 September 1944, the Group was ordered to unload their gear from the ship, return to Bellows Field, and stand down. The men were incredulous. Their hopes of catching up with the war and engaging the enemy seemed dashed. Morale plunged.

Colonel Eugene P. "Moose" Mussett came over from Seventh Fighter Command Headquarters to give the 15th a bromide. Although higher command rarely condescended to justification, he explained the tactical situation. Colonel Beckwith, he disclosed, was in a task force that had been bound for the invasion of Yap Island in the Caroline Group. A Navy carrier strike force had hit the Philippines a few days earlier and had so reduced the Japanese air strength that strategic plans had been altered. The Carolines were to be bypassed in favor of a Philippine invasion. Had the Group proceeded to Yap they would have been stuck there with only the isolated Japanese base at Truk Island within the range of the P-47Ds. They would have traded boredom for monotony.

The Group's glue — the non-coms: (Left to right) Charles Zuercher, Spencer Olsen, Wilbur Howser and Andrew Hymel of the 45th Sq. (Source: Spencer Olsen)

After a move to and from ship and all the packing and unpacking it was hard to find any silver lining in the clouds that seemed to overhang the 15th Group. Nor did subsequent events improve the unit's disposition. Back at Bellows they continued to train pilots for the 318th Fighter Group and two aircraft accidents resulted in serious, though not fatal injuries. When, near month's end, a rotation plan was announced for men with 45 month's overseas service, it appeared to be the final straw — one had to be positively ancient to ever see home again. But perverse fate had one more trick to play. The 45th Squadron's C-47, used by the entire Group for R-and-R to Hilo and the Parker Ranch, was transferred to the 19th Transport Squadron. While Chaplain Jamison could find solemn comfort in reporting no funerals for the month of September, he had to admit that he was "not immune to the mood of

The Group's glue — the non-coms: Left — (left to right) First Sgt. Moore, Tom Walker, and Jakola of the 47th Sq. (Source: John Whitcomb) Right — The bond between airplane drivers and mechanics was strong. Russell Skaggs confers with Bernie Bjorseth by their 47th Sq P-47D. (Source: Russell Skaggs)

A formation of the 15th Group's key men. Col. Beckwith leads the diamond formation of P-47s with (left to right) Buck Snipes, 45th Sq, Jim Vande Hey, 78th Sq, and John Piper, 47th Sq. (Source: Gilmer Snipes)

The beginning of a new era — the first P-51D-20s arrive at Bellows in November 44. (Source: Walter Kreimann)

bewilderment and disappointment" that infected the Group.

October arrived and so did Colonel Beckwith, back from a cruise to nowhere. He found his "keenly disappointed organization" resettling at Bellows Field. It had been occupied during the abortive embarkation by a division of mice, and the 15th had a fight on its hands to recapture the old base. Second Lieutenant Bill Swain of the Group S-2 Section was the acknowledged champion mouse catcher. He was heralded as the "ace of aces" with 29 mice to his credit.

Despite the mice, morale got a big boost when several enlisted men with lots of hash marks on their sleeves, were reassigned to the States. These returnees were the first since the start of the war, and included the 47th's top soldier, First Sgt. Eldred G. Moore. He had been overseas since December 1939. More furloughs were granted and those who had to stay behind were treated to an improbable goat-hunting expedition on Molokai Island organized by Special Services. The hunting of wild goats reportedly required firearms and copious quantities of spirits.

The 318th Fighter Group's mission reports from Saipan were still read with interest and envy. The combination of losses and reassignments for the 318th caused a continuing drawdown on the 15th Group. With an influx of replacement pilots, several of the Group's flying officers returned stateside to new assignments or gunnery school including: Captain Jim Apple, 1st Lt. John Basham, and 1st Lt. John Polk from the 45th; Captain Willie Weaver, 1st Lt. Leigh Hightower, and 1st Lt. William H. Sparks from the 47th; and Captain Marshall Crispen and 1st Lt. Jack Cotter from the 78th.

Likewise, several charter members among the Group's non-commissioned oficers hit the magic 45 months and rotated back to the "old country." Sparks was destined to return by a circuitous route for the final act.

The unit's official history for October closed with a comment reflecting the Group's mood: "The month was weary, stale, flat, and unprofitable."

November 1944 was marked by two major events. Though the 15th remained at Bellows Field in the Pineapple Air Force, they were advised by Seventh Fighter Command to prepare for movement to a combat zone.

The conditioned response was one of bemused skepticism. The official history noted that the announcement "has not generated enough of a flurry to disturb the field mice that sleep so complacently in our offices and shacks." The unit scribe waxed eloquent in his incredulity:

> The reason for this insouciance and otiosity, that would put Rip Van Winkle to shame, is fourfold. First; just about all the supplies that might be needed were acquired when this unit prepared for the move that aborted in September. Secondly, since, on what had turned out to be merely a dry run, the personnel had gone so far as to pack all the equipment and actually load it on the ship, everyone has a pretty good idea of what is needed and will be taken along, how to pack it, and just how long it will take. Thirdly; having been fooled once, no one is going to yell 'Wolf! Wolf!' at us again, particularly since our move has already been delayed several times. And fourthly; since fighter Command is going along on this deal and have undertaken to supply us with all the material, information, S.O.I.s, intelligence 'poop', etc., there is nothing much for us to do except await the eventful day.

The second event kindled considerably more interest. A handful of brand new P-51D-20-NA aircraft arrived at Bellows. The sleek North American "Mustang" was the ultimate fighter. It combined top speed, maneuverability, and high-altitude capability with outstanding range. It was a hot plane, but an honest one with few bad traits. Colonel Beckwith had been briefed on the future mission of the Group utilizing the long-range potential of the P-51, but was not permitted to disclose grand strategy to the rest of the unit. "This made words of encouragement hard to come by."

Crew chiefs and mechanics groaned at yet another conversion from radial back to in-line engines and the need to learn the secrets of a new machine. Inspection soon demonstrated that the P-51 was designed for ease of maintenance. This feature would prove critical in the environment of the last campaign where men and machines would be given the harshest testing.

North American P-51H in flight.

The continuing desire for action may have been responsible for a mid-month accident in the 47th Squadron. During a simulated combat mission, 1st Lt. Richard J. "Spider" Condrick let go with 20 rounds of .50 caliber. Five of the bullets found an unintended target, 1st Lt. Charles J. Cameron's P-47. Cameron landed at Bellows despite four holes in his right wing, one in his left, and a severed hydraulic line to his right wheel brake. Spider would later refine his aim on Japanese targets.

Another operational accident in November again attested to the sturdy construction of the venerable Jug.

Above: Installation of the IFF on a P-51 at Bellows Field. (Source: Jim Vande Hey)

Lt. Frank Lindner died on 13 January 45 exploring the limits of the speedy Mustang. (Source: Jim Vande Hey)

Jim Tapp testing his droppable life raft contraption off Oahu on 11 December 44. Note static line to 110 gal. wing tank. (Source: David Beyl)

Left: Jim Beckwith at Bellows with another "Squirt" ready for the move to combat. (Source: Gilmer Snipes)

Second Lieutenant dick Schroeppel of the 78th Squadron, had a mid-air collision with a P-38 from another unit. In an amazing piece of flying he managed to bring his P-47 back to Bellows minus four feet of wing. Schroeppel, like many other members of the Group, was spending his allotment of good luck. The repeated scrapes with death that were inevitable in this sort of flying would accelerate with future combat. One could not hope to crash airplanes, defy the elements, and face enemy fire indefinitely. For many of these men, good fortune would lapse in the months ahead.

Tragedy of an ironic nature visited the Group with the death of Major Tom Mackey. The popular CO of the 47th Squadron had just returned to the States on leave. He died as a passenger in an Army transport that crashed in a storm over California. Captain John A. Piper, Operations Officer for the 47th, assumed command of the Squadron while Captain Theon E. Markham took over the Operations slot.

As P-51s were added to the inventory, the pace of training quickened and the Group racked up 6,295 hours of flight time, a new monthly record. The transi-

Part of the Group's assault echelon, embarked on the transport, ***Lenawee****, mostly members of the 47th Sq: (Left to right) Front row, leaning on railing: Keisling, Fitzgerald, Unknown, Oronsky, Frick (KIA), Elliott, Tyler, Sanders, Sidebottom, Lapides, Broadbent; middle row, leaning on front row: Dibelka (KIA), Klessig, Blandford, Scanlan (KIA), Van Zandt (KIA), Kinsey, Riley, Strother, Carletti, Jones; back row: Kriss, Weaver (KIA), Johnson, Liddell (KIA), Davis, Addington, Bisky (KPC). (Source: John Whitcomb)*

tion from the big P-47 to the little P-51 was a unique experience. "One flew like a water buffalo and the other like a gazelle," in the view of 2nd Lt. John M. Fitzgerald of the 47th Squadron. The P-47 was landed by holding the nose a bit high and plopping it down on the runway. It was a big strong brute and could take that sort of abuse. Handling the Mustang in a similar fashion caused damage to landing gears and tail assemblies and even created incidents of wings buckling.

The high speed capability of the P-51 also called for caution. Speed in dives was reaching limits never before encountered and setting up the dynamic conditions of compressability. It was considered likely that such a situation caused the Group's first P-51 operational fatality. Second Lieutenant Robert A. Ferris, of the 78th Squadron was lost on 25 November when a wing pulled off and his plane exploded or disintegrated during a steep dive.

Inevitably, the question of P-47 versus P-51 performance was raised to the point of challenge, and late in the month, an unofficial test was conducted. Captain Jim Tapp in a P-51D and Major Emmett Kearney in a P-47D staged a horse race from Bellows to 30,000 feet. The Mustang, making a shorter takeoff run, climbed much more rapidly and won the race to 30,000, but at that rarefied altitude it bested the P-47 in straight and level flight by only 10 m.p.h.

December 1944 was dominated by a feverish conversion to the P-51 Mustang. The Group began the month with 71 Jugs and only 6 Mustangs. By month's end the inventory showed only 11 Thunderbolts remaining and 93 Mustangs mustered at Bellows Field.

An invention that was destined to save the lives of several Seventh Fighter Command pilots was perfected and linked to the P-51. Because of the ever present potential for pilots going down at sea, Captain Jim Tapp had long pondered a droppable rescue kit. He was joined in his independent research by Captain Vic Mollan. The 110-gallon external wing tank of the Mustang finally provided the means to package the kit. The sea-rescue parcel consisted of a zipper type kapok bag and contained: an A-3 life raft, a Gibson Girl radio, a Navy kit of visual signal equipment, and rations. Encased in a modified 110 gallon wing tank, the packet was attached to a QA-3 chest parachute. When the bomb release was triggered the tank would drop away, separate, and a static line would open the parachute. On December 12, Captain Tapp flew the first mission to test the drop rescue kit. Second Lieutenant Charles C. Heil, the 78th Squadron's resident swimming champion, was the guinea pig. The equipment worked so well that Hickam Air Depot began to assemble these kits. Any P-51 equipped with the life-saving drop tank would later be code named "Josephine."

As the few enlisted vets reached the magic number of points and rotated home, their assignments were taken by replacements. Almost unnoticed the Group passed through its first month in three years without using its pilot personnel to nourish the squadrons of other Pacific units.

Pilots logged 4,800 hours largely transitioning to the P-51. Several accidents took place. Most of them resulted from unfamiliarity with the Mustang or from flying it as though it were a P-47. Wings and skin were buckled again in two instances, but only two planes were completely wrecked. Better still, there were no fatalities or serious injuries.

Mechanics and engineering officers continued to learn the intricacies of the new P-51. The installation and modification of a new IFF (Identification Friend or Foe) transponder consumed an inordinate number of man hours. It had originally been located in an area best suited to access by a snake. With their usual ingenuity, the mechanics redesigned the airplane moving the IFF to a location behind the armorplate in a position the battery formerly occupied. The battery was then moved forward to a location above and behind the engine. According to pilots, the modification adjusted

Air echelon of the Group aboard the CVE 86, ***Sitkoh Bay,*** *enroute Guam, January 45. (Source: Jim Vande Hey)*

the center of gravity forward slightly, which seemed to improve the flying characteristics of the plane.

Colonel Beckwith spent the last week of December on Saipan on Detached Service with the 318th Fighter Group. Lew Sanders and his team gave Beckwith a briefing based on their six months of Marianas combat service.

These developments were indicative of a forthcoming move to combat down under, but as the Group's official history stated:

> It just seems impossible to 'keep the iron hot' forever. Eagerness and desire to get into combat had waned into complacency. In athletics it's called being overtrained. Whatever the name for it, or its cause, morale has suffered.

Christmas and New Year's Eve celebrations rounded out the year and did nothing to improve spirits. For many it was the first holiday far from loved ones. For others, it was the fourth.

As January 1945 began, even the worst skeptics were obliged to observe that something was definitely afoot. Combat clothing and front-line gear were issued where lacking. Carbine rifles, with new adjustable sights, were zeroed in on the range and sub-machine guns were allotted to each Squadron. Ammunition was drawn for hand and shoulder weapons.

As the month progressed, unofficial talk pointed toward the Group's participation in operations planned for the Bonin and Volcano Islands. On 21 January terrain models of these islands arrived. The rumors seemed to be taking substance.

When all officers and enlisted men were told to ship home their excess personal gear and the government offered to pay the freight, the certainty of forthcoming action took on a high degree of probability. But when the Group barber chair was sold to the 580th Signal Aircraft Warning Battalion because there wasn't room for it on the ship, that seemed to provide indisputable proof that the 15th was shipping out.

Flight operations were shut down on 19 January. It was none too soon. Not since December 1941 had the Group suffered such a disastrous month. Three accidents had cost the loss of six P-51Ds and all six pilots including three members of the 47th who went down in bad weather during a pre-dawn mission on the 16th.

On 20 January the 78th Squadron left Bellows Field for the last time and, after a "what the Hell" buzz job on the old base, landed their Mustangs at Ford Island. The other two Squadrons followed, and 82 Mustangs eventually assembled at Ford Island for transfer to the aircraft carrier, *Sitkoh Bay*, (CVE86). The final Squadron flights over Honolulu were magnificent spectacles. Second Lieutenant Harold Baccus landed hot at Ford Island Naval Air Station and ground looped his 47th Squadron P-51 "in front of God and everybody." With respectful reproach, a Navy Chief said, "They sure do come in hot when you land with the flaps up, huh, Lieutenant?" Like everyone else, Harold Baccus was more than a little anxious to catch up with the war.

By 8 February the last of the 15th Group's men and equipment had sailed from Honolulu, leaving the Aloha Tower and the Pineapple Air Force in their wake.

Through a certain mystique the unit had become a force. The Group was not a static organization; men had come and gone. Nor was it an inanimate object like a ship or a fortress to which men at arms could associate or establish ties of identity. It was a homeless assemblage of men and things, granted status only by official pieces of paper.

Yet from the fervor of its members, past and present, the 15th Fighter Group assumed certain characteristics — soul and nobility. Because of them it had become a community of purpose, a tradition, a brotherhood.

Chapter V

ASSAULT ON IWO
February 1945 to March 1945

The 15th Fighter Group constituted a veritable armada at sea. The planes and some of the pilots were aboard the *Sitkoh Bay* while the rest of the pilots, ground personnel, equipment, and material were embarked aboard the transports *Berrien, Dashing Wave, Muliphen, Cape San Martin, Cape Georgia Bay, Sea Runner,* and *Lenawee*. After all ships were underway, personnel were advised that their ultimate destination was the island of Iwo Jima.

The CVE *Sitkoh Bay* set course for the Marianas and arrived off Guam on 13 February 1945. The Mustangs were crammed on the carrier deck in four tightly packed rows. Two planes were hooked to catapults in case of an emergency situation. Since the Japanese Navy had largely been rendered *hors de combat* in four years of action, the catapult would only be used for a remote contingency. Yet Major Jim Vande Hey, whose plane was one of those poised for the improbable shot, was less than enthusiastic. Since the P-51 could not return to the carrier, any launch would be a one-way ticket. "Either I had to be close to an island, or I had to go for a swim at the end of the flight," concluded Vande Hey. Jim had been involved in one previously successful carrier operation and was anxious to maintain his perfect record.

The trip proved uneventful and the planes were hoisted over the side to barges, then towed ashore to Orote Field. After the P-51s had been unpickled, they were flown to East Field on Saipan. There, at the home of the battle seasoned 318th Fighter Group, the air echelon found accommodations and quarters. Over beers, they discussed the pending campaign with old friends. Most members of the 318th had been in the Pineapple Air Force, and many of the pilots had trained with the 15th. Colonel Lew Sanders, CO of the 318th and a 15th alumnus, had come to Hawaii in 1941 with Colonel Jim Beckwith, CO of the 15th. Major Phil Rasmussen, who had flown with Sanders in the desperate battle of 7 December 1941, was now his Operations Officer. It was a pleasant class reunion. It was also an opportunity for the pilots to brush up on their flying and bone up on intelligence data.

Things weren't nearly as cheery for the officers and men on the transports *Berrien* and *Lenawee* carrying Group staff and most of the excess of the 45th and 47th Squadron personnel. They arrived off Iwo Jima on 19 February. It was D-Day.

Major Emerson R. Johnson, Group Material Officer, commanded the 15th's assault force. Emerson was a soldier of the old school. He had enlisted in the service in 1928, served as a bugler, librarian, aircraft mechanic, crew chief, and aircraft technical inspector. He was a Tech Sergeant in the 19th Pursuit Squadron on 7 December 1941. Because of his extensive experience, he received rapid promotions and was commissioned a 2nd Lt. on 17 June 1942. He was a "shavetail with whiskers", an officer who had risen through the ranks. Now, as the Group's senior officer present, and one of the oldest, at 38, he was at the focal point of the Pacific War. He recalls vividly the approach to the southeast shore of Iwo Jima:

> The Captain of the *Lenawee* eased our ship in towards Mount Suribachi in what was a calculated act of provocation. Immediately a shell hit ahead of us and slightly to our left. I thought, "Let's not go in any further," but he went slowly forward and the next shell landed ahead and slightly to our right. I thought, "Boy! Now they have us bracketed," but that Captain must have known what he was doing. He made a slow turn to the right and the next shell landed way short of the ship. We could see the shells were coming from a gun in a cave at the base of Suribachi.

Major Johnson and the rest of the men then watched as a torrent of naval shells and bombs were directed at the cave entrance. The Japanese gun fell silent.

For weeks prior to the invasion, Iwo had been bombed relentlessly by Air Force heavies and carrier planes of Task Force 58. Now, eight battleships, six cruisers, and a flotilla of destroyers rained tens of thousands of shells on the tiny island. Never had an enemy target been subjected to such a monumental pre-invasion bombardment by the combined forces of the United States. First Lieutenant Hanry G. "Sandy" Sanders, Intelligence Officer for the 47th Squadron, remembers the spectacle: "The shelling was so heavy we couldn't talk to each other." The barrage was so intense that the island was periodically obscured under an immense pall of dust and smoke.

Nestled in among the warships and transports of Task Force 54, the men on *Lenawee* and *Berrien* had an unforgettable view of the struggle for Iwo Jima. It seemed impossible to the airmen on the transports that any human could have survived the saturation bombardment of those eight square miles of land. It was equally implausible to imagine that the enemy could manage refuge in any man-made shelter from the giant 16 inch battleship rounds that augered deep into the earth before detonation. The preparation gave Emerson Johnson confidence:

The Iwo Jima invasion as seen by the Group's assault echelon from the navy transports

Airmen "squared their jaws" as marines who had died in the ***Lenawee's*** *sick bays were buried at sea. (Source: John Whitcomb)*

Loading into an LCVP from ***Lenawee****.(Source: John Whitcomb)*

Reserves going ashore on Red Beach.(Source: John Whitcomb)

Mount Surabachi just after the flag raising. (Source: John Whitcomb)

The heavy cruiser, ***Tuscaloosa****, approaches the APA* ***Lenawee*** *to replenish her supply of naval ordnance. (Source: John Whitcomb)*

Men of the Group watch a dying Navy TBF hit by enemy fire over Iwo. (Source: John Whitcomb)

I was just sure that there would be little or no resistance for the Marines, and was convinced that we would probably be going in the next day. How wrong I was! When the initial bombing had quieted and the Marines started ashore, the island erupted with fire as the enemy began fighting for the beach.

Men and equipment were getting bogged down on the beaches. Tanks were seen struggling in the soft volcanic ash. Observers onboard the transports could tell that things were not going according to schedule. They sensed that the Marines were catching hell on the Devil's own beachhead.

The worst fears of the Task Force were soon realized as landing-craft from the early waves began to return with an ever increasing stream of casualties. Both *Lenawee* and *Berrien* were pressed into service as hospital ships. It was a sobering sight for the young men of the 15th Group. Emerson Johnson recalls:

> A noticeable change was taking place among the Air Force troops topside. For those who had never seen actual war, first hand, this was a 'growing up fast' time. As the gravely wounded Marines were taken below, my men were blowing their noses and squaring their jaws.

Dr. Jack Lapides, the 47th Squadron's Flight Surgeon, pitched in to assist the ship's overworked mdical staff. "We gave up our quarters to be used as hospital operating rooms and wards," said Sandy Sanders. "Those boys had suffered terribly and we gladly slept on the deck. Our rooms ran red with blood and the smell of death began to materialize."

The same drama was taking place on the transport, *Berrien*. Men of the 45th Squadron helped with the wounded, then assisted in unloading ammunition to resupply the fleet cruisers. By day's end there were bracing minidramas on each ship as Marines who had not survived their wounds were quickly buried at sea.

Air raids took place nightly, adding to the din of battle on land. With flares, tracers, and the hammering of the transport's antiaircraft batteries, the extraordinary show continued almost non-stop. On 21 February, D-plus-2, a Japanese Kamakazi plane smashed into the escort carrier, *Bismark Sea*, and turned her into a raging inferno. As internal explosions racked the ship, she rolled over and sank. Over two hundred of her crew were lost. On D-plus-4 the men on the *Lenawee* saw the Stars and Stripes raised on Mount Suribachi. "For days we had watched the Marines inch slowly up the island," said Major Johnson. "Their tanks and equipment littered the eastern slope. Iwo was by no means secure, but seeing that flag go up was sure encouraging." The 15th Fighter Group's advance party was getting ready to hit the beach the following day.

Their departure was delayed by priority cargoes and rising seas, but the first contingent of the Group boarded at LST late on 24 February 1945, D-plus-5, and departed the security of their transport. According to Emerson Johnson:

> It was after dark when we finally landed, I should say, 'went ashore' for we did not quite reach the beach. After splashing through 12 or 15 yards of surf we were safely on Iwo in the volcanic ash of the eastern slopes of Suribachi. It was one step forward and two backward with full field pack on our backs, a carbine in hand, and a .45 holstered to our belts. You could call it mushing, I guess.
>
> Then a challenge froze us in our fumbling tracks. "Halt! Who goes there?
>
> "Friend, of course.
>
> "What's the password?
>
> "Washington," I responded.
>
> "That's not right," came the answer as we heard the ominous click of the Marine's rifle safety. In a flood of argument, we protested that "Washington" had been the approved password just that morning when we were briefed onboard ship. "Just a minute," said the sentry, now toying with the new arrivals. Calling down the line to the next sentry he asked, "Hey, Joe, what's the password for tonight?"
>
> "Washington," came the distant reply.
>
> "OK," he said. "Pass on but keep your heads down. There's a lot of sniping going on up above. You guys had better find a spot and dig in for the night. This place is dangerous."
>
> "It sure is," I thought, "With sentries who don't know the password."

The Marine's warnings had been both irrelevant and unnecessary. From the first challenge through the next few minutes, punctuated by gunfire, Johnson and his men knew that they had located the front line of World War II.

Digging foxholes in Iwo's loose volcanic ash was like trying to dig a hole in a lake. "All you could do," said Emerson, "was make a depression and jump in before the ash closed around you."

After a restless night, the advance party scouted Airfield No. 1. It had been taken by the Marines, but was not yet clear and was still under enemy fire. The Japanese defenders were being squeezed toward the northern end of Iwo Jima, but they were still full of fight and, incredibly, they were surfacing behind lines from a complex labyrinth of by-passed caves, tunnels and casemated concrete bunkers.

Johnson and his team spend the second night on Iwo in a laboriously excavated and sandbagged super foxhole with a pyramidal tent for a roof. It was just off the end of what they considered an inactive runway. The unscheduled arrival of a pair of battle damaged Navy planes and two bullet holes in the tent propelled the unit into another move the following day.

Additional people coming ashore found that the area assigned to the Group was in a noisy neighborhood. They had dug in near a battery of Marine artillery. These 105 mm giants belched death day or night, on

Landing craft on Red Beach. (Source: Richard MacKenzie)

A Navy PBM (right) surveys the chaos on Iwo's Eastern coast. (Source: Richard MacKenzie)

The earth, churned by shell fire, contained grisly discoveries. (Source: Earl Steggeman)

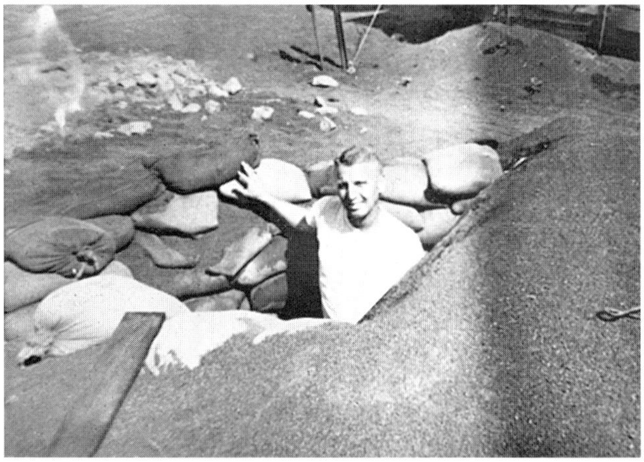

Shoveling in the loose volcanic ash was like digging a hole in water. (Source: R. Edsel Wilcox)

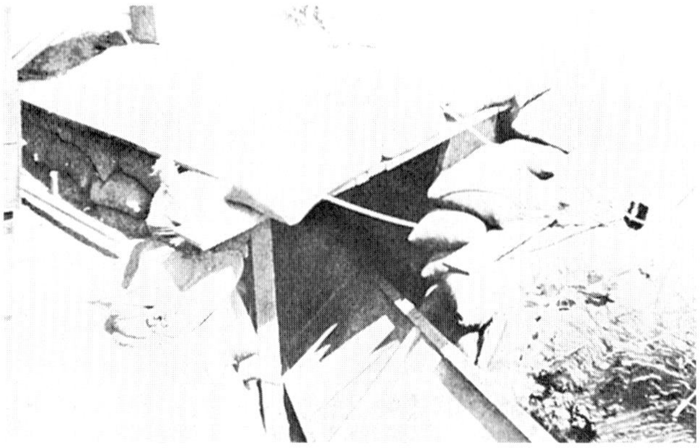

A sandbagged reinforced air raid shelter prepared by men of the 47th Sq. (Source: Henry Weinberger)

A Marine mortar unit in action around the assault echelon's first positions near Red Beach. (Source: Richard MacKenzie)

Emerson Johnson's assault force dug in near a battery of Marine 105mm artillery. (Source: Fred Arnold)

This deluxe foxhole was home to Lt. Clyde Mangum (KIA) of the 78th. (Source: Jim Vande Hey)

call, in ear-splitting barrages. For the first few days the 15th bore no resemblance to a fighting aviation unit. They were occupied with the chores of ground soldiers — digging and reinforcing foxholes, establishing communications, and drawing transport and supplies from the chaotic beach. Weapons were always in hand or close by. K-rations were the only food for three days, and water was for drinking only. It was hard to tell a Captain from a Corporal because all personnel had stripped their uniforms of any insignia of rank. Years earlier the infantry had learned that shiny bars and chevrons attracted sniper fire. Nights were punctuated with the rattle of small-arms fire and the occasional thunder of the 105s, as the whole scene was intermittently illuminated by the blossoming of a star shell.

Remaining portions of the Ground Echelon disembarked from their ships and joined Major Johnson and the assault force on the 4th of March. The entire unit then pitched into the sweaty job of unloading and securing the Group's equipment, supplies and material. The 78th Squadron history told a tale that exemplified the selfless spirit of the Group:

> Everybody from buck private to Major McNevins (Exec) took a hand in the task of converting wilderness and ruin into orderly, protected, serviceable districts. Pilot officers shoveled and hammered. Engineering experts filled sandbags. Crack mechanics lifted boxes and toted crates. Cooks drove stakes. The men resembled less a highly specialized group of aircraft artisans than a labor battalion. What was accomplished was all the more remarkable considering that, with few exceptions, the men had never before been exposed to combat conditions.

By 6 March the Marines had driven a wedge to the northeast coast and isolated most of the remaining defenders into two pockets of resistance around Kitano Point and Tachiiwa Point. The 811th Aviation Engineer Battalion had filled the craters on Airfield No. 1 and cleared the wreckage of battle. The Group was implanted, sandbagged, functional, and ready for the Air Echelon on Saipan.

The 15th Fighter Group was about to enter its last campaign nearly 4000 miles from Wheeler where they had engaged in their first. The destiny that brought them to Iwo Jima was part of a panoramic war strategy.

In October 1944 the first giant B-29 Superfortresses had arrived on Saipan. By 24 November these Twentieth Air Force giants had launched their first strike on the Japanese homeland with a raid on Tokyo. Honshu, Japan's main island, was over 1200 miles from B-29 bases in the Marianas. The round trip was 2570 nautial miles (3000 statute miles) and the bombers were airborne for about 14 hours. Iwo Jima lay near the route to Tokyo, about at the halfway point. Its seizure was viewed as a necessity. Repeated bombing had not seriously impaired the operation of Iwo's airfields. Japanese engineers had long been experts at crater elimination. Aside from stamping out the infernal opposition which Japanese fighters could mount from Iwo, its capture would provide an emergency landing field for damaged B-29s and a base for P-51 escorts.

Iwo, resembling a pork chop, is five miles long and two and one half miles wide. It is part of a string of active volcanic peaks that lay like stepping stones in the Pacific from the Marianas to the very doorstep of Honshu Island. These islands, some no more than spires of rock, were formed a few thousand years ago as lines of weakness in the earth's surface permitted volcanic matter to rise from the ocean floor.

The rugged group of rocky outcroppings, including Iwo, are called Kazan Retto in Japanese, or Volcano Islands. This entire spine of widely interspersed islands, reaching to within 65 miles of Tokyo, is known as the Nanpo Shoto Group. The trenches on either side of the ridge plunge to depths as great as 5,000 feet.

Iwo Jima, literally translated, is sulphur island. It is straddled by two peaks: to the south by the 3,181 foot Minami Iwo Jima, 33 miles away, and to the north by 2,630 foot Kita Iwo Jima, 38 miles distant. These two barren granite monuments served as natural signposts directing flyers to Iwo Jima. Kita was code named "Hotrocks."

The most prominent feature on Iwo Jima is Mount Suribachi, a crater rising 546 feet from sea level.

The situation on D plus 11, 2 March 45. (Source: Harold Hinds)

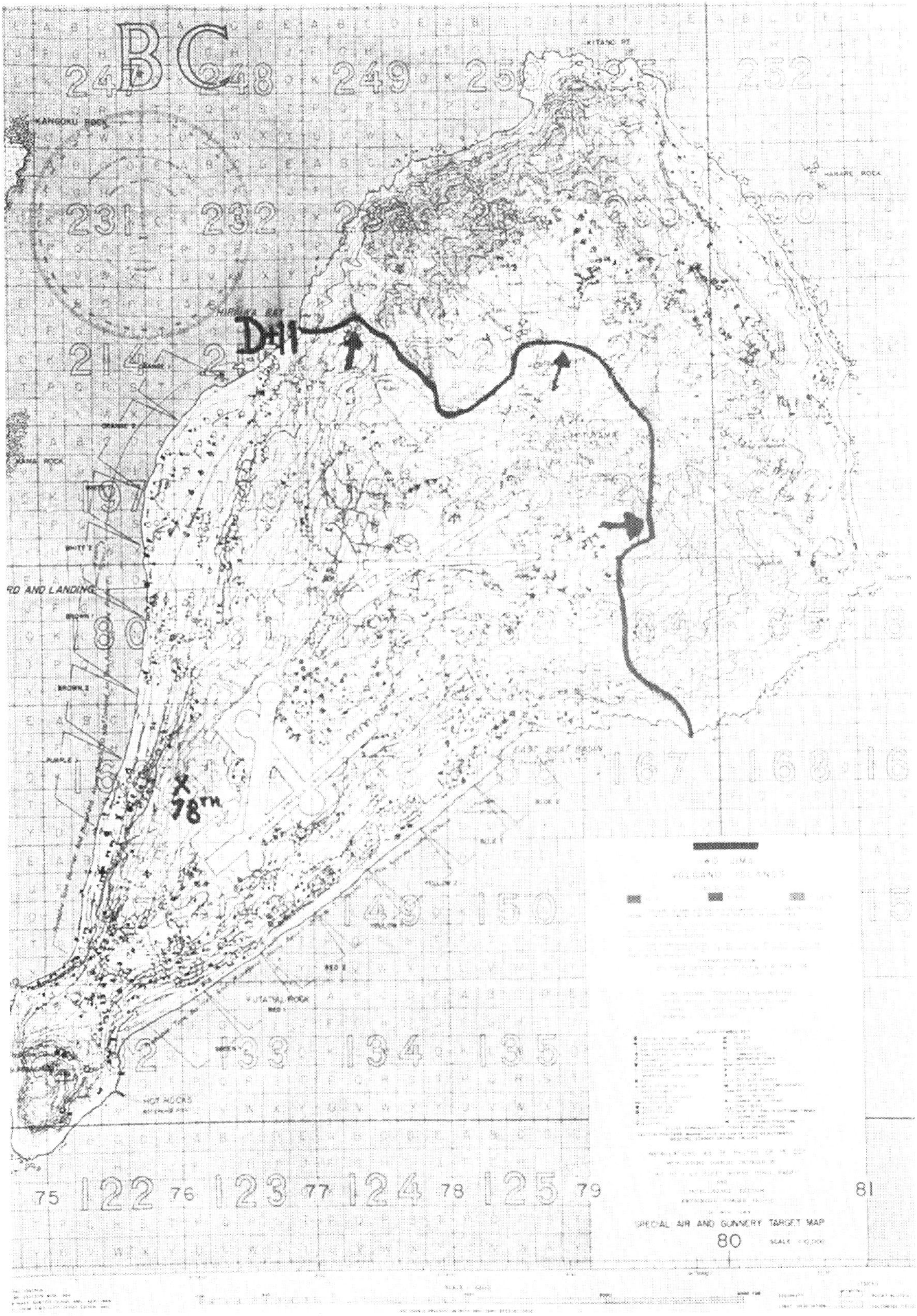

Though most of the rocky island was barren, sugar cane, cocoa, and rice had been cultivated. The methodial bombing and shelling had stripped the island of any pretense of life or vegetation, and churned the volcanic matter into a powdery mass. Dozens of vents or fissures emitting steam and sulphurous vapors coupled with the devastation of bombardment gave the island an unearthly atmosphere.

This was the inhospitable environment that awaited the 15th Fighter Group. On 6 March 1945 Major General Mickey Moore, Chief of the Seventh Fighter Command, led the P-51s of the 47th Fighter Squadron from Saipan to Iwo. General Moore landed the first P-51 and Squadron CO, Major John Piper, was next. Captain Raymond J. "Whitney" Betner, third man down, blew a tail wheel on landing and ground looped with most of the island watching. "I felt sorry for him" said Mickey Moore. "I was sure glad it wasn't me."

On 7 March the rest of the Air Echelon formed up over Saipan and Jim Beckwith led the 45th and 78th Squadrons into Iwo. The 47th Squadron took over the chore of daylight Combat Air Patrol the same day. P-61s of the 6th Night Fighter Squadron arrived for night air defense over "Agate", as the base was curiously called.

The pilots were glad to be getting into action but were appalled at the living conditions. "You should have been here a week ago," was the response of Emerson Johnson's old-timers. First Lieutenant Robert H. Roseberry, 78th Squadron, claimed that the Australian C rations were billy goat and turnips.

Late on 8 March Marine ground units requested air support and the 47th responded. Major Piper led an eight-plane formation attacking Japanese positions in specified map grids on the northern coast. They made one run after another pouring .50 caliber fire into enemy emplacements. With each pass the air coordinator kept urging the P-51s to put their fire closer to the Marine front lines, supposedly marked by yellow cloth panels. The pilots couldn't see the panels and were understandably nervous about hitting their own troops on the first mission where they had fired their guns in anger. But they expended 16,640 rounds of ammunition and the Marines said it was the best job of close air support in two weeks.

The 45th Squadron got into action on 9 March. Major Buck Snipes, Captain Skinny Ennis, and Captain Art Bridge each led eight-plane flights to bomb and strafe Kangoku and Kama Islands. The pilots thought these islands were totally barren rock piles lying close off Iwo's west coast, but the Marines had reported random mortar and rocket fire from them.

Later that same day, the 45th sent up three more missions in close support of Marine units at the north end of Iwo. Colonel Beckwith led one mission while Captains Dwight Butler and Art Bridge led others. Many pilots flew two sorties.

Skinny Ennis recalled, "We were instructed to get airborne as soon as possible to avoid enemy ground fire at the end of the runway." On one hop, Ennis led his flight with such precision that all eight 500-pound bombs fell in a 200-foot circle less than 600 yards from friendly troops. Again the Marines were lavish in their praise. Ennis, the Makin veteran, considered the effort no more than should have been expected from a journeyman carpenter. "It was an ordinary operation. One that we were very good at."

The 78th Squadron took over the ground support role on 10 March flying 45 individual sorties. Major Jim Vande Hey was up three times. Major Jim Tapp and Captain Todd Moore led other missions. Second Lieutenant Gordon H. Scott took an AA hit in his tail section, but landed safely. Colonel Beckwith, Major Snipes, Major Piper, and Captain Bridge acted as air controllers, but found that targets on the north end of Iwo were becoming hard to pinpoint as Marines squeezed the Japanese defense perimeter into a narrow strip along the sea.

On the 11th the Group flew two more ground-support missions and also reached out to interdict nearby Japanese island bases for the first time. A sub-group of the Nanpo Shoto chain, the Bonin Islands, were northeast of Iwo Jima. The nearest was Haha Jima, 120 nautical miles from Iwo; its neighbor, Chichi Jima, was 27 miles further north. Both had been occupied and fortified for decades by the Japanese. Chichi was by far the more important island with an airfield, deep water anchorage, and a seaplane base. It was also a major communications center with sizeable radio and radar facilities. Susaki Airfield on Chichi had been hit repeatedly by Air Force heavy bombers and Navy carrier planes. Although its air defense force had long since been eradicated, Susaki was still used as a staging point for night raiders flying from Japan to Iwo Jima.

Seventeen P-51s of the 47th Squadron each armed with two 500-pound bombs were assigned to the strike. John Piper led his Squadron but both Colonel Beckwith and General Moore accompanied it. Everyone wanted to get in on this first strike!

The carefully planned mission resulted in 22 bomb hits on Susaki, direct hits on small ships in the harbor, and strafing damage inflicted on buildings and a parked transport plane. Though there was considerable antiaircraft fire from both large and small weapons, no one was hit. Air sea rescue forces, a Navy destroyer, and two Catalinas were stationed at appropriate intervals to render aid. The first of many missions to interdict Chichi and Haha Jima took just over 2 hours and was considered a great success. The 47th's official mission report expressed the exhilaration of these men who were finally pasting enemy targets after such extended frustration.

> Excellent mission. Towns on Haha in too good condition to satisfy Invader I (General Moore). Perfect performance of planes, good weather and communications. Briefing good. All pilots agreed was lots of fun.

Colonel Beckwith led the 45th Squadron on a return visit to Chichi and Haha Jima the next day. This time it wasn't quite as much fun. With Chichi Jima largely covered by low hanging clouds, the sixteen P-51s dumped their 500 pounders on Haha. Concentrating on the town of Okimura, they attempted to bomb and strafe the place into a condition that would satisfy Mickey Moore. The Mustangs met with heavy AA at 3,000 feet on their bomb runs and moderate automatic weapons fire on low level strafing runs. First Lieutenant William W. Redus had a two-foot hole blown in his

A Japanese ship bombed and beached on Iwo was used as a spotter post for artillery fire by the enemy as late as 11 March 45. (Source: John Whitcomb)

Concrete reinforced bunkers and strong points resisted the intense bombing and shelling. These underground facilities continued to house Japanese resistors until July 45: Left —(Source: Jim Vande Hey) Right —(Source: Richard MacKenzie)

Unexploded 16 inch battleship rounds dotted the Island. (Source: Walter Kreimann)

This 47th Sq 2½ ton truck was demolished by an enemy land **mine** but S/Sgt. Forrest Chapman and Cpl. Chester Jansen survived. (Source: H. G. Smith)

port wing flap and 1st Lt. Bill Fisher caught a round of machinegun fire in his right wing flap (although he didn't know it until his mechanic discovered the hole.) Dumbo was nearby and reassured Redus on this return to Iwo.

On 13 March it was the 78th Squadron's turn to practice their skills on Chichi. With the Group CO, Jim Beckwith, again leading, sixteen Mustangs bombed and strafed the harbor and airfield. Flak was encountered, but the Squadron came away unscathed.

During the last days of the battle, close support for the Marines on north Iwo Jima had become precision bombing and strafing missions. The Japanese main force had been hemmed into a forest of rocks and canyons known to the Marines as "Death Valley". The enemy, still led by their commander, General Kuribayashi, would not surrender and were fighting tenaciously. Even in this confined space they fought from caves, tunnels, and concrete reinforced defenses. Bombing and strafing in such a narrow pocket from a speeding fighter was no job for amateurs. Most approaches were made from the east over the island so that any long bombs or bullets would splash in the water.

On the 14th of March the Group flew its last close-support strike. Five P-51s were assigned, each hung with two 110 gallon wing tanks carrying a home brew of 60% diesel oil, 40% aviation gasoline, and an instantaneous detonator. They made their target runs as low and slow as possible to ensure accuracy. The fire bombs were dropped on target from an average height of 25 feet. They then followed in trail, making 15 to 20 strafing runs. No return fire was received.

Though it seemed impossible, the Japanese had endured the concentrated and methodical pounding they had been subjected to since 19 February. Many of them merely went to ground, like foxes, and survived underground in hidden caves and tunnels. They generally surfaced at night, and men not bent on mayhem would forage for food and water, then return and hole up again. One plucky Japanese gunner, known as "Pistol Pete", would emerge from his hole at night, lob a mortar shell in the general direction of occupied Iwo and burrow back into his den. One of his shells hit the 78th Squadron's empty command post at 0200 tearing up the office. The same shell shredded the covering tarp on the adjoining foxhole and lacerated several B-4 bags. But its occupants, though unharmed, were humbled.

Night barrages became commonplace and were infectious. Sometimes a random shot by some bypassed Japanese, or a G.I. sentry firing on a Japanese straggler, real or imagined, would set off a chain reaction of shooting. The Americans ventilated each other more often than the enemy in such exchanges. The 15th was fortunate that none of its personnel were ever wounded in these wild shootouts.

The Group's first Purple Heart during Iwo Jima service was won in 'noblesse oblige' fashion, by the Group CO, Colonel Beckwith. After leading a 45th Squadron strike to Haha Jima on 15 March, Beckwith decided to give Kita Rock a close inspection on the return trip. Seeing a landing barge and personnel on the east shore, he strafed his way across the island at 20 feet. Return fire from automatic weapons hit the Colonel's Number 15 in the wings and canopy. One round penetrated the cockpit and knicked him near his lower back and posterior. Undaunted by the wound, Jim Beckwith mounted his P-51 the next day on a Chichi mission.

The 17th of March marked the date of the Group's first fatality. The certainty of death had been present even during training in Hawaii, and it was a foregone conclusion that combat would extract inevitable losses. The first death occured not from Japanese activity but from the weather. While on a routine CAP just north of Iwo Jima, a flight from the 45th Squadron flew briefly through some weather. When the flight emerged, 1st. Lt. Beaver Kinsel had vanished. No one saw the Makin veteran go down, nor did a search find pilot or plane wreckage. This was but the first mysterious demand on life by the elements that periodically stalked the Nanpo Shoto.

On the 18th and 19th of March the Group sent out 52 aircraft in separate sorties assisting in the search for a lost Navy plane. A TBM Avenger had reportedly ditched near Kita. Knowing that the Navy had spared no effort on their behalf in the past, the 15th made a maximum but fruitless effort to locate the downed Navy crew. During this operation Jim Tapp's invention, the five-man droppable life raft, was employed for the first time in combat. Todd Moore flew Josephine carrying the specially rigged wing tank.

Between 17 and 25 March Group Headquarters and the three Squadrons were assigned new areas for their permanent camp. Like groundhogs deciding it was Spring, they came out of their foxholes and began to assemble tents and modest wooden buildings. Clearing and leveling the ground was an unpleasant task as live shells and dead bodies surfaced.

Bomb shelters were also built in the new bivouac though their use was disdained by most. On 24 March there was a discussion of a practice air alert. When the sirens sounded that night the men strolled nonchalantly to the shelters in a rather festive mood. Next morning it was learned that up to eight Japanese intruders had attempted an attack on the island. Night fighters shot down two of the enemy and probably destroyed a third north of Iwo. The drill had been all too authentic. The Japanese were not yet done with Iwo's defenders.

The 15th Group received welcome company on 22 March when the 21st Fighter Group began to arrive with its P-51s. This sister organization was full of 15th vets and old friends from Hawaii. The 21st began to share the duties previously borne by the 15th, flying CAP and missions to the Bonins.

Iwo Jima had seemed to be getting more or less civilized when the war broke out all over again. Although organized resistance had ended a week earlier,

The first elements of the air echelon arrived on 6 March when Brig. Gen. Moore led the 47th Sq up from Saipan. Whitey Betner's plane hit a soft spot in the runway and ground looped. (Source: E. M. Moore)

The 78th Squadron's Command Post: Left — Operational one day. (Source: Jim Vande Hey) Right — Hit by a Japanese mortar round the next. (Source: Jim Vande Hey)

Not the City Dump but the 45th Squadron's living area. (Source: Gilmer Snipes)

Iwo nurtured its own hot water system in sulfur springs. (Source: Gilmer Snipes)

Ground crews and pilots of the 47th Sq watch on Airfield No. 1 as planes of the 45th Sq arrive. 7 March 45. (Source: USAF)

some 300 Japanese surfaced prior to dawn on 26 March. They staged a diabolically clever attack on an encampment containing the 21st Fighter Group, 549th Night Fighter Squadron, and a Signal Battalion. Marines and Seabees rallied to the support of the Seventh Air Force units. After four hours of bitter combat, some of it hand to hand, the enemy force was destroyed. U.S. losses numbered 44 dead and 88 wounded. Included among the 21st Group's casualties were several officers formerly of the 15th, including Group CO, Ken Powell. (See Appendix 11).

Major Sokol, Group Flight Surgeon, Squadron Flight Surgeons Goldman, Lapides, and Lewis and their staffs pitched in to work on five of the wounded.

Though the battle was fought some distance from the 15th Group's camp, and they were never directly involved, the vicious combat had a profound effect on everyone. Security was tightened and weapons were cleaned and kept close at hand. Second Lieutenant John Fitzgerald, of the 47th, took to wearing an old Army campaign hat when he was Officer of the Day. He figured the outline of that old lid would protect him from being shot by another American.

Jim Vande Hey recalls an incident where the OD was meticulously rehearsing the code word with a tent full of pilots scheduled for the dawn CAP. The OD was cautioning them not to get trigger happy when suddenly awakened. Taking exception to the lecture, one pilot commented, "By God, you'd better make sure you know the code and identify yourself, because if you hear a click from my corner, it will be a bolt going back." Captain George Morey, coolly cleaning his .45, added, "If you hear a click over here, it'll be a dud."

The Group took over all air operations on the 26th, allowing the battered 21st to lick its wounds. The 78th Squadron flew two missions to Chichi and the 47th followed with one more. The dive-bombing runs on Chichi and Haha Jima were being done at high speed out of respect for the antiaircraft fire which was becoming particularly intense over Chichi. Bursts had been seen as high as 7,000 feet on prior missions and, with practice, smaller caliber guns were getting more accurate at deck level. Bombing runs were generally being conducted at speeds of 375 to 450 m.p.h. indicated air speed, but some pilots were exceeding 500 m.p.h. fearing flak more than compressibiltiy.

During the early mission of the 26th a six-inch flak hole appeared in 1st Lt. D. B. Moore's right wing and Squadron leader Jim Vande Hey had his wings and tail dented, but both men returned safely. The day's late mission, by the 47th Squadron, was not so lucky. Second Lieutenant John R. Shuler was flying at 450 m.p.h. on Major Piper's wing, strafing Chichi, when his plane took a hit. He started to climb on course for Iwo and reached 4,000 feet altitude. But his oil pressure soon dropped and coolant began gushing from the engine. With his cockpit full of smoke, Shuler rolled the Mustang over and bailed out successfully.

He landed in the ocean about 10 miles off Chichi Jima

Col. Beckwith in No. 15 (far left) leads the 45th and 78th Squadrons across Saipan enroute to Iwo Jima on 7 March. (Source: Jim Beckwith)

as John Piper called for a Dumbo. Shuler seemed to have trouble with his life raft and appeared, to those circling above him, to be struggling in the water. The Catalina appeared in 15 minutes and a Navy destroyer was enroute, but Shuler seemed to be swallowed by the ocean while his mates were orbiting overhead. Eurich L. Bright immediately led another 47th flight out from Iwo to cover the downed pilot but searched without success. The destroyer finally arrived on the scene and found only Lieutenant Shuler's empty life vest, with its straps broken, floating on the surface.

The month ended on a pair of sour notes. A 48-plane training mission was flown from Iwo Jima to Saipan and return. It was to have been a prelude to the equidistant missions the Group would soon fly from Iwo to the Empire. Less than half the formation completed the mission. Several pilots aborted because of an array of mechanical problems and either returned to Iwo early or landed at Saipan.

Colonel Beckwith led the remainder of the Group over Kita Rock, Haha Jima, and Chichi giving the usual abuse, but the Japanese managed to extract a price for the March 31st raid on Susaki. With great cunning and deliberation they set off a land mine as the Mustangs swept over the airfield in low-level runs. With perfect timing they caught 2nd Lt. Lee M. Bargaehar's 78th Squadron P-51 in the explosion. His plane crashed and burned.

The Group had now lost three pilots in action, but considering the early days on Iwo and the amount of random fire thrown in the 15th's direction, they were fortunate not to have suffered heavier casualties. Staff Sergeant Forrest Chapman and Cpl. Chester E. Jansen had suffered the only other bruises when they drove their 47th Squadron 2½ ton truck over a Japanese yardstick mine. The GMC truck was added to the surrounding junk heap, and, though Chapman and Jansen reportedly aged several years, they continued to serve.

Mustangs of the 78th Sq are loaded with 500 pounders for close support of the Marines. Bombs were lifted into the racks by GI muscle. (Source: Jim Vande Hey)

It is hard to say enough for the mechanics who had to fine tune and maintain these planes under the most primitive conditions. Corrosion, always a problem in the ocean islands, seemed to be accentuated by the dust and sulphur. The volcanic grit was, however, an enigma unique to Iwo Jima. There was no way to protect equipment from ingesting this powdery silica. "It was coarse and abrasive," recalled 1st Lt. Ned Baldwin. "It played hell with the maintenance crews. They were really dedicated." Except for rainy days there was a constant cloud of dust hanging over the island stirred up by winds or churning propellers. Engineering officers and enlisted men labored day and night to surmount these two problems and keep the Mustangs in flying condition.

For most of the month the armorers had also performed above and beyond the call. There were no mechanical devices for hanging bombs on the P-51s. Each 500 pounder had to be hoisted into the racks by raw GI muscle.

The proximity of the Marine cemeteries, which were expanding at a gruesome rate, were sobering influences on Jim Beckwith and his command. The high cost of this miserable piece of real estate had far exceeded any strategic estimate. By the time the island was secured, the toll was over 6,800 dead and nearly 20,000 wounded Marine and Navy personnel. The 15th had developed quite an affinity for the Marines who had taken Iwo, and they had a powerful craving to utilize their skills in balancing that casualty ledger.

The Group had earned another battle star on their Pacific Theatre campaign ribbon. They had put in as tough a month on Iwo as any Army Air Force unit had yet experienced. As a result of combat conditions, the boy-scout existence, alternating dust and rain induced mud, cold sleepless nights, bad food, and limited water, the men had been sorely tested. Colonel Beckwith was proud of their ability and willingness to adapt and adjust to the rugged environment. They knew that this was the final campaign, the job they had sought, and for which they had trained. The 47th Squadron's history captured the feeling: "Few complaints were to be heard, for the planes were now serving their purpose and not being wasted on Pineapple Schedules."

April 1945 began with heavy rains that lasted for four days. The Group's foxholes, so lovingly and elaborately fashioned, were turned into catch basins. As the deluge ended, living conditions were about at the ebb. Fortuitously, some uncommon act of advance planning had inagurated the construction of new facilities. The Group began to vacate their miserable makeshift warrens for the luxury of four- and six-man tents, with wooden floors and cots. Mess halls began to function and sulphur water showers were improvised. Though it wouldn't wash the soap from your hair, the hot sulphur water was a blessing. Everyone was pretty ripe after weeks of bird baths from helmets.

Group pilots were being selected by lot for rotation to Oahu for threes weeks rest and recuperation. After 58 missions in 25 days on Iwo, someone finally realized that R-and-R was necessary. The flyers accepted the leave orders, but without much enthusiasm. "We were primed for action." said Leon Sher, "and after a few days in Honolulu, I was bored to death." The 47th Squadron pilot was driven to such lengths that he bought a knitting book along with yarn and needles at Woolworth's and began to fashion dog tag holders for the men who had everything. Sher, "made twelve knitted dog tag holders and gave them out as presents when he got back to Iwo."

Leon and his companions were reflecting their frustration at the possibility of missing the historic event which they knew was about to happen while they were on leave. Japan had been the 15th Group's designated target since they were earmarked for Iwo Jima. The Empire had been their quest since 7 December 1941.

Chapter VI

IWO ESCORT
April 1945 to June 1945

When the pilots were informed of the first Very Long Range (VLR) mission, the briefing was attended by much PR fanfare. Senior commanders and people from all over Iwo crowded the hall along with war correspondents and reporters from *Yank* and *Brief*. Flash bulbs and kleig lights, seldom seen in the Central Pacific, gave the appearance of a Hollywood opening.

It was much more than that. Everyone sensed the aura of history surrounding this mission. U.S. Army Air Force single-engined fighters were preparing to fly 1600 miles round trip to strike at the heart of Japan.

Both the 15th and 21st were slated to put up a force of P-51s to escort 100 plus Superforts of the 73rd Bomb Wing to Tokyo. The target of the B-29s was the Nakajima aircraft plant.

> And gentlemen in England now a-bed
> Shall think themselves accursed they
> were not here,
> And hold their manhoods cheap whiles
> any speaks
> That fought with us upon Saint Crispin's Day."
> *Henry V*, Act IV, Sc. 3

For the men of the 15th Fighter Group it was St. Crispin's Day. For those who had been at Wheeler Field on 7 December 1941 it was also the hour of retribution. It was 7 April 1945.

Only the most experienced pilots were chosen; men with 800 to 1,000 hours. Makin veterans were dominant among the flight and element leaders.

The pilots were up long before dawn. Chaplain Jamison conducted a prayer service and Father Tom Norton administered communion to the Catholic pilots. The sky was still gray when the pilots climbed into their cockpits. Tension was nearly a tangible thing. At 0645 over fifty Merlin engines roared to life on Airfield No. 1.

Ground personnel of the Group, though they could never experience the pilots' emotions, had their own range of feelings. Sandy Sanders felt the sort of "thrill" that "The Star Spangled Banner" evokes. "I wished I could go along and got a cold shiver down my spine as they began taking off."

Colonel Beckwith was off first at 0655 and began to circle near Kita Rock. The Group followed, taking off in pairs at close intervals, and assembled in formation. There were no take-off accidents despite the heavy combat load of fuel and ammunition. In addition to the normal load each plane carried two 110 gallon drop tanks. General Moore had joined the mission and even a unit of spare P-51s were sent out to fill in for planes that might abort. Everyone wanted to be in on this show.

As usual, the mechanical gremlins appeared and began to take their toll. Colonel Beckwith found that his oxygen was not feeding properly and, bitterly, he

Col. Beckwith was constantly in the cockpit during the first weeks on Iwo Jima. (Source: USAF)

P-51s of the 45th Sq taxi out for a close support strike. (Source: USAF via North American)

Final missions against the Japanese forces on Iwo were flown low over the rocky crags of the North coast. It was precision work. (Source: Earl Steggeman)

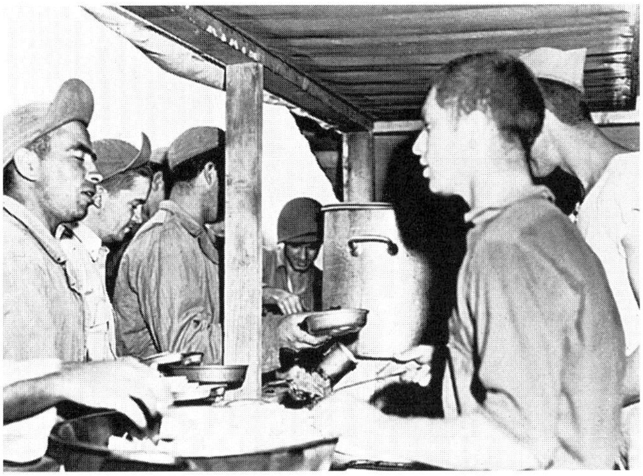

Even hot food was poor to lousy in the early days. The expressions say a lot. 78th Sq. (Source: Jim Vande Hey)

Lt. Ted Saed (standing), 78th Sq Engineering Officer, looks in on the enlisted mess. (Source: Jim Vande Hey)

(Left to right) 47th Sq Lts. Ollie O'Mara and Charlie Jennings (KIA) consider their first meal on Iwo Jima — K-Rations á la carte. (Source: USAF)

47th Sq non-coms, (left to right) Brokop, Cieala, Katsanos, Conway, Pfleiderer and Murray picnic on C-Rations. (Source: R. Edsel Wilcox)

turned back. General Moore found he had a stuck gas switch. Like Beckwith, he swung his P-51 toward Iwo. Several others developed rough engines some 200 miles out and prudently returned.

With fifty P-51s arrayed around him, Major John Piper of the 47th Squadron took over the Group lead. Gil Snipes led his 45th and Jim Vande Hey the 78th. Following three B-29 navigators, they rendezvoused with the strike force at 18,000 feet over Kozu Shima, less than 100 miles from Tokyo. Art Bridge recalls:

> It was a real spectacle. The 29s were just finishing their assembly in a grand circle as we arrived. I could see the lead B-29s were at 12,000 with the rest staggered back all the way up to 18,000. My flight was covering the point and we began to scissor to maintain our airspeed and not get ahead of the bomber stream.

Far behind the main force a lone P-51 piloted by 2nd Lt. Charles C. Heil, doggedly pursued the mission. A reserve pilot from the 78th, Charlie had been ordered north to fill in for one of the aborts. After some 600 miles of solo navigation he was pleased to spot a formation of Superforts and gladly became their lone escort. Puzzled at the absence of his unit, Heil nonetheless took up a protective stance over the B-29s and began to scissor back and forth. He had become the solitary escort for the wrong strike force. The 313th and 314th Bomb Wings were assigned to bomb Nagoya, not Tokyo.

Jim Vande Hey was exhilarated as they spotted Honshu. "The weather was clear. We saw the coast, and old Mount Fujiyama standing out just like it did in the pictures. It was an unmistakeable landmark."

About 1045 the strike force crossed the coast of Japan and enemy fighters began to materialize. The Mustangs, which had flown the inbound leg on their external fuel, dropped their wing tanks and prepared for battle. The bombers were now calling out bogeys from head-on at all altitudes.

Major Snipes released his wing tanks and his engine windmilled to a stop. The gremlins were at work again. His fuel flow had stopped. For two minutes Buck's P-51 fell from 18,000 feet while he frantically sought to restart the engine. At 10,000 feet the Merlin coughed back to life. Snipes and his wingman, 1st Lt. Fred Henderson, climbed back toward the bombers.

Todd Moore spotted the first Japanese pursuit plane down low — a decoy. Major Piper's flight was tantalized by a single low-flying Nick over Sagami Wan (outer Tokyo Bay), then by four single-engined Tojos that came at them head-on, breaking down and away while still out of range. Recognizing the feints and lures, Squadron leaders restrained their eager warriors. "Stay in formation." Within minutes the Japanese fighters began making aggressive passes. Action broke out all along the perimeter of the bomber stream.

Captain Bob Down and 1st Lt. Dick Hintermeier of the 47th finally drew blood with the next Nick. Hintermeier said, "I made a high frontal quartering pass that hit the right engine and set it smoking. Down's bursts struck the canopy and right engine, and the plane burst into flames."

Down, Hintermeier, and 1st Lt. Eurich L. Bright then made 180 degree overhead to stern passes at single-engined Japanese interceptors plummeting through the bombers. Bob Down and Dick Hintermeier each flamed a Tojo while Bright performed the same job on a Tony. A Zeke passed in front of Bright and he poured fire into it. The enemy pulled up, then fell away burning. A twin-engined Japanese aircraft loomed into Bright's sights and he shot it down in flames.

Another Nick, diving from above, attempted to reach the B-29s but Major Jim Tapp and 1st Lt. Phil Maher gave chase. Both pilots closed on the Japanese plane scoring numerous hits and sending it plunging out of the fight. Returning to the main formation, Tapp encountered a single-engined Tony at 20,000 feet. He closed on the enemy plane firing continuously from 800 feet down to 10-foot range. The Tony burned as the pilot jumped.

Tapp then observed a twin-engined Dinah boring head-on into the bomber formation. Jim blacked out momentarily trying to turn into the enemy but avoided pursuit for fear of colliding with the B-29s. This may have been the same Dinah that Major Vande Hey encountered at 18,000 foot altitude. The Japanese pilot, now in a shallow diving turn, was acting like a cat who had just wandered into a room full of dogs. Vande Hey, who was able to turn with him, escorted the Dinah from the formation.

"I think the poor guy was on a local flight and just stumbled into us."

Though he drew fire from the tail gunner, Jim's bursts tore off the left engine cowling and started a fire. The Dinah was last seen smoking in a tight diving spiral. It was out of control.

Over in the 47th's territory yet another stranger wandered into the fray. A single-engined Nakajima "Myrt", a carrier-based recon aircraft, was spotted flying at 15,000 feet to the side of and ahead of the bomber stream. Captain Theon B. Markham led his flight after the Navy plane but it turned into the P-51s. Only Spider Condrick was able to get in a clean shot. His two bursts hit the wing root and the plane plunged to the ground.

Reforming his flight, Ed Markham saw many vapor trails above and ahead of the bombers. Eight twin-engined Nicks began making uncoordinated diving head-on passes on the Superforts. Markham bore in on the nearest and it disintegrated under his long accurate burst.

The 45th was on the right flank of the bomber force not encountering much action. Buck Snipes said:

> The Japanese were making head-on passes. I didn't see any attacks on the bombers from our

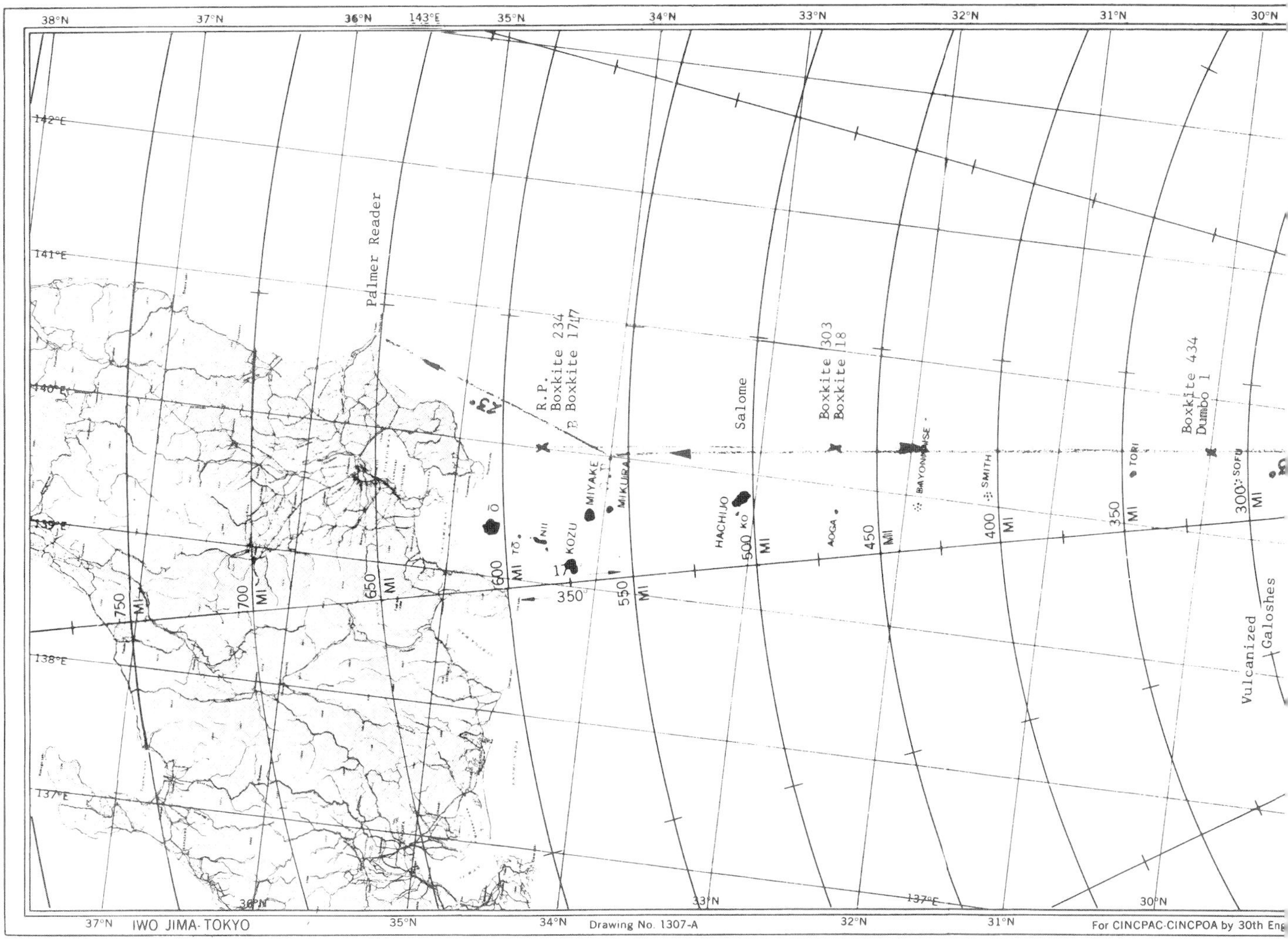

IWO JIMA-TOKYO
Drawing No. 1307-A
For CINCPAC-CINCPOA by 30th Eng
38°N
37°N
36°N
35°N
34°N
33°N
32°N
31°N
30°N
143°E
142°E
141°E
140°E
139°E
138°E
137°E
Palmer Reader
R.P.
Boxkite 234
B Boxkite 1747
Salome
Boxkite 303
Boxkite 18
Boxkite 434
Dumbo 1
Vulcanized
Galoshes
Ō
TO
NII
KOZU
MIYAKE
MIKURA
HACHIJO
AOGA
BAYONNAISE
SMITH
TORI
SOFU
750 MI
700 MI
650 MI
600 MI
550 MI
500 MI
450 MI
400 MI
350 MI
300 MI
350

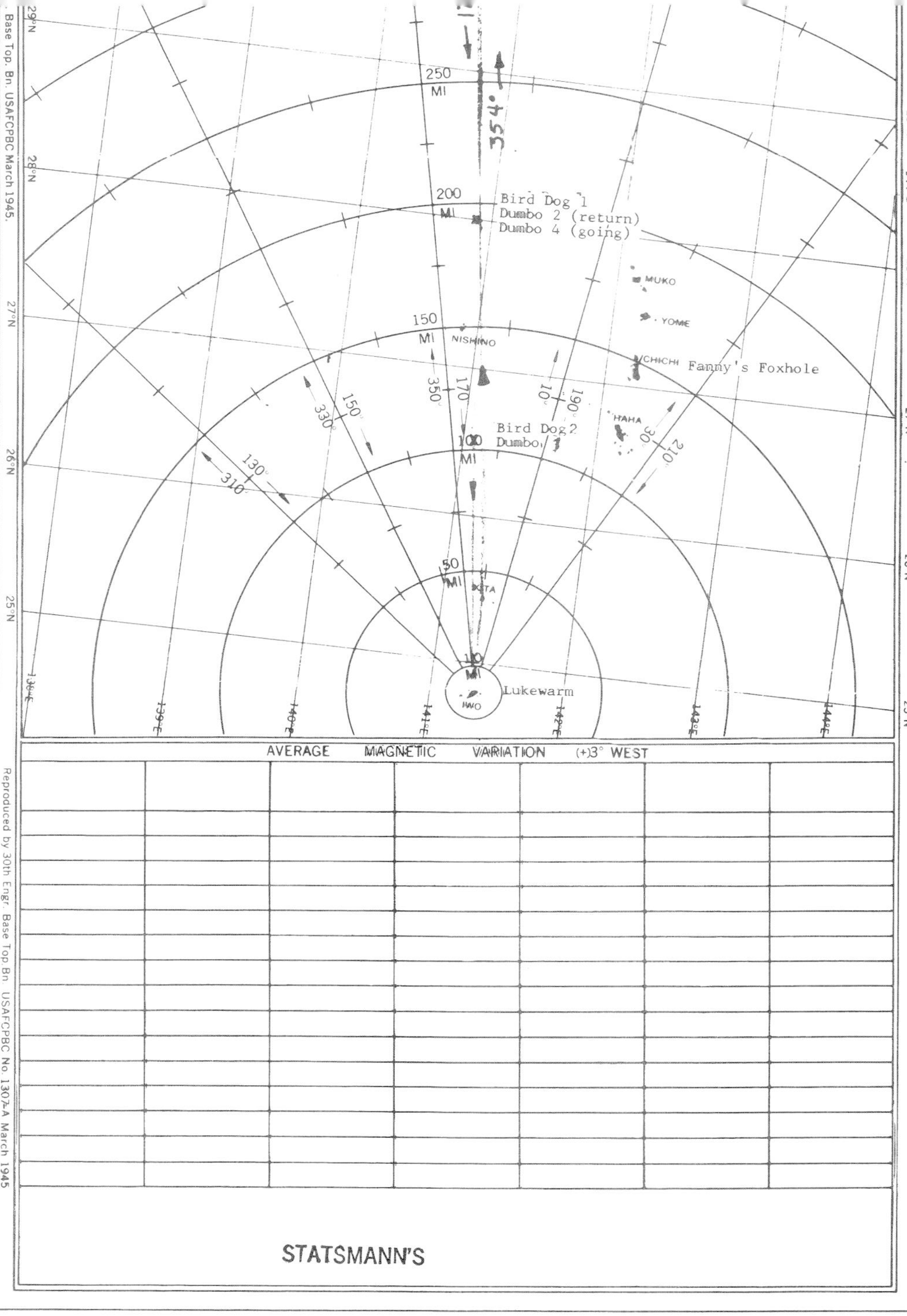

. Base Top. Bn. USAFCPBC March 1945.

AVERAGE MAGNETIC VARIATION (+)3° WEST

STATSMANN'S

Reproduced by 30th Engr. Base Top Bn. USAFCPBC No. 1307-A March 1945

side. Two enemy fighters diving through the lead planes came directly over Henderson and me. We pulled up but couldn't get any lead, and the Japs were past before we could even shoot. I pulled off just before stalling and vowed at the time never to get myself in that predicament again.

Finally, two Nakajima "Tojo" fighters came abreast of the 45th. Snipes and Henderson each selected one.

I hit mine and he smoked but I overran him and lost contact. The one that Henderson shot at made a sharp 90 degree turn in front of me. It was already damaged. I fired at him and the Tojo began to smoke, one wheel dropped down, and the pilot jettisoned his canopy. The canopy barely missed me as the pilot jumped. I was turning toward him as his parachute opened. I'm sure he thought I was going to shoot him, but I couldn't do that.

Captain Al Maltby and 1st Lt. Wesley E. Brown, the other half of Snipes' flight, also had problems with enemy planes making head-on passes. Al stalled out but got a good burst into a Tony that dove straight for the ground and out of sight. Wes Brown took after a twin-engined plane that had just dropped a phosphorous bomb over a group of B-29s. Brown's fire brought flames from the enemy plane and it fell away from the battle in a spiral.

Several other pilots flicked off shots at enemy planes as they swept through the huge formation in frontal assaults. The Mustangs tried to roll in behind the Japanese running the gauntlet of the B-29 gunners. First Lieutenant Quentin G. McCorkle flew into the "dead" zone near the bombers and felt his plane being hit. A B-29 gunner had nearly severed his rudder cable.

Near the front of the formation Captain Todd Moore was leading a flight of the 78th. The diving head-on tactics of the Japanese defenders was causing most of the combat to occur well behind them. Not until reaching the mainland in the Choshi Point area did the Japanese make the mistake of giving Moore an opportunity. From 22,000 feet he spotted several planes below approaching the bombers. Bob Roseberry, Moore's wingman, relates the action:

As we dove, I remember thinking that I had to stick to Captain Moore's wing no matter what happened. He was a veteran and this was my first air action.

We saw four Hamps doing lazy eights in a loose string over the B-29s. Moore closed on the tail of the string and exploded the fourth plane with a short 20 degree deflection shot. At full throttle we closed on the number 3 man and Moore began firing. I was stacked in so close to the Captain that his ejected shell casings were hitting my plane. I flew within 60 feet of the third Hamp. Its bottom was blown out and the plane was burning and falling rapidly out of control.

I fired a short burst at the number 2 Hamp with absolutely no results. Frankly, I was more concerned with sticking to Moore and not getting lost than in getting a Hamp. The two remaining Japanese pulled up and started to roll over and come down on us. I advised Captain Moore, and our entire flight easily dove away and rejoined the B-29s.

Bob Moore, who had destroyed two enemy planes in about 45 seconds, said, "We left the other two Hamps like they were standing still."

Jim Tapp, still in the thick of the battle was now defending a burning B-29 over Tokyo. He peppered another single-engined two-seat aircraft watching it fall out of the fight. Then he turned his attention to a six-plane flight of enemy fighters and sent a Tojo spinning crazily out of control, minus a six-foot wing section.

By 1130 the fury of the battle subsided. The B-29s had sent their cargo of bombs tumbling onto Tokyo and were approaching the Rally Point. Both sides called it quits after some 300 planes had engaged in one of the great air battles of the Pacific War.

The adrenalin was still flowing among the 15th pilots as they alternately savored their victories and sweated their gas supply. They still had nearly three hours of flying ahead of them. Jim Vande Hey became aware that he had been sweating profusely and was hungry. "We all dressed like we were going to the North Pole, and I didn't even take along a candy bar."

Back at Iwo Jima, those who had to stay behind were sweating too, agonizing as friends do when they are powerless to intervene or participate. One P-51 was in certain trouble. First Lieutenant Frank L. Ayers was hustling back with a B-29 code named "Cyclone Charlie." Frank, flying top cover with the 47th Squadron had been one of the last planes to leave the Rally Point. He knew that his Mustang was drinking gasoline faster than it should. An hour out of Tokyo he ran into an overcast and flew on instruments for an hour. As his fuel warning light began to blink, Ayers called the Navy destroyer supposedly stationed 200 miles north of Iwo. He got a prompt and reassuring response but couldn't see the ship because of the overcast. With the last of his gas he eased down through the soup and broke out only 100 feet above the water. There, like a biblical miracle, was the destroyer. Ayers climbed back up into the overcast to gain jumping room and parachuted from his plane. The Navy had him on board within minutes and signaled Agate Base that the lost chick was safe.

Between 1415 and 1430 all of the Group's remaining planes landed. After 7 hours and 35 minutes of grinding overwater flight and nearly 50 minutes of mortal combat with 110 Japanese airplanes, every soul was accounted for. Some had landed with only five to eight gallons of gasoline.

Even Charles Heil had come home from his historic solo flight to Nagoya. He was pretty steamed at first.

A packing crate board on an oil drum gave the Group "brass" an exclusive mess. (Left to right) Lt. Col. Ben Kearney, Deputy CO, and Capt. Hogan Birk, Ops Officer. (Source: Rich Birk)

(Left to right) Lts. John Fitzgerald and Dave Balak of the 47th Sq. John wore the old campaign hat when he was OD so he would not be mistaken for a Japanese. (Source: John Fitzgerald)

(Left to right, foreground) Doc Lewis and Jerry Yellin of the 78th Sq try to forget the evening meal over coffee. (Source: Jim Vande Hey)

This steel pot was one of the most versitile implements of World War II — a wash basin or a helmet. (Source: Jim Vande Hey)

Mess Sgt Young (left) guarding his 78th Sq supplies. (Source: Jim Vande Hey)

Saturday night at the sulfur baths on Blue Beach. (Source: Jim Vande Hey)

"Where were you all?" he kept demanding of the other pilots. "B-29s all over the sky and not one damned 51." His anxiety level was understandable. Over Nagoya his engine had begun to run rough, but he postured bravely against Japanese interceptors and played out the hand. The Superforts, both amused and fascinated by their first and only fighter escort, radioed, "Don't worry, we'll take care of you."

Though three B-29s had been lost over Tokyo, two were definitely brought down as a result of heavy antiaircraft fire. The third might have been lost to enemy fighter action.

B-29 gunners claimed an incredible 80-23-50 (destroyed-probably destroyed-damaged) for the day. Such claims were always suspect in all theatres of combat because of duplicate sightings and simultaneous defensive fire. Eight gunners, all shooting at the same attacker, might each claim individual credit for destruction or at least damage of the enemy craft. Such expansive tallies are even more suspect when P-51s were hit by B-29 fire. It is presumed that they resembled Tonys through the sights of squinting Superfort gunners.

Considering the sheer size of the Japanese attack force, and previous loss ratios suffered by unescorted B-29s, it is certain that the Mustangs provided a much greater level of protection. A B-29 gunner perhaps gave the best testimonial: "The Mustangs were knocking down Japs all over the sky. For a while there during the fight there were enemy parachutes all around us. I'll never forget it."

Neither would the men of the 15th. The weather reports were accurate. The rendezvous was perfect. Their air discipline and fuel management were magnificent. The Group had claimed 17 Japanese planes destroyed, three probably destroyed, and five damaged. They were tired and ached in strange places, but not one complaint was heard. Major Buck Snipes summarized everyone's feelings when he said, "I wouldn't have missed it for all the gold at Fort Knox."

Participants in the first strike on Chichi Jima on 11 March 45 were these 47th Sq members led by Col. Beckwith. (Left to right) Front row: Charlie Jennings (KIA), Ed Markham, Eurich Bright, Beckwith, John Piper, Bob Down, Joe Brunette; back row: Ollie O'Mara, Walter Powell (KIA), Charlie Cameron, Ray Obenshain, Larry Pepin, Jule Mitchell (KIA), Frank Ayers, Fred Grover, Hank Ryniker. (Source: Jim Beckwith)

Chichi Jima Island and Futami Harbor. Both photos taken after VJ-Day. (Source: Earl Steggeman)

In recognition of their pioneer flight and outstanding performance the Group was awarded the Distinguished Unit Citation. (See Appendix 13)

For several days the Group rested, remembered the action of 7 April, and basked in the warm glow of their accomplishment. It was not merely the certain destruction of 17 enemy planes which gave satisfaction; it was also the culmination of so many bygone goals in a near letter-perfect mission. The next mission would not be so unblemished.

The second VLR mission was launched on 12 April 1945. Again the 15th Group was to escort B-29s to Tokyo. After the aborts were replaced by reserve aircraft, 49 Mustangs mustered with Deputy Commander, Major Emmet Kearney, leading.

The trip north was uneventful but the rendezvous did not come off with precision. The P-51s orbited the rendezvous point for 20 minutes consuming precious gasoline before the B-29s arrived. The Squadrons, stacked from 15,000 to 20,000 feet over the bombers, began the run on the target about 1150. Within ten minutes, while the formation was just over the coast of Honshu, the first Japanese planes were spotted.

Single twin-engined enemy planes appeared invitingly on the perimeter of the strike force. If ignored, they attacked the bombers; if pursued, they broke off, trying to lure away the Mustangs. The escorts were damned if they did and damned if they didn't.

Major Kearney, with Lieutenants Harry M. Tyler and Alex Trodahl, peeled off after a Nick flying through the bombers. Kearney fired a long burst and saw the enemy craft dive away smoking.

In the 45th Squadron's zone, Captain Art Bridge observed a Nick preparing to attack the B-29s. As Art and his wingman, 1st Lt. Walter H. Harrigan, turned toward the Nick, three single-engined Japanese fighters began to position themselves ahead of and above the lead bombers. Bridge's flight turned back toward this new menace as the three enemy aircraft dove on the B-29s. Bridge fired at the lead plane as all three unleashed wing rockets at the bombers. Art scored hits on the enemy craft but was forced to turn his attention to more Japanese fighters plunging through the heart of the B-29 formations. His maneuver sent him into the torrent of B-29 defensive fire.

> When we made a pass on four Tojos, we were quite close to the B-29s. A round of .50 caliber Armor Piercing Incendiary (API) came through my cockpit, missed me, and landed in the wing, blowing up in my wings. I was telling this story a few months later back in Hawaii and a B-29 jockey admitted he had seen the whole thing and claimed me for a Tony.

Zooming out of range of the massed guns of the Superforts, Bridge made an orbit to get his bearings and check his condition, then, with Harrigan, scissored above the bombers searching for his unit. Approaching ten nearby P-51s, he was brought up short by Jim Vande Hey's familiar voice on his radio, "If friendly, waggle wings." Bridge and Harrigan waggled instantly and furiously.

The mission leader, "Pilot Ben" Kearney, had engaged another Nick and, with Tyler's help, shot it down. Again a Japanese Zeke was hovering nearby, and used the Nick's dilemma to attack the bombers. Kearney turned back to his position in time and fired a long burst, flaming the Zero.

Captain George Hunter and 2nd Lt. Gerhard "Goldie" Rettberg, the other half of Bridge's flight, had battled the rocket firing Tojos, hitting two. They were unable to follow the diving Japanese but their actions had separated them from the rest of the 45th. They, too, were scissoring above the bombers, trying to rejoin their unit. Spotting what appeared to be a stray P-51, Hunter closed on him, and realized he was about to join up with a Japanese Tony. Though the discovery was now mutual, Hunter was able to fire first and send the Tony down, flaming from the wing roots.

In tight elements, the 47th Squadron had beaten off several attacks. Major John Piper and 2nd Lt. Robert Worton had downed one Nick. First Lieutenant David Stelling and 1st Lt. Joseph A. McCormick had gone after a speedy Mitsubishi Raiden or "Jack". Stelling's plane was suffering from an oil leak which had put a sheen on his windshield. Nonetheless, he pressed his attack and saw hits from both P-51s enter the enemy fighter before it dove away. Charlie Cameron finished the 47th's work for the day by flaming another Nick, sending it into a vertical dive.

Flying the right flank of the bomber stream, the 78th Squadron encountered less action. Major Vande Hey was credited with one enemy aircraft destroyed as was Major Jim Tapp. (His fifth aerial victory in two missions.) First Lieutenant Richard D. Duerr leading 2nd Lt. Gordon A. Christoe had chased off a Zeke, and then spotted a lone Tojo. Duerr scored hits on the enemy plane as he swung across the bomber formation. Looking back, Duerr could not find Christoe. A B-29 gunner, who saw the action over the bombers, observed one of the P-51s turn and head southeast, smoking, in a gentle glide. Jim Vande Hey heard Christoe calling briefly on the radio but could neither contact nor observe him. Christoe was never seen again. It seems most probable that he flew into the B-29's defensive fire.

On the departure route, just west of Yokahama, Captain Skinny Ennis looked back at the results of the 94-plane raid. The Nakajima factory had been the primary target, but in Ennis' view, it was a "square column of smoke" over a section of Tokyo. The enemy seemed to have disengaged as the bombers departed so Ennis was surprised to see a pair of Nicks flying 2000 feet above and parallel to the bomber stream. With 2nd Lt. Alvan E. Roberts on his wing, he started after one while George "Bruiser" Dunlap and 2nd Lt. Dean E. Deckerty went after the second.

> We approached the Nick and closed much too fast. Both shooting at it, we went right over the enemy plane. The target flipped over and dove for a long way in a slow spiral and pulled out, still heading in our direction.
>
> Scrambling to get back on his tail, we dove at full throttle to catch up. My plane began to buffet — something I had never experienced. It was damn scary. I held the sitck with both hands and my knees, and the vibration stopped as I leveled off at low altitude.

At 550 m.p.h. indicated air speed, Ennis and Roberts had been on the razor's edge of compressibility.

> As we pulled out, the target was just approaching my gun sight. We had hit it many times and both shot again. It shuddered under our combined fire, waffled away and just fell from the sky.

Easter Sunday, 1 April 1945. Chaplain Jamison conducts services. (Source: USAF)

7 April 1945

Preparing for the first VLR mission to Tokyo. A wide range of emotions are expressed in the faces of these 78th Sq pilots:

Jim Vande Hey (far left) gives the pre-dawn briefing. (Source: Robert W. Moore)

Todd Moore and "Stinger" are ready. (Source: Robert W. Moore)

"Tapper" is cocked and primed. (Source: Jim Vande Hey)

S/Sgt. Matt Emberson assists Maj. Van. (Source: Jim Vande Hey)

Back from the Empire: Buck Snipes (in the cockpit) and Mort Knox (KIA), 45th Sq, congratulate each other on downing enemy interceptors. (Source: Gilmer Snipes)

Back from the Empire: An exhausted Jim Vande Hey sheds the tools of his trade. (Source: Jim Vande Hey)

7 April 45, back from the Empire: Skinny Ennis, 45th Sq, pooped but delighted. (Source: Rich Birk)

> Roberts and I ended up cruising along the edge of a long bay at not much more than 100 feet. For several miles I was like a tourist, looking at the most beautiful houses and gardens I had ever seen.

The aerial battle was over, but the struggle to get home was just beginning. Mustangs and B-29s headed for the rally point in ragged formations. Not a single B-29 had been lost, but Christoe had vanished. Several other P-51 pilots were in trouble with battle damage, rough engines, or low gas supply.

Some of the 15th's planes had been over the target area on internal fuel for more than an hour. At combat speeds, the Merlin engine swallowed gas at a frightening pace. Many pilots were calling navigator B-29s for direct vectors to Iwo. Others were seeking the location of air sea rescue units on the route. A lot of folks were in trouble this time.

Whitey Betner had left early to find a "Lifeguard" submarine. He had been plagued with blower problems since reaching the rendezvous off Honshu. His 47th Squadron P-51 was now experiencing severe engine vibration. He joined a B-29 on course for Iwo and gave up on the sub. His plane vibrated so violently for 15 minutes that he was unable to read his instrument panel. The shaking subsided, then recurred again periodically. Three hundred and fifty miles from base the B-29, anxious to take the most direct route to Tinian, told Betner that a Dumbo and a destroyer could be found on a heading of 70 degrees about 30 miles down the road. With little enthusiasn, but no alternative, Betner headed his plane for a spot in the middle of no place. His 51 had no homing device.

At the assigned location he eased his wheezing Mustang down to 1000 feet. Visibility was five miles. There was neither Dumbo nor a destroyer to be seen. Betner took a dead reckoning bearing of 170 degrees and plodded on alone.

He finally made radio contact with another Dumbo and a P-61 night fighter. The "Black Widow", sent out to screen the returning aircraft for enemy planes verified Betner's position and heading with its radar. On course, and now approaching Agate Base, the game Captain Betner decided to sweat it out with his recalcitrant beast. He landed with 40 gallons of fuel remaining. As the official unit history so aptly put it: "He managed to return to Iwo Jima by his own initiative and the grace of God."

As the 78th Squadron left the coast of Japan, Jim Tapp noticed a small stream of coolant leaking from his wingman's P-51. The pilot, 2nd Lt. Fred W. White, carried on resolutely toward a Lifeguard sub and a Dumbo stationed some 375 miles north of Iwo Jima. At the appointed location White's engine was smoking badly. He prepared to bail out as the rest of the flight scanned the water and sky for signs of the rescue units. Tapp, calling frantically on the busy radio channels for Dumbo, watched White drop from his stricken plane at 3,000 feet. His parachute never opened. The flight orbited the area of the splash for a few minutes — then, helpless to do any more, they set course for Iwo.

About 290 miles from home, 2nd Lt. Maurice F. Gourley advised his flight leader, Captain Ray L. Obenshain, that he was losing oil pressure. "Obie" led his 47th Squadron flight directly to a destroyer on station 190 miles from Iwo and called in a Dumbo.

As the rest of the flight watched, Gourley jumped at 2,500 feet in what appeared to be a normal bailout. Though he landed close by the destroyer, and the Navy was at his splash point within seconds, the young Lieutenant vanished in the water.

Dean Deckert had an engine that cut out periodically. Each time he assumed he would be taking a swim, but his maverick Mustang kept restarting and eventually got him home.

Major Vande Hey knew it was going to be nip and tuck getting back. The squadron had dropped wing tanks soon after the strike force had formed. He had been over Japan for an hour by the time he reached the Rally Point.

> When we started back I called a B-29 and told him I was low on fuel. I asked him to take me home by the shortest possible route. He said, 'Get on my wings, little brother.'
>
> We went through some weather without difficulty, and about 100 milcs from Iwo he started leading me down through an overcast. He asked

7 April 1945

Back from the Empire: Harold Collins, 78th Sq, tries to unfold himself after 8 hours in the cockpit. (Source: Jim Vande Hey)

Back from the Empire: Sitting on the wing Van tells the ground crews of the big air battle. (Source: Jim Vande Hey)

The 47th Squadron's victors: (Left to right) Dick Hintermeier, Ed Markham, Eurich Bright, Bob Down, Spider Condrick. Bright got three. (Source: Don Broesamle)

Back from the Empire: The Japanese didn't lay a glove on Quentin McCorkle but a B-29 gunner holed his 45th Sq P-51. (Source: USAF).

Back from the Empire: Lt. Charlie Heil, 78th, conducted a lone escort to Osaka. (Source: Jim Vande Hey)

Back from the Empire: After mission interrogation and reliving the great event. (Source: Jim Vande Hey)

me how I was doing, and just then my fuel warning light went on. I said, 'I don't think I'm going to make it.'

The B-29 alerted rescue, Dumbo came out on our heading, and I started saying the rosary. We broke out at 4,000 feet. Iwo was right there ahead of me. I'm a poor swimmer and I was ready to dead stick it from 4,000 feet. I made a straight in approach, dropped my gear, and when I three pointed it, the engine conked out. I didn't even have enough gas to taxi.

General Moore drove up and said, 'How did it go, Van? Were you hit?'

'No sir. Just out of gas and happy to be sitting here on the runway.'

After 40 months in the Central Pacific and 1500 hours of flying Jim Vande Hey had just barely completed the mission. He had gambled his life for the last time; orders were being cut reassigning him to the States.

Purple Flight, from the 47th, had been assigned to fly subcover off the coast of Honshu and were the last to land. They pancaked at 1402. Everyone had flown for at least seven hours, some for nearly eight.

There was no celebration after this mission. The B-29s had been protected admirably, Tapp had become the Seventh's first ace, and the tally was favorable — 11-5-2 for the loss of three planes and three pilots. However, tallies couldn't measure the loss of friends, and the near disasters were cause for concern.

The post mortems were extensive and strident:

Why was the rendezvous twenty minutes late?

Why was the bomber stream so extended? The fighters were over Honshu on internal fuel for too long.

There was too much chatter over the emergency channels. And the homing channel, the DU, had been jammed by pilots who left their transmission switch in the "on" position.

Why weren't the air sea rescue vessels and planes stationed on the direct strike route and the return route?

The B-29s were too slow on the return trip for the most efficient gas consumption of the P-51s.

Why did a B-29, with plenty of gas and navigational gear, abandon Betner?

The 15th Group had cause for distress, but they knew they weren't practicing a science. They were perfecting an art.

Several of the Group's old guard had reached the magic number and were slated for reassignment to the States. It was a complex mathematical formula that culminated in rotation, but for the pilots, the accounting was time and missions minus death. The bottom line was survival.

Colonel Beckwith, Group Commander; Major Kearney, Deputy Commander; Major Snipes, 45th Squadron CO; and Major Vande Hey, 78th Squadron CO had all survived.

As these four veteran officers passed through Hawaii on their return to the U.S., they ran into an old buddy, Lt. Colonel Jack Thomas. The 45th Squadron's old CO had talked himself back into the Seventh Fighter Command. He was going through Oahu enroute to Iwo Jima.

Thomas was bringing 1st Lt. Hayden Sparks, a 47th Squadron vet, with him. Sparks had returned to the States for gunnery training late in 1944 and had been earmarked for shipment to Europe when Thomas, with his strong sense of kinship, "waylaid" him.

Jack Thomas reveled in tales of the VLR missions being flown against the Empire. He relished the prospect of renewed combat and tried to talk Vande Hey into returning.

"He was such a dynamic guy," said Jim, "and so enthusiastic, that he damn near talked me into going back. But after that last VLR mission I figured I'd run out my string of luck." Vande Hey had judged the measure by which one could tempt fate and knew there was an outer limit. Jack Thomas would never draw that fine distinction.

As some of the old leaders moved on, their places were taken by highly qualified veterans, mostly familiar family members. Top job in the 15th Fighter Group went to Lt. Colonel DeWitt Spain. Though wounded in the 26 March attack on the 21st camp, DeWitt had recovered and was back in the cockpit. Now he was back home with the 15th Group.

Group pilots were advised of another Tokyo mission on 15 April. At the final weather briefing on 16 April Fighter Command changed the target to Kyushu, the southernmost of the Japanese home islands.

Attacks by Japanese Kamikazi aircraft were having a devastating effect on the U.S. invasion fleet off Okinawa. Top Pacific commanders felt that an air strike against Kyushu airfields would take the pressure off the Okinawa armada. Such last minute command changes are usually attended by foulups, and the Kyushu mission proved to be no exception.

The preparation time was nil, strip maps were inadequate and late in arriving, and there was insufficient time for pilots to acquaint themselves with the targets. Even the final briefing was a flawed affair. So many people jammed the theatre that pilots in the back heard only snatches of essential intelligence. The pilot's disenchantment with the planning of the 12 April mission was not dispelled by the fiasco that preceded the 16 April mission.

Forty-seven P-51s of the 15th Group, Major Jim Tapp leading, took off rom Iwo Jima intending to rendezvous with the 21st Group. The latter unit was 45 minutes behind schedule, doubtless because of the prevailing confusion which had set this strike in motion. The missed rendezvous was an omen of things to come.

According to doctrine, the Squadrons had strict orders to make but one pass, line abreast, against the heavily defended airfields. The Air Force and the Navy had lost more planes to antiaircraft batteries concentrated at enemy airdromes than to all other causes of

"Bushmasters" who made the historic trip: (Left to right) front row: John Chambers, Bob Carr (KIA), Ernie Hostetler, Vic Mollan, Don Gautsche, Phil Maher; back row: Charlie Heil, Dick Duerr, Bob Beyl, Bob Roseberry, Jerry Yellin, Al Sherran (KIA), Doug Moore, Todd Moore, Doyle Brooks, Leo Evans, and Harold Collins; sitting on wing: Jim Vande Hey, CO, and Jim Tapp. (Source: Jim Vande Hey)

enemy action. You might catch the defenders by surprise on the first high-speed pass, but they were sure to be leading their targets and have refined their aim if a second were attempted.

Jim Tapp groped through haze to lead the attack on Kanoya Airdrome. There were between 50 and 75 aircraft present, mostly twin-engined, well dispersed either in bunkers or camouflaged.

Diving from 10,000 feet at an indicated air speed of 450 to 500 m.p.h., Mustangs of the 78th Squadron hit the Kanoya complex in a loose line abreast at deck level. Only Tapp, his wingman Phil Maher, Todd Moore's flight, and Bob Roseberry managed to get their sights on enemy aircraft during the brief seconds that they strafed the airfield. All other 78th aircraft hit hangars, shops, power plants and antiaircraft emplacements.

The 45th Squadron, led by Capt. Art Bridge, located the target and hedgehopped as low as 15 feet. They drew heavy anti-aircraft and intense automatic weapons fire, arriving after the Japanese gunners had been alerted by the attack of the 78th. Strafing hangars, barracks, and antiaircraft positions, the 45th took considerable abuse. Bridge, Lieutenants Wes Brown, Emerson L. Cyphers, Robert D. Wray all took hits over the target, but managed to limp home.

During this attack the 45th encountered a Japanese air traffic controller who either was strangely detached from the war or was the Oriental equivalent of Harpo Marx. Both Captain Al Maltby and Bruce Campbell, leading strafing flights of P-51s in hell-for-leather dashes across Kanoya, were flashed a green landing light from the control tower. None of the Mustang drivers were inclined to accept the invitation.

The 47th Squadron orbited the rendezvous point according to incomplete instructions and became separated from the rest of the Group. Unableto find the target in the low-hanging haze, and having lost all coordination with other units, they elected to return to the Rally Point and proceed to Iwo Jima.

The mission was a "bust" as far as everyone was concerned. Even those who located the target were grumpy about the meager results. It as doubtful that they had given any succor to the naval forces off Okinawa. The mission might have been called a draw had every plane returned. However, 275 miles from Agate Base, 2nd Lt. James Wightman of the 78th began to have engine trouble. Todd Moore tried to talk him through his mechanical problems for another 25 miles until his engine cut out completely. He bailed out from

Getting ready for the next mission: Vic Mollan checks the maintenance on his 78th Sq P-51. (Source: Jim Vande Hey)

Getting ready for the next mission: Swabbing the guns on Todd Moore's "Stinger." (Source: Jim Vande Hey)

Getting ready for the next mission: "Wee Lona Lee" gets preflighted next door to a B-29. (Source: Jim Vande Hey)

Getting ready for the next mission: Tom McCullough's "Miss Kay" gets tended by some of the 78th's finest. Note dust caps on exhaust stacks. (Source: Jim Vande Hey)

Left — Getting ready for the next mission: Jessie Kneezle checks the belts of .50 caliber ammo going into a 47th Sq Mustang. (Source: USAF)

about 2500 feet but his chute did not open. A Dumbo, summoned earlier, orbited the scene but could not locate Wightman.

The next Empire mission occurred on 19 April 1945. It was the first fighter sweep conducted by the Seventh over Honshu, a shooting ground that was now familiar. Group CO DeWitt Spain led 53 aircraft over Atsugi Airdrome near Yokohama. The 15th was flying high cover for the 21st Fighter Group.

Captain Ennis led the 45th in the initial sweep on Atsugi after the 21st Group had torn up the field. There were many fires left burning by the 21st and Ennis picked out an undamaged transport for his target. "I gave it a long, long burst but it did not catch fire," said Skinny.

Nettled by the attack of the 21st Group, the Japanese flak batteries were delivering an intense and accurate volume of automatic weapons fire. Second Lieutenant Arthur A. Burry took a non-lethal hit as Ennis turned for another pass.

Despite the strafing fighters, one brassy Japanese fighter tried to take off. Lieutenants Jay Slater and Leroy E. Yakish turned in their strafing run and knocked down the Tojo just as its wheels were retracted.

Ennis and Burry ran into another Tojo and gave him a damaging burst before he maneuvered away. Captain Fred Henderson's flight ran into some aggressive Raidens and engaged in a dangerous low-level dog fight. Pulling up inside the enemy fighter, Henderson started firing in a 20 degree deflection shot. Both planes stalled and, as Henderson recovered, the Raiden was in his sights. He fired a burst. The Japanese plane broke into flames and went into a flat spin at 2,000 feet. Second Lieutenant Donald E. Statsman, Henderson's element leader, got behind another Jack and shot its tail off.

First Lieutenant Paul Hunter lost a cylinder in the left bank of his engine shortly after leaving the Rally Point. What seemed like a pending sub rescue turned out to be just a long tough flight. Hunter's crippled and vibrating P-51 incredibly carried him 750 miles back to a landing at Iwo Jima.

Only two enemy fighters got within sight of the 78th Squadron, high cover on this particular mission. One of them made the mistake of getting within reach of CO Jim Tapp. "I made an opposite cross, front quarter, curve of pursuit pass on a Jack that was flying at 8,000 feet," said Major Tapp. "At 1,000 feet range I opened fire and the Jack immediately burst into flames." That fancy long range shot was Jim's sixth aerial victory.

There were a few complaints about target information, the navigation plan and the position of Air Sea Rescue (ASR) units, but on the whole it was considered an excellent mission. The score was 6-0-3 for no losses.

Round the bar that night, Lyman Ennis, pleased with the array of targets, said, "I'd rather make five runs over any target in Japan than one over Mili."

Jim Tapp got four victories on the 7 April mission and another on the 12th to become the Group's first ace. (Source: Todd Moore)

The next long-range mission, another fighter sweep, was scheduled for 22 April 1945. The target was Suzuka Naval Air Base near Nagoya with Akenogahara Airdome as a secondary target. With Lt. Colonel Spain leading, 51 Mustangs proceeded toward Honshu with B-29 navigators. Encountering hazy conditions over the Empire, the Squadrons achieved mixed results.

Some of the 45th had trouble locating the primary target and concentrated their fire on targets of opportunity. Captain Al Maltby had a mission mixed with terror and humor. "My engine was running pretty rough when we reached the Japanese coast," he recalls. "Directly over the airfield at about 10 feet, my engine cut out completely for about 30 seconds. I glided out over the bay before I got it running again." Then, in a moment of comic relief, a lone Japanese, in a rowboat, whanged away at his speeding plane with a pistol.

DeWitt Spain, flying with the 47th Squadron, led the way to a Japanese airfield. With 2nd Lt. Dick Long on his wing, Spain swept over the field at 50 feet strafing three parked Tojos. His tracers hit all three, blowing the wing off one. At the completion of his run, he looked about for Long but could not locate him. Captain Bob Down, leading the next flight, saw Long's P-51 take several hits from ground fire. It pulled up smoking in a sharp climbing turn, but was never seen again.

The next flight of the 47th, led by Ed Markham, had started its strafing run from 6,000 feet and roared over the enemy field, line abreast, at 50 feet drawing intense small arms fire. Pulling off the target, they observed three Zekes at low altitude and gave chase. Markham shot down one and shared the destruction of another with 1st Lt. Henry C. Ryniker.

Dick Hintermeier, leading the last flight over the enemy base, saw an Oscar fly across his path. He gave it a short squirt but his speed carried him past the Japanese fighter. First Lieutenant Harold L. Baccus, following Hintermeier, spotted the enemy craft. "I was able to pull my aircraft into a very tight turn sufficient to

Skinny Ennis (left) and his wingman, Al Roberts, shared a victory for the 45th Sq on 12 April 45. (Source: USAF)

get a good lead. I could see my .50 caliber projectiles stitching the Oscar. Metal fragments were flying off, and he began to smoke as I continued firing, then went into a tight spin at low altitude and crashed.''

Meanwhile, Captain Hintermeier was offered another golden opportunity: ''I had just witnessed Baccus' victory and I rolled out right on the tail of another Japanese fighter, a Tojo. I gave him three bursts and he rolled over and went right into the ground.''

On the way back, Bob Down was busily spraying .50 caliber fire at an assortment of interesting targets when he clipped a high tension wire. The Mustang took the beating and kept on going.

Todd Moore led the 78th Squadron in a sweeping attack of Akenogahara Airfield. Coming over the perimeter of the field, he spotted an Oscar taking off. He closed and fired a long deflection shot ending almost on the enemy's tail. The Oscar whipped over in a spiral roll, crashing and burning on the field.

Second Lieutenant Thomas L. McCullough saw another Oscar at 200 feet over the center of the field. ''I made a head-on pass about 10 degrees off and gave him a three-second burst. He pulled up, and I did too, trying to keep my lead but I couldn't hold it. It didn't matter. He passed over me, rolled on his back, then split S-ed into the ground.''

Returning to the rally point from the sweep, Long's absence was confirmed. The Group also found a perplexed flight from the 47th flying submarine cover. Whitey Betner's unit, operating with a B-29 navigator, had no sooner arrived on station when Lt. Stelling was seen to bail out. A Super Dumbo was on the scene quickly, and the sub arrived in just five minutes. However, Stelling's body could not be located. Since he had made no radio call and there was no enemy action in that area, his loss was mystifying.

Captain Al Maltby nursed his faltering engine all the way back to Iwo Jima. He ran his Merlin at what sounded like its preferred level, which was very slow. After eight hours and five minutes, he landed with just 15 gallons of gas. The trip was etched on his backside as well as his memory. ''I had been sitting on that parachute for so long that here was no feeling in my buttocks. I had to take heat treatments to restore circulation.''

First Lieutenant Nick Hubbuch, Communications Officer for the 78th Squadron, had flown the mission in a navigational B-29 code-named ''Cloud Hopper Charlie''. He assembled useful information which would facilitate future missions. He also reported that the first P-51s returning to the rally point made a head-on pass at the B-29 scaring the wits out of the crew. Even after deadly combat over the mainland, the irrepressible Mustang pilots couldn't resist buzzing the big bird.

The mission was considered a good one, marred only by the losses. The Group had seen only nine enemy planes in flight and had destroyed six. Airdrome strafing had accounted for another 11-3-16. One six- to eight-thousand ton ship and one 100-foot lugger had been left burning by mast height attacks and another dozen ships had been damaged. All in all it had been good hunting.

However, there was the gnawing realization that almost every mission was now costing human lives. The low-level missions were productive in targets, but were taking an inevitable toll. There was also the puzzling loss of the last four men who had parachuted. Clearly, the men of the 15th were captains of their souls, but not the masters of their fate.

Battle damaged B-29s had been plopping down on Iwo Jima since 9 March. On 24 April one came in with severe damage and, unable to stop, crashed into the 15th Group's ramp area. the wounded Superfort came to a grinding halt amidst the parked aircraft of the 45th and a furious fire began. Pilots and mechanics taxied or pushed parked P-51s from the growing blaze. Acts of heroism were common, but none so outstanding as the efforts of three 78th Squadron enlisted men. Sergeants Greco, Lorenczewski, and Sweet, at great risk to themselves, ran to the raging fire, and pulled a wounded crewman from the B-29.

The ground action at Iwo had virtually ended, and living had become less tense. A scattering of Japanese were stilled holed up in the caves on the north end of the Island. Hogan Birk, who ventured out with others on expeditions to the craggy north, recalls the tenacity of the Japanese holdouts. "They couldn't be inveigled out with threats or offers of food and medical aid. Any approach to the caves provoked a volley of shots that quickly discouraged souvenir hunting."

Just as life on Iwo was becoming more relaxed a series of explosions on the southeast beach sent men scurrying for their slit trenches. The unexplained detonations on 25 April were caused by a sentry who had accidentally set off a trip flare near an ammo dump. Before the fire could be extinguished it reached the stored ammunition. Piles of lethal ordnance would periodically erupt, triggering neighboring stores. It was a spectacle to rival the best Fourth of July display, but became tedious after the first few hours.

The grand finale came at 0330 the morning of 26 April when 148 five-hundred-pound bombs were detonated in one cataclysmic roar. Shrapnel showered over the island. Many temporary buildings were collapsed by the explosion. Tent poles were shattered and pegs were jerked from the ground. No "Group" tent escaped damage.

The ammo dump explosion did not respect rank or station. The inside of General Moore's headquarters was exposed as a wall of his Quonset hut was blown in. The Seventh's common chapel was reduced to rags and broken sticks. Lieutenant Colonel Tom Norton, Command Chaplain, was an orphan with nothing but the clothes on his back. A 90 mm rocket had gone through his tent like a runaway locomotive.

Fate had yet another more deadly trick to play on the 15th. This time bad weather was lying in wait, ready to unloose nature's black magic.

The Group had taken off early on 26 April to escort B-29s to Kyushu. Rendezvous was effected with the navigational B-29s on schedule by mission leader, Major Tapp. The Squadrons were a bit strung out as they approached the assembly point. The 45th, last to take off, was trailing the rest of the Group. Captain Bridge, Squadron CO, found that the bomber force was behind all of them.

One hundred miles from Kyushu the mission began to encounter a weather front. Approaching the coast, layered clouds began to confuse and obscure the assembly. The B-29s were stacked in groups from 8,000 to 14,000 feet and began to climb through the worsening overcast. Art Bridge, who had led his Squadron in a back-tracking maneuver to find the Superforts, clung to the bomber formations as they bore through dense cloud layers. The coast only appeared in brief glimpses. none of the fighter pilots could fix their locations, and ducking in and out of the overcast, they struggled to maintain visual contact with each other and the bombers.

The proximity of large units of aircraft in close formation being swallowed by clouds, was an unnerving experience. Some fighters clung tenuously to the B-29s, while others separated and climbed above the overcast. Bridge, climbing through 15,000 feet, received an eerie call from 2nd Lt. Emerson Cyphers of Blue Flight. In a garbled transmission he communicated that he was at 1,000 feet and having trouble. Art ordered him to home in on the B-29 navigator and get a vector for Iwo. Then he called the Blue Flight leader, Mort Knox — no answer. Bridge quickly contacted his other flight leaders. Everyone responded. Cypher's radio fell silent after the first transmission.

Officers of the 78th Sq muster for a class photo on 15 April 45: (Left to right) Front row: Schoenbart, Wayland (KIA), Pena, Fahey, Hostetler, Mollan, Collins, Saed, Miles, Grimes, Mathis (KIA), D. B. Moore, Chism (POW), Maher, Gautsche, Butler, Evans, Martin; middle row: Powers, Carey, Carr (KIA), Bauman, Teresi, Price, Heil, Yellin, Beyl, Vande Hey, CO, Roseberry, Sherren (KIA), Ruby, Kern, Westlund, Marshall, Schroeppel (KIA), Sedam: back row: Scott (POW), Mangum (KIA), Kreimann, Delahunty, Duerr, Owens, McNevins, Tapp, Williams (KIA), Brooks, Merrill, Lewis, Hubbuch, McCullough, Nelson (KIA), Wightman (KIA), Sherbundy. (Source: Walter Kreimann)

The 15th's veteran Squadron Commanders: Buck Snipes, 45th Sq. (Source: USAF)

Repeated calls to Blue Flight elicited only an ominous silence.

Struggling through the same murky overcast, the 78th Squadron was experiencing similar mysterious troubles. Captain Harold Collins began leading his flight through the weather on instruments at 11,000 feet. He had gathered his planes tightly about his P-51. During the climb he noticed that 2nd Lt. Wallace K. Wayland's Mustang began to drop back. Second Lieutenant Doyle Brooks, number four man in the flight, was puzzled to see Wayland dropping past him since his line of flight appeared to be normal.

When Collins failed to raise Wayland on the radio he called the 78th's navigator, "Cloudhopper 2", and advised that one of his chickens was missing. The B-29 immediately informed the nearest submarine, "Darkeyes 35".

Green flight of the 78th was led by an experienced officer of the Seventh Fighter Command, Lt. Colonel John W. Mitchell. As his flight broke out on top of the overcast it was one plane short. Colonel Mitchell's wingman, 2nd Lt. Clyde V. Mangum, had disappeared. Again there had been no call for help, nor was there any response to repeated calls from Mitchell.

Jim Tapp got his flight through, without mishap, to a layer between the undercast and the overcast. Spotting the strike force through holes in the clouds, Tapp attempted to place his unit in a supporting position over the target area. The Mustangs drew fire from the B-29s for their effort, and Phil Maher took a .50 caliber slug through his wing.

The Group never saw the target, never encountered a single enemy aircraft, and saw no AA fire. Keeping a respectful distance from the strike force, they left the target, picked up the navigational B-29s, and began the long trip back.

On return to Iwo the worst fears were realized. Six planes were missing — vanished in the mists off Kyushu without explanation or trace. The 45th Squadron had lost Captain Morton M. Knox, 1st Lt. William W. Redus, 2nd Lt. Emerson L. Cyphers, and 2nd Lt. Robert D. Wray. The 78th Squadron listed 2nd Lt. Wallace K. Wayland and 2nd Lt. Clyde V. Mangum as missing.

At the mission interrogation pilots registered anger and dismay at the late arrival of target photos, B-29s leading multi-plane formations through pea soup conditions, and inaccurate weather forecasting. They even railed against the lack of communications from the dedicated air sea rescue units. This last objection reflected their understandable frustration at the loss of comrades.

They were shadow boxing with an invisible enemy which had, in one mission, taken a greater toll than had been suffered in eight weeks of action against the Japanese. The likeliest explanations for these recent fatalities were zero visibility, disorientation, and mid-air collision.

Such a shroud of weather enveloping an aircraft obscures the horizon and all other visual reference points. A pilot can develop vertigo in a matter of seconds by submitting both to his natural instincts and false messages from the inner ear. This phenomenon can only be avoided by asserting rigid self-discipline and flying by instruments.

Standard procedure in dense overcast was for the flight leader to fly instruments while the others tucked into the tightest possible formation visually guiding on the flight leader or the element leader. This then fostered the next and more horrible peril, mid-air collision. In a tightly knit formation at high speed, the mere touching of wingtips could trigger a chain reaction where planes swatted each other out of the sky. Fighting to control their tumbling planes or to bail out, the endangered pilots rarely had time to radio explanations.

Knox, the Makin veteran, and five others had died violently, yet in a shadowy and unaccountable way that extracted nothing from the enemy. There was no *quid pro quo*. This calamitous engagement with the ill winds of nature was a portent of disasters yet to unfold.

In yet another twist of fate, the 47th lost a plane and pilot on 29 April on a routine test flight. First Lieutenant Alex Trodahl took a recently serviced P-51 on a local hop. Developing engine trouble, he called for an emergency landing. With several members of the unit

The 15th's veteran Squadron Commanders: John Piper, 47th Sq. (Source: USAF)

The 15th's veteran Squadron Commanders: Jim Vande Hey, 78th Sq. (Source: USAF)

watching, he lost power on the approach and his plane settled sickeningly toward the ground. He crashed and died 150 feet short of Runway 24. Trodahl was the only member of the Group buried on Iwo Jima during the entire campaign.

The month of April ended with the Group's seventh VLR mission on the 30th. It was a long and pointless airplane ride to and from Honshu. The 15th was scheduled to meet a strike force of B-29s and escort them to Tachikawa Army Air Arsenal. This important Japanese air depot, with its bomber base and experimental and research facilities, was comparable to our Wright Field. The assumption was that it would be vigorously defended and the Group was emotionally primed for a bitter engagement.

Lieutenant Colonel Spain led 46 Mustangs to the Departure Point. After three orbits he concluded that the bomber force had already left for the target and ordered his force forward to the anticipated battle. Roaming as far west as the Shizuoka area and north of Tokyo, their only sight of Japan was Mount Fujiyama protruding through the overcast, making sport of their long-range effort. After searching diligently for the strike force, Spain was finally rewarded with a distant view of nine B-29s obviously in no distress and in no need of escort. It was just one of those command snafus. The bombers and the fighters had been given different marching orders. Cursing the timing miscues that had sent them on such a vacant endeavor, the Group plodded back to Iwo.

Enemy or not, the Empire trips were gruelling ordeals in a P-51. Bomber crews routinely flew missions of this length in many theatres of combat, but not fighter planes. The bombers had copilots, navigators, and headroom. One could stand up and stretch cramped muscles in a bomber, but not in a P-51. The Mustang's cockpit was a bit roomier than a coffin, but not as long. Strapped into a sitting position on a parachute pack, pilots could neither stand nor lie down. Encumbered with life vest and shoulder holster, they were wired at throat and helmet for radio and piped to oxygen, at high altitudes, through a face mask. They were literally immobilized from the buttocks to the neck and confined in that posture for seven to nine hours. A modicum of relief was afforded by shifting the weight from one cheek of the butt to the other. However, after several hours of abnormal circulation, this therapy failed and the entire rear end went numb. On the return trip some pilots would roll their planes over, trim them for upside down flight, and hang from their shoulder harness for a few moments of unorthodox relief.

Fighters were flown with courage and dedication throughout the world, but nowhere were they flown on such consistently long arduous missions as on the Empire run.

April 1945 had been a paradox for the 15th Fighter Group. It had been both rewarding and perplexing. On seven VLR missions to Japan and twenty more to the Bonin Islands they had performed admirably. They had destroyed 40 enemy planes in aerial combat and another 15 on the ground. Most importantly, the B-29s were getting through to perform their missions with far

Some of the old guard are honored in the shadow of Mount Surabachi. (Left to right) Ben Kearney, Jim Vande Hey, Buck Snipes and Jim Beckwith are awarded Bronze Star Medals by Brig. Gen. Moore prior to Stateside reassignment. (Source: USAF)

fewer losses. However, the Group had paid a heavy price for their success. They had lost 17 aircraft and 13 pilots to a variety of causes. Losses to Japanese action had been expected, but the unseen enemies; bad weather, flawed bailouts, and mechanical malfunction had reaped the most abundant harvest. It was hard to measure risks so ill-defined and often concealed. Bob Roseberry had developed a survival formula that was a combination of diminishing risk with qualified uncertainty. "I figured that if a new pilot got through his first two or three long-range missions he had a good chance to make it."

By 1 May the engineering and maintenance crews had rooted out a series of bugs. Spark plugs were burning up with each long range mission. It was deduced that the problem, apart from seven to eight hours of low cruising speeds, was Iwo's dust and condensation in the fuel. There had also been some gun jamming in the subzero deepfreeze of high altitude combat. As soon as the pilots understood that the prolonged use of the gun heaters would not overload the generators or jeopardize the electrical system, the trouble vanished.

The installation of a directional device, known lovingly as "Uncle Dog" or "DU" was completed on all P-51s. It consisted of two side by side VHF (very high frequency) antennae aft of the cockpit. The unit received the letter U or D in Morse code from a homing station, ground or air. When the pilot adjusted his heading to refine the Morse signals into a steady hum, he had established a compass fix toward the transmitting station. The DU proved a lifesaver and the pilots regarded it highly. Its improper and indiscriminate use had cuased jamming on the early missions, but this was later resolved.

Accommodations at the Iwo Inn were steadily improving. The pilots and ground personnel had advanced from conditions of squalor to a gypsy-like life style. Food continued to be the main complaint. John Fitzgerald, 47th Squadron, recalls their creativity in adapting:

> Our food was rotten in the early months, but we did get an unusually ample quota of booze. The Navy, on the other hand, had great food but led a life of undeserved sobriety. Whenever a Navy ship would call we would barter liquor for steak, eggs, and fruit. We'd all give a portion of our liquor ration to our Supply Officer, Gene Broadbent, who would swap it with the Navy like an old Indian trader. Always suspected, he scraped a few bottles off the top for his own use.

A number of ingenious people designed and built a steam bath to heal and restore the cramped muscles and sore bones of the pilots. Major Joseph "Smokey" Walther, Command Flight Surgeon, had determined to do something about the problems caused by cramming a human body into a fighter plane cockpit for eight hours.

Having noted that there were sulphur springs gurgling beneath the surface of Iwo Jima, Doctor Walther asked the resident detachment of Navy Seabees what it would take to drill a well, install the necessary plumbing, and erect tubs in a Quonset hut. The Navy construction engineers were disinterested until the good doctor offered a trade of fire water for hot water. "Hell," said one, "for that we'll get you a direct hook-up to the Devil's kitchen." And so the Iwo Jima Spa was inaugurated. After debriefing, those pilots who wished, were immersed in the hot sulphur baths, handed a cold beer, then given a massage. The hydrotherapy offered both physical and emotional relief.

Other creature comforts were slowly satisfied as laundries sprang up, horse-shoe pits were laid out, and volley-ball courts appeared. The highlight of the month, however, was the completion and inauguration of the Group's outdoor theater. It was a Rube Goldberg affair made of scrap lumber, packing crates, and bits of mechanical gear gathered from all three squadrons. There were few chairs, but scores of people showed up with their own board or box for the grand opening. The movie was "Whistling in Dixie". A band concert was planned the following night, but a Pacific typhoon canceled the fun and torrential rains washed away part of the Iwo Bijou. Undaunted, the 15th's veterans of adversity rebuilt and broke all previous attendance records a few nights later when folks from all over Iwo came to see "Rhapsody in Blue."

The weather played more mischief than tearing up the theater and blowing down a few tents. It was beginning to be regarded as THE enemy. The official history for May discussed an array of problems which had been encountered and solved. But the weather by its very nature seemed to be "insurmountable."

The B-24 weather reconnaissance flights to Japan were undertaken on a daily basis to help verify the forecasts of staff weather central on Guam. Even this

Gun camera scenes from the 16 April Kyushu mission as seen through the sights of Todd Moore, 78th Sq: Strafing hangars at Kanoya A/D. (Source: Robert W. Moore)

A disappointing handful of aircraft were found scattered about the field. (Source: Robert W. Moore)

Kanoya's power plant gets a dose of .50 caliber fire. (Source: Robert W. Moore)

effort could not augment the science of meteorology when it came to the nature of the Nanpo Shoto. As the weather changed like a chameleon, missions were scheduled and scrubbed with maddening frequency. The Group Intellience Section discussed these planning frustrations in the May history:

> For example, on 1 May we were alerted for a mission on the 4th. On the 2nd the mission was changed to the 3rd. On the 3rd it was postponed until the 4th and on the 4th it was scheduled for the 5th. On the 5th it was canceled.

After the long range mission of 1 May was aborted, the Group was unable to get weather clearance over the Empire for a week. The Squadrons used the time to flog Chichi Jima with over 40 sorties.

Another P-51 Group, the 506th, had arrived on Iwo Jima in early May to beef up the command. During its shakedown a plane from the 506th collided with one from the 15th on a routine flight. Both pilots were lost. Second Lieutenant Bill Edwards, a 45th pilot, was one of those killed. A replacement, Edwards was unknown to the Squadron. He had arrived only eight days before and never lived to fly a VLR mission. Such were the multiple risks that attended the undertaking. For some there were second and third chances, for a few, not even a first.

Orders for a Honshu fighter sweep finally came on 8 May. The Group, with its B-29 navigators, was assigned to fly high cover for the 21st Group. The target was Kisarazu Airfield on the East shore of Tokyo Bay.

With Jim Tapp leading, 42 Mustangs made landfall and proceeded to the target area. No enemy aircraft were encountered but the Group ran into cloud layers at various altitudes and hit nasty rain squalls as they let down to lower levels.

The 21st had stirred up a storm of light and heavy AA fire which even reached up to buffet the covering Squadrons. The 15th Group moved down the coast to a fresh target, Tateyama Airfield, shooting up trains and ships along the way.

The anti-aircraft defenses at Tateyama must have been alerted by the prior attack on Kisarazu. Units of the 15th were met by a flurry of intense AA fire. Captain George Dunlap's flight was buffeted by the barrage at 3000 feet and two of his planes were hit immediately. Dunlap saw 2nd Lt. Roy F. Zalesky's Mustang tumble out of control toward the bay. Second Lieutenant Leroy E. Yakish had also taken a direct hit on the belly of his Mustang. He fought to control the plane for a few moments, then began to veer off, as pilots of the 45th called to him to head for the lifeguard sub or bail out. Sliding into the low hanging clouds, Yakish responded briefly that he had lost his air speed indicator and was on instruments, flying blind. That was his last transmission.

Tapp did not risk a strafing run because of the intense ack-ack and poor weather. A trail of anti-aircraft bursts

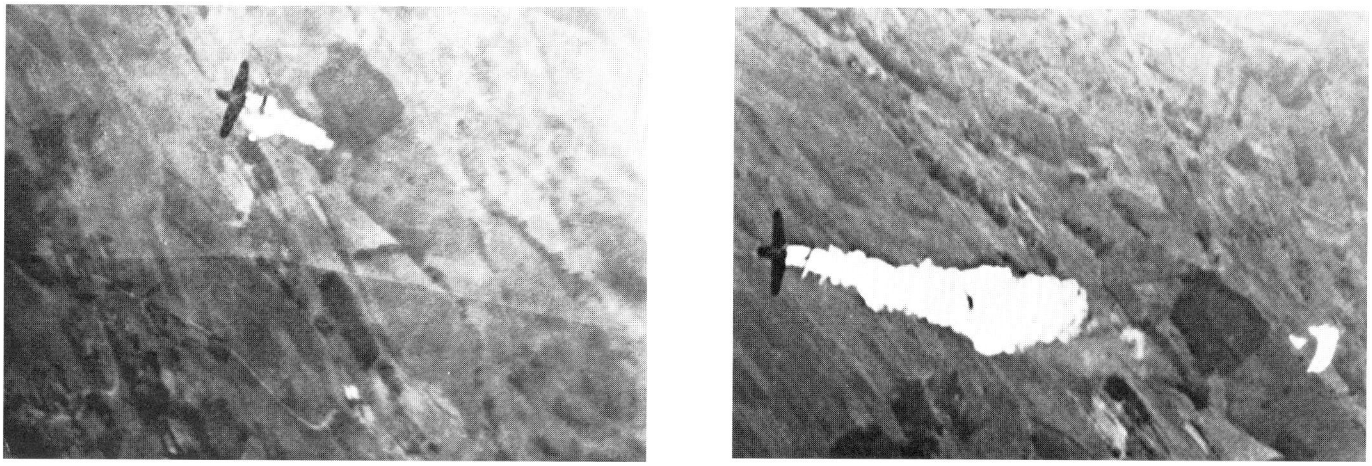

Air action with the 302nd NAG west of Atsugi, 19 April: Don Statsmann, 45th Sq, flames a Raiden or "Jack," then follows as its tail burns off. (Source: Don Statsmann)

Jim Tapp, 78th Sq CO, scores hits on another Jack. The fuselage band marks this Japanese pilot as a flight leader. (Source: Robert W. Moore)

was following Tom McCullough, number 4 man in Ernie Hostetler's flight, with frightening accuracy until the Mustangs pulled away from the airfield.

Reforming at the Rally Point, without Yakish or Zalesky, the remainder of the Group felt blessed to have survived the wicked combination of weather and flak.

Jack Thomas arrived on Iwo in mid-May and it was old home week. He had known many of the pilots as instructor, flight leader, or Squadron Commander. Due to his senior rank he took command of the 15th from DeWitt Spain, who became Group Operations Officer. John Mitchell, a flying school classmate of Thomas', was detailed as Deputy Group Commander. A veteran of the Thirteenth Air Force, Mitchell had flown a long tour in the Solomon Islands where he had scored 8 victories, including the destruction of a Betty which carried Admiral Yamamoto to his death.

Two days after returning, Thomas was in the cockpit, headed for Japan. Spain led the mission because of his long experience on the Empire run. Fifty-nine P-51s were put up but aborts brought the final muster to 48. The Group was ordered to escort B-29s to Tachikawa Airdrome just west of Tokyo.

The weather was favorable enroute but three hours out, forty minutes short of the Departure Point, an enormous weather front loomed. The overcast was solid and stood like a rampart off the coast of Honshu. It ran for 100 miles with its base at 1,000 feet and the tops to 24,000.

With no hope of going around the weather, Spain penetrated the front, climbing from 11,000 feet. Between layers and cloud gaps the Group searched for the strike force but never made visual contact. They even became separated from the navigator B-29s for short periods. By communication with the bomber force it became apparent that the two formations had passed each other, unseen in the overcast. Only God knew how close they came to a monumental mid-air collision. Lt. Colonel Spain ordered a 180-degree turn and led the unit back for the trip home.

The Group was missing one Mustang at the rally point. As the climb through the overcast had started, 2nd Lt. Paul C. Frick began having engine rouble. His 47th Squadron Mustang fell behind as his engine periodically cut out.

Separated from his flight and receiving only broken transmissions from the flight leader, Frick was on his own over the coast of Honshu. With his DU also out of commission, he badly needed a friend.

Spotting a flight of 21st Group P-51s, he tried to tag along. They didn't see him and he couldn't catch them. Next, he encountered seven B-29s and realized he was over land as two flak bursts smudged the haze. Frick established radio contact with one of the Superforts who agreed to lead him back to the Rally Point. With the bomber doing both navigating and communicating, they located a B-29 navigator and started the long trip home. Frick's engine was running so poorly he asked the B-29 to slow down. The Packard Rolls Royce Merlin ran like a Model T but it kept going.

While Thomas was aloft, getting his initiation in the weather frustrations of the region, a secondary front intervened as a threat. Long after the mission had departed, the wind changed and a fog bank settled over Iwo Jima. The island was socked in with zero visibility and the meterologists could not predict when the shroud would lift.

Officers at Agate Base radioed the Groups to suggest a diversion to Okinawa but fuel supply was grossly insufficient. The Mustangs were returning to Iwo whether it was there or not. Grimly the staff alerted all emergency rescue units "to stand by for an impending catastrophe."

Sandy Sanders agonized over the prospect of "pilots who could not be fished from the drink when they could not even be located in the foggy waters."

And then, twenty minutes before the fighters were due back, the improbable seemed to occur. "The wind whipped up," said Sanders, "blew the fog away, the clouds lifted to 6,000 feet, and for an hour and a half the weather held as our pilots swarmed over the island and landed."

John Fitzgerald, flying with one other stray P-51, dropped through the overcast and broke out at 75 feet near Minami Rock. He was south of Iwo and had almost overshot the last landmark for hundreds of miles. He did a 180 to the shaft of open sky that girdled Iwo, and landed safely.

Thirty minutes after the last plane was down, "the wind died, the clouds lowered, and the visibility returned to zero-zero again until ten o'clock that night." Sanders and everyone else had a ready explanation for the phenomenon: "It was a miracle. God was on our side."

They tried again on 24 May and once more weather turned them back. With Lt. Colonel Mitchell leading, 49 Mustangs set out for a sweep of Matsudo Airfield on Tokyo's outskirts. Proceeding north at 9,000 feet, the Group began to encounter heavy clouds about 250 miles out. Climbing through the overcast to 17,500 feet, they were confronted by another wall of towering cumulus clouds that reached beyond 30,000 feet. The B-29 navigators diverted 30 degrees attempting to go around the barrier but found only bigger, cloud formations with ominous blue and black hues. "Cloudhopper 1", the lead B-29, judged them impenetrable and ordered a return to base.

These on-scene judgement calls made eminently good sense to those confronted by the weather. However, there were mutterings among top Pacific air commanders about the increased frequency of weather aborts and achievement of strategic goals. This had the inevitable effect of creating an atmosphere of deficiency that would cause mission leaders to take more risks. Taunting nature would prove more disastrous than doing battle with the visible enemy.

The Matsudo mission was rescheduled and a new batch of pilots were briefed for the take-off on 25 May. Sixty-four planes assembled for the strike.

Action near Nagoya, 22 April 45: Todd Moore gets an Oscar victory in a dangerous low level fight over Akenogahara A/D. (Source: Robert W. Moore)

Blowing a locomotive at Toba. (Source: Robert W. Moore)

A sunken cargo ship, attended by two salvage rigs, is caught by strafing P-51s near the entrance to Nagoya Bay. (Source: Robert W. Moore)

South of Nagoya Bay a mixed flight of 78th and 45th Sq Mustangs attack a small cargo ship on 22 April. Above: Moore scores hits and starts a fire on the first pass. (Source: Robert W. Moore) Left: Bruce Campbell, following Moore, touches off a load of explosives and the ship "disintegrates." (Source: Robert W. Moore)

First Lieutenant Walter Kreimann was looking forward to the mission. He had been on several escort missions to the Empire but had not yet done any airdrome strafing. Walter had a friend from his home town, Hitchcock, South Dakota, an ex-high school coach, serving as a control tower operator. He had promised to give Walt a good rubdown at the Iwo Jima Spa on his return from the next mission. Walter thought "that would be a grand climax to a good mission."

Again a massive front seemed to lie along their route, blocking passage over the Nanpo Shoto. Iwo's dust accompanied the mission and began to clog up the automatic mixture controls. The higher they flew, the leaner the mixture should have been.

> "We were all monkeying around with our carburetor settings which were getting too rich a mixture during the long climb," explained Kreimann. "Everyone was trying to get better fuel efficiency because we felt pretty certain this front would be waiting for us on the way back. Many people began to abort because of rough engines. But this was my first fighter sweep and I got mad and determined that I would not go back. Famous last words."

The front could not be circumvented and the Group climbed, with full combat loads, to 22,000 feet. Thirty-six P-51s aborted along the way. For the remaining 28 it was downhill in clear skies to landfall on Honshu.

With John Mitchell leading, they approached from the east. Lake Imba was their Initial Point, the start of the attack run. Crossing north of Matsudo, they executed a tight 360-degree turn, came in line abreast by Squadrons and plunged from 10,000 feet to near deck level.

Bruce Campbell was gratified by the clear weather and fine array of targets as he led the 45th Squadron across Matsudo. He even gave the Japanese grudging credit for a large cloth dummy in the center of the field that looked like a real airplane from altitude. Peppering hangars and parked aircraft, the 45th could get nothing to burn. It appeared that the Japanese were draining fuel tanks until just before their planes were scheduled for flight.

As they retired from the target, reforming from line abreast to their standard echelons, a bogey was called out at 5 o'clock high. Campbell did a tight 180-degree turn to the left and closed on the tail of a Dinah, firing from 2,000 to 200 feet distance. As Captain Campbell was tearing up the right engine and setting it afire, his wingman, F/O Billy Singleton, was stitching the left engine. With a neat bit of teamwork they destroyed the enemy plane, watching it crash in outer Tokyo as one chute blossomed.

The 45th's committed line of approach to the airfield had yielded little, but the 47th had better luck. Mitchell's unit swept across and found a line of Tojo fighters diagonal to their approach. They laced the seven Tojos with tracers, 2nd Lt. Sam Jones burning one.

Todd Moore was leading the 78th Squadron in its descent and dash over Matsudo though CO Jim Tapp was along. "Tapper", bringing up the rear, was working on another of his special "do it yourself" projects this day. He led Purple Flight which, for the first time, was armed with underwing rockets. This extra load, along with new 165 gallon wing tanks, had left them in the van of the main force.

Moore and Vic Mollan's flights came in from the south and raked their way across the field, setting fire to a Nick (Moore), and puncturing a Tojo (Mollan). Walt Kreimann was flying on Captain Moore's wing:

> "We had been given good aerial recon photos of Matsudo and knew right where the bunkers were. When we started across the field and I put my nose down, I was so surprised to see planes in the revetments just as they had appeared on the photos, that I almost forgot what I was there for. I was a momentary spectator. But I squeezed the trigger and got some direct hits on a Nick, then pulled up doing 350 m.p.h."

Jim Tapp, arriving last with his rocket carriers, knew the previous flights had already stirred up the Japanese gunners. He headed straight into Matsudo from the northeast, assuming the enemy was primed for attackers from the south.

Jim was diverted momentarily by three enemy planes crossing his path. They looked as if they might be attempting a pass on the preceeding squadrons, so, rocket load or not, he pitched into them. The enemy scattered like quail and Tapp returned to his primary mission.

With Phil "Flip" Maher on his wing, Tapp dove on Matsudo from 6,000 feet and leveled at 700 feet:

> "On the way in we fired our .50s at the few known gun positions to keep their heads down. Because of the ammo dump explosion (25 April) we were short of rockets — too short to use them for practice. So we picked two big hangars as targets.
>
> "On getting into range, I salvoed my rockets into one hangar. Flip picked the other and let his fly. As we passed over, the rockets were exploding within, and as soon as we cleared them, we hit the deck, taking evasive action. As usual, Japanese tracers were all over the sky."

Many Group pilots were lost parachuting. Dave Stelling was killed on 22 April jumping from his 47th Sq plane off Honshu. (Source: John Whitcomb)

Ernie Hostetler and 1st Lt. John Patterson, the other half of Purple Flight, volleyed their 12 rockets into a group of buildings judged to be a radio station and adjoining power plant. There were satisfying explosions with bricks and debris flying skyward.

There was boyish elation over the effects of the five-inch High Velocity Aircraft Rockets. Weighing 140 pounds each, these malevolent looking missiles were the size of the rounds fired by the main batteries of Navy destroyers. The results were awesome as fires raged and smoke columns rose to 10,000 feet.

Climbing away from Matsudo, Maher pulled up into his wingman position and advised Tapp that he was still carrying one rocket which had failed to fire:

> I circled to get back in position for a high speed pass. I started at about 8,000 and diving to 5,000 feet, I crossed my fingers and pushed the rocket button again. This time the last rocket went whooshing off. I was relieved that I now had a

A battle damaged B-29 of the 504th Bomb Group made an emergency landing on Airfield No. 1 and crashed into parked aircraft of the 45th Sq. (Source: a. E. M. Moore, b. John Katsanos)

> plane I could fight with because I could hear Bob Moore calling out bandits to the north.

Indeed, Moore had sighted entire squadrons of Japanese fighters and was leading his six planes toward them, oblivious of the odds. Walter Kreimann recalled:

> Todd was an eager beaver. He had a nose for trouble and led us right into a hell of a lot of Zeros. I had a good line of sight on one, no angle, and it blew up, spraying oil all over my windshield. As I looked back I could see the Zeke breaking up and the pilot going down.

Moore had gotten strikes on the first Zeke that crossed his path, then moved on to a five-ship formation where he flamed the last one in line. Encountering another eight Zekes, Moore locked onto the tail end of that formation and exploded the last plane in mid-air.

Captain Vic Mollan, with 2nd Lt. Robert L. Williams as wingman, was behind Moore and able to clean up after him. He attacked the first damaged Zeke and watched it burst into flames.

Mollan then spotted a single Zeke turning into the Mustangs. He made a head-on pass at the enemy plane getting many strikes and saw it explode after it passed over him. Williams was firing at it also. Moments later he glanced back gain. Williams was gone. Mollan called him repeatedly — no response. Lieutenant Williams had crashed over Honshu and was buried by the Japanese. It seems likely that he was the Group's first loss in aerial combat since the action of 7 December 1941.

With many enemy aircraft at higher altitudes and fuel now at a premium, Moore ordered a withdrawal of his remaining five planes. First Lieutenant Bob Coryell found one last Zeke in their way and shot it down enroute to the rally point.

Tapp, in a high-speed climb, had "marched to the sound of the guns" as it were, and located the enemy.

> All at once we seemed to be in the middle of the Japanese Air Force. There were about 60 Jap fighters in all, and fortunately, the great majority were below us and seemed to be in a hurry to get out of the area. I just couldn't wait any longer so I rolled over into an overhead pass on the last flight of three Tojos.
>
> I waited until I was in perfect range and opened fire. I used about ten rounds per gun in one burst and the last Tojo blew up, forcing me to pull up sharply to avoid a collision. Flip followed through and picked off another.
>
> On my sharp pullout I lost Maher and radioed him to head down the Tone River. At Choshi Point heavy Japanese antiaircraft batteries obligingly picked us up and we sighted each other from the flak bursts.
>
> Swinging back over the Peninsula we found that all Japanese planes had cleared out so we switched our attention to ground targets. Since trains all seemed to have pulled into tunnels we went over Tokyo Bay in search of shipping. Near the entrance to the Bay we sighted a small LST-type ship and scored hits on it but didn't succeed in making any serious damage. About five miles further south we sighted another ship, a small freighter.
>
> Determined to get this one, I cut the throttle back so that I could get in a good long burst. Maher and I fired in unison to zero range, and as we passed over the ship it blew up in a mass of flames.
>
> We had spent too long over Japan by this time, and, being low on fuel and ammo, we headed for the last B-29 navigator. The rest of the Group had already left for home. In a short time we sighted 'Dreamboat' orbiting the rally point and we rendezvoused and settled down for the 750-mile trip back to Iwo.

The return flight was begun with no little concern. The weather front that had been surmounted on the trip north still blocked the return route. The 78th Squadron

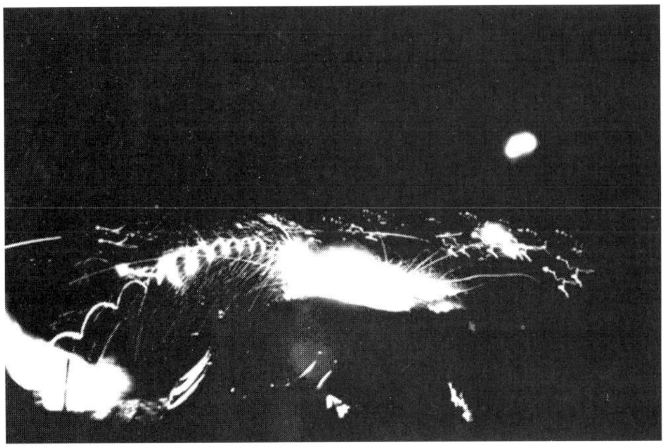

The ammo dump explosion the night of 25-26 April. (Source: E. M. Moore)

Interrogation of 47th Sq pilots after VLR mission of 26 April 45. (Left to right) Walter Powell (KIA), Bernie Bjorseth, Roy June, Howard Weaver (KIA), (head obscured by Asst. Intelligence Officer, Elliott); right rear: Eurich Bright (sandwich in hand) is interviewed by Intelligence Officer, Sandy Sanders. (Source: W. H. Sparks)

Alex Trodahl crashed short of the runway on 29 April 45 and was killed. He was the only member of the Group lost during the Iwo tour who was buried by his comrades. (Source: Bob Scamara)

had seen the most action and left Japan last. Their fuel supply was tightest so they loafed along at 1600 rpms. "A little slower than a washing machine," according to Walt Kreimann.

Climbing slowly and using hand signals to review the battle, Kreimann and Moore were killing time on the way back. Todd Moore's two victories had made him the Group's second ace, with six confirmed kills. Walt had also been Tapp's wingman when he became an ace. He was justifiably proud of being an "ace maker", and of his own kill, confirmed by the gun camera.

> I was as happy as could be, thinking about our success and relishing the thought of that rubdown. We were less than two hours from home. Suddenly I noticed my temperature gauge was rising to the danger point. I began pulling, moving and adjusting every control I had. But nothing helped. I barely had time to advise Captain Moore that I was in trouble when I saw a lick of flame out on the nose of the ship. No sooner had I cracked the hood than the flames were shooting right over the canopy and into the cockpit.
>
> Moore was calling Air Sea Rescue and advising me that we were approaching a Lifeguard sub station but I told him I couldn't hang around any longer.
>
> I shoved the canopy back further, flipped the plane upside down and tried to fall out, according to the book. However, I became stuck half way, with the lip of the hood and the headrest in the middle of my back. I was vertical at about 9,000 feet over the ocean with the engine and the cockpit afire.
>
> The wind had torn off my goggles and I was trying to get free, but the slipstream seemed to hold me there, half in and half out as the plane began to drop.
>
> I finally put my foot on the stick and pushed as hard as I could. That created a twisting motion, and I was wrenched free of the plane — an unorthodox method, to say the least. I pulled the rip cord but never really felt the chute pop open before I hit the water.

Todd Moore and Vic Mollan agonized as they radioed for help and watched Kreimann's burning plane fall from the sky. They did not see Kreimann bail out; they only saw the stricken Mustang hit the water near Tori Shima, 375 miles from Iwo Jima.

Planes of the 78th Squadron were the last to land. Tapp and Maher barely had taxi gas. Walt Kreimann's South Dakota buddy was waiting for him, as promised, on the flight line. He kept asking about him until he got to Captain Mollan. "I'm sorry. Walt won't be coming back."

The Group had shot down nine enemy planes. They had destroyed two and damaged 12 more on the ground. The sinking of one ship and the damaging of another added to the tally, but the lethal effects of the HVAR

8 May 45, Capt. Sandy Sanders interrogates a 47th flight just back from Honshu. (Clockwise from Sanders' left) Ed Markham, Ralph Heintz(POW), Lt. Col. Bob Rogers, Jule Mitchell(KIA). Sgt. Richard MacKenzie is standing wearing baseball cap. In the foreground Howard Weaver (KIA) is debriefed by Elliott. (Source: Richard MacKenzie)

rockets prompted the most enthusiastic discussion in the post-mission interrogation.

The 15th had paid a price. Williams and Kreimann were both presumed lost. No one had made a successful parachute jump since Frank Ayers had bailed out on the first VLR mission.

For 1st Lt. Eldon E. "Cowboy" Westlund, the odds must have seemed inordinately skewed in favor of the enemy and the elements. Since arriving on Iwo in March, all three of his tent mates, Wightman, Wayland, and now Williams had been lost. There weren't many trips free of charge on the Empire run.

Reports of Walter Kreimann's death were, however, greatly exaggerated. After hitting the water like a rocket he had popped to the surface with his life raft intact:

> At first I was euphoric that I had gotten out of the plane alive and made a successful parachute jump. Then, as time passed and the 10 foot swells began, I lost my enthusiasm. I didn't even feel the burns, because of the seasickness. I was violently ill in the middle of the ocean a long way from base.

Seasickness, in desperate circumstances, can grant one a measure of emotional relief. It makes death an almost acceptable alternative. Unknown to Kreimann, however, the Air Sea rescue system was alive and well and doing its damnedest for him:

> I saw a B-29 pass high overhead, then another came toward me but turned back. A moment later he appeared again in the distance, flew a circle high over me and returned the way he had come. I didn't know it at the time, didn't care much, I was so sick — but he was directing a sub to my position. Some time later, near dusk, I heard a clink of metal on metal. I looked behind and there was this long gray thing sliding through the water toward me. I didn't know if it was ours or theirs, but in my condition, I didn't care.

The U.S.S. *Tigrone* (SS 419), Commander Hiram Cassedy, officer in command, plucked Walter Kreimann from the deadly waters of the Nanpo Shoto after a three-hour search. The submarine crew also fetched Walt's parachute from the life raft. Twelve of the 27 panels had been burned or melted. There had been just enough fabric remaining to break his fall. The fire that scorched his parachute had left him with third degree burns on his right leg and less severe burns on his ankles, legs, wrists, and face.

> Ten minutes after I saw the sub I was standing in a hot shower, drinking brandy from a bottle. They gave me some of their clothes, the pharmacists's mate doctored my burns, and I was led to the wardroom. Sitting at a white table cloth with silverware, I was fed a rare steak. It was a hell of a transition in the course of an hour.
>
> Later that night the Captain said, 'You stick around and you'll see me break the record for saves.' By the next day, *Tigrone* had picked up so many survivors from various downed airplanes that we were eating sauerkraut and weiners. It all tasted great to be. When I figure all the long odds I beat, it still makes me quite conservative and very humble.

May had been a month of frustration, with the weather offering formidable opposition while the enemy adroitly avoided combat. The Japanese had been husbanding their resources and their energy for a worthy force. They found it on 29 May 1945 when over four hundred B-29s attacked Yokohama. The 15th sent 53 planes as escort along with 48 from the 21st.

As the strike force approached the IP, Japanese

Sgt. Ralph Federson, crew chief thanks Art Bridge for bringing his P-51 back from a May mission with the 45th Sq. (Source: Art Bridge)

The wreckage of Japan's Iwo based air force: Left — A thoroughly riddled Betty bomber. (Source: Jim Vande Hey) Right — Todd Moore picks at the bones of a Jill, torpedo bomber. (Source: Robert W. Moore)

fighters in large numbers began diving and rolling through the bombers. They displayed aggressive tactics not seen since early April. The P-52 pilots had their hands full protecting the B-29 formations and covering their own tails.

Wheeling about the great bomber stream like angry hornets, Mustangs and Japanese fighters traded blows, oblivious to the intense flak which pockmarked the sky. It became a deadly killing ground as stricken aircraft fell from the high altitude in burning arcs and parachutes blossomed below the battle.

Dogfighting Jacks, Todd Moore was distracted by the sight of a Zeke on the tail of a P-51. Lieutenant (j.g.) Sadanori Akamatsu, a legendary Japanese ace, was surrounded by the 45th Squadron, but was resolutely tearing holes in 2nd Lt. Rufus Moore's Mustang. Captain Moore couldn't dive to assist for fear of a collision with other P-51s milling through the sky. No one could intervene as the veteran enemy pilot sent his prey plunging into the waters off Honshu, while skillfully eluding pursuit. Captain Todd Moore felt a degree of professional respect for the lone aviator who had taken on some 75 Mustangs. "If he had been an American, he would have been awarded the Congressional Medal of Honor."

Captain Joe Powell's flight of the 47th was broken up by two Zekes and two Tojos attacking from astern. Powell and his wingman, Leon Sher, chandelled away from the Japanese but not before Sher's plane had been ripped by 20-mm-cannon fire. One hit had torn away a section of wing and flap while another had gone through his fuselage below the tail, and a third had shattered his canopy and passed through his legs.

The P-51 had lost so much wing area that the stick was "fluttering." Sher struggled toward the Rally Point grateful that the Tojos "didn't follow up on the attack." His flying machine was barely functional. It was no longer a fighting aircraft.

Separated from their flight by vicious engagements over the target, Lieutenants Fred Grover and Warren Reed intercepted four Zekes headed for the bombers. In a swirling duel, Grover shot down two, and Reed probably destroyed one more.

Eurich Bright and George Petrouleas, while departing from the target area, saw two Zekes doing dazzling acrobatic rolls over the B-29s preparatory to an overhead attack. They broke up the act by shooting one Zero into Tokyo Bay.

Jim Tapp led his 78th Squadron into a swarm of single-engined Japanese fighters. Tapp shot down a Zeke with only one operational machine gun while other members of his unit destroyed four more.

Bob Roseberry knew it was going to be a bad day as they reached the coast of Honshu. Major Tapp had just positioned the 78th over the Superforts when bandits were sighted. He ordered the Squadron to drop its wing tanks, in anticipation of imminent action. Two dozen drop tanks cascaded down over the coast of Honshu, but not Roseberry's. He pulled again and again on the release, jerking the Mustang about, trying to dislodge the tanks. Bob Roseberry was going into action over Yokohama still lugging two wing tanks. Despite this impediment to speed and maneuverability, he doggedly pursued the battle.

As several Jacks roared past him from head-on, Roseberry gamely rolled over and went after them, but his P-51 was like a ship dragging anchor. He could neither pursue nor defend. Lurching about, he was inevitably set upon by an enemy fighter. Taking several hits in his internal fuel tanks as well as the unwanted external tanks, he found sanctuary in a cloud layer.

> About this time I realized that I was all by myself over Japan with two wing tanks which refused to come off and a slightly used P-51. My wingman had lost me in the clouds and the Squadron had turned out to sea to join up with the B-29s who were to take us home.

Leading a personal rampage through the area of battle, Todd Moore, flying with the 45th Squadron, had shot down two Jacks and a George. In each case he had

Iwo's black volcanic beaches littered with invasion wreckage were uninviting. (Source: John Katsanos)

A day of yachting and fishing between missions for pilots of the 47th. (Source: John Fitzgerald)

seen his adversaries parachute from their disabled planes. On an impulse, Moore decided to take some gun-camera flicks of the last Japanese to bail out. "As I closed on him he thought I was going to blast him and he started some wild gyrations by pulling on the parachute shroud lines to 'slip' the chute out of my line of fire. He reminded me of a Halloween cardboard skeleton dangling on the end of a set of strings." Flying within 100 feet of the suspended Japanese pilot, Moore rocked his wings in a chivalrous salute to a worthy foe. He felt a great sense of personal saisfaction that in his three victories over enemy aircraft that day he had not "murdered" anyone.

Following Moore and the rest of the 45th Squadron in its wild passage through the bomber stream, wingman Bill Brown had inadvertantly come into the B-29s field of fire. Seven of the big bombers had become victims of flak or fighters and, as the escorts began to lose their cohesiveness in the unfolding brawl, every single-engined fighter plummeting through the tight formation of B-29s was suspect. Brown's plane was riddled by friendly fire and he limped from the combat radioing for a fix on the nearest Lifeguard submarine. The *Pipefish*, (SS 388) lying less than 100 miles off the coast of Japan, heard his call.

For about three quarters of an hour over 600 American and Japanese aircraft and the enemy flak batteries had maintained a level of sustained violence seldom witnessed in the Pacific air war. Over 35 planes from both sides had been destroyed and another 50 probably destroyed or damaged.

More than 100 men had been shot from the sky. The 15th Group had claimed 15-5-12 in the running battle, for the loss of one plane and one pilot, Rufus Moore.

Long after the Japanese had disengaged and landed to lick their wounds, the Mustang pilots were still engrossed in the battle to survive. Over 750 miles of ocean had yet to be crossed before the 15th could stand easy and balance the ledger. Several battle damaged P-51s were struggling toward an uncertain fate.

Bill Brown was the first to go down. Flying his P-51 on a southeast heading he had bailed out successfully near the *Pipefish*. The submarine retrieved him in less than two hours.

Bob Roseberry had used his DU to catch the 78th and its B-29 navigator, but his P-51, "Mrs. Rosie", was spilling gasoline at an irrevocable rate. "I called Major Tapp, the B-29, and everyone else I could think of, and informed one and all that I was going to bail out before we reached Iwo."

Like everyone else in the Group, "Rosie" was aware of the dismal record of those who had lately parachuted. That old phrase, "hitting the silk", had become a bad joke among these pilots. On the 16 April mission Bob had wached Jim Wightman clear his disabled P-51 and fall like a rock to the ocean. The memory of that scene was foremost as his fuel warning lights flashed their silent alarm. He was 60 miles from base.

> Just prior to the last of the gas, I called my wingman and told him I was getting out. For over an hour I had tried to think up some famous last lines but couldn't come up with a thing. So I slid back the hood, unhooked everything but the seat belt and rolled the plane over on its back. I pushed forward on the stick hard and hit the seat belt release, and just like that I was floating in space. It was quiet as Hell.

Tumbling through the sky, Bob was fascinated to see first the ocean, then the sky between his feet. Giving the rip cord what he considered a suitable yank, he realized that nothing was happening. Reaching back to claw at the chute pack he thought, "I wonder if its going to hurt when I hit the water. None of this past life flashing in front of my eyes stuff."

With both hands he gave the rip cord one more Herculean pull and was gratified by a breathtaking jerk as the canopy popped open. His wingman, agonizing above, was certain that the parachute had barely deployed before Roseberry hit the water.

He put out enough dye marker "to cover several acres of ocean", and waited as a P-61 orbited overhead. The Black Widow had summoned the Destroyer Es-

45th Sq officers in front of their tent. (Left to right) Bill Morrow, Adjutant, Don Statsmann, Jim Haglund, Supply Officer, Wes Brown, and Vince Reinert. (Source: Don Scott)

cort, *Brough*, which was several miles away but proceeding at flank speed.

Brown was safe onboard the submarine *Pipefish* and the DE *Brough* was going to fetch Roseberry as the rest of the Group began to pancake on Iwo Jima. Some, with battle damage, made more dramatic landings than others.

After 7 hours and 35 minutes of flying, Leon Sher was returning his battered P-51 to base. He was aware that he had a broken plane but he didn't know the full extent of the damage as he made a cautious approach to Runway 5. He knew that his plane was missing some elementary wing sections but was unable to see his tail wheel damage.

> I didn't know that, and I was trying for a three-point landing on only two points. However, I didn't have enough wing area left and I stalled out too early. All I could do was bury the nose in the ground. The Mustang pitched up vertically but didn't go over and flopped back down breaking its spine. All I got was a slight bruise on the nose from the gunsight.

After a few hours of rubber boating it, Bob Roseberry was helped on board the *Brough*. It wasn't until a couple of sailors came to his assistance that he realized his left arm was hurt. Apparently he had been hit by the tail as he left his plane. He had come close to that deadly contact that had cost the lives of so many other pilots. Roseberry's Law: "Get through the first two VLR missions and you have a chance" had been sorely tested. He had avoided death's mortal warrant at least four times this day. The Navy gave him no opportunity to brood, however:

> The Doctor on the DE checked me over, gave me a straight shot, then put my arm in a sling. That night the Navy got me into a game of hearts and took all the money I had, $10.00. After the game one of the officers suggested that I tell the rest of the pilots to carry more money as it hardly paid to fish us out at only ten bucks a head.

After Roseberry returned with his story of the unexpected dfficulty involved in pulling his rip cord, there was a mass parachute opening exercise on South Field. No one realized how hard it could be. To the contrary, pilots had for years avoided contact with the fabled ring is if it were a grenade pin. No one wanted to risk a chute opening on the ground, or worse, in a cockpit. It never dawned on them that it might not open at all, especially when needed. Perhaps this had been part of the distressing bail-out problem.

Several now P-51D-25 models had arrived on Iwo late in May. They were badly needed, as 13 aircraft had been lost or scrapped during the month. With the D-25 came a new gunsight, the K-14. It incorporated a gyro-actuated optical system that permitted the pilot to "dial in" the wing span of a known target aircraft. The range was then computed for targets from 200 to 800 yards. It was fancy equipment for men who has sharpened their shooting skills on trap ranges.

Another batch of old timers were awarded their tickets home in May. The Group Sergeant Major, James I. Moyer, had been in the Pacific for almost five years. A member of the original cadre, a founding father as it were, Moyer had been at Wheeler Field on 7 December 1941 as a Corporal, and had been wounded in that attack. Makin veterans, Captains Ennis, Henderson, Maltby, and Morey departed the 45th Squadron for the States. The 47th sent Captains Hintermeier, Down, Betner, Obenshain and Pepin home as well as their CO, Major John Piper. Captain Ed Markham assumed command of the 47th.

Deaths and stateside reassignment had left too many gaps in the ranks of the 45th Squadron. It had lost eight officers in action since arrival on Iwo and five more had rotated home. It was therefore necessary to transfer four of the 78th's seasoned pilots, Todd Moore, Harold Collins, John Patterson, and Albert Sherren to the 45th.

Men of the 47th Sq survey the wreckage of their orderly room after passage of a typhoon. (Source: John Whitcomb)

E. E. Westlund   J. R. Wightman   W. K. Wayland   L. R. Williams

Eldon "Cowboy" Wesltund lost all his 78th Sq tent mates during a six-week period. Jim Wightman's engine quit returning from Tokyo on 12 April. His chute failed to open. Wallace Wayland vanished in heavy weather on the Kyushu mission of 26 April. Bob Williams was shot down engaging enemy fighters over Matsudo A/D, Tokyo, on 25 May. (Source: Jim Vande Hey)

Pilots stationed on Iwo Jima were prone to claim that if there was a cloud anywhere in the Pacific it would be hanging around Iwo. This casual observation bore an element of truth. The region was a sort of meteorlogical stewpot. Migratory high pressure systems off the Asiatic continent mingled with Pacific highs in lines of convergence that formed severe weather fronts. These systems moved north with the sun. They were south of the Volcano Islands during the invasion and the early weeeks of Iwo's occupation, but moved north over the Nanpo Shoto through May and June.

These monumental fronts had become the primary nemesis of the Seventh Fighter Command and the Twenty-First Bomber Command. To augment the job of forecasting, B-24s were sent out on daily weather reconnaisance missions to the Empire. Despite these efforts, predicting the weather several hours in advance over such an enormous mass of water was little more than scientific conjecture.

The madness inherent in sending massed formations of planes into such unstable conditions was negated by strategic necessity. The air offensive against Japan could not be deferred. And so it was on 1 June 1945 that the Seventh Fighter Command sent their mightiest strike force yet against the weather. All three P-51 groups had been assembled for the first time to escort a huge force of B-29s on an incendiary raid to Osaka.

Following their B-29 navigators north, 184 Mustangs

*Walter Kreimann made a successful jump from his P-51 on 25 May but was burned. After several hours in the ocean he was resuced by the submarine, **Tigrone.** (Source: National Archives)*

Right: Ollie O'Mara and Monk Baldwin upgraded their standard of living from a tent to this classy shack. (Source: Ned Baldwin)

Below: Capt. Dwight Butler (on cowling) and other officers and EM admire 45th Sq Mustangs as they return from a mission. (Source: USAF)

were arrayed in group and squadron formations. The 15th, flying the middle position with 59 planes, formed part of that impressive force. Two hundred and fifty miles out, they began to encounter scattered cumulus clouds in layers. As the weather thickened, a B-29 weather ship ahead of the strike force gave coded advice that it had penetrated the front without difficulty and was proceeding on course to Osaka — "The oranges are sweet".

Before long the formation had entered a cathedral opening among the towering cumulus and they began an orbit while Group leaders and B-29 navigators conferred, with difficulty, by radio. The psychological pressure to push on, to accomplish the mission, was unstated but present. Over half of the Seventh Fighter Command's May sorties had aborted.

The front seemed to run from the ocean to heights far above the formation. Monk Baldwin thought the tops were near 70,000 feet. Lieutenant Colonel Jack Thomas, leading the 15th, agreed to proceed through what appeared to be a ragged hole to the north.

Minutes later, at a point some 375 miles from base the hole closed and the great gaggle of P-51s entered a solid bank of clouds. Visibility was reduced dangerously and turbulence was soon encountered. Thomas called for the B-29 navigators to deviate from their course or climb, but radio communications in the electrically charged atmosphere were breaking up. His pleas went unanswered.

As visibility went to zero, B-29s, fighter leaders, and planes flying on each other's wings began to lose visual contact. Suddenly the magnificent cohesive force was a jumble of disorganized individuals in a seething cauldron of the foulest weather. Seeking holes and light spots in the clouds, the pilots were like men trapped in a mine trying to tunnel their way to daylight.

"It was as thick as anything I've ever flown in," said Monk Baldwin, leading a flight from the 47th Squadron. "I couldn't see my number 3 and 4 men and started to climb with Allen White only five feet off my wing." Harry Van Zandt and Howard Liddell, the rest of Baldwin's flight, lost contact with each other and Van Zandt was swallowed by the weather.

Pilots lost horizons and were buffeted by a symphony of convection currents as rain pelted their canopies. Strapped in their coffin-like cockpits, they sweat profusely battling to control their bucking planes and the mental terror of vertigo as all reference to the known world vanished.

Charlie Klessig's P-51 was snapped over like a leaf in the wind and fell, spinning, for 3,000 feet before he recovered control.

Flying in a B-29 as a communications coordinator, 1st Lt. W. Malcomb Parry of the 45th Squadron was horrified as the accompaning fighters were consumed in the grey non-dimensional limbo. The radio chatter from dozens of Mustangs made it clear that a tragedy had inexorably been set in motion.

During the 15th's very struggle to stay airborne a B-29 navigator began leading part of the 506th Group in a 180-degree turn out of the weather. That turn led them blindly into the 15th's territory. Jack Thomas was appalled to see two 506th planes coming at him from right angles. He could read the numbers of the Mustangs as they sliced through his four-plane flight. Thomas pulled up sharply to avoid a collision and found himself alone. First Lieutenant Ken Dahlquist dove to avoid mid-air contact and his plane fell into a spin. He recovered at 3,500 feet. Lieutenants Jack Nelson and Don White were swept from the sky.

"May Day! May Day! I'm bailing out!" continuously crackled over the earphones as collisions, excess icing or turbulence sent planes tumbling toward the dark waters of the Nanpo Shoto. Those frantic calls were interspersed with desperate appeals for vectors. So many men were using their directional units and ASR frequencies that the channels became jammed and useless. Squadron leaders were ordering some units to return while others groped forward, fearing less the enemy ahead than the unseen terror behind.

In ones and twos, through the murky atmosphere, they would unexpectedly break into an open cavity and there find another lost stranger or an orbiting B-29. Planes of varying squadrons and groups would rally to each other and cling together like terrified wayfarers in a savage and foreign land. Occasionally, through holes in the overcast, pilots caught glimpses of P-51s spinning down in a descent of death.

Those who headed north, out of determination or desperation, took different paths to Osaka. Charles Cameron and his wingman, newcomer Major Truman Anderson, lost the rest of the 47th's Blue Flight when they entered the overcast. Cameron went down on instruments to a mere 50 feet over the water. As both ceiling and visibility improved he led his two-plane force higher and found a group of B-29s in a clear pocket at 8,000 feet. They were being escorted by two strays, 1st Lt. Phil Schlamberg of the 78th Squadron and a P-51 from the 21st Fighter Group.

Captain Joe Brunette's Maple Red Flight also tried to go below the weather. He broke out at 4,000 feet in a clear pocket with his wingman, 2nd Lt. Eric Hutchison, and found Purple Flight from the 78th Squadron, but Brunette had lost both Scamara and Lawrence Lortie from his 47th flight.

Jim Tapp, leading Purple Flight, had Cecil Grimes and Phil Maher glued to his wingtips. With Brunette's two planes the sorry little force percolated into the clear at 23,000 feet and found part of the B-29 strike force rallying at the departure point. Three more P-51s of the 21st Group joined the escort for the run over Osaka.

Bob Scamara, who did a solo act after losing contact with the flight and his wingman, Lortie, " . . . was frantically trying to fly instruments and keep a lookout for other planes that might be chewing into me at any second. After a few minutes went by without a collision, I breathed a little easier and began to climb, trying to get above the clouds."

Unable to find the top of the overcast, Scamara went back down, still on instruments, and broke out in a clear pocket at 3,000 feet. Alone on a heading for Osaka, Bob heard an order given to return to base. Having just woven his way through the charnel house of rotten weather and spinning aircraft, he had little incentive to turn back, and rather fancied his lonely quest.

As the ceiling slowly lifted he climbed back to 10,000 feet, where he had been when weather first engulfed the formation. In the distance he spotted a B-29 leading a four-plane flight of Mustangs.

> My first impulse was to join up, but this would place me under their control, so I just followed behind, climbing to 22,000 feet and came out at the bombers' rendezvous point off the coast. On reaching Osaka I saw B-29s going over the city in waves. The target was a fiery mass with smoke rising to over 25,000 feet right up to the overcast. I watched as the bombers entered the smoke column on a northerly course and came out on a 90 degree heading flying easterly. I decided to fly with them in escort position. Since I still had my wing tanks, I had plenty of gas, so after escorting the first wave, I returned to the bomber stream and picked up another wave. I was the only P-51 in sight and had to keep a respectful distance from the B-29s. They fired at me everytime I got too

Maintaining and servicing the Mustangs: T/Sgt. Marvin Udesen works over the guns on No. 191, a "Dogpatch" aircraft. (Source: Russell Bishop)

Maintaining and servicing the Mustangs: An engine change by 47th personnel. (Source: USAF)

Maintaining and servicing the Mustangs: Boresighting the guns on a 47th plane, Ser. No. 4-463914. T/Sgt. Tom Walker in the cockpit. Source: Russell Bishop)

Maintaining and servicing the Mustangs: Transporting belts of .50s to 47th Sq Mustangs. (Source: Russell Bishop)

> close. Not surprisingly, they couldn't imagine I was one of them.

Neither could the Japanese believe that any American escort fighters had gotten through. A lone twin-engined Nick began to let down right in front of the intrepid Lt. Scamara for a leisurely pass at a B-29.

> I whipped around to get behind him, dropping my wing tanks in the process, and applying full throttle. Then the engine quit.

Bob Scamara's mind spun like a gyro. He was alone, 25,000 feet over Japan, with a dead engine. If the B-29 gunners didn't nail him on the way down it seemed certain that the Japanese would get him. For a few seconds he was paralyzed with fear. Then he realized that in his eagerness to attack the Nick he had forgotten to throw the fuel switch. The Merlin was trying to suck gas from the wing tanks now tumbling earthward. Switching to his internal fuel, the engine coughed back to life.

> As I approached the Nick I fired at his left side. Pieces started to fly off, his landing gear flopped down and he began to burn. I had almost overrun him and had to throttle power back all the way to stay behind. I crossed over through the fire to his right side giving him another burst. Then, still coasting, I came up alongside and watched. The cockpit was a mass of flames. As one wing dropped off, then the other, the Nick fell into a spin burning all the way down.

Scamara had now lost sight of the bombers. With the overcast still present, no other planes about, and the route home filled with dark clouds, Bob felt a sense of panic. Calling on various radio channels he established contact with a B-29. He was given a vector for Iwo and felt a surge of reassurance.

Major Tapp's flight had arrived over Osaka hauling a load of rockets. After flying the long trip north and contemplating another encounter with the weather front on the way back, he didn't intend to perform any low-level antics. They salvoed their rockets in the

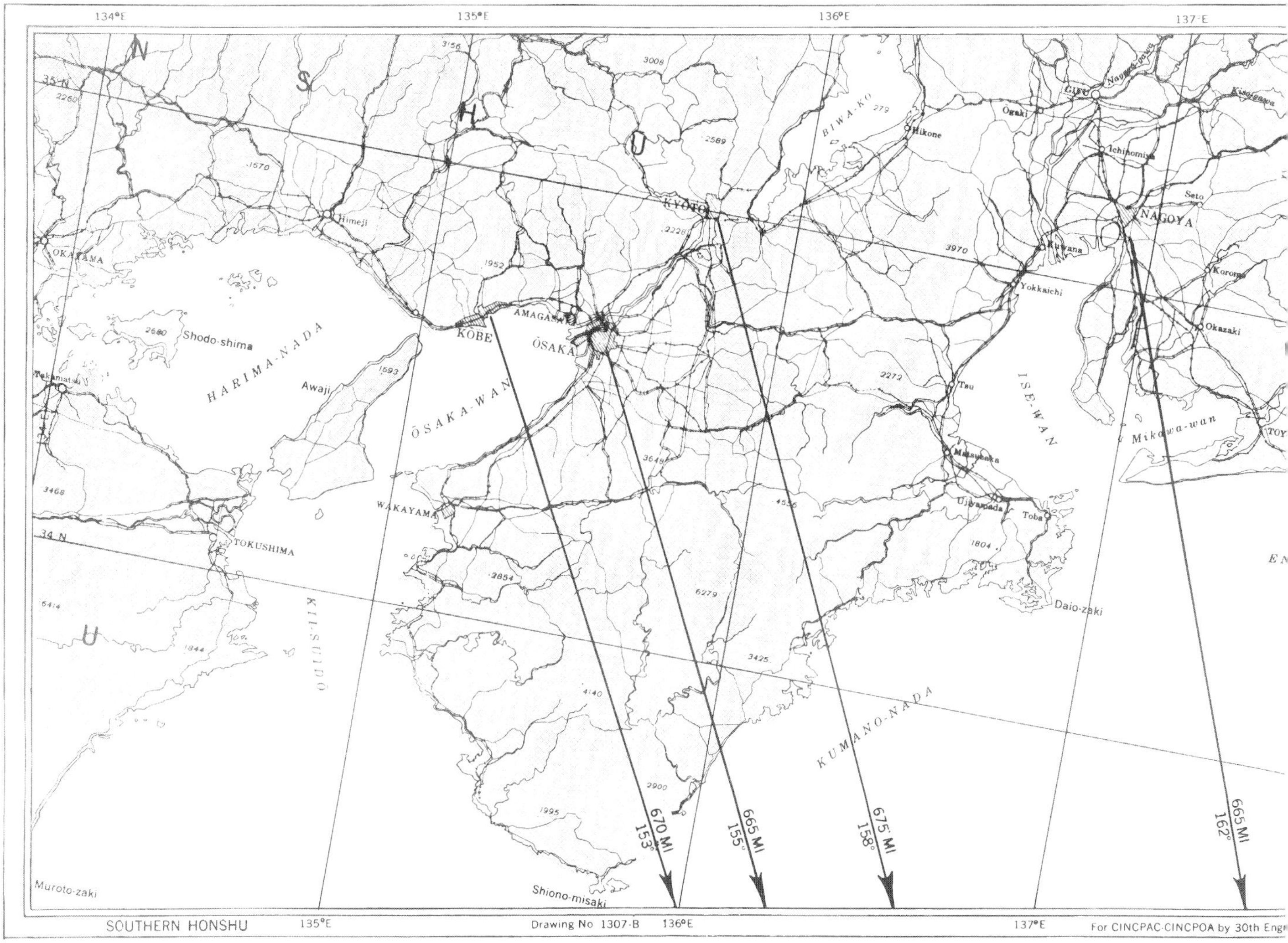

134°E
135°E
136°E
137°E
35°N
34°N
KYOTO
NAGOYA
KOBE
OSAKA
AMAGASAKI
Himeji
OKAYAMA
Shodo-shima
HARIMA-NADA
Awaji
OSAKA-WAN
WAKAYAMA
TOKUSHIMA
KII-SUIDO
Takamatsu
Hikone
Ogaki
GIFU
Ichinomiya
Seto
Kuwana
Yokkaichi
Okazaki
Tsu
ISE-WAN
Mikawa-wan
Toba
Daio-zaki
KUMANO-NADA
BIWA-KO
Shiono-misaki
Muroto-zaki
670 MI 153°
665 MI 155°
675 MI 158°
665 MI 162°
SOUTHERN HONSHU
Drawing No 1307-B
For CINCPAC-CINCPOA by 30th Engr

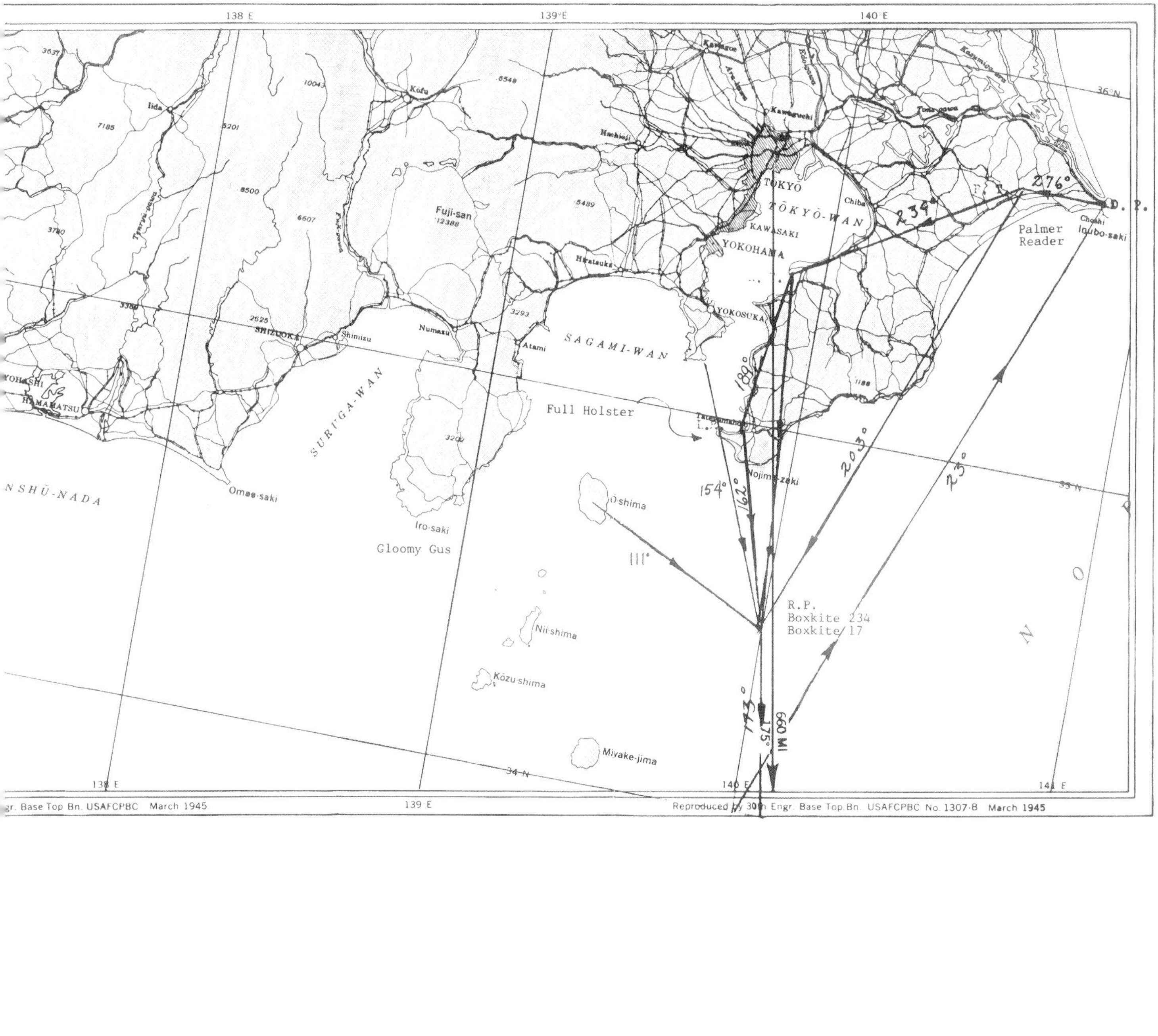
138 E
139 E
140 E
TOKYO
TŌKYŌ-WAN
KAWASAKI
YOKOHAMA
YOKOSUKA
Chiba
Hachioji
Kawaguchi
Kofu
Iida
Fuji-san
Hiratsuka
Numazu
Atami
Shimizu
SHIZUOKA
HAMAMATSU
SAGAMI-WAN
SURUGA-WAN
NSHŪ-NADA
Omae-saki
Iro-saki
O-shima
Nii-shima
Kōzu-shima
Miyake-jima
Nojima-zaki
Choshi
Inubo-saki
36 N
35 N
34 N
Full Holster
Gloomy Gus
Palmer
Reader
I.P.
R.P.
Boxkite 234
Boxkite 17
276°
234°
189°
203°
73°
154°
162°
111°
173°
175°
660 MI
141 E
Reproduced by 30th Engr. Base Top.Bn. USAFCPBC No. 1307-B March 1945
Engr. Base Top Bn. USAFCPBC March 1945

Parachuting had become a near fatal exercise and a practice sling was rigged. (Source: John Sullivan)

general direction of Osaka, scanned the sky for enemy planes, then tacked onto some returning B-29s.

Cameron and Anderson, following their B-29s over Osaka, caught some flak for their trouble. Anderson's plane was damaged at the IP. Then they fended off a lone Zeke before returning to the Rally Point and joining a B-29 navigator.

Back at Agate Base radio intercepts made it apparent that this had been a flawed mission. The first planes had returned after only four hours with gaps in their ranks and stories of the prodigious weather front and its nether world of terror. Small flights of mixed Mustangs and B-29s had begun to pancake about noon. It would be four more agonizing hours before the planes that had penetrated the front would return.

The flight line was packed wth people waiting in small nervous knots. Pilots, mechanics and ground staff scanned the sky counting planes and searching for friends. Chaplains Jamison and Norton paced the line with officers from Fighter Command staff.

Walter Kreimann, freshly returned from his tour of duty with the Navy, was delighted to be back and anticipated a hero's welcome. Instead, he was greeted by long faces.

"I couldn't figure out what was wrong until I finally got someone to talk. The planes were trickling back, but not enough of them."

Monk Baldwin returned with a B-29 navigator and fifteen P-51s from various units. The navigator, Walnut 7, had seen a pilot parachute below the front, and Monk had scoured the waters at low level for half an hour without success. He landed at 1245.

Predictably, the weather had edged south toward Iwo Jima and many pilots used the DU to home in on the island.

Those who had made it to Osaka were the last to return. Joe Wagner, flying alone through the clouds and rain, landed at 1415. Tapp, Grimes, and Maher followed. Brunette, Hutchison, and Schlamberg landed about 15 minutes later. Cameron and Anderson pancaked at 1525. Bob Scamara was the last P-51 down. He had been in the cockpit for nearly nine hours.

Malcomb Parry, in his B-29 navigator, was last member of the Group to land. He had been airborne for 10½ hours with a grandstand seat and all the communications equipment at his command to monitor the unfolding tragedy. He verified the scope of the loss and certified the events that had enveloped the mission. He was "deeply distressed that a considerable number of fine young men had died" in a mission which "probably should have been aborted." Because of his commanding view of the operation he was asked to prepare a written report for higher authority. Lieutenant Colonel Thomas reassured him that he should "tell it like it was."

The Seventh Fighter Command hadn't suffered such a blow since the Japanese attack on Wheeler Field. Twenty-seven Mustangs had failed to return. Air sea rescue units, working in the same terrible weather, picked up two pilots of the 506th Fighter Group before day's end. However, that seemed to erase the final lingering hope.

The sadness within the 15th Fighter Group was deep and inconsolable. They had lost ten comrades — not to the enemy, but to weather. The survivors were exhausted and shaken by the ordeal.

Then the frustration and anger took over. Why had the weather ship given them the green light? Why did the B-29 navigators lead them into such deplorable weather? Why hadn't they diverted as Thomas had requested? Why the bad communications? Every member of the Group was touched by the disaster. They felt as if they were actors in a Shakespearean tragedy.

These men had never shrunk from danger; indeed they had sought mortal combat. But in the fearsome arithmetic of war's bookkeeping they perceived the cost to be greater than the gain.

There was an investigation. General Hap Arnold, Chief of the Army Air Forces, even showed up to ask questions. Of couse, there was no real fault finding, nor could there be. It was the war that had brought them to this god forsaken place in the Pacific. And it was the war that sent them up in fragile machines to defy gravity, the enemy and the elements. It was 750 miles from Iwo to the Empire and death held all the prerogatives along that perilous route. These men had consciously placed themselves in harm's way the day they pinned on their wings.

A tropical depression, with its attendant foul weather, mercifully kept the Group earthbound for the next several days. It also curtailed air/ sea rescue units as the storm swelled into a full-fledged typhoon by 6 June. Iwo was battered by wind and rain.

North of the Bonins, cruising above the Nanpo Shoto Trench, the submarine *Trutta* was submerged at 200 feet procceding toward Lifeguard station off Honshu, some 400 miles north. Even at that depth, mountainous seas rocked the ship. Surfacing briefly at dawn, Lt. Commander F. P. Hoskins, skipper of the *Trutta*, recorded waves of forty to fifty feet. He and his bridge crew were lashed by 100 knot winds. The 1500-ton submarine was being tossed about like a piece of driftwood. Hoskins cleared the bridge and sought the safety of the depths. Two hundred feet below the waves *Trutta* still rolled up to 10 degrees.

At 1330 Hoskins rose to periscope depth. The barometer had hit bottom and was rising. Seas were moderate and *Trutta* had to get up speed to get on station. The submarine finally surfaced and began churning northward. That forenoon, 7 June, lookouts spotted the unmistakable flash of a yellow rubber life raft on a swell, dead ahead. Proceeding toward this bit of flotsam, without much conviction, the crew was amazed to find it occupied by a living human being.

After six full days at sea, 2nd Lt. Arthur A. Burry, a member of the 45th Squadron, had been miraculously found. He was located about 300 miles north northwest of Iwo Jima and about 50 miles west of Sofu Gun rock. He had been thrown from his raft countless times in the howling typhoon of the 6th. Burry was weak from hunger and exposure, had suffered delirium during his final night at sea, but he perked up once aboard the submarine.

The balance sheet for the VLR mission of 1 June 1945 was finally closed. Fate had stealthily snatched ten pilots from the Group's roster and then, almost mystically, had given one back.

The Field Order for 7 June looked like a re-run of the 1 June mission. All three P-51 Groups were scheduled to escort over 400 Superforts to Osaka.

The 47th Sq lines up for a pre-takeoff photo before the ill-fated mission of 1 June 45. Six of them were lost in a weather front a few hours later: (Left to right) Front row: John Fitzgerald, Bob Andersen, Paul Frick (KIA 1 June), Al Dibelka (KIA 1 June), Harry Van Zandt (KIA 1 June), Ed Markham, CO, Joe Brunnette, Charlie Cameron, Don Locke; standing: Sam Jones, Don White (KIA 1 June), Charlie Jennings (KIA 1 June), Bob Scamara, Ollie O'Mara, Allen White, Howard Liddell (KIA 14 June), Monk Baldwin, Joe Wagner, Erick Hutchison, Charlie Klessig, Roy June, Emil Schroeder (KIA 1 June). (Source: John Whitcomb)

The exercise began badly as Lt. Leon Sher crashed on take-off. Because of a faulty tail wheel assembly he skewed off the runway just before his plane had reached flying speed. He rode it to a grinding crash over some bunkers near the end of the runway. He was out of his plane "before it had come to a stop" with gasoline from the wing tanks exploding behind him.

Leon stumbled into the nearest sanctuary to avoid the fire and landed on a Marine officer who was the regular occupant. Totaly unsympathetic to the aviator's plight, the Marine roared, "Get the hell out of here."

Sher felt like a drunk who had come home and

The grand opening of the 47th Squadron's new Officers Club: Left — The "Dogpatchers" bar. Right — Brig. Gen. Mickey Moore (center, hat under arm) attended the gala. Maj. Ed Markham, Sq CO, stands at the General's left. (Source: John Fitzgerald)

entered the wrong house. Stunned from the harrowing escape all he could think of was, "Gee! I'm sorry. I didn't mean to jump into your foxhole." Thirty years later he had a casual meeting with the same Marine. "Those guys are sure mean. He was still mad at me for jumping into his damn foxhole."

As the rest of the 47th roared over the burning wreckage, Aviation Engineers scraped the P-51 out of the way, added a few feet of volcanic ash and lengthened the runway right over it. Staggering back to the Squadron area, Sher caught more verbal flak.

Captain Chet Oster, Squadron Engineering Officer, wanted to know, "Where's your plane?"

Pointing wearily in the direction of the crash, Sher answered, "They buried it."

"Well, you'd better get the Form 5 out of it, or you'll end up paying for that thing."

Leon smiled as he contemplated the possible punishment they could extract from him in restitution for an unaccounted P-51. Maybe they's send him home.

After eight other aborts, less dramatic than Leon Sher's, the strike force was whittled down to 46 planes from the 15th Group. Lieutenant Colonel DeWitt Spain was mission leader, and this time a Squadron CO, Major Ed Markham, rode along in a B-29 as mission coordinator.

There was almost total cloud cover all the way from the rendezvous to the coast of Honshu. There, the clouds built up to 15,000 feet completely obscuring the target and most of Honshu Island. Climbing high above the overcast, the Group took up position several thousand feet above the bombers and had a panoramic view of the strike.

As black flak smudged the white clouds at the B-29s' altitude, a single Nick appeared to try a forlorn pass. Major Moore was after him like a panther and sent the enemy plane flaming through the cloud layer.

Retiring from the target, the weather cleared over the ocean and the Group pilots could clearly pick out the Lifeguard subs and the rescue destroyers on the return trip. Everything was in place and working to perfection. All planes made it back to Iwo after some seven hours and forty minutes. The weather had been a pussycat. This mission had been a piece of cake.

A fighter sweep of Kagamigahara Airdrome near Nagoya was ordered for 8 June, but was totally thwarted by weather. Climbing to 22,000 feed on course through an overcast, the Group was soon facing a front with buildups to over 30,000 feet. The Mustangs were only 60 miles away from Iwo and mission leader Lt. Colonel John Mitchell was not about to preside over a repeat of the 1 June disaster. He aborted the mission.

On 10 June the Group went into the breech again, bound for a sweep of Atsugi Airdrome at Tokyo. Many B-29 units were also ticketed for targets around the Japanese capital and arrived somewhat ahead of the mustang.

The Japanese had a complex visual air-raid-warning network as well as a radar warning system. However, their radar lacked range, only providing about 55 minutes notice. The ground spotters were useful for inland targets but provided scant advance warning of attacks on east coast cities. The radar, furthermore, was seldom able to detect fighters or to determine if bombers were accompanied by fighters. With a paucity of interceptors, the Japanese had decided to use a tactical plan to expend their defensive effort against the B-29s and avoid contact with U.S. fighters. Apparently they had assumed that the B-29s were coming in unescorted on this particular day.

Within minutes of leaving the IP the 47th Squadron got into a dogfight with Franks while still at 15,000 feet. The entire Group dropped wing-tanks and proceeded to engage over forty enemy aircraft in scattered battles above and around the bomber stream. The action was so intense that they never did get down on the deck to strafe Atsugi. It was the kind of air battle to which the Group had been looking forward.

Bogies were being called in from all directions and

Tally Ho's were being sung out with youthful passion and exuberance.

Major Wayne Wells, Group Operations Officer, led his flight into some Franks. Warren Reed said, "They were stacked from 3,000 to 6,000 feet below us going the opposite direction. We did a wingover and peeled down after them."

Major Wells let the first two go but then latched onto the tail of the formation. His first target blazed at the wing roots, then advancing up the line he "burned another fighter in the flight ahead."

The Franks scattered and tried to turn back into the P-51s. One was trying to maneuver into position for a shot on 1st Lt. Jule Mitchell, but stalled out right in front of Warren Reed. "I gave him a quick burst and had to roll the ship to miss him. I was about 50 feet away when the Frank caught fire."

The fourth member of Wells' flight, Major Truman Anderson, was flying Wells' wing. "It was the first time I'd ever gotten that close to a Japanese airplane. The one I got for sure did a slow split-S in front of me. I hit him right in the canopy and when I last saw him he was spiralling down."

Hearing the 47th call out the first contact, Major Todd Moore, leading the 45th, waded into the action with the Franks and destroyed one for his eleventh victory.

Lieutenant Colonel John Mitchell, leading the mission, joined with Major Howard Sutterlin to burn a Hamp. Sutterlin then teamed up with First Lieutenant Fred Grover to share another victory while Grover split an Oscar with 2nd Lt. Malcolm Sedam in a neat bit of team effort. Fred Baumann added another victory to the 78th's daily bag on his birthday. Doyle Brooks "tore the tail off" one Zeke and got his second Zeke in a screaming 4000 foot dive at 450 m.p.h.

Enroute to the rally point the 78th was jumped by an aggressive flight of cannon equipped Kawanishi "George" fighers. Doyle Brooks was calling out a radio warning of the attack, but Tom McCullough was trying to DU his flight to a navigator B-29 and didn't hear the alarm. Tom spotted the enemy just as they engaged.

> He turned into me and I automatially turned back into him, but I got hit first. I temporarily lost control of the plane and ended up on the deck before I took charge again. I contacted a B-29 for assistance and he told me he had to drop his bombs first. So I followed him back to Japan while he made his delivery.

Doyle Brooks and Paul Martin each shot up one George to end the engagement and the Group reformed at the Rally Point minus McCullough.

Flight Officer Billy Singleton landed with only 15 gallons of gas and Tom McCullough logged eight hours, much of it trying to fly his damaged plane behind a B-29. "They throw off the damnedest prop wash." However, the noses were all there when counted — everyone had survived and that was what counted.

The mood at interrogation was one of "exhilaration." Bob Worton kept asking if anyone else had heard the Japanese voice on A Channel saying, "American boy, American boy, come down and get little Jap boy!" No one had gone down and the flak had not taken its usual toll. For the first time in weeks the Japanese had slugged it out in the air. The Group destroyed 16, probably got four more and damaged eight.

Along with the routine hazing of Chichi Jima each three or four days, the Group took their regular turns at CAP. Interceptions of bogies generally turned out to be errant B-29s or Navy carrier planes. During one of those seemingly dull missions, 2nd Lt. Ed Liddell of the 47th, disappeared in the early mists of a dawn patrol. It was believed that pilot and plane went down about 15 miles north of Iwo Jima on 14 June though no wreckage was ever found.

Most air alerts on Iwo had come at night when CAP was the responsibility of the P-61s of the 548th and 549th Night Fighter Squadrons. These heavily-armed, radar-equipped planes were adept at finding the Japanese hecklers, but the enemy began using a jet or rocket assisted auxiliary unit to give them the thrust necessary for escape. Lt. Colonel Jimmy Alford, an old grey beard with the Command, in charge of night fighter operations, decided to try having the speedy Mustangs of the 15th ride shotgun with the P-61s. He picked a couple of his proteges for the experiment: Monk Baldwin and Joe Brunette. Both had first trained and served as single-engined pilots with the 6th Day and Night Fighter Squadron on Oahu and had transferred to the 47th Squadron before the trip to Iwo Jima.

On two nights in June, Brunette and Baldwin took off with P-61 Black Widows to exercise their cat eyes. The official history called the experiment "unprecedented" but the test failed largely because the three high-speed aircraft had too much trouble staying together without colliding. "It was blacker than the inside of a cow," recalled Monk.

However, these night sorties by the P-51s inspired Major Wells, Group Operations Officer, to fantasize about night VLR missions. The B-29s had begun night raids on Honshu and Wells reasoned that the Japanese night fighters wouldn't be expecting an escort. "You'll have a field day," he said.

By his own admission Monk Baldwin was a "civilian at heart" all the time he was in the service, so he was barely tolerant in his response to his superior. "Now can you imagine flying 750 miles at night over water and ever coming back home? You lead the first night mission and I'll go with you."

The judgement of the veteran night-fighter pilots prevailed, so there were never any VLR missions in the dark. Baldwin considered each completed daylight VLR trip a minor miracle based on his law of averages. It was with good reason. Monk was just a few weeks from a one-way ticket to the Empire.

The Group set off for Osaka on 15 June, but aborted

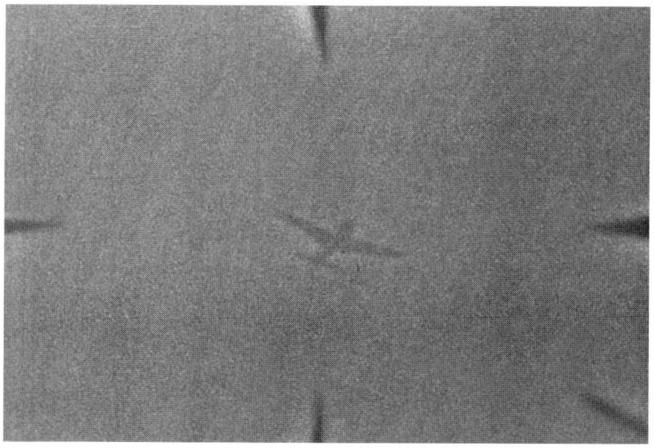

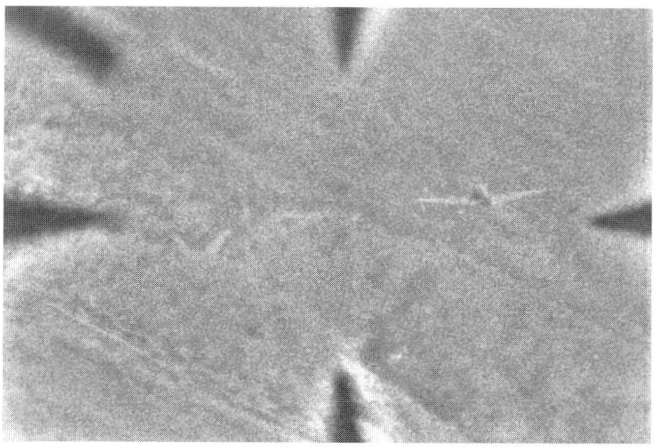

The Group fought a furious air battle against superior numbers of enemy fighters on 23 June 45 over Honshu. They scored 9 - 1 - 15, losing three P-51s and one pilot. Scamara and Scanlan were surrounded by Japanese fighters and Scanlan was lost. The sequence of gun camera shots show some of Bob Scamara's encounters as he shot down three and damaged seven enemy planes. (Source: Bob Scamara)

the mission when a weather ship flying ahead of the strike ran into an insurmountable front and returned.

The mission had started badly as Captain Joe Fitzsimmons lost his engine just after takeof. Without sufficient altitude to jump, he ditched his 78th Squadron P-51 just off the beach at Iwo Jima with an audience of thousands. He jettisoned the canopy, cut the switches and tried to bring the Mustang down nose high in a soft surfing attitude. But the underside airscoop acted like an instant anchor. "She just mushed into the water on her belly," said Fitzsimmons.

No question about it, the P-51 was a great airplane, but a lousy boat. Still in the cockpit, the pilot was under ten feet of water almost instantly. Though aching from cracking his nose on the gunsight, Joe released his straps and belt and shot to the surface when he inflated his Mae West. The Navy had him back ashore within an hour.

In the middle of June the 15th Group sent up 44 planes in an old fashioned, Pineapple Air Force type aerial review. The formation flew over Iwo Jima to honor several of their own who were being awarded medals by General Hap Arnold. Among those decorated were Major Tim Tapp, who won the nation's second highest award, the Distinguished Service Cross. Tapp also received the D.F.C. Major Todd Moore had the Silver Star and D.F.C. pinned on by General Arnold and Bob Scamara recieved the Silver Star.

Knowing that Moore was a Squadron CO and an 11-victory ace, the Commanding General of the Army Air Forces was obliged to ask, "How old are you, son?" Todd had recently turned 23. It was a young man's game, but even the young matured quickly in the bracing atmosphere of the Empire run.

Even an aborted mission, such as the one of 19 June, contained the elements of near disaster. The strike got out only 200 miles when it was forced to turn back by an impenetrable front. All planes landed safely, but the excitement had occurred as several heavily burdened fighters cracked up during take off. Joe Brunette walked away from his wrecked P-51 as did 2nd Lt. Ed Bates, but 2nd Lt. Robert Thornton was seriously hurt when the wing tanks on his 45th Squadron Mustang exploded. He was dragged from the wreckage with second- and third-degree burns.

Second Lieutenant John Fitzgerald was taking off as Joe Brunette's wingman and nearly became the fourth accident of the day. As Brunette's plane veered out of control and ground looped, Fitzgerald had to do some fancy footwork to avoid being a party to Brunette's trouble.

> I started to reduce power, scissored out of his way, then poured the power on, trying to take off. I felt certain that I couldn't brake to a stop before I reached the end of the runway.
>
> As I crossed the end of the strip I had barely horsed my plane off the ground. I was flying but not very well. I dipped into a shallow spot beyond the end of the runway and the ground crews back down the field lost sight of me for a moment. I was skimming over rocks and tents just a few feet off the ground on the brink of crashing when I crossed over a downslope leading to the beach. This put more air under me so I lowered the nose just a bit to gain flying speed.

Fighting his way along the invisible tightrope between flying and stalling, John Fitzgerald was dueling with the laws of physics and "sweating blood." By this time the rest of the 47th Squadron was roaring off the airfield and passing over John's struggling Number 191. They were banking to look down and were waving at him. At first he thought they were congratulatory waves; then he recognized they were of the frantic variety:

> I suddenly realized what all the signals meant; my gear and flaps were still down. In my white-knuckled attempt to get airborne I had neglected to retract wheels and flaps.

Once the aircraft was cleaned up, 191 flew like a bird. This mission had been a cliff hanger before the Group had even rendezvoused, and after the order to abort, it didn't even count as a sortie. It was nothing more than a dangerous airplane ride.

The weather cooperated on the next attemped VLR mission. With Jack Thomas leading, 54 Mustangs set out to strike Tokyo area airfields on 23 June 1945.

On this particular day the enemy was up in force and although they may have intended to engage B-29s all they found were Mustangs. The Superforts were not out this day.

The Japanese air defense force was, by this time, a mixture of green, poorly trained pilots and a scattering of veterans who had survived years of war. Air-sea rescue, as the Americans devoutly practiced it, had been disdained by the Japanese high command. In a reverse dogma, they had squandered their trained and dedicated aircrews in the early stages of the conflict with fatalistic Bushido philosophy. As the Allied vise closed on Japan, it became apparent that these experienced flyers were a perishable commodity not renewable through a seasonal harvest. By the time this imperative had become self-evident, it was too late to recall those who had been cast off. However, even inexperienced Japanese pilots when led by skilled veteran officers could be aggressive and persistent. On 23 June the sky over Honshu was filled with belligerent combatants on both sides.

Just four minutes after leaving the departure point the 47th Squadron was jumped by many enemy fighters who had been waiting at higher altitude. Making overhead, head-on, and high side passes the Franks broke up the P-51 formations as pilots wrenched their planes about to avoid streams of tracers.

Bob Scamara, an element leader in Harold Baccus' flight, "rolled over on my back, dove a little, then pulled back up" just in time to get behind a Frank that had overshot the formation. Chasing the enemy plane into a cloud bank, Bob was surprised to see that his wingman, Jack Scanlan, had stayed with him through the violent maneuvers.

Harold Baccus' Yellow Flight, of the 47th, had been scattered and damaged by the onslaught. His wingman, 2nd Lt. Lamar Christian, had been hit and his plane fatally damaged. Harold lashed out at the enemy fighters hitting two Franks as he protected Christian. Fighting his way toward the sea, Baccus sent out distress calls to Dumbo and the nearest Lifeguard sub. There was no response but the two planes headed for the station some 30 miles offshore.

Lieutenant Colonel Thomas, flying with the 47th Squadron, had avoided the first vicious attack. He and his wingman, F/O Fronnie Jones had then pitched into the Franks and each shot down one. Thomas had perforated another, but had to let him go as the convulsive air battle alternately made the hunter the hunted.

Frank Ayers, leading the 47th's Green Flight, had lost his three wingmates in the first wild maneuvers of the dog fight. Alone, he got on the tail of a Frank and exploded it, then went after another. His tracers started the Japanese fighter smoking and its right landing gear dropped as it dove for cover into a cloud.

Turning back to find his Squadron mates, Ayers was weaving to cover his own backside.

> I had turned left and saw nothing and then turned back and saw a Jack right on tope of me with

In the aftermath of the 23 June VLR mission, the sub, ***Trepang,*** *rescued Frank Ayers and Lamar Christian. After a month of "Lifeguard" duty the sub docks at Guam with 30 Army aviators. Ayers is standing seventh from the left and Christian is standing far right arm in sling. (Source: National Archives)*

> tracers blazing out of his wings. He was on me alright. He knocked an eight inch hole in my right wing and the top of the cowl was riddled from prop spinner right to the windshield. Gas sprayed all over my canopy but didn't burn. I dove away and started back.

With a brief respite in the air action, Scamara and Scanlan had joined up with Jack Thomas and his flight and were proceeding toward assigned ground targets. Again they were attacked from above and behind, this time by six Georges. "I was flying about one quarter mile abreast of the Colonel," recalls Bob Scamara, when he turned into me. I knew that meant Japs on my tail so Scanlan and I quickly turned, passed Thomas, and pulled up into a mess of enemy planes."

Scanlan hit one and Scamara sent another plunging down on fire into Lake Kasumiga-ura. A wild dogfight ensued and Scamara thought the whole Japanese air force must be after him and his wingman. Things were happening so rapidly tha Scamara couldn't get his K-14 computing gunsight to compute fast enough. He was going through a series of hectic aerobatic maneuvers flicking off bursts and cursing himself because he seemed to be just missing the streaking Japanese fighters. He finally broke out of the hornet's nest on the tail of one enemy plane and followed it to the deck, scoring hits. The Japanese fighter began a tree-top escape to the north and Scamara decided not to follow deeper into Japan.

Glancing over his shoulder for the first time in several minutes Scamara was relieved to see his faithful wingman. Through all those gyrations Jack Scanlan was still flying with him. Bob and Jack had been friends since flying school at Luke Field and had implicit trust in each other. They made a great team.

Climbing and heading back south, the two lone Mustangs flew abreast, about one quarter mile apart so they could watch each other's tails.

> It wasn't long before we were tapped again. They were really out to get us. I called a warning to Jack and a flight of Zekes was on us. We tore right back at them.
>
> If there was ever a time to run for it, that was the moment, but I don't think either of us ever considered it. All we could think of was to kill those devils. I saw Jack get one but there were a few too many, more than I could count.
>
> After I had rolled out of a turn and could see Jack, I knew it was a little too late for me to help him. There were two Zekes sneaking up on his tail. I was heading toward him and yelling over the radio for him to do something, but he flew straight and level. His radio must already have been hit. I came on firing and calling him, but the Japanese fighters hit him in the wings and set him on fire. I could see his ammunition exploding as he pulled up, rolled over, and jumped.

As Scanlan floated down in his parachute over the Chiba Peninsula, he was surrounded by menacing enemy fighters. Scamara tore into them like an enraged bull until only two of his six guns were still firing. With Japanese planes still above him and his ammunition almost completely expended, he dove for the deck and headed for the rally point at full throttle. In the vicious and protracted battles he had expended over 1800 rounds of .50 caliber ammunition shooting down three and damaging seven enemy aircraft.

After the initial engagement with Franks in which 2nd Lts. Endrew G. Elliott and Robert C. Burnett of the 47th had each drawn blood, they were scattered and disorganized by the superior numbers. Elliott found himself alone and was about to be attacked by an estimated 25 Jacks flying in a long string formation. He applied full power and outdistanced the enemy fighters.

The 78th Squadron was proceeding to Shimodate Airdrome as planned without enemy interference. As usual, those venomous HVAR rockets were carried, this time by eight P-51s. Captain Nelson Merrill led the airfield strike, disintegrating a hangar with rockets and destroying or damaging six planes on the ground with strafing passes. The 78th was impressed with the ingenuity of Japanese airdrome defenses. For the first time, four barrage balloons were sighted tethered between three and four thousand feet over an airfield. Dummy aircraft or junk hulks were also in wide use at Shimodate.

Neither the 78th nor the 45th Squadrons experienced serious aerial resistance. It seemed that the enemy interceptors had staked out an air superiority area into which the 47th Fighter Squadron had stumbled. The plan had been effective. Scanlan was down on Japanese soil, hopefully a prisoner, while Christian and Ayers were preparing to join the Navy.

Baccus had led Lamar Christian as close to the rescue submarine as the faltering P-51 would allow. Lamar took to his chute, breaking his collar bone as he hit the ineludible tail, but landed alive five miles north of the Lifeguard submarine *Trepang*. Frank Ayers followed close behind:

> As I got over the edge of Tokyo, ground fire tore all but a couple of inches off my right aileron and blew some more holes in the wing and fuselage. It knocked the hell out of things. I was going wide open and could only coax 240 m.p.h. out of her.

Six more Japanese fighters began to follow Frank's battered Mustang so he put the nose down and added a little more speed. The Japanese gave up the chase figuring, correctly, that Ayers' P-51 didn't have much flying time remaining.

Lieutenants Allen White and Leon Sher, who were flying sub cover, met Frank Ayers as he limped over *Trepang*. They were amazed that he was still airborne. The fuselage of the Mustang had a hole behind the cockpit "big enough for a man to jump through." With the usual difficulty Ayers tried to extricate himself from the P-51. Though he was an expert at the exercise, it took two tries before he could overcome the slipstream and fall free. His chute opened beautifully and he waved cherrily to White and Sher. Any successful bailout and rescue was cause for relief. Frank was twice blessed, having previously completed a jump and DD rescue on 7 April. He was picked up within minutes by the *Trepang* which had just taken Christian aboard.

The rest of the Group had already left the Rally Point enroute back to Iwo Jima when White and Sher felt secure in relinquishing their cover for the submarine. They chased the last B-29 navigator for 40 minutes before catching him.

Sher barely touched down on the end of the runway at Iwo when his engine died. White's engine ran out of gas half way down the strip. They had been airborne for eight hours and fifteen minutes.

The interrogation after the mission was tense and somber. The Group took little satisfaction in their nine air victories. They had lost three planes and while Christian and Ayers appeared to be safe, Scanlan's fate was unknown.

Trying to sort out the facts, Sandy Sanders was debriefing a shocked and listless Bob Scamara. When he asked about the lopsided dogfight with the Zeros, Bob said quietly, "One of them shot down Jack. They weren't going to do that to my buddy." It wasn't until one year later that Scanlan's true fate was revealed. Wounded and taken prisoner in Chiba Prefecture, he was released by local military authorities to a vigilante mob that lynched him.

Reflecting on the intensity of the bruising 1640 mile mission, Harold Baccus thought it was the toughest yet — "the ultimate test of nerve and stamina."

June ended with two disappointing ventures; one an escort to Nagoya on the 26th and the last, an aborted fighter sweep to Tokyo.

John Mitchell, leading the VLR escort of 26 June, played cloud tag with a few unaccomodating enemy interceptors. An ace of long experience and great repute, Lt. Colonel Mitchell got his sights on a Zeke and exploded it. Second Lietuenant Doug Reese of the 45th put a burst into a lone Tony and its pilot parachuted. For 47 other pilots it was just seven boring hours in a cramped cockpit with a canteen of water and some candy for nourishment and a packet of Benzedrine pills to keep them awake.

The next day Lt. Colonel Thomas led the Group north for 400 miles before an advance weather ship reported a front barring the route. It ran from the deck up to 35,000 feet. Thomas turned the Group around and put them in a string formation to give Tori Shima Island a thorough hosing of .50 caliber fire. There was a landing craft on one shore and other signs of obvious military activity. Though Tori Shima was not particularly menacing, it gave Thomas vicarious pleasure to fire his guns at anything enemy.

So ended June 1945, a month of general bordeom and frustration interspersed with moments of stark terror. The Group had lost eleven pilots in those brief encounters with fate.

Attrition of a more pleasant nature had also changed the complexion of the 15th. Major Art Bridge was reassigned to the States turning over command of his

45th Squadron to Captain Harold Collins. Other pilots of the 45th, all Makin veterans, who returned home included Captains George Hunter, Bruce Campbell, Bill Fisher, and George Dunlap. Captains Vic Mollan and Lucien Parish of the 78th also got their tickets stateside as did Group officers Lt. Colonel DeWitt Spain and Major Rich Birk. Likewise, a few Master and Tech Sergeants won rotation, some after more than four years of service with the 15th.

Air leaders, Jim Tapp, Todd Moore, and Ed Markham got all too brief leaves. Captain Merrill took temporary command of Tapp's 78th Squadron and Captain Walter Powell of Ed Markham's 47th.

Second Lieutenants who had learned the nuances of fighter operations under these veterans, advanced in rank and responsibility to take over leadership positions. Many new pilots arriving from the training fields of the U.S. filled in the wingman slots. It was a rather strange "pilgrim's progress" dominated by durability and death.

With another month behind them the men of the Group had improved their lot. Mess halls had been built to replace the tents, and Quonset huts had sprung up for many essential services. The 47th even completed the Group's first Officer's Club with a grand opening on 20 June. A massive party eventually involved members of all three Squadrons, Group officers, and even the Seventh Fighter Command staff. Few men were afflicted with excessive sobriety under these pressure laden conditions and the party was a real blow out.

Nature put on another of its shows the following day as a typhoon came howling out of the Pacific. The 78th's Command Post was wrecked and the 45th's Day Room tent was draped over a new mess hall. Men who had been spitting out dust 24 hours earlier were now wading through mud.

Despite the grind of flying combat missions, the Group was further burdened by the need to train replacement pilots. Those who had been on the Empire missions, regardless of rank or air hours, were like steel forged in fire. The deadly routine of sorties conferred a degree of mechanical efficiency that no amount of Stateside training could yield. It was necessary to give incoming replacements extensive ground indoctrination and flight trainings before they ventured out on VLR sorties.

Major Moore expounded on the extraordinary environment in which the Group operated:

> No matter how well trained, new fighter pilots and even vets from the European Theatre must learn the facts of life out here — how to conserve fuel on long-range missions, and that it's one thing to climb over a weather front and something else again to climb back.

The Seventh Fighter Command's leading ace had learned, during his long apprenticeship, that teamwork was an essential ingredient in the mix of success and survival. This was, after all, the killing business.

> The flight is made up of two elements, the first consisting of the flight leader and his wingman, the second of the element leader and his wingman. On the defensive, mutual support tactics are based on the two elements turning in on each other in case of attack. The Japanese just won't attack four planes in mutual support. On the offensive, the flight leader makes the initial pass and does most of the shooting. The wingman stays off his guns unless he gets a setup shot — too much danger of his ricochets hitting the flight or element leader. Besides it's their eyes and ears we want to warn of approaches on the leader's tail. The element leader and his wingman stay in close mutual support. Most of the planes that get shot up are the ones that lose track of their leader.

The Group had developed their long-range capability to a high degree. After rendezvous they would set a cruising speed of about 205 m.p.h. indicated air speed for the run to Japan. With the Merlin engine set at about 2400 rpm., an auto-rich mixture, and a manifold pressure of about 35 inches, they would approach the Departure Point having consumed most of the fuel in their wing tanks.

After jettisoning external wing tanks, the pilots switched to the fuselage tank. This 85 gallon tank lay just aft of the cockpit. At about half full the sloshing gasoline could cause control reversal resulting in a snap roll. Thus in the early minutes of activity over the Empire it was devoutly to be wished that one could get the fuselage tank below half full before embarking on aerial combat.

At combat power settings the 85-gallon tank was generally drained by the time the Mustngs had been recalled to the rally point. If things went as planned they flew home on the two 92-gallon internal wing fuel tanks. The ideal altitude was 10,000 feet where, with a power setting of 1800 rpm.'s and indicating about 210 m.p.h., the P-51 consumed 40 gallons per hour. These factors all culminated in a theoretical supply of fuel sufficient for a comfortable margin of safety returning over the 750 or 800 miles to Iwo Jima. However, this cruise control rationale rapidly came unraveled if any one of several unplanned events occurred: dropping external tanks too soon, weather enroute, battle damage, the malfunction of some portion of the plane's infernal gadgetry, orbiting another plane in trouble, or bad navigation. There were no pit stops and no way stations, just the limitless sea.

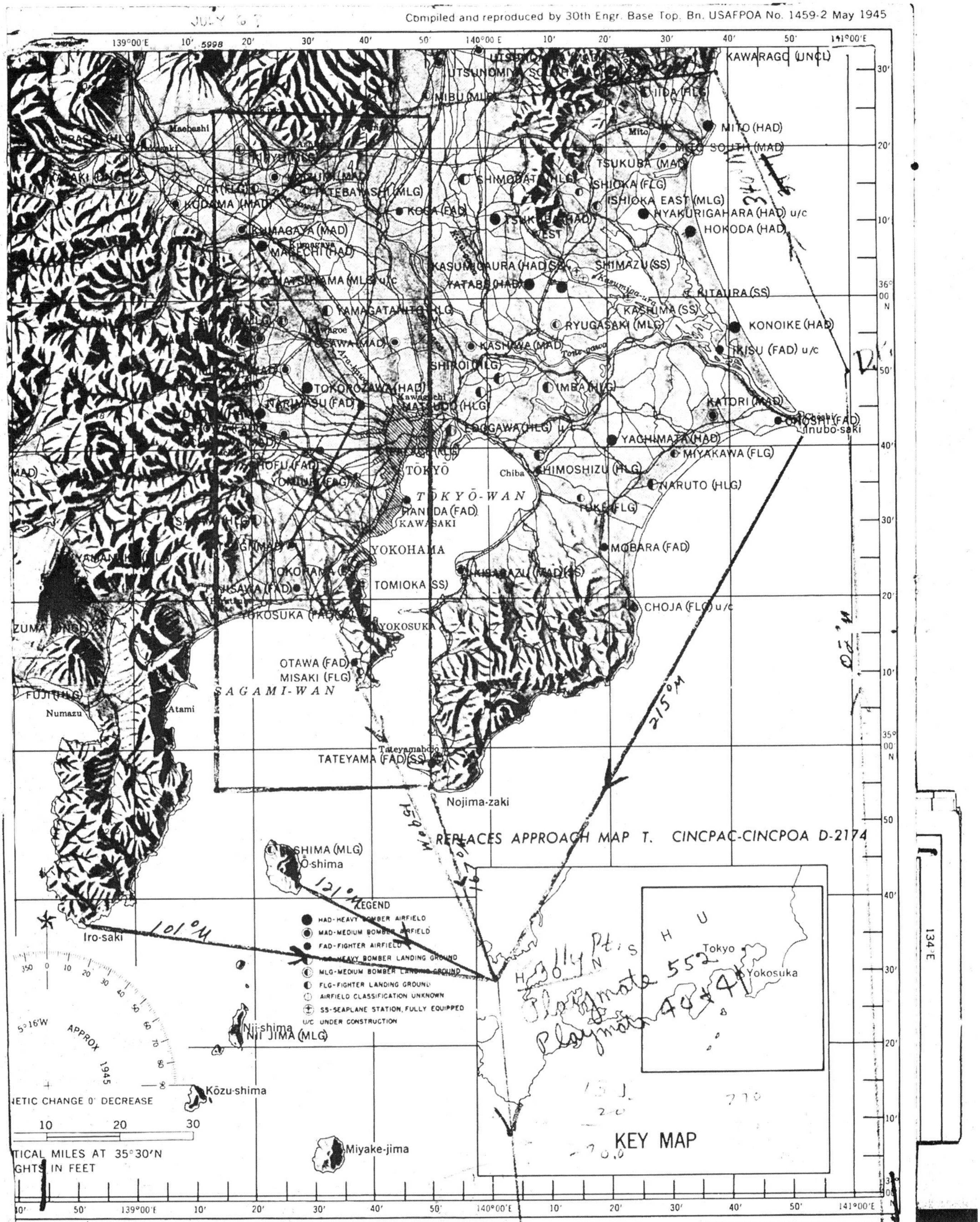
Compiled and reproduced by 30th Engr. Base Top. Bn. USAFPOA No. 1459-2 May 1945
KAWARAGO (UNCL)
MITO (HAD)
TSUKUBA (MAD)
SHIOKA (FLG)
ISHIOKA EAST (MLG)
HYAKURIGAHARA (HAD) u/c
HOKODA (HAD)
KASUMIGAURA (HAD SS)
SHIMAZU (SS)
KITAURA (SS)
KASHIMA (SS)
RYUGASAKI (MLG)
KONOIKE (HAD)
IKISU (FAD) u/c
TOKOROZAWA (HAD)
IMBA (HLG)
KATORI (MAD)
CHOSHI (FAD)
Inubo-saki
YACHIMATA (HAD)
MIYAKAWA (FLG)
SHIMOSHIZU (HLG)
NARUTO (HLG)
TŌKYŌ
TŌKYŌ-WAN
HANEDA (FAD)
KAWASAKI
YOKOHAMA
TOMIOKA SS)
MOBARA (FAD)
CHOJA (FLG) u/c
YOKOSUKA
OTAWA (FAD)
MISAKI (FLG)
SAGAMI-WAN
Numazu
Atami
TATEYAMA (FAD) (SS)
Nojima-zaki
REPLACES APPROACH MAP T. CINCPAC-CINCPOA D-2174
Ō-shima
Iro-saki
LEGEND
HAD-HEAVY BOMBER AIRFIELD
MAD-MEDIUM BOMBER AIRFIELD
FAD-FIGHTER AIRFIELD
MLG-MEDIUM BOMBER LANDING GROUND
FLG-FIGHTER LANDING GROUND
AIRFIELD CLASSIFICATION UNKNOWN
SS-SEAPLANE STATION, FULLY EQUIPPED
U/C UNDER CONSTRUCTION
101°M
121°M
215°M
Nii-shima
NII JIMA (MLG)
Kōzu-shima
Miyake-jima
Tokyo
Yokosuka
KEY MAP
Playmate 552
NERAL APPROACH CHART
MAY 1945
RESTRICTED
File 7B-8
CINCPAC-CINCPOA NO. 1

A flight of 45th Sq P-51s headed for Japan. (Source: USAF)

Chapter VII
EMPIRE SWEEP
July 1945 to August 1945

With the Allies closing in on the Japanese Home Islands the main thrust of the strategic air offensive changed to night raids by the XXI Bomber Command. The Seventh Fighter Command adjusted their tactics from one of bomber escort to fighter sweeps. Defeating enemy air power by direct aerial confrontation had become a spotty business at best. June had offered only two chances for major aerial engagements. The command structure believed that repeated fighter sweeps of airfields, shipping, and other targets of opportunity provided the best hope to cripple Japanese air power and damage other essential facilities.

The 15th set about implementing this new strategy, but they would pay a price. The Group had been equipped with the wrong tools for the new assignment. The Mustang was conceived and designed as a high altitude, long range, air supremacy fighter. Escort of B-29s and air superiority over the Japanese had been the Group's original mandate. Now they were going to use the right plane for the wrong job.

Low-level strafing had already been acknowledged as the most dangerous employment for fighters. Colonel John Mitchell, in an after action summary, more pointedly discussed the necessity of a rugged plane, one that could fly through its own richochets. "The in-line engine aircraft is too vulnerable to make it a suitable airplane for strafing." Its cooling system was too susceptible to AA fire placed as it was under the aircraft.

Chichi Jima had received little attention from the Group in June but periodic reconnaissance flights had detected an unusual amount of activity for a supposedly bypassed and beleagured garrison. Despite the tons of bombs and rockets and the thousands of rounds of

John Fitzgerald and Crew Chief, Gaillard Andrews, in front of No. 198. (Source: John Fitzgerald)

Harry Tyler and Crew Chief, John Supple. (Source: W. H. Sparks)

(Left to right) Walter Powell (KIA), S/Sgt Emil Kline and Unknown EM. (Source: W. H. Sparks)

S/Sgt. James N. Lindsay, painter extraordinaire, who decorated the 47th Mustangs. (Source: W. H. Sparks)

machine-gun fire which had bathed Chichi the Japanese were up to something there. The 15th sent an eight-plane rocket unit from the 78th Squadron to attack small boats in Futami Harbor on 3 July. What appeared to be a routine milk run turned into an unmitigated tragedy.

Just about 1000, after the last low-level pass had been completed, 1st Lt. Dick Schroeppel pulled up sharply with his plane ablaze. No one knew if he had been hit by flak; none was seen.

Schroeppel had no time to gain altitude nor did he have the opportunity to coast away from the island. It was jump or burn. At 1006 he parachuted from low altitude, making a successful jump. He drifted down well into the waters of Futami Harbor. Charlie Heil, flying Josephine, dipped down low over his comrade but Schroeppel waved him off as he successfully shucked his chute harness and boarded his one-man life raft.

While two 78th P-51s climbed for altitude and began radioing Agate Base for ASR assistance, the others set up a gunnery pattern. As Schroeppel paddled furiously toward the open sea, his Squadron mates strafed the nearby coast of Chichi. There were ominous splashes rising around the downed pilot as Japanese gunners began to get the range.

Dick's progress was agonizingly slow and the currents were working against him, but the P-51s made pass after pass covering him. They strafed guns, people, and even suspicious rocks. After 30 minutes of intense high speed runs they were nearly out of ammunition and running low on gas.

Thirteen planes of the 45th Squadron destined to bomb Haha Jima were diverted to Chichi to take up the watch. They arrived as Schroeppel was being swept onto a rocky point on the northern tip of the harbor entrance. While planes of the 78th raced back to Iwo Jima, the 45th Mustangs set up a string formation and began a relentless barrage on the cliffs over-hanging the haggard pilot.

The entire Group and the 4th ER Sq fought a losing battle for Dick Schroeppel on 3 July 45 off Chichi Jima. (Source: Jim Vande Hey)

More help was on the way; the Seventh pulled out all stops to save their trapped pilot. A B-17 Superdumbo, equipped with a large motorized lifeboat, as well as a Catalina had been dispatched from Iwo Jima. Both planes were from the 4th Emergency Rescue Squadron. Major Wayne Wells, Group Operations Officer, had been up early that morning doing some recon over the Bonins when he heard the radioed distress call. Wells and his wingman, 2nd Lt. Donald Locke, spotted Schroeppel resting on the rocks and joined in the covering operation. Occasionally they strafed the shore line and burned a couple of small wooden boats that otherwise would have been ignored.

Shortly after noon the B-17 piloted by 1st Lt. Claude L. Bodin, Jr. arrived on the scene. With a Mustang flying between him and the shore line, Bodin lined up his "Flying Dutchman" for a low slow run across the harbor mouth and over the rocks where Schroeppel had taken refuge. None of the B-17 crew could spot the downed pilot and they circled out to sea awaiting developments.

The angry P-51s were still zooming over the rocky point flailing the walls and rim of the cliff with saturation fire. At 1223 they saw Schroeppel move from his rocky hiding place to release some dye marker. Still game and using his head, he was trying to mark his position and give those aloft some idea of the drift of the current.

Wells and Locke had become desperately low on fuel and had to leave. They pancaked at 1245, Wells with 15 gallons of fuel remaining and Locke with 8. Their ammunition, 1800 rounds per plane, was completely expended. As they landed, 22 planes from the 78th were preparing to take off as the next relay. A flight of five 47th Squadron P-51s were being readied.

Using the dye marker as a reference, Lieutenant Bodin wheeled his lumbering B-17 in for another run. While the Mustangs went through desperate maneuvers to keep the enemy pinned down, the B-17 parachuted its boat at 1240. The lifeboat drop was almost perfect. It landed within 100 yards of the target, close by the outlying reefs.

As Group pilots peered anxiously through their canopies they spotted their cornered comrade on the edge of the rocks, stripping to his shorts. Exhausted as he must have been, the intrepid Schroeppel moved out of hiding and began to swim for his life. Fighting his way through the surf, the currents, and around the reefs, he reached the boat and tumbled in. The wearying exercise had alternately drained and exhilarated the spectators in the circling planes.

But now the Japanese had a naked target and an unobstructed field of fire. Despite the vengeful Mustangs they opened up on the big life boat with mortars, machine guns, and small arms. Their murderous fire turned the water white even as the P-51s savaged the enemy gunners with a deluge of .50 caliber slugs.

Both sides fought ferociously, absorbed in a battle

Airdrome strafing, Tokyo area, 4 July 45: Left — The scattered white dots are enemy tracers feeling for the 47th's Mustangs. Right — Leon Sher is almost at taxi level as he tears up parked Zekes. (Source: Leon Sher)

G. H. Scott

A. W. Sherren

R. L. Carr

Gordon Scott, 78th Sq, was shot down and taken prisoner on the 4 July sweep. Al Sherren and Bob Carr were both lost to the 78th Sq on 8 July 45, picked off by Japanese fighters. (Source: Jim Vande Hey)

that assumed an importance far out of proportion to the Pacific conflict. For the men on the cliffs and those in the airplanes, the war had boiled down to a symbolic struggle for the death or life of a single man.

At 1330 an OA-10A, Catalina, arrived over the harbor. It made several runs over the battered boat where Schroeppel could be seen lying in the bottom. Despite the presence of reefs, tricky currents, and swells, Captain Robert B. Richardson asked Agate Base for permission to land. Fighter Command told Richardson to proceed at his discretion. Unhesitatingly he prepared to go in.

With a Lufbery Circle of P-51s covering, the big Dumbo made a long, difficult approach and touched down. As it taxied near the lifeboat, the cliffs and beach became alive with sniper fire. This was more than the abused and frustrated Japanese on Chichi had ever hoped for, an enemy flying boat taxiing within range.

Despite the continued hail of fire from the P-51s, mortar shells cascaded in geysers around the Catalina and bullets rang off its metal skin. Captain Robert C. Anderson, a Flight Surgeon, leaned from a side gun blister as they circled the lifeboat three times. Schroeppel lay motionless in a pool of blood, his left leg almost torn from his body. The Doctor confirmed what had been feared for some time by those aloft — Schroeppel was dead.

With enemy fire still falling on and around the Catalina, Richardson gunned the engines and took off upwind straight away from the island. He called the circling P-51s and informed them that they had been unable to retrieve Schroeppel's body.

The strafing of Chichi stopped. Then, with few words, planes of the 78th Squadron formed a string and, Viking style, with their remaining ammunition, they sank the lifeboat with Dick Schroeppel's body.

"It was better that way," said 1st Lt. Jerry Yellin. "We were Dick's best friends. We didn't want his body washed ashore with those sons of bitches."

Successive VLR airfield sweeps of 4 and 5 July produced virtually no air action and a disappointing 13-3-23 in claims for enemy ground losses. The Group lost one pilot, 1st Lt. Gordon H. Scott, who bailed out over Japan, became a prisoner and survived to be repatriated. Several P-51s were damaged by ground fire but all returned safely.

Another brace of airfield raids was staged on 8 and 10 July with somewhat better results and proportionately higher casualties. Again the enemy was nonexistent in the air or would furtively leap from hiding to pick off single P-51s. First Lieutenant Robert L. Carr of the 78th and Captain Al Sherren of the 45th were both shot down in this fashion on the 8th. Second Lieutenant David Wilson of the 78th was wounded and went down short of Iwo Jima but was rescued by a destroyer. Six other Group aircraft were damaged as the unit claimed two in the air and 19-3-15 on the ground.

On 10 July the Group tallied seven planes destroyed on the ground while losing three planes and receiving damage to four more. First Lieutenant Frederick Ernst was killed in action while Ollie O'Mara was rescued by a lifeguard sub and Harold Collins was scooped out of the ocean in another improbable open-sea, high-wave rescue by a Dumbo of the 4th Emergency Rescue Squadron.

Sam Jones came within an eyelash of being another fatality when a bullet creased his helmet. He dug it out of his headrest after landing. "I guess it almost had my name on it."

Clearly the ground strikes were extracting a heavy toll of men and aircraft from the 15th. At this rate every aircraft in the Group would be shot down or damaged in a month. The enemy had begun to husband their scarce

Leon Sher attacked a corvette type naval vessel in Outer Osaka Bay on 10 July and touched off the ready magazine behind the forward turret. (Source: Leon Sher)

aircraft and fuel, utilizing a static or zone defense. While this tactic proved quite useless against B-29 raids, it forced our fighters to search out Japanese air strength on the ground. With a masterful use of straw dummies, camouflage, and derelict airplanes, the enemy not only forced U.S. planes into more dangerous searches for targets but they employed the juiciest looking false targets to lure U.S. fighters into flak traps. The operational aircraft were often found hidden "along highways, under trees, and in camouflaged revetments two to four miles from the airfields," according to the Command history. Pilots of the 15th conducted these hazardous endeavors without any noticeable loss of precision, but they considered themselves most vulnerable in such low level charges. Todd Moore said, "Strafing is the most dangerous work known to man, since speed and coordination are our only defenses when we're in that low." Bob Scamara thought encountering Japanese in the air afforded "a gay old time," but airfield strafing was like going up against "a firing squad."

As an aside to the airdrome mission of the 10th, Leon Sher took a big bite of the Japanese Navy. Coming out of a run on Hanshin Airfield near Osaka, Sher instinctively jerked his plane about in a wild evasive maneuver as he saw 20 mm tracers coming at him like glowing baseballs. He lost his flight mates with his aerobatics and joined up with Don Scott and others of the 45th Squadron. Sher relates:

> I was headed toward the coast when I saw this ship in a little bay. I thought it was a freighter and I might as well give it a squirt. I didn't know it was a warship until I was within a mile or so and all those red balls began coming at me. I decided, on impulse, to go ahead and everyone else broke off toward other targets. I came in at a steep angle and bore in close, shooting long bursts. I got so close I could see a sailor's belt buckle. I came down off the mast, flat out, everything to the firewall. I was going so fast I just barely cleared the water and avoided a high speed stall as I dished out.

Leon Sher had blown the ready magazine of the CD30, a destroyer escort, seriously damaging the ship, and recorded the pillar of fire and smoke on gun-camera film. He made another pass, then decided he had gambled enough for one day. Strafing airfields was bad, but strafing naval ships with multiple AA batteries was considered near fatal.

Photo reconnaissance finally determined that the recent flurry of activity at Chichi Jima involved the installation of a mobile radar station. It was a neat device to give the Empire advance warning of fighter strikes enroute up the Nanpo Shoto chain.

The Group participated in a total of eight Bonin Island missions during July to take out the radar unit and shipping. Ostensibly the strikes were also considered training runs for new pilots, but they became all too realistic. After the loss of Schroeppel on 3 July, 2nd Lt. Enon W. Harvey crashed into Futami Harbor just 10 days later. A replacement pilot, Harvey had been assigned to the Group only two weeks before he was killed. Bob Worton was killed near Chichi later on that month in a mid-air collision with a plane from the 21st Group on what was also dubbed a training mission, and 1st Lt. John Allen was shot down, but rescued by combined ASR units. The Chichi Jima milk runs had

F/O Robert Miller took heavy tail damage from flak over Nagoya on 15 July but brought his 45th Sq P-51 back to Iwo. (Source: E. M. Moore)

cost the Group four planes and three pilots in one month.

The last five VLR fighter sweeps of July were bruising affairs, starting with a Nagoya strike on the 15th. Heavy AA fire was encountered at 10,000 feet on approach to the target and light weapons fire became intense over Okazaki and Kowa. Running the gauntlet over the bullet-swept fields, six P-51s were hit. Two crashed carrying Jule Mitchell and 2nd Lt. Ronald Johnston to their deaths. First Lieutenant Paul Chism got just enough altitude to bail out and was taken prisoner. The Mustangs destroyed eight and damaged another eleven parked aircraft.

Flight Officer Robert A. Miller nursed his damaged P-51 to the rally point, then prayed it back to Iwo Jima. With half of his left stabilizer and rudder shot away, he brought his plane in for a hot, rough landing. Ground crews of the 45th watching his approach, "cheered with relief" as his plane rolled to a stop.

The Group CO had led a strike to Chichi Jima on 18 July and wasn't supposed to be on the VLR mission to Nagoya that next day. However, on 19 July the venturous Thomas climbed back into the cockpit with a "what the hell" attitude.

The 78th Squadron, carrying rockets as usual, was last to take off and, unable to catch the rest of the Group to effect rendezvous, turned back. The two remaining Squadrons successfully diverted around a front and followed the west shore of Ise Bay to Nagoya. From 10,000 feet over Kakamigahara Airdrome, Lt. Colonel Thomas directed the 45th to attack while he flew top cover with the 47th.

Hayden Sparks was part of the reserve flight circling at altitude over Kagamigahara. Just as the 45th was observed completing its run over the airfield, Thomas called Sparks on the radio and told him to get on his wing.

Leading the 47th Squadron down from its top cover position, Thomas peeled off and dove on the Japanese field. Sparks tucked in as close as he could get. "My pride made me determined not to lose him."

In a near-verticle dive Thomas plunged toward the target at an alarming rate of descent. Glancing in turn from his friend and leader to the view through his whirling propeller, Sparks saw that Thomas was diving toward a twin-engined Japanese bomber taxiing across the Airdrome. As his high speed indicator swung past 450 mph he also noted that the two-plane element with them was beginning to pull out of the dive. Thomas, however, continued his reckless descent.

Lining up the Betty in their sights, the two Mustangs began to fire bursts as they plummeted past the 505 mph air speed red line. At a point near pullout, with their air speed indicators near 600 mph, both planes entered compressibility.

Thomas' plane suddenly disintegrated, the wings folding back and pieces flying off. As stunned pilots of the 47th Squadron watched, Lt. Colonel Jack Thomas rocketed to his Valhalla.

Sparks was also about to transcend the limits of aero-dynamic pressure. "I lost complete control. The stick was flopping around between my knees, beating the hell out of me."

As Sparks reached the moment of critical "flutter" and observed Thomas' plane shatter, he instinctively pulled back on his throttle. The buffeting stopped but the Mustang turned sideways and continued its rapid descent. With the stick in the pit of his stomach, fighting the rudder pedals to correct the slide, he began to pull out.

There was a point on Kagamigahara where both friend and foe expected the P-51 to impact as it reached the end of its long dive. It was a Japanese gun emplacement. Sparks roared over the pillbox, no more than a few feet in the air, as Japanese soldiers dove from the structure, convinced that fiery entombment was near.

Hayden Sparks had escaped the crushing dynamics

Lt. Col. John Mitchell, one of the men who got Adm. Yamamoto, succeeded Thomas as Group C. (Source: E. M. Moore)

of compressibility and had recovered the use of his control surfaces just before he had run out of sky. He made it back to Iwo Jima, but his P-51 was junked. Most of its rivets had been pulled loose.

Inexplicably, the Japanese separated Thomas' body from the wreckage of his plane and buried him. (He was later reburied in Golden Gate National Cemetery.) Perhaps the manner of his death had caused the enemy to pay this final tribute to a fallen warrior.

The loss of their leader and friend stunned the 15th Fighter Group but there was no time out for mourning, no let up in the effort. The Group had 46 planes over the Nagoya area the next day. The Japanese threw up a torrent of intense and accurate fire from Okazaki, downing two planes over the target and damaging eight more. Captain Joe Walker of the 45th and 1st Lt. Jack H. Collie of the 78th were killed in action.

It had been almost impossible to pick out the dummies and derelicts from the real planes. The Group only claimed one aircraft destroyed and 10 damaged, then were reduced to strafing and rocketing a steam roller, hangars, and fishing boats. Clearly the damage inflicted was not a fair exchange for the price paid. The Japanese had won this round.

The sweep of 28 July was such a dismal quest for the Japanese air arm that the Group saw none in the air and forlornly claimed only four damaged aircraft on the ground around three Tokyo airfields. The region was so bereft of primary targets that the pilots roamed the countryside strafing targets of opportunity. Monk Baldwin began a new career working on the Japanese railroads, by blowing the Group's first locomotive. Other pilots hit a radar station and shipping, blowing the boiler

Group Commander, Jack Thomas, shortly before his death on 19 July 45. (Source: W. H. Sparks)

Hayden Sparks was Thomas wingman in the fatal dive over Kagamigahara A/D. (Source: W. H. Sparks)

of a DE (destroyer-escort). Flak was less of a factor and due to some divine providence, no one was lost.

Fighter Command was baffled by the discrepancies between aerial recon reports of aircraft on enemy fields and actual damage reports by the fighters. The variance involved the Japanese facility for passing off counterfeit dummies and wrecks as bonafide fighting aircraft. Only by close examination inherent in low-level strafing could the genuine article be separated from the bogus. Such eyeballing and peeking under camouflage netting presented the P-51s as juicy targets for AA batteries. The enemy even faked false runways and painted X marks over active runways and made mock trees that turned out to be flak towers. With few planes, parts, or pilots, the Japanese were going to extraordinary lengths to husband airpower for the invasion of the Homeland that both sides assumed was imminent.

The Group gave it one more try on 30 July, the last VLR effort of the month. It was a hollow exercise. No enemy aircraft were seen airborne or on the Nagoya airfields. Groping for something worthwhile to blast, the Group unleashed is rockets and machine-guns on factories and a power station between Nagoya and Osaka. Pulling out across Ise Bay, they strafed a small ship which returned heavy machine-gun fire.

About 25 miles down the coastline Captain Walter Powell experienced an explosion that left a two foot hole in his fuselage. Powell, the 47th's Acting CO, turned the flight over to the element leader and at 2,200 feet, he turned out to sea as his unit called a rescue sub. His engine was overheating and spilling coolant, and Powell was slowly losing his slim altitude advantage.

With 2nd Lt. Bill Barlow on his wing, he struggled onward in what was shaping up to be a very brief flight. Barlow saw the coolant door blow off and flames lick back from the exhaust. At only 800 feet Powell jettisoned his canopy preparatory to bailing out, but the plane split S-ed into the ocean hitting the water head-on.

Several planes orbited the area for a time as Super Dumbos arrived and a submarine was summoned. Bill Barlow was the last to leave, flying home alone after all hope had faded. The 15th had lost another veteran leader.

Due to no lack of determination or dedication on their part, the Group had achieved little in July 1945 for the loss of 13 pilots and 23 aircraft. According to strategic plan, they were pressing the Japanese to the wall and the cornered enemy was lashing back. Japanese flak was becoming increasingly effective, as Group records noted, " with all the practice they have been getting."

John Mitchell had replaced his friend and classmate, Jack Thomas, as CO of the 15th and Captain Ernie Hostetler had taken over as Acting Commander of the 47th after the death of Walter Powell.

The pilots were acutely aware that their survival odds were worsening. The U.S. was winning World War II, but at the current rate of attrition, none of those who had arrived with the Group on Iwo would live to see the end. There were some morale problems and a fatalistic attitude began to manifest itself. However, dwelling on past and future losses was a form of self-indulgence that could dull one's cutting edge. Instead of offtime melancholy they engaged mostly in tomfoolery.

(Left to right) Monk Baldwin, George Petrouleas, Ed Markham, and Eurich Bright after a water fight in the 47th Club. (Source: John Fitzgerald)

One of the longest running gags was putting a lit cigarette in someone's pocket. Doc Lapides is the victim as he dances with Phil Oransky. Sam Jones is about to drop the cigarette as Roy June observes. (Source: John Fitzgerald)

They played hard in keeping with their trade. Most of the nonsense took place at the Officer's Club. The 78th built their club, complete with fireplace, out of native volcanic stone. On its inauguration the sulphur gas trapped in the stones blew up as it warmed. Bob Roseberry couldn't recall more than one fire in that fireplace.

At the 47th "O" Club, Monk Baldwin had gone to exceptional lengths to entertain his Squadron mates. With an old generator from a Japanese truck he had "wired" the bar. When a visiting fireman would drop by, Monk playing the gracious host, would say, "Try our booze, it'll give you a real jolt." The unwary visitor would accept a glass and lean into a prearranged puddle on the bar. Monk then hit the switch and gave him a shock which delighted the local fraternity.

Monk and Spider Condrick were constantly outdoing each other with practical jokes, but when Condrick went back to the States to gunnery school, Monk turned his trickery loose on Tom Leaver, Armament Officer. Monk would almost rather let the air out of big Tom's mattress than shoot up a locomotive.

However, the longest enduring gag was putting a lit cigarette in someone's pocket. "That was just about the funniest damn thing in the world at that time," recalled John Fitzgerald. The joke backfired on John one night as he was pursued out of the club by one of his victims. Tearing around the Club in the dark, he collided with one of the many overhangs on a Quonset building. They had been prefectly engineered to protrude at head height. Doc Lapides needed several stitches to close the gash on Fitzgerald's forehead.

By late July 45 Iwo had become so civilized that the walkways in the 45th Sq area were marked with stones. (Source: Robert W. Moore)

More air power had come to Iwo Jima in late July with the arrival of the 414th Fighter Group. The casual veterans of the 15th viewed the 414th's brand new P-47Ns with their auto pilots and other gadgetry as something of a paradox. The 15th's mechanics were still scrounging for parts from old wrecks to make their weary Mustangs flyable. The U.S. war machine, now in high gear, could readily disgorge 100 new P-47s but no P-51 spare parts.

Just as the newcomers arrived, the last Japanese soldier on Iwo climbed out of his cave and surrendered. At long last things were secure on Iwo Jima, but over Japan there was still a battlefield in the shell-shocked sky.

World War II was approaching its climax as the Group flew north on 2 August 1945, but for the 15th Fighter Group and its old enemy, this was just another bloody round. Passing high over one vacant airfield after another near Nagoya, the Group finally attacked

Paint chipped and battle worn Mustangs of the 47th Sq taxi out for another VLR mission. (Source: W. H. Sparks)

Left —Ralph Heintz was shot down and taken prisoner on 3 August. (Source: Ralph Heintz) Right —Walter Powell (left), standing with Joe Brunette, was killed in action on 30 July 45. (Source: W. H. Sparks)

Bob Beyl survived a hit that shattered his canopy. (Source: David Beyl)

A hit on No. 159 of the 47th perforated the fuselage and poppea rivets loose. (Source: Earl Steggeman)

Komaki Airdrome. They saw only five grounded aircraft, some thought to be inoperative, and could only claim one destroyed and one damaged.

Flying through a blizzard of ack-ack over Komaki, the Group moved on through a continuing barrage to hit rails and shipping. Monk Baldwin saw a train in the distance as the Japanese spotted the hedgehopping P-51s. They unhooked the locomotive from the cars and raced toward a tunnel. Monk's .50 calibers caught the locomotive before it gained refuge. There was never any question about a railroad engine being "probably" destroyed. "If you hit them just right," said Baldwin, "they blew real good."

Leon Sher and his wingman got another locomotive and several cars. "I just love working on the railroads," recalled Sher.

It was like a shooting gallery for both sides this day. Eight Mustangs were damaged, but all returned to base though there were two crash landings. This was the day for which that old Air Corps adage was intended: "It's a good landing if you can walk away from it."

There was no respite as Lt. Colonel Mitchell led the Group to Tokyo the following day. The 41 pilots were astounded at the enemy's endless bag of tricks. In addition to a swarm of dummy Japanese aircraft, they saw what appeared to be a B-29 on Tsukuba Airfield. It also appeared to be a dummy but, fake or not, it was probably a flak trap. No one took the bait.

There were orange and red box kites tethered at two fields and a pair of barrage balloons at 2500 feet over Kasumigaura. The 45th Squadron shot down the two gas bags, with World War I visions dancing through their heads. There was also a smoke screen set up to shield the hangars at the same field.

Flak was relatively moderate until the Group reached Katori Airfield near the coast. The 78th Squadron's rocket carriers had made the first pass while the 47th flew high cover. Moderate inaccurate automatic weapons fire was encountered by the first wave, but the

A look of weary apprehension prevails in this 7 August photo of 47th Sq pilots bound for a Tokyo airfield sweep. (Left to right) Front row: Harry Tyler, Dave Balak, Ed Markham, CO, Hayden Sparks, Bill Dow, Al Olivier; back row: Hank Ryniker, Ernie Sorgnit, Marvin Loveless, Francis Kinsey, Joe McCormick, Charlie Doughty, Bob Scamara, and Bob Kriss. Note strip maps in leg pockets. (Source: W. H. Sparks)

Japanese were alerted and primed as the 47th Squadron came in for their run.

Extemely heavy fire met Ernie Hostetler's fourteen P-51s. Enemy tracers filled the air over Katori feeling for the Mustangs as they raced across the field. The Squadron destroyed nine grounded planes, but paid the price as intense accurate antiaircraft fire found five of them.

Harold Heintz was hit as he started his strafing run but he bore in on his target tearing it to shreds with his .50s. His engine began to run rough as he pulled up and headed for the sea. With coolant streaming from his engine and the temperatures crossing the red line limits, Ralph struggled to reach the coast. Just five miles beyond the shoreline of Honshu he jumped.

Hayden Sparks and Martin Gilbride circled their flight mate and covered him while summoning a Dumbo. Sparks had also received flak damage but stayed over the downed Heintz until Dumbo arrived and dropped another supply packet. With word that a submarine was enroute, Sparks and Gilbride waggled their wings and headed south.

Harold Baccus' Mustang was also mortally wounded and he was trying to put some distance between himself and the Japanese coastline. His heart beat increased as he passed over a Japanese destroyer hugging the Honshu shore. As his plane spewed coolant and gasoline, his flight was dashing about like retrievers trying to locate a Dumbo or a submarine.

Harold got about 20 miles offshore when his engine quit and the time for parachuting was at hand. He hit the water successfully and, like Heintz, was able to board his liferaft, but Dumbo couldn't land and there was a knot of uneasiness because the Japanese destroyer was closer to both downed flyers than the nearest lifeguard sub.

With the skies devoid of friendly aircraft, Ralph Heintz and Harold Baccus each lived out their own dramas.

The sight of the P-51s and the Catalina hovering over Heintz had not gone unnoticed. Just after the last U.S. plane left, a flight of Zekes appeared. They made four strafing runs each on the downed pilot and his raft. Heintz dove each time like a duck, surfacing briefly to peer at the hunters. The enemy had scattered the supply packet, punched three holes in the life raft, but never laid a glove on the stalwart Heintz. With calm resolution he used an onboard repair kit to patch his raft, re-inflated it, and climbed aboard for a night of aimless drifting.

Baccus, meanwhile, was adrift further out to sea and was being blown south across the black and inhospitable waters of the Nanpo Shoto. That evening a ship came churning past him and Harold fired a flare. Knowing that it was Japanese he figured even imprisonment was preferable to rafting it on the Pacific. If the Japanese saw his flare, they didn't think him worth retrieving or killing. At midnight, like a magical sea-monster, the submarine *Balao* slid out of the darkness to rescue him.

With the dawn of 4 August Ralph Heintz was still adrift off the coast of Honshu. Passing through minefields, he spotted enemy ships between himself and the shore and sat helplessly awaiting his fate.

Before dawn the next morning he was washed ashore by the surf. Exhausted, he hid among the sand dunes

Above — Crew Chief, Arthur Mongelli, and his well traveled P-51D-25. This plane was flown by Lt. Col. John Mitchell and others. The score and mission hash marks are for the aircraft. (Source: R. Edsel Wilcox)

Right — Bernie Bjorseth (not shown) and "Cedric Cesspool," 47th Sq, survived 15 VLR missions to the Empire. (Source: Russell Skaggs)

and slept the day through awakening the next morning to the sound of nearby voices. He played hide and seek among the sand dunes for a few hours until one of the numerous clam fishermen spotted him. Ralph still had his .45, but couldn't bring himself to shoot a defenseless fisherman.

Within hours he was tied to a post in the nearby village and "figured that was about it," but a Japanese policeman took charge and trotted him off in handcuffs, like a prize catch, through several small villages. There was some hitting and spitting but less than he feared and no more than he expected.

After being turned over to Japanese Military Police, he was put on a train for Tokyo. Enroute, the train was strafed but "no one seemed to get hurt and we moved on." Ralph couldn't help but wonder which unit had done such a shabby job of strafing. (It wasn't the 15th). He eventually arrived at a POW camp where he languished until liberated near the end of August.

The Group was enroute to Tokyo area airfields again on 6 August with 51 Mustangs, while history was being made a few hundred miles west of them by a lone B-29 with a single bomb. About 0815 the first atomic bomb was dropped on the city of Hiroshima obliterating nearly five square miles and eventually causing 148,000 casualties. As a raging fire wind from the apocalyptic explosion was sweeping through Hiroshima the 15th Fighter Group was diving into the flak over Sagami searching vainly for enemy aircraft.

In retrospect, this mission and all future ones were like the machinations of a deranged high command. With a weapon in hand which could erase whole communities of humans, these superb aerial knights were

The 45th Sq with a B-29 navigator northbound for Honshu. (Source: USAF)

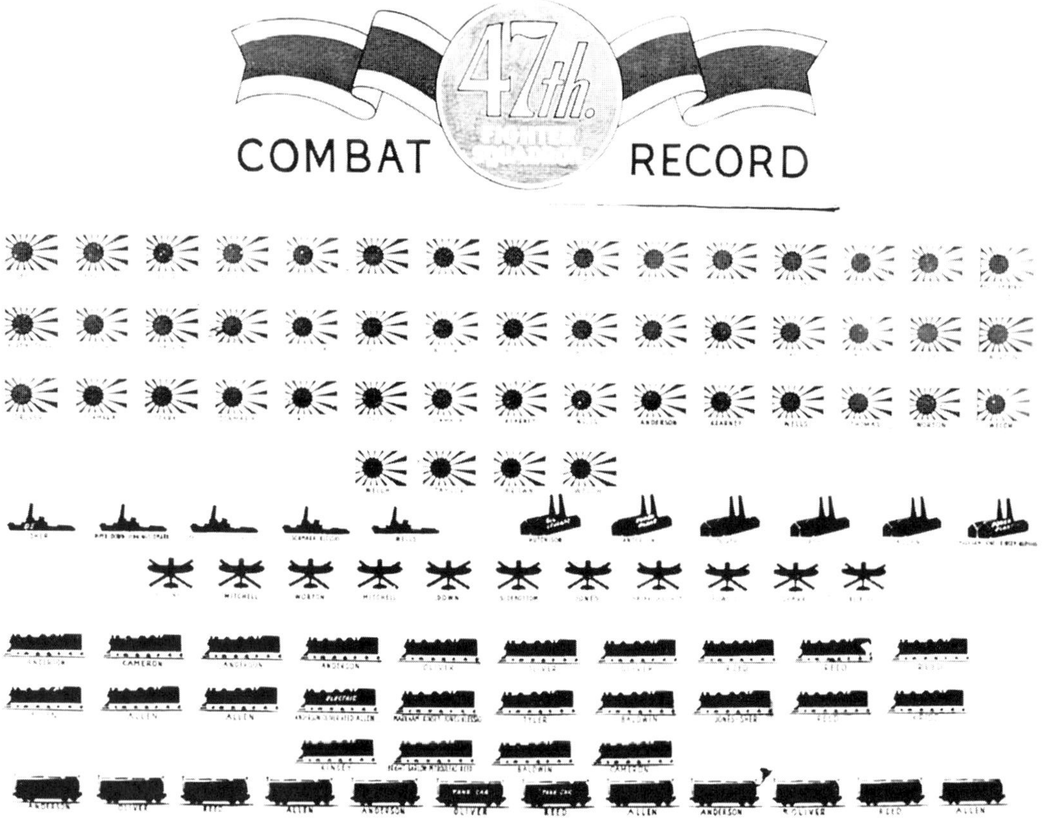

The 47th Squadron's final tally. (Source: Richard MacKenzie)

sent through a hailstorm of anti-aircraft fire to shoot up boxcars, knock holes in brick walls, and break windows.

Six P-51s were damaged, four went down. Goldy Rettberg of the 45th was the first to bail out. He parachuted into Tokyo Bay and was never seen again.

Bones Weaver was hit by AA fire when he was down on the deck. As he fought to gain altitude and reach the sea, Japanese gunners all along the route seemed to concentrate on his smoking plane. The 47th Squadron rallied to his defense diving at enemy batteries with return fire. Weaver had gotten his stricken plane up to about 2,000 feet and was approaching the coast when he was hit several more times. In a spilt S, the Mustang began a descent toward death. Weaver jumped at no more than 100 feet. Warren Reed, braving the enemy fire, dropped down to 15 feet. He could clearly see Weaver's lifeless body crumpled on the beach, the parachute canopy partially enshrouding him.

Reforming over the Bay one of the pilots heard a Japanese voice on the radio say, "Very sorry, boys. Come back tomorrow."

Monk Baldwin had been in one of the planes covering Weaver's retreat and began to wonder if he would have a tomorrow.

> We had drawn heavy fire from a factory just south of Yokohama and spotting the source of the tracers I pulled around for another pass. That was a mistake. They got me good. The first round that hit my plane must have been a pretty big one, a 40 mm. I took such a shot in the wing that it flipped me over on my back. The next hit, probably a 20 mm righted the ship.

Monk's Mustang was reduced to a pile of scrap aluminum with tail and aileron surfaces shot away, his hood shattered, gas gushing from his wing and the plane on fire. With a mighty effort he got the plane up to 1,000 feet altitude and staggered toward the Rally Point.

Commander Fred Gunn, skipper of the submarine, *Scabbardfish*, was on lifeguard station at the Rally Point. He was cruising on the surface barely 25 miles from the Honshu coast off the approach to Sagami Bay when he began to receive distress calls on the ASR channel. There were three battle damaged P-51s wobbling toward the Lifeguard.

Monk Baldwin, 1st Lt. Frank Seymour of the 21st Fighter Group, and 2nd Lt. Stan Moore of the 47th Squadron were all homing in on the *Scabbardfish*. They appeared in close order with Baldwin in the lead. Unstable as his plane was he rolled it over and "popped right out" over the sub. "Captain Gunn was waiting for me like a fielder for a fly ball," said Monk, who was only in the water for a few minutes.

What with all the circling Mustangs, the *Scabbardfish* asked Moore if he could bail out between the sub and Seymour. Stan responded, "Hey, this is the first time I've ever done this. I'm no expert." Captain Gunn wasn't insistent and rather seemed to enjoy the air

Todd Moore and "Stinger VII" near the end of the long campaign. (Source: USAF)

show as he scooped up one pilot after another. "It looked," thought Gunn, "like the graduating class at Fort Bragg."

Major Todd Moore, mission leader, was not a man who suffered futile missions gladly. He fumed at the loss of four planes and two men dead for a meaningless trip to Sagami, a deserted and burned-out airfield.

That night, the men of the 15th Fighter Group heard President Truman announce that the first atomic bomb had been dropped on Hiroshima. The pilots, who had flown so many hundreds of hours from so many "nasty places," had trouble accepting the reality of the announcement. They had spent years chipping away at the enemy with small victories, leaving their dead along the way. Those bitter skirmishes had seemed so relevant, and now they were told that a single B-29 had vaporized an entire city.

One would have assumed that the historic event of 6 August 1945 would have brought an end to the war, but there were still three more missions to fly — three more times into the pernicious skies.

The very next day after Hiroshima, the Group escorted B-29s to Honshu. No enemy planes rose to challenge the raiders. Even the Japanese anti-aircraft fire was "inaccurate and meager." One plane went down 250 miles from Iwo after developing a coolant leak, but the pilot, Bob Carey, was rescued. Bob Kriss landed with just 13 gallons of gas.

Two days later, 9 August, the second nuclear bomb was dropped on an already reeling Japan. This bomb erased one and one half square miles of Nagasaki, causing some 70,000 casualties.

The Japanese government had been considering surrender when the first atomic bomb struck. They communicated their intent through the Swiss Government shortly after the second bomb exploded over Nagasaki. However, the war technically continued between procedural messages and replies.

Major Wayne Wells led the Group in a Tokyo escort

Don Scott and No. 75 of the 45th made it through the campaign. (Source: Don Scott)

mission on 10 August. Scissoring along the edge of the bomber stream, they encountered a handful of brave but ineffective Japanese fighters making uncoordinated approaches to the bombers.

In brief action between the IP and the target, Ollie O'Mara led a flight from the 47th Squadron after a distant flight of enemy planes. They damaged all four but the Japanese aircraft had no stomach for the uneven action and dove away in the smoke haze over Tokyo. The 45th Squadron was able to press their attack more closely and shot down a Tony and a Tojo. They were the first victory for 1st Lt. Bill Farrell and the twelfth for Major Todd Moore.

Swallowing their usual dose of benzadrine, the Group pilots settled down for the trip back to Iwo Jima. It was counted as a great mission. Everyone was making the return flight.

That night they clustered around to hear Armed Forces Radio announce that the Japanese had made a surrender offer. It was almost over, but not quite. They "sweated out" four more days of formal negotiations. "Nobody wanted to get shot down at that point," said Leon Sher.

However, there would be a final accounting, the last round of a scheduled 15 rounder. On 14 August 1945 the pilots of the 15th Fighter Group were briefed for the last VLR mission.

Iwo Jima reverberated to the roar of aircraft engines as all four groups of the Seventh Fighter Command prepared to escort bombers or strike enemy airfields. The 15th had been assigned to sweep airfields in the Nagoya area.

With Todd Moore leading, 46 Mustangs assembled for the final charge. He had been advised that if the surrender came through "officially," the mission would be called back. The code word "Utah" would be flashed to a B-29 navigator as the signal to abort and return.

They found the skies empty over Honshu. Not a single Japanese plane arose to engage the fighters.

Proceeding with their valedictory, the Group investigated several fields and found them devoid of air operations. A lone Frank was strafed at Komaki and a Betty at Toyohashi, but neither would burn. The Squadrons turned their attention to rail lines and marshalling yards where much rolling stock seemed to be deserted. With rockets and machine guns they battered locomotives, freight cars, roundhouses and power plants.

All Japan seemed to have stopped, like a broken watch, except for the AA gunners, who continued to dispute the sky. The Group drew fire at every airfield and from several towns.

First Lieutenant Philip Schlamberg was suddenly missing from the 78th's formation near Futagawa. Major Markham, CO of the 47th, and 1st Lt. Elmer Owens of the 78th were both losing oil as they headed for the Rally Point. Lieutenants Allen, Sher, and Kinsey of the 47th had also been hit as had Major Fitzsimmons and Lieutenants Westlund and Coryell of the 78th.

Todd Moore led the tattered formation out of Honshu alerting the Air/Sea Rescue units in a tense exercise that had become all too routine. Ed Markham was the next to go. He bailed out at the Rally Point as the sub cover flight hovered around him. He parachuted successfully and was picked up in a record five minutes by an old friend of the 15th, *Tigrone*.

Lieutenant John Allen had jettisoned his canopy over the *Tigrone* knowing he had an oil leak, but since his oil pressure was up, he decided to try to get closer to home. He tagged on to the first B-29 and asked for an express trip back to Iwo Jima.

Owens nursed his plane to within 100 miles of the base before it quit. He bailed out and was rescued by a destroyer.

Sher's engine kept cutting out as he coddled his plane along. Leon, by his own admission, "crashed a lot" and was determined not to be the final statistic in the casualty records of World War II.

Thirty minutes out of Honshu, Moore surveyed the battered remnants of the Group, then the voice of irony split his earphones. The signal, "Utah," was flashed from Agate Base. The war was over. Todd felt no comfort or elation, only a "terrible frustration" at the loss of Phil Schlamberg.

Allen landed as the last of his oil vanished. The other five damaged Mustangs all managed to reach Iwo. As pilots from the last strike unwound their individual knots of emotion the island began a two-day holiday. Jim Tapp, unfolding his six-foot frame from the cockpit found it "difficult to comprehend that the war had been over for two hours."

Reactions to the outbreak of peace were varied and ran the gamut of emotional expression. Most of those on Iwo were surprised, even shocked at the suddeness of it all. They were expecting another beachhead airfield operation. Bob Roseberry said, "We assumed the next stop was Japan. We already had the code name for the invasion, OLYMPIC, and were starting the packing process."

There was a lot of drinking and an equal amount of sober reflection, as those who had started on Iwo "marveled" that they were still alive. "There wasn't any wild celebration in the 15th," said Sandy Sanders. "These boys were burned out. They were just drained."

Five members of the Group toasted VJ Day at sea abroad rescue vessels. Harold Baccus put in an 18-day tour of duty with the Navy and was in on the sinking of two enemy ships while learning the submarine trade.

Monk Baldwin and Stan Moore, still aboard the submarine *Scabbardfish,* were patrolling off Hokkaido Island when the good news arrived. The sub was packed with an assortment of rescued Army and Navy aircrews. Monk recalls the unbridled joy when Captain Gunn passed the word, then gave the ship's crew all the medicinal brandy and his passengers a pint of Old Overholt rye whiskey. "About fifteen of us shared that pint so no one man got much, but it was a great feeling and no one complained."

At Camp Omurii on Tokyo Bay, Ralph Heintz and scores of other prisoners were astonished when told by their bewildered guards that the Emperor had broadcast a surrender decree. Ralph was touched by the happiness, prayers, tears and the gritty patriotism of the men who had suffered as prisoners for years. But he missed the comradeship of his Squadron mates at this moment of victory.

Anticipating some unknown future operations, the Command staff quickly organized new peacetime operating and training procedures. Neither high performance military aircraft nor their pilots could lie idle like stacked rifles. So it was into the cockpit and into the blue for the Mustangs and their drivers. The orders did not generate much enthusiasm as John Fitzgerald remembers:

> Suddenly no one wanted to fly. We were all survivors. Guys who had willingly flown in combat didn't want to risk getting killed in a dumb operational accident. But the CO made it unmistakably clear that the planes had to be flown to be kept in shape and he was in charge of the rotation orders.
>
> So we bored around the island like it was a primary training school in Texas. Nobody wanted to get out of sight of Iwo. With all those hot fighters tooling around the same air space it was dangerous as hell — worse than a VLR mission.

The Group was even required to fly back up the old Nanpo Shoto Chain on some airpower demonstration flights culminating in a "flyover" of the battleship *Missouri* during the signing of the peace treaty. While this evoked some general grumbling it was well organized and the ASR forces along the route were a monument to planning.

Rotation policies were soon employed, and as new men arrived and old timers left in droves, morale was generally high. The shooting had ended.

Bob Scamara had completed 15 VLR missions and eight more to the Bonins. Fifteen trips to the Empire and back was what the Command had defined as a tour of duty. The life expectancy of a pilot was measured in hours, about 110. Bob and others had reached that elusive goal, but many had fallen in quest of victory. Of the 166 officer pilots who had originally landed on Iwo Jima, 43 had been lost including three POWs — a grisly 25% loss ratio. Counting replacement pilots killed, the Group had suffered 50 casualties in the final air offensive against the Empire. There had been another 21 pilots rescued by ASR units between Iwo and Japan. From 7 December 1941 to 14 August 1945, 134 officers and enlisted men of the Group had died in the long campaign. Another 43 of their alumni had fallen in other theatres of operation.

Epilogue

This history hopefully has been something more than a mere chronicle of events. Within the limitations imposed by cryptic, incomplete records and sincere but failing memories, it is an honest accounting of the saga of the 15th Fighter Group.

Though the members of the Group have shared much with me in the assembly of this history, I was not one of them. While they have reminisced, laughed, and on occasion, shed a tear with me, I did not serve with them.

It would therefore be presumptuous to conclude this history attempting to define the essence of their shared experience. Only they can do that. Only with their own first person views can we seek to capture the affinity which bound together this extraordinary band of brothers:

James M. Vande Hey, Brigadier General, USAF (Ret.), Real Estate Developer, Austin Texas:

> It was a great war with the greatest bunch ever assembled.

Leon P. Sher, Captain, USAF (Ret.), Board of Equalization, State of California

There was implicit trust among us, great esprit de corps, and team spirit. I've never seen anything like it since.

Emerson R. Johnson, Colonel, USAF (Ret.), Prospect, Pennsylvania:

There was nothing I wouldn't have done for those boys, and I believe they felt the same about me.

E.P. "Mickey" Moore, Major General, USAF (Ret.) 1907-1981:

They would go incredible distances, fly their hearts out, and those who managed to return were so crippled we had to help them from their cockpits. There were none finer.

Ned H. Baldwin, Captain, USAF (Ret.), Auto dealer, St. Petersburg, Florida:

The old veteran pilots were extraordinarily brave men. If you didn't go home after about two years out there, the chances were you got killed.

Robert W. Moore, Major, USAF (Ret.), Business Executive, Glasgow, Kentucky:

I would do it all again if I could turn the clock back.

During the closing toast at a 47th Squadron reunion in 1980, Sandy Sanders, Lt. Colonel, USAF (Ret.) was trying to characterize the profound qualities that had given the organization its inner greatness. Suddenly he summoned the words that were uncharacteristic of fighting men: "What we had for each other was love."

With smiles of satisfaction and not a few misty eyes, every glass was silently raised. That said it all.

Capt. Bob Beyl, 78th Sq, and "Gloria Beth" sporting 16 VLR mission hash marks sometime after VJ-Day. (Source: David Beyl)

Appendix I

Headquarters 15th Pursuit Group (P)
Wheeler Field, T.H.
5 August 1941

Operations Memorandum)
Pilot Qualification
Number 14)

1. *Reference:*
15 Pur Gp Cir. 15-5 & 15-7

2. *Upon recommendation of the Commanding Officers of organizations to which they are assigned or attached the following officers are announced as qualified check pilots and pilots of aircraft as indicated and as instrument check pilots where noted:*

a. Check Pilots

AUSTIN, G.H. Captain — A-12, AT-6, B-12, B-18, P-26, P-36.
BLANCHARD, P.W., Jr. Major — AT-6, A-12, P-36, P-40.
KINGHAM, A.R. Captain — AT-6, P-26, P-36, OA-9.
BECKWITH, J.O. 1st Lt. — P-26, P-36, A-12, AT-6, B-12.
SANDERS, L.M. 1st Lt. — P-26, P-36, AT-6.
SCHWARTZ, W.H. 1st Lt. — AT-6, A-12, B-18, P-36, P-40.
SUMMERS, T.B. 1st Lt. — P-26, P-36, AT-6.
THOMPSON, H.E. 2nd Lt. — AT-6, P-36, P-40.
TYER, A.W. Captain — AT-6, B-12, B-18, OA-9, P-26.
WILMOT, W.B. 1st Lt. — AT-6, B-12, P-26, P-36, P-40.

b. Pilots

AKRE, R.O.S. Major — B-18, OA-8, OA-9.
BECKWITH, J.O. 1st Lt. — P-40.
BROWN, V.V.D. 1st Lt. — 0-47, B-18, A-12, AT-6, P-26, P-36, P-40.
BUCKLAND, S.E. 1st Lt. — B-18, P-26.
CORDS, H.H. 2nd Lt. — P-40 (Day Only), P-36, AT-6, P-26, A-12.
COX, J.A. 2nd Lt. — P-36, P-26, AT-6, A-12 (Day Only).
DAVIS, E.S. 2nd Lt. — P-40, P-36, AT-6.
GABRESKI, P.S. 2nd Lt. — AT-6 (Day Only), P-36 (Day Only).
HANEY, W.F. 2nd Lt. — AT-6, P-36 (Day Only).
HAYES, W.L., Jr., 1st Lt. — B-18.
HOUNSOM, J.M. 2nd Lt. — P-36, A-12, AT-6, P-26.
KINGHAM, A.R. Captain — B-18.
LAWRENCE, N.W., Jr. 2nd Lt. — AT-6, P-36 (Day Only).
LITTLE, J.E. 2nd Lt. — AT-6, P-36 (Day Only).
MAGOFFIN, M.D. Captain — P-36, A-12.
MARTIN, W.P. 2nd Lt. — A-12, AT-6, O-47, P-26, P-36.
MOORE, M.A. 1st Lt. — P-26, P-36, P-40, AT-6, A-12, B-12, OA-9.
NELSON, H.C. Captain — P-26, O-47.
NORRIS, O. 2nd Lt. — P-40, AT-6, P-36.
PARRETT, C.M. 2nd Lt. — AT-6, P-26.
POWELL, J.H. 2nd Lt. — AT-6, P-36 (Day Only).
RASMUSSEN, P.M. 2nd Lt. — P-36, (Day Only), AT-6.
RIGLEY, O.H., Jr. 1st Lt. — P-36 (Day Only).
ROGERS, R.J. 1st Lt. — P-26, AT-6.
SANDERS, L.M. 1st Lt. — P-40 (Day Only), B-12.
SAWYER, J.R. 2nd Lt. — P-40, P-36, A-12, AT-6.
SHIFFLET, F.B. 2nd Lt. — AT-6 (Day Only), P-36 (Day Only).
STERLING, G.H. 2nd Lt. — AT-6, P-36 (Day Only).
SUMMERS, T.B. 1st Lt. — B-18, A-12, B-12.
TAYLOR, K.M. 2nd Lt. — AT-6, P-36 (Day Only).
TAYLOR, W.E. 1st Lt. — A-12, AT-6, B-18.
THACKER, J.M. 2nd Lt. — P-40 (Day Only), P-36, AT-6.
THORGERSON, J. 2nd Lt. — A-12, AT-6, P-26, P-36.
TINDAL, L.N. Major — OA-9, 0-47, P-36, OA-8, B-18, B-12.
TYER, A.W. Captain — A-12, P-36.
WEBSTER, J.J. 2nd Lt. — P-26.
WELCH, G.S. 2nd Lt. — AT-6, P-26.
WIGLEY, R.C. 2nd Lt. — AT-6, P-26, P-36, A-12.
WILKINS, J.C. 2nd Lt. — A-12, AT-6, B-12, P-40 (Day Only), P-36, OA-9, O-47.
WILMOT, W.B. 1st Lt. — A-12.
WRETSCHKO, J.C. 2nd Lt. — AT-6, P-26, P-36.

c. Instrument Flight Check Pilots:

AUSTIN, G.H. Captain
BECKWITH, J.O. 1st Lt.
BUCKLAND, S.E. 1st Lt.
HAYES, W.L. 1st Lt.
WINGHAM, A.R. Captain
NORRIS, O. 2nd Lt.
SANDERS, L.M. 1st Lt.
SCHWARTZ, W.H. 1st Lt.
SUMMERS, T.B. 1st Lt.
TAYLOR, W.E. 1st Lt.
TYER, A.W. Captain
WILKINS, J.C. 2nd Lt.
WILMOT, W.B. 1st Lt.
WRETSCHKO, J.C. 2nd Lt.

By order of Major Tindal:
A.R. KINGHAM,
Captain, Air Corps,
Group S-3.

OFFICIAL:
A.R. KINGHAM,
Captain, Air Corps,
Group S-3.
Distribution:
"B"

Appendix II
7 December 1941
Aerial Combat Sorties Flown During Japanese Attack

Pilot	Squadron	A/C Flown	Sorties	Enemy Aircraft Claims Destroyed	Probables	Damaged	Comments
Brown, Harry, 2nd Lt.	47	P-36	1	1	1		
Dains, John, 2nd Lt.	47	P-36, P-40	2				KIA 7 Dec. 41
Moore, Malcolm, 1st Lt.	46	P-36	1			1	Died Post-WW II
Rasmussen, Philip, 2nd Lt.	46	P-36	1	1			
Rogers, Robert, 1st Lt.	47	P-36	1		1		
Sanders, Lewis, 1st Lt.	46	P-36	1	1	1		
Sterling, Gordon, 2nd Lt.	46	P-36	1	1			KIA 7 Dec. 41
Taylor, Kenneth, 2nd Lt.	47	P-40	2	2	2		
Thacker, John, 2nd Lt.	46	P-36	1				
Webster, John, 1st Lt.	47	P-36	1			1	Missing SWP, 24 Feb. 44
Welch, George, 2nd Lt.	47	P-40	2	4			KPC 1954
			14	10	5	2	

Appendix III

Ground Casualities, 7 December 1941

Killed In Action

Headquarters Squadron:
Mitchell, John G., Cpl.
Walker, Lumus E., Cpl.
Chambers, Eugene P., P.F.C.
Schott, Robert L., P.F.C.
Shattuck, Robert R., P.F.C.
Vidoloff, Russell P., Pvt.

45th Squadron:
Buss, Robert P., Cpl.
Allen, Robert G., Pvt.

46th Squadron:
Plant, Donald D., P.F.C.

72nd Squadron:
Burns, Edward J., First Sgt.
Depolis, Frank J., S/Sgt.
Everett, James, S/Sgt.
Free, Paul B., S/Sgt.
Good, Joseph E., S/Sgt.
Guthrie, James E., S/Sgt.
Price, John A., S/Sgt.
Cashen, Malachy J., Cpl.
Baker, George W., P.F.C.
Creech, William C., P.F.C.
Cebert, Dean W., Pvt.
Goucy, Allen E. W., Pvt.
Hull, Robert L., Pvt.
Leslie, George G., Pvt.

Wounded In Action

Headquarters Squadron:
Baker, Leonard A., S/Sgt.
Nuttall, Roland L., S/Sgt.
Bennett, Howard A., S/Sgt.
Price, Walter J., Sgt.
Moyer, James I., Cpl.
Dodd, Harry O., P.F.C.
Durbin, Noel E., Pvt.
Ewers, James F., Pvt.
Neidzwiecki, Robert R., Pvt.
Richards, John N., Pvt.
Strong, Kenneth E., P.F.C.

45th Squadron:
Smith, Edwin G., First Sgt.
Baldwin, Robert H., S/Sgt.
Zuercher, Charles P., Cpl.
Gremore, Kenneth W., P.F.C.
Suffern, Richard, Pvt.
Zangari, Anthony A., Pvt.

46th Squadron:
Westhaver, Clayton M., Sgt.

47th Squadron:
Holley, Lester W., P.F.C.

72nd Squadron:
Carr, James W., M/Sgt.
Fay, John A., S/Sgt.
Dabney, Fred A., Sgt.
Davenport, James M., Sgt.
Ames, George C., Cpl.
English, James T., Cpl.
Kelly, Henry T., Cpl.
Klahn, Lester W., Cpl.
Steff, Jonah A., Cpl.
Bellue, Thomas E., P.F.C.
Kawa, Russell J., P.F.C.
Salloum, Naif J., P.F.C.
Fitzsimons, Robert G., Pvt.
Kimble, Thomas P., Jr., Pvt.
Tillett, George, Pvt.

Summary:

Killed in Action	23
Wounded in Action	34

Appendix IV

Decorations Awarded for Gallantry in Action On 7 December 1941

Name and Rank	Decoration
Rogers, Robert J., Capt.	Silver Star
Sanders, Lewis M., Capt.	Silver Star
Webster, John J., Capt.	Silver Star & Purple Heart
Brown, Harry W., 1st Lt.	Silver Star
Moore, Malcolm A., 1st Lt.	Silver Star
Rasmussen, Philip M., 1st Lt.	Silver Star
Taylor, Kenneth M., 1st Lt.	Distinguished Service Cross and Purple Heart
Thacker, John M., 1st Lt.	Silver Star
Welch, George S., 1st Lt.	Distinguished Service Cross
Dains, John L., 2nd Lt.	Silver Star and Purple Heart (Posthumous)
Sterling, Gordon H., 2nd Lt.	Distinguished Flying Cross and Purple Heart (Posthumous)
Fay, Charles A., S/Sgt.	Silver Star and Purple Heart
Ames, George C., Cpl.	Silver Star and Purple Heart
Tillett, George, Cpl.	Silver Star and Purple Heart

Note: The above honors were awarded on General Orders between 5 January 1942 and 1 July 1942.

Appendix V

Transfers and Reassignments

Name and Rank	Date of Transfer	Unit Sq / Grp	Theatre	Comments
Abel, George L., 1st Lt.	3 Oct 42	80/8	SWP	
Alger, Martin P., 2nd Lt.	3 Oct 42	9/49	SWP	4V; Capt.
Amato, Justin C., 1st Lt.	5 Dec 43	/18	SWP	
Anderson, Don C., 2nd Lt.	7 Aug 43	44/18	SWP	
Armstrong, Robt. E., 2nd Lt.	23 Apr 43	4/52	MTO	4V; Capt.
Artwohl, Arpod J., 1st Lt.	14 Dec 43	68/347	SWP	
Austin, Gordon H. Maj.	11 Feb 42	/325	MTO	2V; Grp CO; Lt. Col.
Babel, John S. 1st Lt.	3 Oct 42	 40/35	SWP	3V; Capt.
Baker, Richard H. 2nd Lt.	22 Apr 43	339/347	SWP	KIA 3 Jul 43
Barker, John W. 2nd Lt.	22 Apr 43	339/347	SWP	
Barnes, Samuel T. 2nd Lt.	29 Aug 42	68/347	SWP	
Barnes, William D. 1st Lt.	22 Apr 43	68/347	SWP	
Barrington, Carter 2nd Lt.	14 Dec 43	67/347	SWP	KIA 5 Mar 43
Barton, John E. 1st Lt.	23 Mar 43	6NFS	SWP	
Bauer, Robt. L. 2nd Lt.	29 Aug 42	67/347	SWP	KIA 1 Feb 43
Bayley, Edwin T. 1st Lt.	20 Oct 42	67/347	SWP	
Bellows, Donno C. 2nd Lt.	16 Oct 42	339/347	SWP	1V; 1st Lt.
Benner, John G. 1st Lt.	19 Oct 42	7/49	SWP	2V; Capt.
Bennett, Earl C. 1st Lt.	9 Mar 43	6NFS	SWP	1V; Capt.
Blair, Leland B. 2nd Lt.	23 Mar 43	80/8	SWP	3V; 1st Lt.
Blakely, Warren A. 2nd Lt.	16 Oct 42	8/49	SWP	2V; 1st Lt.
Boal, Robert P. 1st Lt.	23 Feb 43	339/347	SWP	
Bock, Kenneth E. 2nd Lt.	5 Jun 43	7/49	SWP	
Bodge, John H. 2nd Lt.	14 Dec 43	67/347	SWP	KIA 12 Mar 44
Borders, Andrew J. 1st Lt.	4 Jun 43	70/18	SWP	KIA 14 Sep 43
Bowerman, Robt. K. 2nd Lt.	27 Aug 43	35/8	SWP	1st Lt.
Bradner, Jack F. 2nd Lt.	17 Apr 43	6NFS	SWP	
Briccola, J.A. 2nd Lt.	Apr 44	339/347	SWP	
Brown, Harry W. 1st Lt.	3 Oct 42	431/475 9/49	SWP	5V; Capt.
Brown, Herschel A. 1st Lt.	23 Feb 43	68/347	SWP	Capt.; KIA 22 Feb 44
Brown, Keith S., 2nd Lt.	3 Mar 43	41/35	SWP	1V; 1st Lt.
Byers, Rex A. F/O	23 Apr 43	44/18	SWP	1V; KIA 25 Dec 43
Carr, Samuel R. 2nd Lt.	4 Jun 43	44/18	SWP	KPC Jul 43
Carriger, Wm. R. 2nd Lt.	5 Dec 43	418NFS	SWP	KIA 16 Jan 44
Carter, James A. 2nd Lt.	26 Mar 43	8/49	SWP	1V; 1st Lt.

Chandler, George T. 1st Lt.	2 Feb 43	339/347	SWP	5V; Capt.
Chandler, James A. 2nd Lt.	26 Mar 43	7/49	SWP	
Cheney, Francis J. 2nd Lt.	5 May 43	12/18	SWP	1st Lt.
Chewning, Samuel H. F/O	5 Jun 43	8/49	SWP	
Clapper, John W. 2nd Lt.	19 Oct 42	40/35	SWP	3V; Capt.
Cleague, Ralph T. 2nd Lt.	1 Jul 43	433/475	SWP	2V; 1st Lt.
Cleveland, Howard M. 2nd Lt.	4 Jun 43	70/18 44/18	SWP	2V; Capt.
Cohen, Joseph F/O	1 Jul 43			
Cohn, John A. 2nd Lt.	1 Jul 43	431/475	SWP	2V; 1st Lt.
Coleman, William E. F/O	11 Jun 43	6NFS	SWP	
Collins, Orval B. Capt.	21 Apr 43	67/347	SWP	Maj.; KIA 21 Mar 44
Connolly, Robert J. 2nd Lt.	7 Aug 43	44/18	SWP	2V; Capt.
Crain, Franklin 2nd Lt.	23 Apr 43	44/18	SWP	1V; 1st Lt.
Croft, Robert W. 2nd Lt.	26 Mar 43	7/49	SWP	1V; 1st Lt.
Crow, Robert J.H. 2nd Lt.	7 Aug 43	44/18	SWP	KIA 12 Oct 43
Crowley, John F. 2nd Lt.	29 Mar 43	7/49	SWP	
Daggitt, Wm. E. 2nd Lt.	30 Aug 42	/347	SWP	
Dames, William H. 1st Lt.	Apr 44	548NFS	CP	1V; Capt.
Danson, Warren R. 2nd Lt.	19 Aug 42	35/8	SWP	1V; Capt.
Daugherty, F.R. Capt.	12 Aug 43	12/18	SWP	2V; Maj.
Davis, F/O	May 44	5RadCalU	CP	
Davis, Emmett S. Capt.	18 Aug 42	35/8	SWP	3V; Grp CO; Lt. Col.
Davis, Jack A. 1st Lt.	23 Feb 43	339/347	SWP	
Deangelo, Antonio M. 1st Lt.	14 Dec 43	68/347	SWP	
Debernarde, Arthur W. 2nd Lt.	30 Aug 42		SWP	13th AF; KPC
Dempsey, Timothy M. 2nd Lt.	21 Aug 42			
Dick, Frederick E. 2nd Lt.	14 Dec 43	7/49	SWP	5V; Capt.
Donack, Percy F/O	27 Aug 43	22B Grp	SWP	KPC 12 Mar 44
Downie, James D. Capt.	21 Apr 43	/347	SWP	
Dreckman, Harold G. 2nd Lt.	2 Feb 43	44/18	SWP	2.5V; Capt.
Drier, William C. 2nd Lt.	29 Mar 43	8/49	SWP	6V; Capt.
Dunbar, Harvey L. 2nd Lt.	30 Aug 42	12/18	SWP	
Duren, Gaylor G. Capt.	29 Sep 43	68/347	SWP	
Dwyer, William H. 2nd Lt.	27 Aug 43	35/8	SWP	1V; 1st Lt.
Egan, William R. 2nd Lt.	14 Dec 43		SWP	5th AF; KPC
Epling, Fenton G. 2nd Lt.	14 Dec 43	7/49	SWP	1V; 1st Lt.; KPC
Farkas, Raymond G. 2nd Lt.	7 Aug 43	44/18	SWP	.5V
Farrell, Roger J. 2nd Lt.	3 Mar 43	41/35	SWP	1V; 1st Lt.
Feiler, William J. 2nd Lt.	18 Aug 42	35/8	SWP	1V; Capt.
Felts, Marion C. 2nd Lt.	14 Dec 43	8/49	SWP	5V; 1st Lt.
Fenimore, Jack A. 2nd Lt.	22 Jul 43	7/49	SWP	1V; 1st Lt.
Fennell, John S. 2nd Lt.	5 May 43	44/18	SWP	
Fetch, Robert M. 1st Lt.	23 Feb 43	68/347	SWP	2V
Fiedler, William F. 2nd Lt.	30 Aug 42	68/347 70/18	SWP	5V; Capt.; Died of injuries 30 June 43
Flack, Nelson D. 2nd Lt.	29 Mar 43	8/49	SWP	5V; Capt.
Florence, John E. 1st Lt.	23 Mar 43	6NFS	SWP	
Forsythe, Homer A. 1st Lt.	23 Aug 42	/18	SWP	
Fradin, Walter F/O	5 Dec 43			
Francis, Magnus D. 2nd Lt.	3 Mar 43	44/18	SWP	3.5V; 1st Lt.
Franks, James H. 2nd Lt.	14 Dec 43	7/49	SWP	2V; 1st Lt.
Gabreski, Francis S. 1st Lt.	16 Oct 42	61/56	ETO	28V; Lt. Col.; POW
Gessler, George W. 1st Lt.	Apr 44	12/18	SWP	2V;
Gilchrist, Devin H. 2nd Lt.	29 Sep 43	36/8	SWP	KIA 26 Dec 43
Gill, James H. 2nd Lt.	21 Aug 42	12/18	SWP	1V; 1st Lt.; KIA 13 May 43
Glascock, Edward T. 2nd Lt.	27 Aug 43	8/49	SWP	3V; 1st Lt.
Gorham, Calvin C. 2nd Lt.	30 Aug 42	70/18	SWP	1V; 1st Lt.
Gours, Charles A. 2nd Lt.	29 Sep 43	8/49	SWP	KIA 28 Sep 44

Graebner, Lawrence A. 2nd Lt.	21 Aug 42	12/18	SWP	1st Lt.
Grandjean, John H. 1st Lt.	21 Apr 43	67/347	SWP	
Gresham, Billy M. 2nd Lt.	1 Jul 43	432/475	SWP	6V; Capt; KPC 2 Oct 44
Guinee, Robert P. 2nd Lt.	2 Feb 43	19/318	CP	Capt.
Haher, John G. 2nd Lt.	23 Jul 43	7/49	SWP	3V; Capt.
Haney, William F. 1st Lt.	3 Oct 42	40/35		
		9/49	SWP	8V; Lt. Col.
Harris, Charles A. 2nd Lt.	30 Aug 42	68/347	SWP	2V; 1st Lt.
Harris, Robert C. 2nd Lt.	5 Dec 43	67/347	SWP	
Harter, Victor G. 2nd Lt.	29 Aug 42	339/347	SWP	Capt.
Hartsfield, John H. 2nd Lt.	14 Dec 43	41/35	SWP	1st Lt.; KIA 14 Feb 44
Heckerman, Arthur 2nd Lt.	29 Sep 43		SWP	5th AF
Hedrick, Howard A. 2nd Lt.	1 Jul 43	432/475	SWP	4V; Capt.
Heen, Roy L. 2nd Lt.	21 Aug 42	12/18	SWP	
Hefelfinger, Charles 2nd Lt.	7 Aug 43	44/18	SWP	
Henry, Roger H. 2nd Lt.	3 Mar 43	88/80	CBI	Capt.; KIA 29 Jul 45
Henze, Irwin W. 1st Lt.	18 Aug 42	40/35	SWP	Capt.
Hill, Herbert H. 1st Lt.	3 Oct 42	41/35	SWP	KIA
Honaker, William F. 2nd Lt.	4 Oct 42	12/18	SWP	1V; 1st Lt; KIA 20 Aug 43
Hornaday, Warren G. Capt.	23 Mar 43	6NFS	SWP	KIA 7 May 43
Horton, John W. 2nd Lt.	19 Oct 42	40/35	SWP	3V; Capt.
Hoyle, James W. 1st Lt.	2 Feb 43	339/347	SWP	1V; KIA 17 Jul 43
Imberg, Ralph R. 1st Lt.	23 Feb 43	44/18	SWP	KIA 1 Aug 43
Jameson, George T. 1st Lt.	21 Apr 43	339/347	SWP	
Jennings, Theo B. 1st Lt.	2 Feb 43	44/18	SWP	1V; Capt.
Jett, Verl E. 1st Lt.	19 Aug 42	36/8		
		431/475	SWP	7V; Lt. Col.
Johns, Kenneth 1st Lt.	19 Aug 42	8/49	SWP	2V; Capt.
Johnson, Bruce B. 1st Lt.	10 Jun 43	6NFS	SWP	
Jordan, Herbert H. 1st Lt.	19 Aug 42	40/35		
		433/475	SWP	
		435/479	ETO	3V; Maj.
Jurgenson, Elmer V.	23 Feb 43	/347	SWP	2V; Capt.
Kaempher, Robert E. Capt.	43	28PRSq	CP	Maj.
Kannamer, Earl W. 2nd Lt.	30 Aug 42			
Kasper, Mark T. 1st Lt.	10 Jun 43	80/8	SWP	1V; Capt.
Kee, Harrison E. 2nd Lt.	29 Mar 43	8/49	SWP	Capt.
Kephart, Thomas G. 1st Lt.	23 Feb 43	70/18	SWP	KPC 20 Mar 43
Kneen, Charles E. 1st Lt.	3 Oct 42	35/8	SWP	Capt.
Knox, John G. 2nd Lt.	1 Jul 43	431/475	SWP	KIA 13 Sep 43
Kofahl, Harold E. Capt.	7 May 42	/86	MTO	Grp CO; Col.
Kriechbaum, Philip E. 2nd Lt.	23 Jul 43	8/49	SWP	Capt; KIA 10 Dec 44
Kuck, Frederick G. 2nd Lt.	23 Mar 43			
Kurt, Edward J. 2nd Lt.	21 Aug 42	/8	SWP	1st Lt.
Lake, Arvel M. F/O	5 Dec 43			
Lambert, Floyd E. 1st Lt.	19 Aug 42	36/8	SWP	Capt.
Laughlin, Joseph L.	28 Feb 43	379/362	ETO	1V; Maj.
Lawrence, Henry W. Capt.	31 Apr 43	339/347	SWP	
Ledford, Linn W. 2nd Lt.	5 Dec 43	418NFS	SWP	
Lee, Averette T. 2nd Lt.	23 Jul 43	8/49	SWP	2V; 1st Lt.
Lesicka, Joseph J. 1st Lt.	23 Feb 43	44/18	SWP	9V; Capt.
Lewis, Jackson B. 1st Lt.	2 Feb 43	68/347	SWP	KIA 27 Feb 43
Lipman, Norman H. 1st Lt.	23 Feb 43		SWP	13th AF
Low, Martin E. 1st Lt.	19 Aug 42	433/475	SWP	Maj.
		40/35		
Lustic, Stanley J. 2nd Lt.	May 44	19/318	CP	7V; 1st Lt.
MacNicol, George M. Maj.	20 Jan 43	/82	MTO	Grp CO; Col.
Martin, William T. Capt.	18 Aug 42	35/8	SWP	1V; 1st Lt.
McCabe, Robert F. 1st Lt.	19 Aug 42	36/8	SWP	Capt.

McCelland, Howard M. 1st Lt.	19 Aug 42	35/8	SWP	3V; Capt.
McDonnell, Robert E. 2nd Lt.	17 Aug 43	6NFS	CP	
McInnis, Lawrence A. 2nd Lt.	27 Aug 43	7/49	SWP	
McIvor, William T. 2nd Lt.	17 Apr 43	6NFS	CP	
McKeon, Joseph T. 2nd Lt.	21 Aug 42	35/8		
		433/475	SWP	
		77/20	ETO	6V; Capt.
McLeod, Robert W. 1st Lt.	23 Mar 43	6NFS	SWP	
Miller, Robert B. 2nd Lt.	May 44	73/318	CP	.25V; 1st Lt.
Mitchell, Milton H. 2nd Lt.	27 Aug 43		SWP	5th AF
Montrose, Paul R. 2nd Lt.	23 Feb 43	68/347	SWP	
Moore, Allan 2nd Lt.	14 Sep 42	12/18	SWP	Capt.
Moore, Malcolm A. Capt.	19 Oct 42	40/35	SWP	1V; Grp CO; Lt. Col.
Morriss, Paul V. 2nd Lt.	1 Jul 43	431/475	SWP	5V; Capt.
Mulliken, Kenneth E. 1st Lt.	15 Jul 43	44/18	SWP	
Nagy, Louis J. 1st Lt.	19 Aug 42	40/35	SWP	1V
Newell, Kenneth C. 2nd Lt.	23 Feb 43	339/347	SWP	
Njus, Casper M. 2nd Lt.	3 Mar 43	44/18	SWP	1st Lt.
Oldham, Rufus 2nd Lt.	Apr 44	70/18	SWP	
Osborne, Philip W. 2nd Lt.	Apr 44	70/18	SWP	
Palmer, James M. 2nd Lt.	16 Oct 42	41/35	SWP	1V; 1st Lt.
Paris, Joel B. 2nd Lt.	14 Dec 43	7/49	SWP	9V; Capt.
Peck, Donald L. 2nd Lt.	23 Feb 43	68/347	SWP	
Peek, Robert M. 1st Lt.	15 Jul 43	339/347	SWP	
Perkins, John H. 2nd Lt.	20 Aug 42	36/8	SWP	1V; 1st Lt.
Perkins, John T. 2nd Lt.	3 Mar 43			
Polhamus, Richard P. 2nd Lt.	26 Mar 43	8/49	SWP	Capt.
Pollock, Lumuel E. 2nd Lt.	4 Jun 43	7/49	SWP	1V; 1st Lt.
Powell, Kenneth R. Lt. Col.	20 Apr 44	/21	CP	Grp CO; Col.
Price, John E. 2nd Lt.	4 Jun 43	44/18	SWP	
Prince, Tony 2nd Lt.	16 Oct 42	41/35	SWP	1V; Capt.
Randolph, Roy E. 2nd Lt.	29 Sep 43	36/8	SWP	1V; 1st Lt.
Rasmussen, Philip M. 1st Lt.	3 Oct 42	/8	SWP	
		/318	CP	1V; Lt. Col.
Richardson, Melvin W. 2nd Lt.	23 Mar 43			
Rieser, Robert E. 1st Lt.	6 Jul 43	333/318	CP	Capt.
Ritala, Robert E. 2nd Lt.	14 Sep 42			
Rogers, Jay G. 2nd Lt.	14 Dec 43		SWP	Died, non-battle
Sallings, Robert W. 2nd Lt.	5 Dec 43	67/347	SWP	
Sanders, Lewis M. Maj.	26 Nov 42	7FtrCom		
		/318	CP	Grp CO; Col.
Sapp, Marion L. 2nd Lt.	14 Sep 42	12/18	SWP	KIA Dec 42
Sauve, Richard H. 1st Lt.	19 Aug 42	35/8	SWP	
Sawyer, Jerome R. 1st Lt.	29 Aug 42	67/347	SWP	1.5V; Capt.
Secord, Frederick H. 1st Lt.	23 Mar 43	6 NFS	CP	
Sherman, Robert B. 2nd Lt.	4 Jun 43	8/49	SWP	1V
Shifflet, Fred B. 1st Lt.	21 Aug 42	39/35	SWP	KIA 3 Mar 43
Shuler, Lucien B. 1st Lt.	2 Feb 43	44/18	SWP	7V
Shoaff, Charles M. 2nd Lt.	14 Dec. 43	8/49	SWP	Injured in Crash
Smith, J. Floyd 2nd Lt.	14 Dec 43			
Smith, Grant R. 1st Lt.	23 Feb 43	44/18	SWP	
		318/325	MTO	2V; Capt.
Smith, Lewis C. 2nd Lt.	4 Jun 43	7/49	SWP	2V; 1st Lt.
Smith, Robert C. 2nd Lt.	11 Jun 43	36/8		
		8/49	SWP	4V; Maj.
Smith, Thomas W. 2nd Lt.	5 May 43	37/14	MTO	1V; 1st Lt.
Squires, Carl M. 2nd Lt.	22 Apr 43	339/347	SWP	1st Lt.; KIA 8 Nov 43
Steinman, John W. 2nd Lt.	5 May 43	/347	SWP	
Stellmacher, Theo. H. 2nd Lt.	23 Mar 43			Died 12 Mar 45

Stratton, Eldon E. 1st Lt.	20 Oct 42	12/18	SWP	1V; Capt.; KIA 30 Aug 43
Straub, David 2nd Lt.	5 May 43	68/347	SWP	
Streete, Alex B. Capt.	28 Jan 42	6NFS	CP	
		68/347	SWP	
		463/507	CP	Maj.
Suggs, Laurine S. 2nd Lt.	20 Sep 43	7/49	SWP	1V; 1st Lt.
Summers, Thomas B. Capt.	15 Oct 42	7FrtCom		
		/318	CP	
		32PrvSq	CBI	.5V; Lt. Col.
Tate, Lyndell P. 2nd Lt.	21 Aug 42	41/35	SWP	Capt.
Taylor, Charles A. 1st Lt.	15 Jul 43	/18	SWP	
Taylor, Garrett E. 2nd Lt.	15 Jul 43	/347	SWP	1st Lt.
Taylor, Kenneth M. 1st Lt.	Aug 42	44/18	SWP	Maj.
Thorgerson, John Capt.	18 Aug 42		SWP	5th AF
Tomberg, Robert M. 2nd Lt.	1 Jul 43	433/475	SWP	2V; Capt.
Tomkins, Frank D. 1st Lt.	19 Oct 42	80/8		
		432/475	SWP	4V; Maj.
Toole, Richard A. 1st Lt.	3 Oct 42	35/8	SWP	
Tucker, Robert E. 2nd Lt.	4 Oct 42	339/347	SWP	
Tucker, Robert G. 2nd Lt.	16 Oct 42	12/18	SWP	
Tullis, Robert W. 2nd Lt.	29 Aug 42	/347	SWP	
Tuttle, Ralph E. 2nd Lt.	9 Apr 43	6NFS	SWP	1V; 1st Lt.
Twichell, Wallace B. Capt	21 Apr 43	67/347	SWP	
Tyer, Aaron W. Capt.	23 Dec 41	/18	SWP	Grp CO; Col.
Uhrenholdt, Kenneth V. 2nd Lt.	14 Dec 43	67/347	SWP	1st Lt.
Veirs, Evan I. 2nd Lt.	Sep 43	72/318		
		7FtrCom	CP	Capt.
Vogt, John E. 2nd Lt.	Sep 43	19/318	CP	5V; Capt.
Voss, John D. Capt.	28 Apr 43	44/18	SWP	2.5V; KIA 8 Nov 43
Wade, Ralph V. 2nd Lt.	21 Aug 42	12/18	SWP	
Walden, Stanley F. 1st Lt.	23 Feb 43	44/18	SWP	
Waldman, William M. 1st Lt.	19 Aug 42	432/475	SWP	1V; Capt.
Warren, Robert M. 2nd Lt.	29 Sep 43		SWP	5th AF
Warrick, Thomas D. 2nd Lt.	19 Oct 42		SWP	5th AF
Waters, Richard L. 1st Lt.	10 Apr 43		SWP	KIA 7 Jul 44
Wayne, Harry W. Capt.	10 Jun 43	419NFS	SWP	KPC 8 Jan 44
Webster, John J. Capt.		2ProAir Svc Sq	CP	Maj.; Vanished on ferry flight 24 Feb 44
Welch, George S. 1st Lt.	3 Oct 42	36/8		
		80/8	SWP	12V; Maj.
Wells, Joseph C. F/O	6 Aug 43	/347	SWP	
Wells, Perry P. 2nd Lt.	14 Sep 42	12/18	SWP	1.5V; 1st Lt.
Wells, Travis D. 2nd Lt.	7 Aug 43	44/18	SWP	1st Lt.; KIA 6 Jan 44
Wells, William D. 2nd Lt.	23 Feb 43	6NFS	SWP	
West, William L. Capt.	23 Apr 43	/347	SWP	
Wheeler, Richard A. 2nd Lt.	22 Apr 43	44/18	SWP	4V; 1st Lt.
Whitaker, Gordon 2nd Lt.	4 Oct 42	12/18	SWP	KIA 29 Apr 43
White, Floyd 2nd Lt.	14 Sep 42	12/18	SWP	1V
Wigley, Roy Capt.	Aug 43	531FBSq	CP	Maj; KIA 18 Jan 44
Winternitz, David R. 2nd Lt.	4 Jun 43	8/49	SWP	1V; 1st Lt.
Works, David P. 2nd Lt.	4 May 43	70/18	SWP	1V; 1st Lt.
Young, Edward L. 2nd Lt.	23 Apr 43	67/347	SWP	1V; Capt.
Zabel, Joel D. 1st Lt.	3 Oct 42	35/8	SWP	
		41/35		
Zuniga, Nicanor A. 2nd Lt.	14 Dec 43	7/49	SWP	1V; 1st Lt.

All available information relates to service after transfer from the 15th Fighter Group. Comments include World War II aerial victories, group command, last known rank, and casualty status where facts are known and applicable.

Appendix VI

Operational Fatalities, 1942-1945

Name, Rank	Date	Sq.	Aircraft	
Freeman, Philip D., 2nd Lt.	22 Jan 42	47th	P-40B	
Tighe, Edward J., 2nd Lt.	30 Mar 42	47th	P-40E	
Sullivan, Raymond T., 2nd Lt.	12 Apr 42	47th	P-26A	
Cox, James A., Capt.	18 May 42	72nd	P-36A	
Norris, Othneil, 1st Lt.	24 Jun 42	46th	P-39D	
Oblak, Joseph, 2nd Lt.	12 Jul 42	Hq Sq	P-36A	
Kelley, Clifton P., 2nd Lt.	4 Sep 42	45th	P-40B	
Morene, Edwin, Jr., 2nd Lt.	6 Sep 42	72nd	P-40	
Miller, William M., 2nd Lt.	17 Sep 42	47th	P-40E	
Fluhrer, Henry L., 2nd Lt.	9 Oct 42	45th	P-40B	
Conrad, Henry L., 2nd Lt.	12 Nov 42	45th	P-40B	
Haggerty, Donald H., 2nd Lt.	12 Nov 42	46th	P-39D	
Corbett, Harry G., 2nd Lt.	21 Dec 42	46th	P-40E	
Dwyer, Lane W., 2nd Lt.	10 Jan 43	47th	P-40E	
Domack, Eugene R., F/O	5 Mar 43	46th	P-40E	
Cocke, Benjamin B., 2nd Lt.	6 Mar 43	46th	P-39D	
Shakespeare, James W., 2nd Lt.	20 Mar 43	45th	RP-40B	
Kennedy, Raymond E., 2nd Lt.	28 Mar 43	45th	RP-40B	
Stanton, Edward C., 2nd Lt.	10 Apr 43	47th	P-40E	
Biorn, Robert S., 2nd Lt.	1 May 43	47th	P-40E	
Ironmonger, Sidney W., 2nd Lt.	2 May 43	78th	P-40K	
Litsis, Leon A., 2nd Lt.	3 May 43	78th	P-40K	
McCullough, John J., 2nd Lt.	8 May 43	47th	P-40E	
Horchler, Clarence W., 2nd Lt.	10 Jun 43	78th	P-40K	
Ruddell, Cyril D.E., Capt.	18 Jun 43	47th	P-40E	
Cook, James V., F/O	19 Jun 43	47th	P-40E	
Lewis, Gordon M., 1st Lt.	12 Jul 43	45th	P-40B	
Tews, Wilbur A., 2nd Lt.	12 Jul 43	45th	P-40B	
Bertsch, Frederick G., 1st Lt.	15 Jul 43	45th	P-40B	
Hamilton, James W., 2nd Lt.	17 Jul 43	47th	P-40E	(died 5 Aug 43)
Place, Harold C., 1st Lt.	24 Jul 43	47th	P-40N	
Hurlburt, Murray L., 2nd Lt.	18 Sep 43	46th	P-39Q	(Canton)
Enos, Phillip J., 2nd Lt.	3 Oct 43	78th	P-40K	
Southerland, Bill, Maj.	9 Dec 43	78th	P-40K	
Snyder, Verne B., 2nd Lt.	28 Dec 43	45th	P-40K	(Nanomea)
Bush, John S., 2nd Lt.	7 Feb 44	47th	P-47D	
Murray, Carl P., 2nd Lt.	23 Mar 44	46th	P-39Q	
Cameron, Daniel M., 2nd Lt.	23 Mar 44	46th	P-39Q	
Fennell, Thomas F., 2nd Lt.	26 Mar 44	46th	P-39Q	
Green, Robert E., 2nd Lt.	1 Apr 44	78th	P-47D	
Blankenship, Rex H., 1st Lt.	6 Apr 44	46th	P-39Q	
Shoulder, James V., 2nd Lt.	26 Apr 44	47th	P-47D	
Nordstrom, Herbert A., 2nd Lt.	21 May 44	78th	A-24RA	
Sliwa, Raymond D., 2nd Lt.	9 Jun 44	47th	P-47D	
Foster, Cly E., 2nd Lt.	10 Jun 44	47th	P-47D	
Edmonson, Howard M., 1st Lt.	14 Jun 44	78th	P-47D	
Schauman, Edwin A., 2nd Lt.	14 Jun 44	45th	P-47D	
Spadoni, Marino E., 2nd Lt.	20 Jun 44	47th	P-47D	
Loe, Robert E., 2nd Lt.	12 Jul 44	45th	P-47D	
Mohler, Philip B., 2nd Lt.	17 Jul 44	45th	P-47D	
Dean, William L., 2nd Lt.	30 Jul 44	47th	P-47D	
Ferris, Robert A., 2nd Lt.	25 Nov 44	78th	P-51D	
Bonham, William H., 2nd Lt.	8 Jan 45	45th	P-51D	
Olson, Bernard L., 2nd Lt.	8 Jan 45	45th	P-51D	

Lindner, W.J., 2nd Lt.	13 Jan 45	78th	P-51D	
Gromada, Frank, Capt.	16 Jan 45	47th	P-51D	
Rudolph, Shipley, 2nd Lt.	16 Jan 45	47th	P-51D	
Tripp, James L., 2nd Lt.	16 Jan 45	47th	P-51D	
Trodahl, Alex, 1st Lt.	29 Apr 45	47th	P-51D	(Iwo)
Edwards, William B., 2nd Lt.	22 May 45	45th	P-51D	(Iwo)

Appendix VII

Fighter Aircraft Lost
In Operational Accidents, 1942

Type	Number
P-26	1
P-36	3
P-39	6
P-40	21
	31

Appendix VIII

Pilot's Combat Record
46th Fighter Squadron, 15th Fighter Group
The Marshall Islands Campaign

Pilot Name	Total Combat Sorties	Total Sorties Time	Total Combat Patrol	Comments re aerial vics, awards, KIA
2nd Lt. Robert H. Amon	8	20:50	26:35	AM
2nd Lt. Ben R. Bryant	8	20:45	21:40	AM
2nd Lt. Chas. E. Bryant	10	23:50	31:10	AM
2nd Lt. Edward H. Bryant	10	22:00	32:30	AM
1st Lt. Geo. M. Brown	10	24:30	10:20	AM
2nd Lt. James A. Burrows	10	26:25	29:20	AM
2nd Lt. Robert E. Clark	10	24:00	14:40	AM
2nd Lt. John C. Cox	8	18:40	25:25	AM
2nd Lt. Geo. E. Dunstan	8	22:10	24:10	AM
Capt. Clifford G. Erdman	5			PH, KIA
Capt. Paul Fojtik	7	18:30	4:15	AM, PH
1st Lt. Jack V. Garnett	11	25:50	13:15	AM
1st Lt. Fred J. Gibson	11	25:20	21:15	AM
1st Lt. William A. Higgins	11	24:00	28:30	AM
2nd Lt. Carl J. Hubbard, Jr.	10	26:10	29:35	AM, PH
1st Lt. Edgar F. Huffman	10	25:10	26:20	AM
1st Lt. Robt. B. Kessler	11	24:35	35:05	AM
1st Lt. Thomas W. Lewis	19	44:00	37:20	½ Vic, AM 1/OLC
2nd Lt. Owen P. McCaul	10	25:45	33:15	AM
1st Lt. Joseph P. McHale	10	27:25	15:40	AM
2nd Lt. Carl P. Murray	10	22:25	31:50	AM, PH
1st Lt. Raymond J. Popson	9	20:20	25:30	AM
2nd Lt. Thomas O. Quinn	10	23:50	24:45	AM
2nd Lt. Cranston B. Rader, Jr.	11	31:05	21:55	AM
Capt. Lamar A. Ramos	9	23:35	31:45	AM
2nd Lt. J. G. Rattigan	1			KIA
F/O Felix P. Scott	10	21:50	33:50	1 Vic, AM 1/OLC
Maj. DeWitt S. Spain	10	25:00	21:40	AM
Lt. Col. John M. Thacker	10	23:20	12:00	1 Vic, AM 1/OLC
1st Lt. Ben C. Warren	12	27:35	16:25	½ Vic, AM 1/OLC

Note: Sorties and hours logged are from an official Squadron tabulation and do not include aborted missions.

Appendix IX

Pilot's Combat Record
45th Fighter Squadron, 15th Fighter Group
The Marshall Islands Campaign

Pilot Name	Total Combat Sorties	Comments re aerial vics, awards, and KIA
1st Lt. John J. Apple	10	1 Vic, AM 2/OLC
2nd Lt. John H. Basham	12	AM 1/OLC
2nd Lt. Jacob J. Bishop	10	AM
1st Lt. Herbert D. Boone	11	1 Vic, AM 2/OLC
1st Lt. Arthur H. Bridge	20	DFC, AM 2/OLC, PH
1st Lt. Dwight R. Butler	19	1 Vic, DFC, AM 2/OLC
1st Lt. Bruce S. Campbell, Jr.	18	AM 2/OLC, PH, DFC
2nd Lt. John S. Chambers	18	AM 2/OLC
2nd Lt. Jack G. Cotter	6	AM
2nd Lt. Richard D. Duerr	7	AM
2nd Lt. George H. Dunlap	18	DFC, AM 1/OLC
2nd Lt. Marsden J. Dupuy	8	AM
1st Lt. F. Lyman Ennis	18	DFC, AM 1/OLC
2nd Lt. William J. Fisher	12	AM 1/OLC
2nd Lt. Lloyd A. Harvey	9	AM, PH, KIA
2nd Lt. Fred A. Henderson	17	DFC, AM 1/OLC
2nd Lt. Russell L. Hendrickson	17	DFC, AM 1/OLC
2nd Lt. Eugene P. Horton	19	DFC, AM 1/OLC
2nd Lt. Richard H. Hintermeier	7	1 Vic, AM 1/OLC, PH
2nd Lt. George H. Hunter, Jr.	19	DFC, AM 1/OLC
2nd Lt. Paul W. Hunter	11	AM
Maj. Gordon R. Hyde	4	AM (15th Grp Ops Off)
2nd Lt. Robert C. Jackson	19	1 Vic, DFC, AM 2/OLC
2nd Lt. Beaver A. Kinsel	9	AM
2nd Lt. Morton M. Knox	18	1 Vic, DFC, AM 2/OLC
2nd Lt. David E. Kriger	8	AM
1st Lt. James A. Loulan, Jr.	5	AM
2nd Lt. Albert E. Maltby	10	AM 1/OLC
1st Lt. Robert W. Moore	17	1 Vic, DFC, AM 2/OLC
1st Lt. George C. Morey	19	DFC, AM 1/OLC
2nd Lt. John W. Polk	17	DFC, AM 1/OLC
Capt. Fred A. Shirley	16	DFC, AM 1/OLC
2nd Lt. Jay W. Slater	7	AM
Capt. Gilmer L. Snipes	14	1 Vic, AM 2/OLC
Lt. Col. Julian E. Thomas	18	DFC, AM 1/OLC
Maj. Harry M. Thompson	19	1 Vic, DFC, AM 2/OLC
Capt. James M. Vande Hey	9	2 Vics, DFC, AM 1/OLC
1st Lt. Alfred O. Williams	16	DFC, AM 1/OLC

Note: Records of hours logged were not retained in USAF archives. Sorties indicated are from mission reports and do not include routine CAP or aborted missions.

Appendix X

Casualty Analysis of Original Iwo Jima Pilot Officers

Group Headquarters:
Beckwith, J.O., Col.**
Kearney, E.L., Jr., Maj.
Birk, R.W., Capt.

45th Squadron:
Snipes, G.L., Maj.
Bridge, A.H., Capt.
Butler, D.R., Capt.
Campbell, B.S., Jr., Capt.
Ennis, F.L., Capt.
Hunter, G.H., Capt.
Knox, M.M., Capt.
Maltby, A.E., Capt.
Morey, G.C., Capt.
Brown, Wes. E., 1st Lt.
Dunlap, G.H., Jr., 1st Lt.
Fisher, W.J., 1st Lt.
Harrigan, W.N., Jr., 1st Lt.
Henderson, F.H., Jr., 1st Lt.
Hunter, P.W., 1st Lt.
McCorkle, Q.G., 1st Lt.
Runton, W.C., 1st Lt.
Slater, J.W., 1st Lt.
Walker, J.D., 1st Lt.
Kinsel, B.A., 1st Lt.
Bates, E.F., 2nd Lt.
(Brown, Wm. E., 2nd Lt.)**
(Burry, A.A., 2nd Lt.)**
Condon, F.C., 2nd Lt.
Cyphers, E.L., 2nd Lt.
Deckert, D.E., 2nd Lt.
Dennis, C.A., 2nd Lt.
Edwards, L.C., 2nd Lt.
Garey, R.R., 2nd Lt.
Gowan, G.F., 2nd Lt.
Hosey, P.E., 2nd Lt.
Joyner, L.K., 2nd Lt.
Kemske, R.P., 2nd Lt.
Kester, J.E., 2nd Lt.
Klein, M.L., 2nd Lt.
Lettie, S.G., 2nd Lt.*
Lortie, L.J., 2nd Lt.
Moore, R.S., 2nd Lt.
Redus, W.W., 2nd Lt.
Reese, C.D., 2nd Lt.
Reinert, V.V., 2nd Lt.
Rettberg, G.C., 2nd Lt.
Richins, J.G., 2nd Lt.
Roberts, A.E., Jr., 2nd Lt.
Scott, D.H., 2nd Lt.
Statsmann, D.E., 2nd Lt.
Thornton, R.M., 2nd Lt.*
Wanamaker, J.A., 2nd Lt.
Watt, R.W., Jr., 2nd Lt.
Wilder, H., Jr., 2nd Lt.
Wray, R.D., 2nd Lt.
Yakish, L.E., 2nd Lt.
Zalesky, R.F., 2nd Lt.
Combs, E.P., F/O

47th Squadron:
Piper, J.A., Maj.
Betner, R.J., Capt.
Down, R.R., Capt.
(Markham, T.E., Capt.)
Obenshain, R.L., Jr., Capt.
Pepin, L.T., Capt.
Powell, W.H., Capt.
(Ayers, F.L., 1st Lt.)**
(Baccus, H.L., 1st Lt.)
(Baldwin, N.H., 1st Lt.)
Bjorseth, B.P., 1st Lt.
Bright, E.L., 1st Lt.
Brunette, J.P., 1st Lt.
Cameron, C.J., 1st Lt.
Carletti, A.J., 1st Lt.
Condrick, R.J., 1st Lt.
Hintermeier, R.H., 1st Lt.
Jennings, C.E., 1st Lt.
McCormick, J.A., 1st Lt.
Mitchell, J.C., Jr., 1st Lt.
Ryniker, H.C., 1st Lt.
Stelling, D.G., 1st Lt.
Trodahl, A.E., 1st Lt.
Balak, D.S., 2nd Lt.
Barlow, W.E., 2nd Lt.
Dibelka, A., Jr., 2nd Lt.
Doughty, C.C., 2nd Lt.
Elliott, A.C., 2nd Lt.
Frick, P.C., 2nd Lt.
Fitzgerald, J.M., 2nd Lt.
Gourley, M.F., 2nd Lt.
(Grover, Fred T., 2nd Lt.)
Heintz, R.N., 2nd Lt. ***
Jones, S.S., Jr., 2nd Lt.**
June, R.E., 2nd Lt.
Kinsey, F.M., 2nd Lt.
Klessig, C.E., 2nd Lt.
Kriss, R.J., 2nd Lt.
Lidell, H.F., Jr., 2nd Lt.
Locke, D.F., 2nd Lt.
Long, R.M., 2nd Lt.
(O'Mara, O.E., Jr., 2nd Lt.)
Reed, W.G., Jr., 2nd Lt.
Scamara, R.S., 2nd Lt.
Scanlan, J.V., 2nd Lt.
Schroeder, E.A., Jr., 2nd Lt.
Sher, L.P., 2nd Lt.
Shuler, J.R., 2nd Lt.
Sidebottom, W.K., 2nd Lt.
Tyler, H.M., 2nd Lt.
Van Zandt, H.M., 2nd Lt.
Wagner, J.F., 2nd Lt.*
Weaver, H.R., 2nd Lt.
White, A.D., 2nd Lt.
White, D.O., 2nd Lt.
Worton, R.A., 2nd Lt.

78th Squadron:
Vande Hey, J.M., Maj.
Tapp, J.B., Maj.
(Collins, H.D., Capt.)
Hostetler, E.W., Capt.
Merrill, N.P., Jr., Capt.
Mollan, V.K., Capt.
Moore, R.W., Capt.
Parish, L.E., Jr., Capt.
Beyl, R.H., 1st Lt.
Carr, R.L., 1st Lt.
Chambers, J.S., 1st Lt.
Duerr, R.D., 1st Lt.
Maher, P.J., Jr., 1st Lt.
Moore, D.B., 1st Lt.
Patterson, J., Jr., 1st Lt.
(Roseberry, R.H., 1st Lt.)*
Ruby, R.C., 1st Lt.
Sherren, A.W., 1st Lt.
Yellin, J., 1st Lt.
Bargaehr, L.M., 2nd Lt.
Bauman, F.A., 2nd Lt.
Brooks, D.T., 2nd Lt.
Butler, C.R., Jr., 2nd Lt.
(Carey, R.F., Jr., 2nd Lt.)
Chism, P.E., 2nd Lt.***
Christoe, G.A., 2nd Lt.
Coryell, R.C., 2nd Lt.
Dahlquist, K.R., 2nd Lt.
Evans, L.B., 2nd Lt.
Gautsche, D.L., 2nd Lt.
Gibson, A.R., 2nd Lt.
Grimes, C.C., Jr., 2nd Lt.
Heil, C.C., 2nd Lt.
Korb, L.L., 2nd Lt.
(Kreimann, W.W., 2nd Lt.)**
Mangum, C.V. 2nd Lt.
Martin, P.A., 2nd Lt.
Mathis, D.T., Jr., 2nd Lt.
McCullough, T.L., 2nd Lt.
Miles, D.S., 2nd Lt.
Montgomery, F.B., 2nd Lt.
Nelson, J.O., 2nd Lt.

(Owens, E., 2nd Lt.)
Schlamberg, P., 2nd Lt.
Schroeppel, R.H., 2nd Lt.
Scott, G.H., 2nd Lt.***
Sedam, M.M., 2nd Lt.
Sherbundy, R.E., 2nd Lt.
Wayland, W.K., 2nd Lt.
Westlund, E.E., 2nd Lt.
Wightman, J.R., 2nd Lt.
Williams, R.L., 2nd Lt.
White, F.W., 2nd Lt.

Legend:
(Italic face) - KIA or KPC
***POW
**WIA
*Operational Injury
(ASR)

Appendix XI

Former 15th Officers
Casualties In Iwo Jima Ground Action
26 March 45

Killed In Action
1st Lt. Daniel J. Mahaney (Statistical Officer)

Wounded In Action
Col. Kenneth R. Powell
Maj. John S. Hudson
Maj. DeWitt S. Spain
Capt. George M. Brown
Capt. Jack V. Garnett
Capt. William A. Higgins
Capt. Raymond B. Kessler
Capt. Thomas W. Lewis
Capt. Herbert C. Swigart (S-2 Officer)
1st Lt. Thomas O. Quinn
1st Lt. Felix P. Scott

Appendix XII

Pilots Participating In VLR Mission of
1 June 1945
By Squadron And Flight

45th Squadron
Red: Maj. Moore, Capt. Higgs, Lt. Richins, *Lt. Burry**
Yellow: Lts. Walker, Mahony, Scott, Bates
Blue: Lt. Col. Mitchell, Lts. Reese, Rettberg, Joyner
Green: Capt. Collins, Lts. Hodgins, Runton, Ernst
Red Reserve: Lts. Sherren, Garey, Gowen, Hosey

47th Squadron
Red: Maj. Markham, Lts. Jones, O'Mara, Klessig
Yellow: Lts. *Jennings, Dibelka, Schroeder, Frick*
Blue: Lt. (Cameron), (Maj. Anderson) Lts. June, (Wagner)
Green: Lts. Baldwin, *Van Zandt,* White A., Liddell
Maple Red: Capt. (Brunette), Lts. (Hutchison), (Scamara), Lortie** (45th)

78th Squadron
Red: Lt. Col. Thomas, Lts. Dahlquist, *Nelson, White D.*** (47th)
Yellow: Capt. Hostetler, Lts. Owens, Coryell, (Schlamberg)
Blue: Capt. Fitzsimmons, Lts. Butler, Scott, Korb
Green: Capt. Duerr, Maj. Sutterlin, Lt. Brooks, *Mathis*
Purple: Maj. (Tapp), Lts. (Grimes), (Maher)

Key:
(Italic face) - lost in weather
( ) reached target
* rescued 7 Jun 45
** reserves

Colonel Beckwith, the Group CO, in his own plane.

Appendix XIII

Headquarters 15th Fighter Group AAF
A.P.O. No. 86

General Orders
Number 27

20 November 1945

Award of Distinguished Unit Badge

General Orders No. 106, Headquarters Twentieth Air Force, dtd 13 November 1945, cites the 15th Fighter Group, AAF for outstanding performance of duty in action against the enemy in a citation extracted therefrom and reading as follows:

Distinguished Unit Citation — As authorized by Executive Order 9396 (Sec I, WD Bul 22, 1943), superseding Executive Order 9075 (Sec III, WD Bul 11, 1942), and under the provisions of paragraph 2d(1), Section IV, Circular No. 333 WD 1943, and letter, Headquarters United States Army Strategic Air Forces, file AG 200.6, subject: "Distinguished Unit Badge," dated 11 October 1945, the following units are cited for outstanding performance of duty in action against the enemy:

The 15th Fighter Group is cited for outstanding performance of duty in armed conflict with the enemy. On 7 April 1945 the group led the first long range escort mission of XXI Bomber Command B-29's against the Japanese mainland. The flight necessitated careful and coordinated planning and required outstanding flying and tactical skill to navigate more than 800 miles from their base on Iwo Jima, rendezvous with the bombers, escort them over the highly important Nakajima Aircraft Factory, Musashino Plant, near Tokyo, and return to their newly won base. The objective was within the most strongly fortified and heavily-defended enemy zone airfields guarding the city. The target was located within the inner anti-aircraft defenses of the Japanese capital. Ground crews worked brilliantly and tirelessly to prepare the planes for this mission, which presented problems never before encountered in the Pacific. The group dispatched this maximum effort of fifty P-51 aircraft from Iwo Jima only a short time after the island was secured from the enemy and before the runways were suitable for proper operation. The heaviest opposition encountered up to this time was met over the target area both from hostile fighters and from flak. One hundred and sixty-five aggressive enemy intercopters made 531 attacks on the bomber stream protected by the gallant and intrepid fighter pilots, but only one B-29 was lost to enemy aerial action. The P-51 pilots of the 15th fighter Group flew fearlessly through extensive and accurate flak and destroyed seventeen enemy aircraft, probably destroyed one, and damaged six. The protection afforded by fighter escort allowed the B-29's to fly by daylight at lower altitudes than was previously practicable. The exceptional achievement of this organization, resulting from outstanding leadership, professional skill, courage and devotion to duty, reflects the highest credit on the 15th Fighter Group and the Army Air Forces.

* * * * *

Appendix XIV

Iwo Jima Combat Losses
March to August 1945

Name and Rank	Sq.	Date
Kinsel, Beaver A., 1st Lt.	45	17 Mar 45
Shuler, John R., 2nd Lt.	47	26 Mar 45
Bargaehr, Lee M., 2nd Lt.	78	31 Mar 45
Christoe, Gordon A., 1st Lt.	78	12 Apr 45
Gourley, Maurice F., 2nd Lt.	47	12 Apr 45
White, Fred W., 2nd Lt.	78	12 Apr 45
Wightman, James R., 2nd Lt.	78	16 Apr 45
Long, Richard M., 2nd Lt.	47	22 Apr 45
Stelling, David C., 1st Lt.	47	22 Apr 45
Cyphers, Emerson L., 2nd Lt.	45	26 Apr 45
Knox, Morton M., Capt.	45	26 Apr 45
Mangum, Clyde V., 1st Lt.	78	26 Apr 45
Redus, William W., 1st Lt.	45	26 Apr 45
Wayland, Wallace K., 1st Lt.	78	26 Apr 45
Wray, Robert D., 2nd Lt.	45	26 Apr 45
Yakish, Leroy E., 2nd Lt.	45	8 May 45
Zalesky, Roy F., 2nd Lt.	45	8 May 45
Williams, Robert L., 1st Lt.	78	25 May 45
Moore, Rufus S., 2nd Lt.	45	29 May 45
Dibelka, Albert, Jr., 2nd Lt.	47	1 Jun 45
Frick, Paul C., 2nd Lt.	47	1 Jun 45
Jennings, Charles E., 1st Lt.	47	1 Jun 45
Lortie, Lawrence J., 1st Lt.	45	1 Jun 45
Mathis, Daniel T., Jr., 1st Lt.	78	1 Jun 45
Nelson, Jack O., 1st Lt.	78	1 June 45
Schroeder, Emil A., Jr., 1st Lt.	47	1 June 45
White, Donald O., 1st Lt.	47	1 Jun 45
Van Zandt, Harry M., 2nd Lt.	47	1 Jun 45
Liddel, Howard F., Jr., 2nd Lt.	47	14 Jun 45
Scanlan, John V., 1st Lt.	47	23 Jun 45
Schroeppel, Richard H., 1st Lt.	78	3 Jul 45
* Scott, Gordon H., 1st Lt.	78	4 Jul 45
Carr, Robert L., 1st Lt.	78	8 Jul 45
Sherren, Albert W., Capt.	45	8 Jul 45
Ernst, Frederick R., 1st Lt.	45	10 Jul 45
Harvey, Enon W., Jr., 2nd Lt.	45	13 Jul 45
* Chism, Paul E., 1st Lt.	78	15 Jul 45
Johnston, Ronald E., 1st Lt.	47	15 Jul 45
Mitchell, Jule C., Jr., 1st Lt.	47	15 Jul 45
Thomas, Julian E., Lt. Col.	Grp	19 Jul 45
Collie, Jack H., 1st Lt.	78	20 Jul 45
Walker, Joe D., Capt.	45	20 Jul 45
Worton, Robert A., 1st Lt.	47	27 Jul 45
Powell, Walter H., Capt.	47	30 Jul 45
* Heintz, Ralph N., 2nd Lt.	47	3 Aug 45
Rettberg, Gerhard C., 1st Lt.	45	6 Aug 45
Weaver, Howard R., 2nd Lt.	47	6 Aug 45
Schlamberg, Philip, 1st Lt.	78	14 Aug 45

* Denotes POW.

Appendix XV

Air/Sea Rescues
March, 1945 to August, 1945

Date	Pilot	Squadron	Rescuing Unit
7 Apr 45	Ayers, Frank L., 1st Lt.	47	DD
25 May 45	Kreimann, Walter W., 1st Lt.	78	SS *Tigrone*
29 May 45	Brown, William E., 2nd Lt.	45	SS *Pipefish*
29 May 45	Roseberry, Robert H., 1st Lt.	78	DE *Brough*
7 Jun 45	Burry, Arthur A., 2nd Lt.	45	SS *Trutta*
15 Jun 45	Fitzsimmons, Joe, Capt.	78	Surface Craft
23 Jun 45	Ayers, Frank L., 1st Lt.	47	SS *Trepang*
23 Jun 45	Christian, Lamar H., 2nd Lt.	47	SS *Trepang*
3 Jul 45	Grover, Fred T., 1st Lt.	47	Mine Sweeper
8 Jul 45	Wilson, David F., 2nd Lt.	78	DD
10 Jul 45	Collins, Harold D., Capt.	45	4th ER Sq.
10 Jul 45	O'Mara, Oliver E., Jr., 1st Lt.	47	SS *Steelhead*
18 Jul 45	Allen, George B., Jr., 1st Lt.	47	4th ER Sq.
23 Jul 45	Worton, Robert A., 1st Lt.	47	4th ER Sq.
1 Aug 45	Unknown	45 or 78	Surface Vessel
3 Aug 45	Baccus, Harold L., 1st Lt.	47	SS *Balao*
6 Aug 45	Baldwin, Ned H., 1st Lt.	47	SS *Scabbardfish*
6 Aug 45	Moore, Stanley A., 1st Lt.	47	SS *Scabbardfish*
7 Aug 45	Carey, Robert F., Jr., 1st Lt.	78	4th ER Sq.
14 Aug 45	Markham, Theon E., Maj.	47	SS *Tigrone*
14 Aug 45	Owens, Elmer, 1st Lt.	78	DD

Appendix XVI

Aerial Combat Claims by Date of Mission

Date of *Mission*	*Pilot*	*Sq.*	*Dest*	** Aerial Claims ** *Prob*	*Damaged*
7 Dec 41	Brown, Harry W., 2nd Lt.	47	1	1	
7 Dec 41	Moore, Malcolm A., 1st Lt.	46			1
7 Dec 41	Rasmussen, Philip M., 2nd Lt.	46	1		
7 Dec 41	Rogers, Robert J., 1st Lt.	47		1	
7 Dec 41	Sanders, Lewis M., 1st Lt.	46	1	1	
7 Dec 41	Sterling, Gordon H., Jr., 2nd Lt.	46	1		
7 Dec 41	Taylor, Kenneth M., 2nd Lt.	47	2	2	
7 Dec 41	Webster, John J., 1st Lt.	47			1
7 Dec 41	Welch, George S., 2nd Lt.	47	4		
23 Oct 43	Snipes, Gilmer L., Capt.	45	1		
15 Jan 44	Scott, Felix P. F/O	46	1		
16 Jan 44	Lewis, Thomas M., 1st Lt.	46	.5		
16 Jan 44	Thacker, John M., Maj.	46	1		
16 Jan 44	Warren, Benjamin C., 1st Lt.	46	.5		
26 Jan 44	Apple, John J., 1st Lt.	45	1		
26 Jan 44	Basham, John H., 2nd Lt.	45		1	
26 Jan 44	Boone, Herbert D., 1st Lt.	45	1		
26 Jan 44	Butler, Dwight R., 1st Lt.	45	1		
26 Jan 44	Hintermeier, Richard H., 2nd Lt.	45	1		
26 Jan 44	Jackson, Robert C., 2nd Lt.	45	1		
26 Jan 44	Knox, Morton M., 2nd Lt.	45	1		
26 Jan 44	Maltby, Albert E., 2nd Lt.	45		1	
26 Jan 44	Moore, Robert W., 1st Lt.	45	1		
26 Jan 44	Thompson, Harry M., Maj.	45	1		
26 Jan 44	Vande Hey, James M., Capt.	45	2		
7 Apr 45	Bridge, Arthur H., Capt.	45			.5
7 Apr 45	Bright, Eurich L., 1st Lt.	47	3		
7 Apr 45	Brown, Wesley E., 1st Lt.	45	1		
7 Apr 45	Brown, Wesley E., 1st Lt.	45		1	
7 Apr 45	Campbell, Bruce S., Capt.	45		.5	
7 Apr 45	Condrick, Richard J., 1st Lt.	47	1		1
7 Apr 45	Down, Robert R., Capt.	47	1.5		
7 Apr 45	Dunlap, George H., 1st Lt.	45			.5
7 Apr 45	Henderson, Fred H., Jr., 1st Lt.	45			1
7 Apr 45	Hintermeier, Richard H., 1st Lt.	47	.5		
7 Apr 45	Hunter, George H., Jr., Capt	45		.5	1
7 Apr 45	Knox, Morton M., Capt.	45	1		
7 Apr 45	Maltby, Albert E., Capt.	45		1	
7 Apr 45	Markham, Theon E., Capt.	47	1		
7 Apr 45	Moore, Robert W., Capt.	78	2		
7 Apr 45	Snipes, Gilmer L., Maj.	45	1		
7 Apr 45	Tapp, James B., Maj.	78	4		1
7 Apr 45	Vande Hey, James M., Maj.	78	1		
7 Apr 45	Walker, Joe D., 1st Lt.	45		1	
12 Apr 45	Bridge, Arthur, H., Capt.	45		.5	
12 Apr 45	Cameron, Charles J., 1st Lt.	47	1		
12 Apr 45	Duerr, Richard D., 1st Lt.	78			1
12 Apr 45	Dunlap, George H., 1st Lt.	45	1		
12 Apr 45	Ennis, Francis L., Capt.	45	.5		
12 Apr 45	Grover, Fred T., 1st Lt.	47	.5		

12 Apr 45	Harrigan, Walter H., 1st Lt.	45		.5	
12 Apr 45	Henderson, Fred H., Jr., 1st Lt.	45		.5	
12 Apr 45	Hunter, George H., Jr., Capt.	45	1	1	
12 Apr 45	Kearney, Emmett L., Jr., Maj.	Grp	1.5	1	
12 Apr 45	McCormick, Joseph A., 1st Lt.	47			.5
12 Apr 45	O'Mara, Oliver E., Jr., 2nd Lt.	47	.5		
12 Apr 45	Piper, John A., Maj.	47	1		
12 Apr 45	Redus, William W., 2nd Lt.	45		.5	
12 Apr 45	Reinert, Vincent V., 2nd Lt.	45		.5	
12 Apr 45	Rettberg, Gerhard C., 2nd Lt.	45		1	
12 Apr 45	Richins, Joseph C., 2nd Lt.	45	1		
12 Apr 45	Roberts, Alvan E., Jr., 2nd Lt.	45	.5		
12 Apr 45	Statsmann, Donald E., 2nd Lt.	45		.5	
12 Apr 45	Stelling, Dave G., 1st Lt.	47			.5
12 Apr 45	Tapp, James B., Maj.	78	1		
12 Apr 45	Tyler, Harry M., 1st Lt.	47	.5		
12 Apr 45	Vande Hey, James M., Maj.	78	1		
19 Apr 45	Barry, Arthur A., 2nd Lt.	45			.5
19 Apr 45	Campbell, Bruce S., Capt.	45	1		
19 Apr 45	Dennis, Ceil A., 2nd Lt.	45			.5
19 Apr 45	Ennis, Francis L., Capt.	45			.5
19 Apr 45	Henderson, Fred H., Jr., Capt.	45	1		.33
19 Apr 45	Kester, John E., 2nd Lt.	45			.33
19 Apr 45	Slater, Jay W., 1st Lt.	45	.5		
19 Apr 45	Statsmann, Donald E., 2nd Lt.	45	1		.33
19 Apr 45	Tapp, James B., Maj.	78	1		
19 Apr 45	Wells, Wayne L., Maj.	Grp	1		.5
19 Apr 45	Yakish, Leroy E., 2nd Lt.	45	.5		
22 Apr 45	Ayers, Frank L., 1st Lt.	47		.5	
22 Apr 45	Baccus, Harold L., 1st Lt.	47	1		
22 Apr 45	Hintermeier, Richard H., Capt.	47	1		
22 Apr 45	Long, Richard M., 2nd Lt.	47			.5
22 Apr 45	Markham, Theon E., Maj.	47	1.5		
22 Apr 45	McCullough, Thomas L., 2nd Lt.	78	1		
22 Apr 45	Moore, Robert W., Capt.	78	1		
22 Apr 45	Ryniker, Henry C., 1st Lt.	47	.5		
22 Apr 45	Spain, DeWitt, Lt. Col.	Grp			1.5
22 Apr 45	White, Donald O., 2nd Lt.	47		.5	1
30 Apr 45	Moore, Robert W., Capt.	78		1	
25 May 45	Campbell, Bruce S., Capt.	45	.5		
25 May 45	Coryell, Robert C., 1st Lt.	78	1		
25 May 45	Kreimann, Walter W., 1st Lt.	78	1		
25 May 45	Maher, Philip J., 1st Lt.	78	1		
25 May 45	Mollan, Victor K., Capt.	78	1.5		
25 May 45	Moore, Robert W., Capt.	78	2.		
25 May 45	Singleton, Billy J., F/O	45	.5		
25 May 45	Tapp, James B., Maj.	78	1		1
25 May 45	Williams, Robert L., 1st Lt.	78	.5		
29 May 45	Bjorseth, Bernard P., 1st Lt.	47			.5
29 May 45	Bright, Eurich L., Capt.	47	1.5		
29 May 45	Cameron, Charles J., 1st Lt.	47	1	1	
29 May 45	Carey, Robert F., 2nd Lt.	78		1	
29 May 45	Carr, Robert L., 1st Lt.	78	.5		
29 May 45	Collins, Harold D., Capt.	78	1		1
29 May 45	Duerr, Richard D., Capt.	78	1		
29 May 45	Edwards, Lloyd C., 1st Lt.	45		.5	1
29 May 45	Grover, Fred T., 1st Lt.	47	2		
29 May 45	Hunter, George H., Jr., Capt.	45			.5
29 May 45	Mathis, Daniel, 2nd Lt.	78	.5		

29 May 45	McCorkle, Quentin G., 1st Lt.	45			1
29 May 45	Moore, Robert W., Capt.	45	3		
29 May 45	Moore, Rufus S., 1st Lt.	45			.5
29 May 45	Olivier, Albert G., Jr., 2nd Lt.	47			.5
29 May 45	Petrouleas, George C., 2nd Lt.	47	.5		
29 May 45	Reed, Warren G., Jr., 1st Lt.	47		1	
29 May 45	Reinert, Vincent V., 2nd Lt.	45		.5	2
29 May 45	Schroeppel, Richard, 2nd Lt.	78	.5		
29 May 45	Slater, Jay W., 1st Lt.	45	1	1	1
29 May 45	Tapp, James B., Maj.	78	1		
29 May 45	Tyler, Harry M., 1st Lt.	47	.5		
29 May 45	Worton, Robert A., 2nd Lt.	47	.5		
29 May 45	Yellin, Jerome, 1st Lt.	78	.5		
1 Jun 45	Scamara, Robert S., 1st Lt.	47	1		
7 Jun 45	Moore, Robert W., Maj.	45	1		
10 Jun 45	Anderson, Truman F., Maj.	Grp	1		
10 Jun 45	Bauman, Frederick A., 1st Lt.	78	1		
10 Jun 45	Bjorseth, Bernard P., 1st Lt.	47	.5		
10 Jun 45	Brooks, Doyle T., 1st Lt.	78	2		1
10 Jun 45	Grover, Fred T., 1st Lt.	47	1		
10 Jun 45	Hawkins, James P., 2nd Lt.	78		.5	.5
10 Jun 45	Higgs, Owen J., Capt.	45			1
10 Jun 45	June, Roy E., 1st Lt.	47	.5		
10 Jun 45	Martin, Paul A., 1st Lt.	78		1	
10 Jun 45	McCorkle, Quentin G., 1st Lt.	45			1
10 Jun 45	Merrill, Nelson P., Jr., Capt.	78	1	.5	1.5
10 Jun 45	Mitchell, John W., Lt. Col.	Grp			1
10 Jun 45	Mitchell, Jule C., Jr., 1st Lt.	47	1		
10 Jun 45	Moore, Robert W., Maj.	45	1		
10 Jun 45	Powell, Walter H., Capt.	47	1	1	
10 Jun 45	Reed, Warren G., Jr., 1st Lt.	47	1		
10 Jun 45	Sedam, Malcolm M., 1st Lt.	78	.5		1
10 Jun 45	Sutterlin, Howard D., Maj.	Grp	1.5		
10 Jun 45	Thornton, Robert M., 1st Lt.	45			1
10 Jun 45	Walker, Joe D., Capt.	45		1	
10 Jun 45	Wells, Wayne L., Maj.	Grp	2		
10 Jun 45	Worton, Robert A., 2nd Lt.	47	1		
23 Jun 45	Ayers, Frank L., 1st Lt.	47	1		
23 Jun 45	Baccus, Harold L., 1st Lt.	47			2
23 Jun 45	Burnett, Robert C., 2nd Lt.	47	1		
23 Jun 45	Elliott, Andrew C., 2nd Lt.	47			1
23 Jun 45	Jones, Fronnie A., Jr., F/O	47	1		
23 Jun 45	Maher, Philip J., 1st Lt.	78		1	
23 Jun 45	McCormick, Joseph A., 1st Lt.	47			1
23 Jun 45	Moore, Stanley A., 1st Lt.	47			1
23 Jun 45	Olivier, Albert G., Jr., 2nd Lt.	47			1
23 Jun 45	Scamara, Robert S., 1st Lt.	47	3		7
23 Jun 45	Thomas, Julian E., Lt. Col.	Grp	1		1
23 Jun 45	Walker, Joe D., Capt.	45	1		1
23 Jun 45	Worton, Robert A., 2nd Lt.	47	1		
26 Jun 45	Mitchell, John W., Lt. Col.	Grp	1		
26 Jun 45	Reese, C. Douglas, 2nd Lt.	45	1		
26 Jun 45	Richins, Joseph G., 1st Lt.	45			1
1 Jul 45	Sutterlin, Howard D., Maj.	Grp	1		
8 Jul 45	Condon, Frederick C., 1st Lt.	45		1	
8 Jul 45	Coryell, Robert C., 1st Lt.	78	1		
8 Jul 45	Fitzsimmons, Joe, Capt.	78	1		
8 Jul 45	Reese, C. Douglas, 2nd Lt.	45	1		
16 Jul 45	Mitchell, John W., Lt. Col.	Grp	2		

19 Jul 45	Brown, Wesley E., Capt.	45	1		
19 Jul 45	Edwards, Lloyd C., 1st Lt.	45	1		
19 Jul 45	Hodgin, William H., 1st Lt.	45	1		
19 Jul 45	Kester, John E., 1st Lt.	45	1		
19 Jul 45	Sparks, William H., 1st Lt.	47	1		
19 Jul 45	Statsmann, Donald E., 1st Lt.	45	2		
19 Jul 45	Worton, Robert A., 1st Lt.	47	1		
10 Aug 45	Farrell, William J., 1st Lt.	45	1		
10 Aug 45	Googe, John W., F/O	47			1
10 Aug 45	June, Roy E., 1st Lt.	47			.5
10 Aug 45	Moore, Robert W., Maj.	45	1		1
10 Aug 45	O'Mara, Oliver E., Jr., 1st Lt.	47			2
10 Aug 45	Powell, Harold E., F/O	47			.5
			133.00	29.00	54.00

Appendix XVII

Aerial Combat Claims by Pilot

Date of *Mission*	*Pilot*	*Sq.*	*Dest*	** Aerial Claims ** *Prob*	*Damaged*
10 Jun 45	Anderson, Truman F., Maj.	Grp	1		
26 Jan 44	Apple, John J., 1st Lt.	45	1		
22 Apr 45	Ayers, Frank L., 1st Lt.	47		.5	
23 Jun 45	Ayers, Frank L., 1st Lt.	47	1		
22 Apr 45	Baccus, Harold L., 1st Lt.	47	1		
23 Jun 45	Baccus, Harold L., 1st Lt.	47			2
19 Apr 45	Barry, Arthur A., 2nd Lt.	45			.5
26 Jan 44	Basham, John H., 2nd Lt.	45		1	
10 Jun 45	Bauman, Frederick A., 1st Lt.	78	1		
29 May 45	Bjorseth, Bernard P., 1st Lt.	47			.5
10 Jun 45	Bjorseth, Bernard P., 1st Lt.	47	.5		
26 Jan 44	Boone, Herbert D., 1st Lt.	45	1		
7 Apr 45	Bridge, Arthur H., Capt.	45			.5
12 Apr 45	Bridge, Arthur H., Capt.	45		.5	
7 Apr 45	Bright, Eurich L., 1st Lt.	47	3		
29 May 45	Bright, Eurich L., Capt.	47	1.5		
10 Jun 45	Brooks, Doyle T., 1st Lt.	78	2		1
7 Dec 41	Brown, Harry W., 2nd Lt.	47	1	1	
7 Apr 45	Brown, Wesley E., 1st Lt.	45		1	
7 Apr 45	Brown, Wesley E., 1st Lt.	45	1		
19 Jul 45	Brown, Wesley E., Capt.	45	1		
23 Jun 45	Burnett, Robert C., 2nd Lt.	47	1		
26 Jan 44	Butler, Dwight R., 1st Lt.	45	1		
12 Apr 45	Cameron, Charles J., 1st Lt.	47	1		
29 May 45	Cameron, Charles J., 1st Lt.	47	1	1	
7 Apr 45	Campbell, Bruce S., Capt.	45		.5	
19 Apr 45	Campbell, Bruce S., Capt.	45	1		
25 May 45	Campbell, Bruce S., Capt.	45	.5		
29 May 45	Carey, Robert F., 2nd Lt.	78		1	
29 May 45	Carr, Robert L., 1st Lt.	78	.5		
29 May 45	Collins, Harold D., Capt.	78	1		1
8 Jul 45	Condon, Frederick C., 1st Lt.	45		1	
7 Apr 45	Condrick, Richard J., 1st Lt.	47	1		1
25 May 45	Coryell, Robert C., 1st Lt.	78	1		
8 Jul 45	Coryell, Robert C., 1st Lt.	78	1		

19 Apr 45	Dennis, Ceil A., 2nd Lt.	45			.5
7 Apr 45	Down, Robert R., Capt.	47	1.5		
12 Apr 45	Duerr, Richard D., 1st Lt.	78			1
29 May 45	Duerr, Richard D., Capt.	78	1		
7 Apr 45	Dunlap, George H., 1st Lt.	45			.5
12 Apr 45	Dunlap, George H., 1st Lt.	45	1		
29 May 45	Edwards, Lloyd C., 1st Lt.	45		.5	1
19 Jul 45	Edwards, Lloyd C., 1st Lt.	45	1		
23 Jun 45	Elliott, Andrew C., 2nd Lt.	47			1
12 Apr 45	Ennis, Francis L., Capt.	45	.5		
19 Apr 45	Ennis, Francis L., Capt.	45			.5
10 Aug 45	Farrell, William J., 1st Lt.	45	1		
8 Jul 45	Fitzsimmons, Joe, Capt.	78	1		
10 Aug 45	Googe, John W., F/O	47			1
12 Apr 45	Grover, Fred T., 1st Lt.	47	.5		
29 May 45	Grover, Fred T., 1st Lt.	47	2		
10 Jun 45	Grover, Fred T., 1st Lt.	47	1		
12 Apr 45	Harrigan, Walter H., 1st Lt.	45		.5	
10 Jun 45	Hawkins, James F., 2nd Lt.	78		.5	.5
7 Apr 45	Henderson, Fred H., Jr., 1st Lt.	45			1
12 Apr 45	Henderson, Fred H., Jr., 1st Lt.	45		.5	
19 Apr 45	Henderson, Fred H., Jr., Capt.	45	1		.33
10 Jun 45	Higgs, Owen J., Capt.	45			1
26 Jan 44	Hintermeier, Richard H., 2nd Lt.	45	1		
7 Apr 45	Hintermeier, Richard H., 1st Lt.	47	.5		
22 Apr 45	Hintermeier, Richard H., Capt.	47	1		
19 Jul 45	Hodgin, William H., 1st Lt.	45	1		
7 Apr 45	Hunter, George H., Jr., Capt.	45		.5	1
12 Apr 45	Hunter, George H., Jr., Capt.	45	1	1	
29 May 45	Hunter, George H., Jr., Capt.	45			.5
26 Jan 44	Jackson, Robert C., 2nd Lt.	45	1		
23 Jun 45	Jones, Fronnie A., Jr., F/O	47	1		
10 Jun 45	June, Roy E., 1st Lt.	47	.5		
10 Aug 45	June, Roy E., 1st Lt.	47			.5
12 Apr 45	Kearney, Emmett L., Jr., Maj.	Grp	1.5	1	
19 Apr 45	Kester, John E., 2nd Lt.	45			.33
19 Jul 45	Kester, John E., 1st Lt.	45	1		
26 Jan 44	Knox, Morton, M., 2nd Lt.	45	1		
7 Apr 45	Knox, Morton M., Capt.	45	1		
25 May 45	Kreimann, Walter W., 1st Lt.	78	1		
16 Jan 44	Lewis, Thomas M., 1st Lt.	46	.5		
22 Apr 45	Long, Richard M., 2nd Lt.	47			.5
25 May 45	Maher, Philip J., 1st Lt.	78	1		
23 Jun 45	Maher, Philip J., 1st Lt.	78		1	
26 Jan 44	Maltby, Albert E., 2nd Lt.	45		1	
7 Apr 45	Maltby, Albert E., Capt.	45		1	
7 Apr 45	Markham, Theon E., Capt.	47	1		
22 Apr 45	Markham, Theon E., Maj.	47	1.5		
10 Jun 45	Martin, Paul A., 1st Lt.	78		1	
29 May 45	Mathis Daniel, 2nd Lt.	78	.5		
29 May 45	McCorkle, Quentin G., 1st Lt.	45			1
10 Jun 45	McCorkle, Quentin G., 1st Lt.	45			1
12 Apr 45	McCormick, Joseph A., 1st Lt.	47			.5
23 Jun 45	McCormick, Joseph A., 1st Lt.	47			1
22 Apr 45	McCullough, Thomas L., 2nd Lt.	78	1		
10 Jun 45	Merrill, Nelson P., Jr., Capt.	78	1	.5	1.5
10 Jun 45	Mitchell, John W., Lt. Col.	Grp			1
26 Jun 45	Mitchell, John W., Lt. Col.	Grp	1		
16 Jul 45	Mitchell, John W., Lt. Col.	Grp	2		

10 Jun 45	Mitchell, Jule C., Jr., 1st Lt.	47	1		
25 May 45	Mollan, Victor K., Capt.	78	1.5		
7 Dec 41	Moore, Malcolm, A., 1st Lt.	46			1
26 Jan 44	Moore, Robert W., 1st Lt.	45	1		
7 Apr 45	Moore, Robert W., Capt.	78	2		
22 Apr 45	Moore, Robert W., Capt.	78	1		
30 Apr 45	Moore, Robert W., Capt.	78		1	
25 May 45	Moore, Robert W., Capt.	78	2		
29 May 45	Moore, Robert W., Capt.	45	3		
7 Jun 45	Moore, Robert W., Maj.	45	1		
10 Jun 45	Moore, Robert W., Maj.	45	1		
10 Aug 45	Moore, Robert W., Maj.	45	1		1
29 May 45	Moore, Rufus S., 1st Lt.	45			.5
23 Jun 45	Moore, Stanley A., 1st Lt.	47			1
12 Apr 45	O'Mara, Oliver E., Jr., 2nd Lt.	47	.5		
10 Aug 45	O'Mara, Oliver E., Jr., 1st Lt.	47			2
29 May 45	Olivier, Albert G., Jr., 2nd Lt.	47			.5
23 Jun 45	Olivier, Albert G., Jr., 2nd Lt.	47			1
29 May 45	Petrouleas, George C., 2nd Lt.	47	.5		
12 Apr 45	Piper, John A., Maj.	47	1		
10 Aug 45	Powell, Harold E., F/O	47			.5
10 Jun 45	Powell, Walter H., Capt.	47	1	1	
7 Dec 41	Rasmussen, Philip M., 2nd Lt.	46	1		
12 Apr 45	Redus, William W., 2nd Lt.	45		.5	
29 May 45	Reed, Warren G., Jr., 1st Lt.	47		1	
10 Jun 45	Reed, Warren G., Jr., 1st Lt.	47	1		
26 Jun 45	Reese, C. Douglas, 2nd Lt.	45	1		
8 Jul 45	Reese, C. Douglas, 2nd Lt.	45	1		
12 Apr 45	Reinert, Vincent V., 2nd Lt.	45		.5	
29 May 45	Reinert, Vincent V., 2nd Lt.	45		.5	2
12 Apr 45	Rettberg, Gerhard C., 2nd Lt.	45		1	
12 Apr 45	Richins, Joseph C., 2nd Lt.	45	1		
26 Jun 45	Richins, Joseph C., 1st Lt.	45			1
12 Apr 45	Roberts, Alvan E., Jr., 2nd Lt.	45	.5		
7 Dec 41	Rogers, Robert J., 1st Lt.	47		1	
22 Apr 45	Ryniker, Henry C., 1st Lt.	47	.5		
7 Dec 41	Sanders, Lewis M., 1st Lt.	46	1	1	
1 Jun 45	Scamara, Robert S., 1st Lt.	47	1		
23 Jun 45	Scamara, Robert S., 1st Lt.	47	3		7
29 May 45	Schroeppel, Richard, 2nd Lt.	78	.5		
15 Jan 44	Scott, Felix P., F/O	46	1		
10 Jun 45	Sedam, Malcolm M., 1st Lt.	78	.5		1
25 May 45	Singleton, Billy J., F/O	45	.5		
19 Apr 45	Slater, Jay W., 1st Lt.	45	.5		
29 May 45	Slater, Jay W., 1st Lt.	45	1	1	1
23 Oct 43	Snipes, Gilmer L., Capt.	45	1		
7 Apr 45	Snipes, Gilmer L., Maj.	45	1		
22 Apr 45	Spain, DeWitt, Lt. Col.	Grp			1.5
19 Jul 45	Sparks, William H., 1st Lt.	47	1		
12 Apr 45	Statsmann, Donald E., 2nd Lt.	45		.5	
19 Apr 45	Statsmann, Donald E., 2nd Lt.	45	1		.33
19 Jul 45	Statsmann, Donald E., 1st Lt.	45	2		
12 Apr 45	Stelling, Dave G., 1st Lt.	47			.5
7 Dec 41	Sterling, Gordon H., Jr., 2nd Lt.	46	1		
10 Jun 45	Sutterlin, Howard D., Maj.	Grp	1.5		
1 Jul 45	Sutterlin, Howard D., Maj.	Grp	1		
7 Apr 45	Tapp, James B., Maj.	78	4		1
12 Apr 45	Tapp, James B., Maj.	78	1		
19 Apr 45	Tapp, James B., Maj.	78	1		

25 May 45	Tapp, James B., Maj.	78	1		
29 May 45	Tapp, James B., Maj.	78	1		
7 Dec 41	Taylor, Kenneth M., 2nd Lt.	47	2	2	
16 Jan 44	Thacker, John M., Maj.	46	1		
23 Jun 45	Thomas, Julian E., Lt. Col.	Grp	1		1
26 Jan 44	Thompson, Harry M., Maj.	45	1		
10 Jun 45	Thornton, Robert M., 1st Lt.	45			1
12 Apr 45	Tyler, Harry M., 1st Lt.	47	.5		
29 May 45	Tyler, Harry M., 1st Lt.	47	.5		
26 Jan 44	Vande Hey, James M., Capt.	45	2		
7 Apr 45	Vande Hey, James M., Maj.	78	1		
12 Apr 45	Vande Hey, James M., Maj.	78	1		
7 Apr 45	Walker, Joe D., 1st Lt.	45			1
10 Jun 45	Walker, Joe D., Capt.	45		1	
23 Jun 45	Walker, Joe D., Capt.	45	1		1
16 Jan 44	Warren, Benjamin C., 1st Lt.	46	.5		
7 Dec 41	Webster, John J., 1st Lt.	47			1
7 Dec 41	Welch, George S., 2nd Lt.	47	4		
19 Apr 45	Wells, Wayne L., Maj.	Grp	1		.5
10 Jun 45	Wells, Wayne L., Maj.	Grp	2		
22 Apr 45	White, Donald O., 2nd Lt.	47		.5	1
25 May 45	Williams, Robert L., 1st Lt.	78	.5		
29 May 45	Worton, Robert A., 2nd Lt.	47	.5		
10 Jun 45	Worton, Robert A., 2nd Lt.	47	1		
23 Jun 45	Worton, Robert A., 2nd Lt.	47	1		
19 Jul 45	Worton, Robert A., 1st Lt.	47	1		
19 Apr 45	Yakish, Leroy E., 2nd Lt.	45	.5		
29 May 45	Yellin, Jerome, 1st Lt.	78	.5		
			133.00	29.00	54.00

Appendix XVIII

Aerial Combat Claims
Emeny Aircraft Claimed as a Result of Strafing

Date of *Mission*	*Pilot*	*Sq.*	* * **Ground Claims** * * *Dest*	*Prob*	*Damaged*
16 Apr 45	Maher, Philip, 1st Lt.	78			1
16 Apr 45	Moore, Robert W., Capt.	78			2
16 Apr 45	Roseberry, Robert H., 1st Lt.	78			1
16 Apr 45	Tapp, James B., Maj.	78			2
19 Apr 45	Ennis, Francis L., Capt.	45	1		
22 Apr 45	Ayers, Frank, 1st Lt.	47			.5
22 Apr 45	Butler, Charles R., Jr., 2nd Lt.	78	.5		
22 Apr 45	Campbell, Bruce S., Capt.	45	1.5		
22 Apr 45	Carey, Robert F., Jr., 2nd Lt.	78	1		
22 Apr 45	Down, Robert R., Capt.	47	1		
22 Apr 45	Duerr, Richard D., 1st Lt.	78	1		
22 Apr 45	Evans, John R., 2nd Lt.	78		1	
22 Apr 45	Long, Richard M., 2nd Lt.	47			.5
22 Apr 45	Merrill, Nelson P., Jr., Capt.	78	1.5		
22 Apr 45	Mollan, Victor K., Capt.	78	2	1	
22 Apr 45	Moore, Douglas B., 2nd Lt.	78	1.5		2
22 Apr 45	Ruby, Robert, 1st Lt.	78	.5		
22 Apr 45	Scott, Gordon H., 2nd Lt.	78	.5		
22 Apr 45	Sidebottom, William K., 2nd Lt.	47	1		
22 Apr 45	Spain, DeWitt S., Lt. Col.	Grp	1		

22 Apr 45	Westlund, Eldon E., 2nd Lt.	78	1		
22 Apr 45	White, Donald O., 2nd Lt.	47		.5	1
25 May 45	Brunette, Joseph P. Capt.	47			1
25 May 45	Coryell, Robert W., 1st Lt.	78			1
25 May 45	Jones, Samuel S., 2nd Lt.	47	1		1
25 May 45	Kreimann, Walter W., 1st Lt.	78			1
25 May 45	Kriss, Robert J., 2nd Lt.	47			1
25 May 45	Mitchell, John W., Lt. Col.	Grp			1
25 May 45	Mollan, Victor K., Capt.	78			1
25 May 45	Moore, Robert W., Capt.	78	1		3
25 May 45	Tillman, David, 2nd Lt.	47			1
25 May 45	Weaver, Howard R., 2nd Lt.	47			.5
25 May 45	White, Allen D., 1st Lt.	47			.5
23 Jun 45	Brooks, Doyle T., 1st Lt.	78	1		
23 Jun 45	Collie, Jack H., 1st Lt.	78		.5	
23 Jun 45	Fahey, Joseph H., Jr., 2nd Lt.	78			1
23 Jun 45	Killion, William F., 2nd Lt.	78	1		
23 Jun 45	Merrill, Nelson P., Capt.	78			1
23 Jun 45	Montgomery, Franklin B., 1st Lt.	78	1		
23 Jun 45	Moore, Douglas B., 1st Lt.	78		.5	
4 Jul 45	Baccus, Harold L., 1st Lt.	47			2
4 Jul 45	Bright, Eurich L., Capt.	47			.5
4 Jul 45	Cameron, Charles J., Capt.	47		1	
4 Jul 45	Edwards, Lloyd C., 1st Lt.	45	1		
4 Jul 45	McCormick, Joseph A., 1st Lt.	47		1	
4 Jul 45	Olivier, Albert G., Jr., 2nd Lt.	47			.5
4 Jul 45	Scamara, Robert S., 1st Lt.	47			2
4 Jul 45	Sher, Leon P., 1st Lt.	47			1
4 Jul 45	Worton, Robert A., 1st Lt.	47	1		
5 Jul 45	Wells, Wayne L., Maj.	Grp			1
8 Jul 45	Combs, Elbert P., F/O	45	2		
8 Jul 45	Condon, Frederick C., 1st Lt.	45		1	
8 Jul 45	Gowan, Gerald F., 1st Lt.	45	1		
8 Jul 45	Joyner, Lawrence K., 1st Lt.	45	1		
8 Jul 45	Mitchell, Jule C., Jr., 1st Lt.	47	1		
8 Jul 45	Petrouleas, George C., 2nd Lt.	47			1
8 Jul 45	Sparks, William H., 1st Lt.	47			1
8 Jul 45	Tillman, David, Jr., 2nd Lt.	47			1
10 Jul 45	Balak, David S., 1st Lt.	47	.5		
10 Jul 45	Collins, Harold D., Capt.	45	2		
10 Jul 45	Doughty, Charles C., 2nd Lt.	47	.5		
10 Jul 45	Forman, Willis O., 2nd Lt.	47			1
10 Jul 45	Jones, Fronnie A., Jr., F/O	47	1		
10 Jul 45	Mitchell, Jule C., Jr., 1st Lt.	47	1		
10 Jul 45	Moore, Robert W., Maj.	45	1		
10 Jul 45	Robinson, Walter J., 1st Lt.	45	1		
19 Jul 45	Balak, David S., 1st Lt.	47		.5	
19 Jul 45	Petrouleas, George C., 2nd Lt.	47			1
19 Jul 45	Powell, Walter H., Capt.	47	1		
19 Jul 45	Worton, Robert A., 1st Lt.	47		.5	
20 Jul 45	Grover, Fred T., 1st Lt.	47			1
2 Aug 45	Hutchison, Eric W., 2nd Lt.	47			1
2 Aug 45	Moore, Robert W., Maj.	45	1		
3 Aug 45	Brucker, Wilber R., 1st Lt.	78			1
3 Aug 45	Burnett, Robert C., 2nd Lt.	47	1		
3 Aug 45	Coryell, Robert C., 1st Lt.	78			1
3 Aug 45	Gilbride, Martin, 1st Lt.	47	1		
3 Aug 45	Heintz, Ralph N., 1st Lt.	47	1		
3 Aug 45	Hostetler, Ernest W., Capt.	47	1.5		

3 Aug 45	Klessig, Charles E., 2nd Lt.	47	.5		
3 Aug 45	Korb, Louis L., 1st Lt.	78			1
3 Aug 45	Locke, Donald F., 1st Lt.	47	1		
3 Aug 45	Powell, Harold E., F/O	47	1		
3 Aug 45	Scamara, Robert S., 1st Lt.	47	1		
3 Aug 45	Sparks, William H., 1st Lt.	47	1		1
14 Aug 45	Coryell, Robert C., 1st Lt.	78			1
14 Aug 45	Fahey, Joseph H., Jr., 2nd Lt.	78			1
			44.00	9.00	45.50

Appendix XIX

Unit Commanding Officers from Activation to August 1945

Group Commanders

Name, Rank	From	To
Maj. Lorry M. Tindal	6 Dec 40	19 Sep 41
Maj. Paul W. Blanchard	20 Sep 41	11 Feb 42
Lt. Col William S. Steele	12 Feb 42	4 Mar 43
Lt. Col Sherwood E. Buckland	5 Mar 43	26 Sep 43
Col. James O. Beckwith, Jr.	5 Mar 43	26 Sep 43
Lt. Col. DeWitt Spain	16 Apr 45	15 May 45
Lt. Col. Julian E. Thomas	15 May 45	19 Jul 45
Col. John W. Mitchell	19 Jul 45	

Squadron Commanders

45th Squadron

Maj. Aaron W. Tyer	1 Dec 40	23 Dec 41
Capt. Harold E. Kofahl	24 Dec 41	7 May 42
Maj. Thomas B. Summers	8 May 42	15 Oct 42
Maj. George M. MacNicol	16 Oct 42	20 Jan 43
Capt. Joseph L. Laughlin	20 Jan 43	28 Feb 43
Lt. Col. Julian E. Thomas	1 Mar 43	3 Apr 44
Maj. Gilmer L. Snipes	4 Apr 44	16 Apr 45
Maj. Arthur M. Bridge	16 Apr 45	3 Jun 45
Capt. Harold D. Collins	4 Jun 45	18 Jul 45
Maj. Robert W. Moore	19 Jul 45	

46th Squadron

Capt. Thomas C. Musgrave	1 Dec 40	24 Feb 41
Maj. Lewis M. Sanders	25 Feb 41	18 Nov 42
Maj. Kenneth R. Powell	19 Nov 42	23 Apr 43
Lt. Col. John M. Thacker	23 Apr 43	3 Apr 44
Maj. DeWitt S. Spain	4 Apr 44	Trf. to 21st Grp.

47th Squadron

Capt. Gordon H. Austin	1 Dec 40	11 Feb 42
Capt. Joseph F. Hunker	12 Feb 42	15 Sep 42
Capt. Jack M. Hounsom	16 Sep 42	28 Feb 43
Maj. Norval K. Heath	1 Mar 43	15 Apr 44
Maj. Thomas W. Mackay	16 Apr 44	6 Nov 44
Capt. John A. Piper	7 Nov 44	26 May 45
Maj. Theon E. Markham	26 May 45	11 Jun 45
Capt. Walter N. Powell	12 Jun 45	30 Jul 45
Capt. E. Hostetler	30 Jul 45	4 Aug 45
Maj. Theon E. Markham	5 Aug 45	

72nd Squadron

Capt. James O. Beckwith, Jr.	5 Oct 41	9 Oct 42
Maj. Robert J. Rogers	10 Oct 42	Trf. to 318th Grp.

78th Squadron

Lt. Col. Sherwood E. Buckland	6 Mar 43	25 Mar 43
Maj. Gordon R. Hyde	26 Mar 43	22 May 43
Maj. Bill Southerland	22 May 43	9 Dec 43
Maj. Emmett L. Kearney, Jr.	10 Dec 43	13 Apr 44
Maj. James Vande Hey	14 Apr 44	16 Apr 45
Maj. James B. Tapp	16 Apr 45	16 Jun 45
Maj. Joe Fitzsimmons	16 Jun 45	5 Aug 45
Maj. James B. Tapp	6 Aug 45	

Appendix XX

Headquarters 15th Fighter Group AAF
A.P.O. No. 86

General Orders
Number 13

10 August 1945

Credit For Battle Participation

1. Under the provisions of paragraph 1 and 2, General Orders Number 17, Headquarters United States Army Forces Middle Pacific, dated 6 August 1945, the following-named officers and enlisted men, organizations indicated, are entitled to wear a bronze service star on the Asiatic-Pacific Campaign Ribbon for participation in the Air Offensive, Japan Campaign, at some time during the period 11 March 1945 to 31 July 1945 inclusive:

Headquarters 15th Fighter Group AAF

Col. James O. Beckwith, Jr.
Lt. Col. Dean E. Mansfield
Lt. Col. Julian E. Thomas
Major Truman F. Anderson
Major Richard W. Birk
Major Bernard Genis
Major Emerson R. Johnson
Major Emmett L. Kearney, Jr.
Major John E. McDonald
Major Joseph H. Rilcy
Major Charles R. SoKol
Major Wayne L. Wells
Capt. Charles T. Blandford
Capt. Clarence J. Duellman
Capt. Irving A. Frankel
Capt. Herman N. Frye
Capt. Albert L. Jamison
Capt. Donald P. Lightbown
Capt. Hyman D. Lipsitz
Capt. James E. Quinn
1st Lt. Dean E. Deckert
1st Lt. John S. Fisher
1st Lt. James J. Healy
1st Lt. James C. Lucus
1st Lt. Edwin P. Kerr
1st Lt. Joseph A. Pizuti
1st Lt. William S. Swain
WOJG Charles W. Bivens
WOJG Curtis L. Davis
F/O Haskell T. Teagarden

M Sgt. Albert G. Fuhrman
M Sgt. Evan R. Kimmel
M Sgt. James I. Moyer
M Sgt. Charles H. Pinn
M Sgt. Leon F. Retzlaff
M Sgt. William H. Scherner
T Sgt. Howard J. Arnberg
T Sgt. John E. Avery
T Sgt. Wilson D. Bowden
T Sgt. Robert B. Clifford
T Sgt. Melvin C. Hendricks
T Sgt. Harry W. Lynch
T Sgt. Monroe Messinger
T Sgt. Gordon H. Powell
T Sgt. Frank L. Withrow
S Sgt. Leo E. Beavers
S Sgt. Arthur Clayton
S Sgt. Robert O. Frederick
S Sgt. Frank Harned
S Sgt. Edwin Hatoff
S Sgt. James R. Hillman
S Sgt. George Laminsky
S Sgt. Gennaro S. Maiorino
S Sgt. Marvin C. May
S Sgt. Joseph A. Paradis
S Sgt. Willard B. Phillips
S Sgt. Arthur D. Reid
S Sgt. Jack Scholder
S Sgt. Sidney C. Sewell
S Sgt. George W. Williams
S Sgt. Charles T. Worthington
Sgt. Richard F. Arnold
Sgt. Charles A. Boyer
Sgt. James A. Brown
Sgt. Dominick A. Cerretani
Sgt. Julius E. Doering
Sgt. Pearl E. Dooley
Sgt. Benjamin H. Edge
Sgt. Edwin Frederick
Sgt. Lewis T. Grayner
Sgt. Frederick J. Haag
Sgt. Paul E. Hunter
Sgt. Jack R. Malone
Sgt. Alfonso M. Moreno
Sgt. Emil R. Morris, Jr.
Sgt. Thomas F. Rice
Sgt. Fred B. Shelton, Jr.
Sgt. Wilbur E. Tiabrt
Cpl. Jesse B. Anderson
Cpl. Jerome Bockstein
Cpl. Arthur W. Brown
Cpl. Herman Busch
Cpl. William Collins
Cpl. Hubert W. Cunningham
Cpl. Arthur Frederick, Jr.
Cpl. Guido J. Giaquinto
Cpl. Peter R. Greenwald
Cpl. Wesley J. Henry
Cpl. George H. Knierim
Cpl. Clinton V. Langley
Cpl. Theodore V. Lubanski
Cpl. Donald J. Lupiani
Cpl. Carl F. Miller
Cpl. Augustas A. Napolitano
Cpl. Worth D. Overton
Cpl. Clifford G. Patton
Cpl. Robert B. Temple
Cpl. James V. Webb
Cpl. Wendell J. Workman
Pfc. James H. Baker
Pfc. Ben Benkowski
Pfc. Sebastian B. Bosco
Pfc. Walter L. Carr
Pfc. Patrick J. De Santis
Pfc. Albert Elias
Pfc. Rueben R. Fiebelkorn
Pfc. Graham C. Gibson, Jr.
Pfc. Arthur J. Giese
Pfc. Sam Halsband
Pfc. Frank W. Handzel
Pfc. Willie F. Johnston
Pfc. Enock Maxim
Pfc. James J. McDonald
Pfc. John C. McInnis
Pfc. Vernile M. Montierth
Pfc. Nathan M. Nall
Pfc. George L. Passama
Pfc. George Potter
Pfc. Eugene C. Wakefield
Pvt. Russell B. Seamster

45th Fighter Squadron AAF

Major Arthur H. Bridge
Major David A. Kyzer
Major Robert W. Moore
Major Gilmer L. Snipes
Capt. Dwight R. Butler
Capt. Wesley E. Brown

Capt. Bruce S. Campbell, Jr.
Capt. Harold D. Collins
Capt. George H. Dunlap, Jr.
Capt. Francis L. Ennis
Capt. William J. Fisher
Capt. Allan M. Goldman
Capt. James W. Haglund
Capt. Fred H. Henderson, Jr.
Capt. Owen J. Higgs
Capt. George E. Hunter, Jr.
Capt. Paul W. Hunter, Jr.
Capt. Morton M. Knox
Capt. Albert E. Maltby
Capt. George C. Morey
Capt. William J. Morrow
Capt. John Patterson, Jr.
Capt. Albert W. Sherren
Capt. Jay W. Slater
Capt. Joe D. Walker
1st Lt. Edward F. Bates
1st Lt. Elmer L. Bishop, Jr.
1st Lt. Arthur A. Burry
1st Lt. Frederick C. Condon
1st Lt. Ceil A. Dennis
1st Lt. Hugh S. Edgerton
1st Lt. Lloyd C. Edwards, Jr.
1st Lt. Frederick R. Ernst
1st Lt. William J. Farrell
1st Lt. Robert R. Garey
1st Lt. Gerald F. Gowan
1st Lt. Charles H. Grant
1st Lt. Walter N. Harrigan, Jr.
1st Lt. William N. Hodgin
1st Lt. Patrick E. Hosey
1st Lt. Lawrence K. Joyner
1st Lt. Robert P. Kemske
1st Lt. John E. Kester
1st Lt. Beaver A. Kinsel
1st Lt. Marvin L. Klein
1st Lt. Samuel G. Lettie
1st Lt. Lawrence J. Lortie
1st Lt. John M. Mahony
1st Lt. Quentin G. McCorkle
1st Lt. Herman F. Miller
1st Lt. John T. Murdock
1st Lt. William M. Parry
1st Lt. William W. Redus
1st Lt. Charles D. Reese
1st Lt. Vincent V. Reinert
1st Lt. Gerhard C. Rettberg
1st Lt. Joseph G. Richins
1st Lt. Alvan E. Roberts, Jr.
1st Lt. Walter J. Robinson, Jr.
1st Lt. Wilson C. Runton
1st Lt. Donald H. Scott
1st Lt. John F. R. Scott, Jr.
1st Lt. Donald E. Statsmann
1st Lt. Robert M. Thornton
1st Lt. Joseph A. Wanamaker
1st Lt. Ross W. Watt, Jr.
1st Lt. Farley W. Wheelwright
1st Lt. Henry Wilder, Jr.
2nd Lt. Harry R. Allers
2nd Lt. John R. Botting
2nd Lt. John R. Brownlow
2nd Lt. William Brown, Jr.
2nd Lt. Grover C. Carico, Jr.
2nd Lt. Robert W. Carr
2nd Lt. Emerson L. Cyphers
2nd Lt. William B. Edwards
2nd Lt. Robert W. Fullmer
2nd Lt. Enon W. Harvey, Jr.
2nd Lt. Robert G. Hooks, Jr.
2nd Lt. Donald J. Koenig
2nd Lt. Rufus S. Moore, Jr.
2nd Lt. Robert D. Wray
2nd Lt. LeRoy E. Yakish
2nd Lt. Roy F. Zalesky
F/O Elbert P. Combs
F/O Robert A. Miller, Jr.
F/O Grady L. Patterson, Jr.
F/O Robert G. Poole
F/O Billy J. Singleton
F/O Stephen C. Yednock
1st Sgt William J. Ward
M Sgt James R. Beardsley
M Sgt Donald V. Furman
M Sgt James M. Moore
M Sgt Willard M. Turner
M Sgt Augusta Wingerter
T Sgt John F. Baznik
T Sgt Richard M. Hefner
T Sgt Andrew J. Hymel
T Sgt Paul Jaroscak
T Sgt Ernest F. Koshinz
T Sgt Robert E. Lee
T Sgt John O. Leitzke
T Sgt William T. Lowthrorp, Jr.
T Sgt Melvin L. Lukehart
T Sgt William M. Major
T Sgt Joseph A. Morrone
T Sgt Virgil E. Price
T Sgt Theron R. Varner
T Sgt Clyde Voges
T Sgt George A. Walker
T Sgt Merrill E. West
T Sgt John L. Zakrajsek
S Sgt Edward M. Anthony
S Sgt Ted Arbury
S Sgt Frank D. Baechler
S Sgt John C. Barling
S Sgt Joseph B. Barnao
S Sgt Charles B. Beasley, Jr.
S Sgt Frank F. Beatty
S Sgt Curtis Campbell
S Sgt James L. Clampitt
S Sgt Leon E. Cohen
S Sgt James P. Coleman
S Sgt Charles C. Covert
S Sgt Marshall W. Davidson
S Sgt John K. DeLaFrance
S Sgt Samuel L. Dixon
S Sgt Lewis G. Donald, Jr.
S Sgt Arthur J. Eardley
S Sgt Arthur Y. Epperson
S Sgt Alfred A. Erickson
S Sgt Walter W. Forrey
S Sgt Marion L. Friend
S Sgt Richard P. Gottschalk
S Sgt Wayne E. Graves
S Sgt Edward J. Grucella
S Sgt Tom A. Hamilton
S Sgt Raymond M. Harms
S Sgt Chester F. Herwig
S Sgt Horace N. Huff
S Sgt John Ihnat, Jr.
S Sgt Bernard H. Inge
S Sgt Peter A. Jacobson
S Sgt Frank R. Jadrich
S Sgt Marvin W. Jaeger
S Sgt Victor J. Kaczmarski
S Sgt Charles A. Knittle
S Sgt Richard W. Koehring
S Sgt Marion F. Kopytkiewicz
S Sgt Harold L. Kramp
S Sgt Albert N. Kuhn
S Sgt Henry J. Lane
S Sgt Alfred P. Laurendeau
S Sgt Nathaniel L. Littlefield
S Sgt Paul L. Mahan
S Sgt Ernest A.J. McGuire
S Sgt Victor F. McKee
S Sgt Lemuel D. Meriweather
S Sgt Edward J. Mondro
S Sgt Louis E. Moore
S Sgt Upton N. Morse
S Sgt Joseph V. Pozniak
S Sgt Pirl C. Robinson
S Sgt Thomas A. Rogan
S Sgt Frank J. Rubino
S Sgt Enio J. Ruotsi
S Sgt John J. Rutkowski
S Sgt John J. Savu, Jr.
S Sgt Tony Skaro
S Sgt Harold A. Stump
S Sgt Leland S. VanDusen
S Sgt Albert E. Vegiard
S Sgt John Vess, Jr.
S Sgt Fred D. Whittier
S Sgt Leland B. Williams
S Sgt Monroe C. Wills
S Sgt Steve F. Zaurski
S Sgt Elmer J. Zehr
S Sgt Donald H. Zobel
Sgt Ralph N. Barassi
Sgt Leo J. Barclay
Sgt John C. Bixler

Sgt Paul W. Black
Sgt Phil Blackwell, Jr.
Sgt John J. Bolan
Sgt Woodrow W. Bradford
Sgt Joseph F. Bullock
Sgt Kenneth Buse
Sgt Elmer B. Cleveland
Sgt James E. Coley
Sgt Lloyd J. Counsell
Sgt Dominic A. Cussary
Sgt Jack Diamond
Sgt John G. Diczban
Sgt Kenneth R. Dill
Sgt Durward N. Dye
Sgt Charles C. Eutsler
Sgt Carroll J. Evanson
Sgt Henry F. Falbe
Sgt Floyd M. Fannon
Sgt Richard H. Farrington
Sgt Bernard Fishkin
Sgt Ira H. Frumberg
Sgt Jack A. Gianlombardo
Sgt Bruno L. Hakala
Sgt Samuel Hochberg
Sgt Fred M. Houda
Sgt Leo H. Hughes, Jr.
Sgt Charles J. Howe, Jr.
Sgt Donald E. James
Sgt John J. Keegan
Sgt Curtis S. Knowles
Sgt Edgar G. Koepke
Sgt Pete Kovalsky
Sgt Eli Kramer
Sgt Darwin L. Lesher
Sgt James R. Light II
Sgt Sulpicio A. Matulak
Sgt Emilio D. Mazzeo
Sgt David A. Monk
Sgt Lawrence F. Montgomery
Sgt Bernard E. Mott
Sgt Thomas E. Muldowney
Sgt Harold M. Mundie
Sgt John J. Murphy
Sgt Nicholas H. Murray
Sgt Ruel O. Oliphant
Sgt Clifford A. Paige
Sgt Albert L. Pettey, Jr.
Sgt Earl G. Robinson
Sgt James R. Rudd
Sgt Asa L. Seals
Sgt Jess D. Shaw
Sgt Willie F. Shelton
Sgt William R. Smith
Sgt Edward L. Stellwagen
Sgt Thomas C. Tasker
Sgt Jesse M. Thompson
Sgt Joseph Tilvickas
Sgt Miles R. Troyer
Sgt Henry Vasil
Sgt Eustagon B. Wabinga
Sgt Richard L. Wheeler
Sgt Roy H. Wuornos
Sgt Frank J. Ziegler
Cpl Cyril J. Adams
Cpl Samuel S. Amendola
Cpl Robert H. Bean
Cpl Coburn M. Black
Cpl Harold A. Blowers
Cpl Wallace E. Boyles
Cpl Cecil H. Boyuls, Jr.
Cpl George W. Bramwell
Cpl Henry J. Breiner
Cpl Howard A. Bush, Jr.
Cpl Pio F. Cabudol
Cpl Harold A. Caisse
Cpl George Caprio
Cpl Robert B. Church
Cpl Ralph J. Clark
Cpl Joseph Cristino
Cpl Hugo P. Curran
Cpl Gene L. Davis
Cpl Frank DiPrima
Cpl James H. Dougherty
Cpl Mick J. Dragesavich
Cpl Richard J. Edwards
Cpl Leo R. Ethier
Cpl Ralph E. Feddersen
Cpl Desford E. Fencil
Cpl Nelson B. Fortner
Cpl Harlan R. Hanna
Cpl Harold C. Harless
Cpl Maurice P. Healy
Cpl H. B. Hensley
Cpl John W. Iler
Cpl Arch J. Hood
Cpl Mark S. Jasper
Cpl Hilarius P. Jost
Cpl John J. Knoch
Cpl John Kovalchick
Cpl Carl Lingen
Cpl Ralph G. Mannara
Cpl Herbert T. Martin
Cpl Robert E. McAdow
Cpl Hillard C. McDaniel
Cpl Alvin K. Nelson
Cpl Francis R. O'Hara
Cpl Andres G. Pagaran
Cpl Anthony W. Patynik
Cpl John J. Payesko
Cpl William E. Penney
Cpl Thomas Polino
Cpl Raymond A. Pyle
Cpl James G. Rice
Cpl Carl C. Russell
Cpl Rene Sanchez
Cpl Roland P. Smith
Cpl James T. Starkey
Cpl Kenneth J. Stevens
Cpl Alvin Studemann
Cpl Calvin B. Talley
Cpl Daniel H. Teer
Cpl Emery C. Toth
Cpl Nicholas F. Trabesh, Jr.
Cpl Robert L. Trickey
Cpl Frederick O. VanKirk
Cpl Harold W. Walther
Cpl Evan J. Ward
Cpl Rallo J. Warren
Cpl Mack A. Webb
Cpl Vernon G. Wollin
Pfc Harold O. Anderson
Pfc Perry E. Babcock
Pfc Wallace J. Bechard
Pfc Robert W. Beekman
Pfc Kiley T. Bowan
Pfc Chester L. Carbone
Pfc Bernard V. Corbett
Pfc Ernest W. Corthals
Pfc Elwood W. Cundiff
Pfc William A. Day
Pfc Joseph R. DeMarco
Pfc Vincent R. DeSano
Pfc Frank Friedman
Pfc Robert E. Gaunt
Pfc Stanley V. Guild
Pfc John Hagman, Jr.
Pfc Glenn M. Hague
Pfc Noble Hartgraves
Pfc Joe E. Hillman
Pfc Harry J. Holocinski
Pfc James M. Ivey
Pfc Clarence H. Lorenzen
Pfc Wilmer L. R. McSwain
Pfc John J. O'Brien
Pfc William J. Patton
Pfc Angelo E. Provitola
Pfc Glen F. Randall
Pfc Charles L. Rotenberry
Pfc Charles J. Rottau
Pfc Samuel Sabino
Pfc Adolph D. Sackmann
Pfc Vincent J. Santillo
Pfc Arthur Scheihing
Pfc Paul Turner
Pfc Louis A. Wiener
Pfc Nathan W. Wood
Pfc Frederick W. Young
Pvt Robert S. Eberhardt
Pvt Earl B. Neher, Jr.

47th Fighter Squadron AAF

Major Fred E. Larson
Major Theon E. Markham
Major John A Piper
Major Clarence L. Strother
Capt Frank L. Ayres
Capt Ned H. Baldwin
Capt Harold L. Baccus
Capt Raymond J. Betner
Capt Bernard P. Bjorseth
Capt Eurich L. Bright
Capt Joseph P. Brunette
Capt Charles J. Cameron
Capt Richard J. Condrick
Capt Robert R. Down
Capt Richard H. Hintermeier
Capt Ernest W. Hostetler
Capt Ormal E. Kiesling
Capt Jack Lapides
Capt Fred K. Martin
Capt Ray L. Obenshain, Jr.
Capt Cletus J. Oster
Capt Lawrence T. Pepin
Capt Walter H. Powell
Capt Henry G. Sanders
1st Lt. George B. Allen, Jr.
1st Lt. David S. Balak
1st Lt. Austin J. Bisky
1st Lt. Eugene A. Broadbent
1st Lt. Wilson S. Campbell
1st Lt. Albert J. Carletti
1st Lt. William A. Dow, Jr.
1st Lt. Charles R. Edens
1st Lt. Andrew C. Elliott
1st Lt. Martin Gilbride
1st Lt. Fred T. Grover
1st Lt. Preston O. Howard, Jr.
1st Lt. Charles E. Jennings
1st Lt. Samuel S. Jones, Jr.
1st Lt. Roy E. June
1st Lt. Francis M. Kinsey
1st Lt. Thomas M. Leaver
1st Lt. Donald F. Locke
1st Lt. Joseph A. McCormick
1st Lt. Jule C. Mitchell, Jr.
1st Lt. Stanley A. Moore
1st Lt. Oliver E. O'Mara, Jr.
1st Lt. Philip Oronsky
1st Lt. Warren G. Reed, Jr.
1st Lt. Henry C. Ryniker
1st Lt. Wallace Saunders, Jr.
1st Lt. Robert S. Scamara
1st Lt. John V. Scanlan
1st Lt. Emil A. Schroeder, Jr.
1st Lt. Leon P. Sher
1st Lt. Ernest F. Sorgnit
1st Lt. William H. Sparks
1st Lt. Dave G. Stelling
1st Lt. Alexander E. Trodahl
1st Lt. Harry M. Tyler
1st Lt. Allen D. White
1st Lt. Donald O. White
1st Lt. Robert A. Worton
2nd Lt. Robert N. Andersen
2nd Lt. William M. Barlow
2nd Lt. Robert C. Burnett
2nd Lt. Lamar M. Christian
2nd Lt. Albert Dibelka, Jr.
2nd Lt. Charles C. Doughty
2nd Lt. John R. Evans
2nd Lt. John M. Fitzgerald
2nd Lt. Willis O. Forman
2nd Lt. Paul C. Frick
2nd Lt. Maurice F. Gourley
2nd Lt. Ralph N. Heintz
2nd Lt. Ronald E. Johnston
2nd Lt. Erick W. Hutchison
2nd Lt. Donald L. Kiggins
2nd Lt. Charles E. Klessig
2nd Lt. Robert J. Kriss
2nd Lt. Howard F. Liddell, Jr.
2nd Lt. Richard M. Long
2nd Lt. Albert G. Olivier, Jr.
2nd Lt. George C. Petrouleas
2nd Lt. William K. Sidebottom
2nd Lt. John R. Shuler
2nd Lt. David Tillman, Jr.
2nd Lt. Lester A. Twigg, Jr.
2nd Lt. Harry M. VanZandt
2nd Lt. Joseph F. Wagner
2nd Lt. Howard R. Weaver
F/O John W. Googe
F/O Fronnie A. Jones, Jr.
F/O Marvin C. Loveless
F/O Harold E. Powell
CWO Ernest E. Addington
1st Sgt Lefther Vasilion
M Sgt Ver Wayne Beach
M Sgt James E. Gassaway
M Sgt Thurman H. Lackey
M Sgt John M. MacQuarrie
M Sgt Edward J. Rooney
M Sgt George E. Schug
M Sgt Thomas W. Walker
T Sgt Florian H. Corressel
T Sgt Claude L. Ditrick
T Sgt Eugene J. Drapeau
T Sgt Richard L. Gaunt
T Sgt Jack C. Goodloe, Jr.
T Sgt Jack M. Gray
T Sgt Dermont M. Gross
T Sgt Fred Harland
T Sgt William T. Hebert
T Sgt Robert D. King
T Sgt Argo M. Parrello
T Sgt George H. Nelson
T Sgt Robert E. Rogers
T Sgt Marvin C. Udesen
T Sgt Frank W. Weibel
T Sgt Charles L. Williams, Jr.
T Sgt Stephen Wojcik
S Sgt Gaillard E. Andrews
S Sgt Chester H. Baker
S Sgt Clarence B. Blecker
S Sgt Anthony A. Belesi
S Sgt George F. Bergin
S Sgt Carl W. Blecker
S Sgt Malcolm H. Bowles
S Sgt Forrest Bowser
S Sgt William R. Ceroli
S Sgt Willis Chaplin, Jr.
S Sgt Forrest E. Chapman
S Sgt Edwin J. Cmaidalka
S Sgt William J. Crossin
S Sgt Enett M. Davidson
S Sgt Peter S. DeFusco
S Sgt Lewis D. Dickerhoof
S Sgt Walter L. Downey
S Sgt Rodney C. Eline
S Sgt Roy K. Elliott
S Sgt William E. Ellis
S Sgt Harry E. Ewing
S Sgt Charles J. Fontenot
S Sgt Timothy J. Glynn
S Sgt John R. Gossett
S Sgt Kenneth Grace
S Sgt Raymond L. Griffin
S Sgt Cosker Hairelson
S Sgt Cletus N. Hamm
S Sgt Raymond H. Hammersmith
S Sgt Eugene Harrell
S Sgt Lyndell C. Harrison
S Sgt Robert W. Hogan
S Sgt Everett E. Jeter
S Sgt Lowell C. Johnson
S Sgt John B. Kirby
S Sgt Emil O. Klein
S Sgt Stanley Kutz
S Sgt James N. Lindsay
S Sgt Armando Lucarelli
S Sgt Charles E. Manz
S Sgt Harold R. Mattson
S Sgt John B. Mauldin
S Sgt Thomas R. McCain
S Sgt Thomas I. McGuire
S Sgt Donald G. Mickle
S Sgt Arthur Mongelli
S Sgt Michael R. Paez
S Sgt Joseph Pipek
S Sgt Donald W. Potter
S Sgt James S. Porter
S Sgt Juan R. Reototar
S Sgt Bernard J. Riley
S Sgt Harry E. Roberts
S Sgt Lester J. Saucier

S Sgt Stanley L. Sherfick
S Sgt Ralph W. Simpson
S Sgt Russell A. Skaggs
S Sgt Lester G. Skidmore
S Sgt Constantino J. Stefani
S Sgt Leonard L. Steffy
S Sgt Earl J. Steggeman
S Sgt John B. Supple
S Sgt William Thomas
S Sgt Jerrold C. Tipler
S Sgt Marvin W. Toovey
S Sgt Fred L. Whidden
S Sgt Roscoe E. Wilcox
S Sgt Stanley J. Winiasz
S Sgt Columbus L. Woods, Jr.
S Sgt Ralph Wright
S Sgt Charles S. Wylie
S Sgt Joseph Zdeb
Sgt Phillip R. Altman
Sgt Dominic A. Armiano
Sgt Samuel J. Baker
Sgt Stanley R. Baker
Sgt Paul Balicik
Sgt Carl W. Benson
Sgt Robert P. Bintz
Sgt Robert E. Branagan
Sgt Edward W. Brokop
Sgt Frank W. Bryce
Sgt Clarence J. Bucholz
Sgt William Burchett
Sgt Peter M. Cacciatore
Sgt Walter S. Carlton, Jr.
Sgt Raymond G. Cole
Sgt Paul A. Conn
Sgt Cecil O. Craig
Sgt Joseph L. Czopek
Sgt Lawrence J. Dempster
Sgt Frank Donnerbouer
Sgt William P. Downs
Sgt Edward G. Duty
Sgt Elmer R. Edmonds
Sgt John W. Flagg
Sgt Vance W. Garry
Sgt Claud Gibbs
Sgt Thomas J. Harding
Sgt William E. Howard
Sgt Francis H. Huck
Sgt Kenneth M. Jaranson
Sgt Wilbur L. Kiser
Sgt Jesse W. Kneezle
Sgt Marvin E. Kness
Sgt Trevor G. Kopp
Sgt Walter Kozakiewicz
Sgt John F. Kulo
Sgt Richard J. S. MacKenzie
Sgt Adam E. Majewski
Sgt George F. McCoy
Sgt Patrick J. McDermottroe
Sgt William A. Miller
Sgt Harold H. Mott
Sgt Ludwik Myszkowski
Sgt Louis Novalich, Jr.
Sgt Louis T. Ouellette
Sgt Harold E. Pancoast
Sgt Bryon P. Pfeifer
Sgt Joseph F. Pletka
Sgt James Ploska
Sgt Roy E. Price
Sgt Lansing P. Pruyn
Sgt Joseph F. Pulec
Sgt David Redlo
Sgt Salvatore A. Restivo
Sgt Kenneth F. Robbins
Sgt William A. Ross
Sgt William R. Ruffner
Sgt Kenneth E. Schock
Sgt James H. Snively
Sgt Charles C. Stevens
Sgt John D. Sullivan
Sgt Don R. Swick
Sgt Herbert F. Taft
Sgt Reynold R. Wagenknecht
Sgt John M. Whitcomb
Sgt Walter N. Williams
Sgt Peter P. Wiszuk
Cpl Maurice R. Acker
Cpl James Albert
Cpl Frederick C. Arnold
Cpl Robert E. Barnett
Cpl Christie F. Bashore
Cpl Michael Bayba
Cpl Michael J. Beck
Cpl Russell A. Bishop
Cpl George E. Boddiford, Jr.
Cpl Joseph A. Boller, Jr.
Cpl Rosario J. Brocato
Cpl Charles E. Bush
Cpl John F. Butterworth, Jr.
Cpl Alesio Cicala
Cpl Arthur L. Clifton
Cpl Ralph E. Crean
Cpl George B. Cummings
Cpl Barnett R. Davis
Cpl Gordon T. Duffy
Cpl Henry M. Ervin
Cpl Garrett E. Everson, Jr.
Cpl Jacque W. Fagan
Cpl William H. Fritts
Cpl Henry H. Garrett
Cpl John R. Gideon
Cpl Ray J. Cirogietti
Cpl John D. Grigsby
Cpl Joseph P. Halowi
Cpl Joseph L. Hawthorne
Cpl Ray B. Haynes
Cpl Roy E. Hollenbach
Cpl Kenneth E. Houchin
Cpl Chester E. Jansen
Cpl Ross E. Kearby
Cpl W. M. Kelley, Jr.
Cpl Joel R. Kerr, Jr.
Cpl John T. Katsanos
Cpl Robert J. Klein
Cpl Elmer C. Lackey
Cpl Alfred J. Manning
Cpl Angelo M. Marino
Cpl Walter F. Martin
Cpl William J. Meagher, Jr.
Cpl Martin J. Meyers
Cpl Alex R. Murray
Cpl Howard D. Haidig
Cpl Raymond D. Ormond
Cpl Charles A. Pierce
Cpl John R. Rega
Cpl William Ridosh
Cpl James A. Riley
Cpl Harvey L. Risberg
Cpl Cedrick D. Ross
Cpl Harry W. Skeen
Cpl Howard C. Smith
Cpl Charlie Stalnaker
Cpl James B. Stewart
Cpl Donald E. Stover
Cpl William L. Sullivan
Cpl John E. Sutton
Cpl Virgil F. Ward
Cpl Willie T. Weeks
Pfc Robert D. Adams
Pfc Kenneth C. Butera
Pfc Anthony R. Cetkosky
Pfc Charles A. Collier
Pfc Francis J. Conway
Pfc Robert J. Cousins
Pfc Dwight R. Davis
Pfc Charles R. Delbridge
Pfc Eldred L. Durkee
Pfc How Fong
Pfc Leonard A. Freeman
Pfc Stanley S. Freiburg
Pfc John A. Fuller
Pfc Paul F. Golden
Pfc Arlie A. Gray
Pfc Kelly G. Grigsby
Pfc Edmund G. Harbers
Pfc John R. Hewitt
Pfc Robert J. Hughes
Pfc Peter J. Kennedy
Pfc Francis K. Lea, Jr.
Pfc Horace Long
Pfc Cornelius J. Lucey
Pfc Bennie Naumowich
Pfc Edward B. Nowisak
Pfc Joseph L. Perretto
Pfc John A. Pfleiderer
Pfc Fred Rasmussen
Pfc Bruce M. Reeder
Pfc Harold M. Rosner

Pfc Frank J. Ruggero
Pfc Howard R. Sawatski
Pfc Edward A. Schnase
Pfc Anthony B. Sgroi
Pfc Albert W. Shay
Pfc Ira E. Shenk
Pfc Stanley Silverman
Pfc Herbert G. Smith
Pfc Elmer M. Strandberg
Pfc Merton A. Thoreson
Pfc Stephen C. Tuohey
Pfc Charles W. Veshine
Pfc Henry G. Weinberger
Pfc Edward R. Wheeler
Pfc Robert N. Winterhoff
Pfc Charles J. Wroblewski
Pfc Gilbert C. White

78th Fighter Squadron AAF

Major Joe Fitzsimmons
Major James R. McNevins
Major James B. Tapp
Major James M. VandeHey
Capt Robert H. Beyl
Capt John S. Chambers
Capt Harold D. Collins
Capt Joe Delahunty
Capt Richard D. Duerr
Capt Ernest W. Hostetler
Capt Julius Lewis
Capt Max L. Marshall
Capt Nelson P. Merrill, Jr.
Capt Victor K. Mollan
Capt Lucien E. Parish, Jr.
Capt Robert H. Roseberry
Capt Ephriam M. Rosset
Capt Robert C. Ruby
Capt Theodore J. Saed, Jr.
Capt Jerome Yellin
1st Lt. Frederick A. Bauman
1st Lt. Doyle T. Brooks
1st Lt. Wilber R. Brucker
1st Lt. Charles R. Butler, Jr.
1st Lt. Robert F. Carey, Jr.
1st Lt. Robert L. Carr
1st Lt. Paul E. Chism
1st Lt. Gordon A. Christoe
1st Lt. Jack H. Collie
1st Lt. Robert O. Coryell
1st Lt. Kenneth R. Dahlquist
1st Lt. Leo B. Evans
1st Lt. Donald L. Gautsche
1st Lt. Arden R. Gibson
1st Lt. Cecil C. Grimes, Jr.
1st Lt. Charles C. Heil
1st Lt. James M. Hilliard, Jr.
1st Lt. Nicholas J. Hubbich, Jr.
1st Lt. Marvin Kern
1st Lt. Louis L. Korb
1st Lt. Walter W. Kreimann
1st Lt. Thomas L. McCullough
1st Lt. Philip J. Mather, Jr.
1st Lt. Paul A. Martin
1st Lt. Clyde V. Mangum
1st Lt. Daniel T. Mathis, Jr.
1st Lt. Leo P. Michaelides
1st Lt. Daniel S. Miles
1st Lt. Franklin B. Montgomery
1st Lt. Douglas B. Moore
1st Lt. Herbert S. Neeshan
1st Lt. Jack O. Nelson
1st Lt. Elmer Owens
1st Lt. John Patterson, Jr.
1st Lt. Frank Pena, Jr.
1st Lt. Albert W. Powers
1st Lt. Stewart I. Price
1st Lt. Philip Schlamberg
1st Lt. Gordon H. Scott
1st Lt. Richard H. Schroeppel
1st Lt. Malcolm M. Sedam
1st Lt. Robert E. Sherbundy
1st Lt. Albert W. Sherren
1st Lt. Nicholas F. Teresi
1st Lt. Wallace K. Wayland
1st Lt. Robert L. Williams
2nd Lt. Lee M. Bargaehr
2nd Lt. William J. Crawford
2nd Lt. John R. Evans
2nd Lt. Joseph H. Fahey, Jr.
2nd Lt. Joseph P. Gutierrez
2nd Lt. James F. Hawkins
2nd Lt. James E. Hilburn
2nd Lt. William F. Killion
2nd Lt. Leroy M. Lancaster
2nd Lt. William M. McLean
2nd Lt. Freddie H. Murff
2nd Lt. Donald K. Olson
2nd Lt. Jerome Schoenbart
2nd Lt. Ralph L. Venamon
2nd Lt. David T. Wilson
2nd Lt. Fred W. White
2nd Lt. James R. Wightman
F/O Casimir Bielaczyc
F/O Robert W. Cowles
F/O Rudolph J. Habe
F/O Thomas H. Temple
F/O Richard H. Trotter
1st Sgt Clayton H. Haywood
M Sgt Harold J. Blattner
M Sgt Lyman O. Blochberger
M Sgt Harold E. Krone
M Sgt Harry Liberman
M Sgt Edward M. Makiavcic
M Sgt Donald J. Rise
M Sgt Ray Wright
T Sgt William L. Adams
T Sgt Alphonse W. Bilewicz
T Sgt Warren W. Carpenter
T Sgt Arthur Clement
T Sgt William M. Deckert
T Sgt Robert Greco
T Sgt Joseph Guldan
T Sgt Trinon H. Hubbard
T Sgt Hugh W. Leggett
T Sgt William C. Meads
T Sgt Roman J. Milkowski
T Sgt Charles S. Morgan
T Sgt Herbert E. Neumann
T Sgt Dean O. Pope
T Sgt Blair H. Record
T Sgt J. W. Stone
T Sgt Kenneth J. Sweet
T Sgt Charles C. Watson
S Sgt Robert M. Allen
S Sgt George R. Ammerman
S Sgt Claude W. Bagwell
S Sgt Francis A. Beaudette
S Sgt Ricardo Blanco
S Sgt Francis L. Boch
S Sgt William H. Bradicich
S Sgt Richard W. Brooks
S Sgt William B. Caplan
S Sgt Clifford H. Catto
S Sgt James H. Chisholm
S Sgt Edward D. Connors
S Sgt Micahel T. Cossack
S Sgt Arnold W. Coursey
S Sgt Frank Craig
S Sgt James W. Dougherty
S Sgt James R. Ellis
S Sgt Mathew A. Emberson
S Sgt Gaylord M. Ewing
S Sgt Steve Fedoush
S Sgt Raymond C. Flaherty
S Sgt Charles J. Gebauer
S Sgt Avery W. Gordon
S Sgt Gerald L. Hamlin
S Sgt Fred D. Heaton
S Sgt Eugene Horvath
S Sgt Joseph Hospodar
S Sgt Stanley J. Hradsky
S Sgt Charlie J. Hunter, Jr.
S Sgt Leland S. Hyde
S Sgt Theophilus L. James, Jr.
S Sgt Reginald T. Kirby
S Sgt Robert J. Kirn
S Sgt Joseph G. Korte
S Sgt Robert M. Kruer
S Sgt Donald E. Lapp
S Sgt Bertram G. Leveroos
S Sgt William Littman
S Sgt Albert J. Lorenczewski

S Sgt William E. Mausling
S Sgt Reavis H. McCallum
S Sgt Orville H. McDonald
S Sgt William E. McGann
S Sgt Albert H. McLellan
S Sgt Harold E. Mercer
S Sgt Anton J. Meyer
S Sgt Henry F. Ott
S Sgt Donald H. Pasch
S Sgt Percy F. Perkins
S Sgt Joseph N. Petesch
S Sgt Lawrence F. Petesch
S Sgt Joseph L. Plotz
S Sgt Oliver C. Randall, Jr.
S Sgt Clifford D. Richardson
S Sgt Allen E. Rickett
S Sgt Thomas M. Rini, Jr.
S Sgt Irving Rosner
S Sgt James W. Rows
S Sgt Leland E. Rozell
S Sgt Ralph W. Ruppert
S Sgt Donald P. Scott
S Sgt Lloyd M. Scott, Jr.
S Sgt Walter F. Shea
S Sgt Samuel C. Stephenson
S Sgt Howard F. Stewart
S Sgt Herman W. Surratt
S Sgt Wilbur D. Turlington
S Sgt Wendell L. Wilson
S Sgt Ray L. Wilt
Sgt Richard K. Alvin
Sgt William R. Arnold
Sgt Frederick E. Bolander
Sgt John F. Bonney
Sgt Roy M. Brown
Sgt Rollin M. Case
Sgt Alve B. Claiborn
Sgt Frank Cobb
Sgt Quinton A. Cody
Sgt Donald Cook
Sgt George A. Cook
Sgt William J. Cotter
Sgt Michael Cristinzio
Sgt John Crossnohere
Sgt Harrison E. Culver
Sgt Edward Dagnais
Sgt Gilbert H. Dell
Sgt James C. Delisa
Sgt Merlin Dixon
Sgt James T. Donnelly
Sgt Lemmetj E. Drown
Sgt Frank Felstein
Sgt David Fessler
Sgt Henry W. Frenzel
Sgt William Gibb
Sgt Marshall J. Gooley
Sgt Vernon S. Gordon
Sgt Charlie S. Greer
Sgt Robert P. Hanchan
Sgt Richard F. Hartlieb
Sgt Leo A. Henderson
Sgt Robert J. Hinderliter
Sgt Andrew J. Horan
Sgt Robert W. Hubert
Sgt Clifford M. Jackson
Sgt Harold L. Jaffe
Sgt John B. Johnson
Sgt Hughy E. Jones
Sgt Fred Kehl
Sgt John F. Kulo
Sgt Arthur H. Krueger
Sgt Robert O. Lockwood
Sgt Perry J. Maines
Sgt Manuel W. Marshall
Sgt Howard J. Matteola
Sgt William F. McClain, Jr.
Sgt Charles J. Montanti
Sgt Charles H. Moore
Sgt John A. Nagy
Sgt Henry E. Nardini
Sgt Elmer J. A. Nickel
Sgt Alan H. O'Neal
Sgt Dezo Patonai
Sgt Edward W. Paulson
Sgt Richard H. Pease
Sgt Leslie A. Riege
Sgt Joaquin Robledo, Jr.
Sgt Melvin J. Schwebke
Sgt Joseph R. Sherwood
Sgt Joseph T. Siebieda
Sgt Irving E. Silverstein
Sgt Robert H. Sweatmon
Sgt Franklin L. Sweet
Sgt Lewis L. Thomas
Sgt Joseph A. Valatka
Sgt John H. Willbanks
Sgt Bernard J. Wyley
Sgt Raymond P. Young
Cpl Frank S. Abraham
Cpl Albert H. Ackerson
Cpl Victor W. Adams
Cpl Raymond T. Armstrong
Cpl Carl W. Aufderheide
Cpl Robert G. Belschner
Cpl Max Berger
Cpl Irving Blaustein
Cpl Gordon C. Boughton
Cpl Daniel A. Byrnes
Cpl Lawrence W. Camarigg
Cpl Alfonse J. Campanaro
Cpl Jack H. Cambell
Cpl Lee I. Carter
Cpl Marvin L. Cermeli
Cpl Leo G. Chouinard
Cpl Maurice J. Cline
Cpl Raymond P. Clouthier
Cpl John D. Conroy
Cpl Frank T. Denczek
Cpl Lester O. Dice
Cpl Corneal W. Ellington, Jr.
Cpl Buford I. France
Cpl Nicholas F. Galarza
Cpl Everett L. Giffin
Cpl Kenneth E. Grieme
Cpl Howard C. Heath
Cpl Clements H. Hentges
Cpl Owen W. Hoskins, Jr.
Cpl Clarence W. Kelley
Cpl Joseph Kotlik
Cpl Boleslaw Kowalski
Cpl John E. Krauss
Cpl Jack L. Landon
Cpl Michael C. Layman
Cpl Edward Lefkoski
Cpl George H. Lemoyne
Cpl Thomas R. Levesque
Cpl Robert N. Martone
Cpl Michael Melnick, Jr.
Cpl Daniel J. Mongno
Cpl Charles P. Moyer, Jr.
Cpl Walter R. Mullervy
Cpl William O. Neumann
Cpl Robert L. Noon
Cpl Clair A. Palmer
Cpl Arthur Patton
Cpl Fred L. Pennacchi
Cpl Thomas A. Perkins
Cpl Charles E. Proulx
Cpl Ralph G. Reed
Cpl William J. Reynolds
Cpl John H. Schmid
Cpl Martin M. Sheridan
Cpl Walter A. Sommers
Cpl Elmer E. Springstroh
Cpl Bertram J. Stark
Cpl Ernest P. VanNorden
Cpl Fred Vespo
Cpl Vernon R. Wells
Cpl Philip H. Weymouth
Pfc Francisco M. Ayala
Pfc Charles F. Bahde
Pfc Frank P. Balester
Pfc James A. Ballou
Pfc Moses J. Baroudi
Pfc Donald J. Bessette
Pfc William Bourgeois
Pfc Steven Bukata
Pfc James A. Carlson
Pfc Robert L. Chatman
Pfc Raymond D. Cooksey
Pfc Joseph J. Davis
Pfc Stanley D. Deiter
Pfc Harry D. Ely
Pfc William J. English
Pfc Johnnie T. Garrison
Pfc Keith A. Hopper
Pfc William Johnson

Pfc Manuel Luis, Jr.
Pfc Cleo J. Lutz
Pfc Carleton E. Markham
Pfc Harry K. Marx
Pfc George F. McCutcheon
Pfc Giles J. Menter
Pfc Ernest A. Midwinter, Jr.
Pfc John T. Misskerg
Pfc Nicholas Mudzik
Pfc William J. Neary
Pfc William D. Newman
Pfc George L. Peterson
Pfc Ira D. Schnider
Pfc James J. Sclafani
Pfc Earl T. Stoken
Pfc Allen L. Strauss
Pfc John Tate
Pfc James V. Torre
Pfc Edward J. Vargo
Pfc Joseph Weinstock
Pfc Carl Whaley
Pfc Richard A. Wheeler
Pfc H. W. Whitmire
Pfc Daniel Yevtich
Pfc John F. Zuverl
Pvt Ernest D. Clayton

By Order of Lt. Col. Mitchell:

Joseph H. Riley
Major, Air Corps,
Adjutant.

Official:
Joseph H. Riley,
Major, Air Corps,
Adjutant

Distribution: "B"

Documentary Sources

Unit histories from Albert F. Simpson Historical Research Center, Maxwell Air Force Base, Alabama, reviewed:

Fifth Fighter Command
Seventh Air Force
Seventh Fighter Command
Thirteenth Fighter Command
Hawaiian Air Force
Hawaiian Interceptor Command
Fourteenth Pursuit Wing
8th Fighter Group
15th Fighter Group
18th Fighter Group
21st Fighter Group
35th Fighter Group
49th Fighter Group
58th Fighter Group
318th Fighter Group
347th Fighter Group
348th Fighter Group
475th Fighter Group
506th Fighter Group
4th Emergency Rescue Squadron

Bibliography

Army Times Publishing Company. Editors of *Pearl Harbor and Hawaii: A Military History*. New York: Bonanza Books, no date.

Barker, A.J. *Pearl Harbor*. New York: Ballantine Books, 1969.

Clark, Blake. *Remember Pearl Harbor*. New York: Harper and Brothers, 1943.

Craven, Wesley Frank and Cate, James Lea, editors. *The Army Air Forces in World War II,* Volumes I, IV, and V. Chicago: University of Chicago Press, 1948.

Dull, Paul S. *A Battle History of the Imperial Japanese Navy (1941-1945)*. Annapolis, Md.: Naval Institute Press, 1978.

Fuchida, Mitsuo and Okumiya, Masatake. *Midway: The Battle That Doomed Japan, The Japanese Navy's Story*. Edited by Clarke K. Kawakami and Roger Pineau. Annapolis, Md.: Naval Institute Press, 1955.

Hoehling, A.A. 7 December 1941: *The Day the Admirals Slept Late*. New York: Kensington Publishing Corp., 1978.

Howard, Clive and Whitely, Joe. *One Damned Island After Another*. Chapel Hill: University of North Carolina Press, 1946.

The Japanese Air Forces in World War II: The Organization of the Japanese Army and Naval Air Forces, 1945. New York: Hippocrene Books, Inc., 1979.

Karig, Walter, Commander, and Kelley, Welbourn, Lieutenant. *Battle Report: Pearl Harbor to Coral Sea*. New York: Farrar and Rinehart, Inc., 1944.

Lockwood, Charles A., Vice Admiral, and Adamson, Hans Christian, Colonel. *Zoomies, Subs and Zeros, Heroic Rescues in World War II by the Submarine Lifeguard League*. New York: Greenberg: Publisher, 1956.

Lord, Walter. *Day of Infamy*. New York: Holt, Rinehart and Winston, 1957.

Millis, Walter. *This is Pearl: The United States and Japan — 1941*. New York: William Morrow and Company, 1941.

Morgenstern, George. *Pearl Harbor: The Story of the Secret War*. New York: The Devin-Adair Company, 1947.

Morison, Samuel Eliot. *History of United States Naval Operations in World War II*. Volumes III, IV, VII, VIII and XIV. Boston: Little Brown and Company, 1962.

Newcomb, Richard F. *Iwo Jima*. New York: Holt, Rinehart and Winston, 1965.

Olson. *Operational History of the Seventh Air Force, 6 November 1943–31 July 1944*. United States Air Force Historical Study Number 38. Available through the Albert F. Simpson Historical Research Center, Maxwell Air Force Base, 1945.

Olson. *Operational History of the Seventh Air Force, 7 December 1941–6 November 1943*. United States Air Force Historical Study Number 41. Available through the Albert F. Simpson Historical Research Center, Maxwell Air Force Base, 1945.

Portens, Stanley D. *And Blow Not the Trumpet*. Palo Alto, Calif.: Pacific Books, 1947.

Schuler, Frank and Moore, Robin. *The Pearl Harbor Cover-Up*. New York: Pinnacle Books, 1976.

Sunderman, James F. Editor, *World War II in the Air, The Pacific,* New York: Bramhall House.

Theobald, Robert A. *The Final Secret of Pearl Harbor: The Washington Contribution to the Japanese Attack*. New York: The Devin-Adair Company, 1954.

Tillman, Barrett. *The Dauntless Dive Bomber of World War Two*. Annapolis, Md.: Naval Institute Press, 1976.

Toland, John. *But Not in Shame: The Six Months After*

Pearl Harbor. New York: Random House 1961.

———. *The Rising Sun: The Decline and Fall of the Japanese Empire. 1936-1945*. New York: Random House, 1970.

United States Air Force Credits for the Destruction of Enemy Aircraft, World War II. United States Air Force Historical Study Number 85. Available through the Albert F. Simpson Historical Research Center, Maxwell Air Force Base, 1978.

United States Army Forces Far East Headquarters, Military History Section. *Pearl Harbor Operations: General Outline of Orders and Plans*. Japanese Monograph No. 97. Available through the Department of the Army; Office of the Chief of Military History, 1953.

United States Army Forces Far East, Headquarters and Eighth United States Army (Rear). *Air Defense of the Homeland*. Japanese Monograph No. 23. Available through the Department of the Army, Office of the Chief of Military History, 1956.

———. *Homeland Air Defense Operations Record*. Japanese Monograph No. 157 (Includes Nos. 157, 158, 159). Available through the Department of the Army, Office of the Chief of Military History, 1952.

United States Congress, Joint Committee on the Investigation of the Pearl Harbor Attack. *Pearl Harbor Attack*. Washington D.C.: U.S. Government Printing Office, 1946, 39 volumes.

United States Department of Defense. *The Magic Background of Pearl Harbor*. Volumes I-V and Appendices. Washington D.C.: U.S. Government Printing Office, 1977.

United States Strategic Bombing Survey. *Interrogations of Japanese Officials*. Washington D.C.: U.S. Government Printing Office, 1947.

Wohlstetter, Roberta. *Pearl Harbor: Warning and Decision*. Stanford, California: Stanford University Press, 1962.

John W. Lambert

John Lambert is a businessman by vocation (Chairman and Chief Executive Officer of Twin City Barge, Inc.) and a military historian by avocation.

The Long Campaign is the culmination of 30 years study and research of the Pacific air war and the first of a World War II history series.

Lambert served in the United States Air Force from 1948 to 1952, and was assigned to the Fifth Air Force in Japan and Korea during 1950 and 1951.

He lives in St. Paul, Minn. and Captiva Island, Fla. with his wife, Dolly, and his dog, Alex.